BAD SAMARITANS

First World Ethics and
Third World Debt

BAD SAMARITANS

First World Ethics and
Third World Debt

Paul Vallely

ORBIS BOOKS

Maryknoll, New York 10545

The Catholic Foreign Mission Society of America (Maryknoll) recruits and trains people for overseas missionary service. Through Orbis Books, Maryknoll aims to foster the international dialogue that is essential to mission. The books published, however, reflect the opinions of their authors and are not meant to represent the official position of the society.

First published in Great Britain by Hodder and Stoughton, 47 Bedford Square, London WC1B 3DP, and in the United States by Orbis Books, Maryknoll, NY 10545

Typset in Great Britain
Printed in the United States of America

ORBIS/ISBN 0-88344-668-5

For my father

Contents

INTRODUCTION

'Such being the nature of our subject and such our way of
arguing in our discussions of it, we must be satisfied with
a rough outline of the truth.'

Aristotle

It was when they took the murdered man's shoes that I
realised I was rich. Today I cannot remember much else
about him. Was he a mining engineer returning from a
holiday back home in England? Was he an expatriate salesman in Lusaka who had arrived at the airport for a short
business tour? I knew at the time. But today all I can
remember is that they took his shoes, and his watch.

Two days after the murder I arrived at the same airport in
Ndola in the once prosperous Copper Belt in the north of
Zambia. I took the same road to the principal mining town
of Kitwe. This was the area of great mineral wealth which,
in the heady days after independence, was set to make
Zambia the most affluent state in black Africa. It was not to
be. The world was plunged into recession and copper fell
dramatically in price. The Copper Belt spiralled into decline.
Today it is at its lowest ebb yet. Prices rise constantly because
of inflation and the rampant black market. Unemployment

is at record levels. Tens of thousands of Zambians now live in the squalid shanty towns to which they once flocked from the rural farmlands in the hopes of big money and an affluent lifestyle with Western consumer goods in plenty.

It was small wonder then that the highway between the two main towns was regularly beset by robbers. It was they who had stopped the taxi in which the man was travelling from the airport after arriving on the evening plane. His driver ran away in fear and the robbers took the vehicle into a nearby wood. The man's wallet was in his suitcase, which was locked in the boot of the car. The driver had taken the key when he fled. So the robbers hacked the man to death and then took his shoes and watch.

I stood in the airport and looked at mine. Sturdy, comfortable leather shoes with rubber soles, inexpensive but suitable for trekking around Africa. They had cost me thirty-five pounds, I recalled. I looked at the watch. I tried to think how much it had cost me. It had been so cheap that when I bought it I had not even fixed the amount in my mind; it was about seventeen pounds, perhaps. Enough to be worth killing for.

Such an incident could, of course, have happened in the night-time streets of any major Western city. It could be an image of modern attitudes to the value of human life. It could be a reflection of a degree of desperation which most of us are fortunate enough never to experience. But there, in that small town in northern Zambia, it seemed to me to sum up a truth about the gap between the First and Third Worlds. What was too small even to register on the consciousness in one place was a matter of life and death in the other. Suddenly I became aware that so many of the perspectives I had always accepted without even thinking were supported by a whole raft of questionable assumptions. It was a moment of insight as important for me as the one which overwhelmed me when I first entered an Ethiopian refugee camp when even the flesh on my body seemed truly to be a luxury.

This is a book about the heavy burden of debt which is being carried by the Third World. It explains how the mechanisms of international finance transmit that burden so that it falls upon the shoulders of the very poorest people in those countries. It then considers what are the implications of those who, like me, profess a Christian faith and asks what responsibilities we have in working towards a solution of the problem.

I am not an economist or a theologian. I hope that will be accounted a virtue by readers who are themselves neither. Most books on such a subject begin by sketching the overall framework in which the problem exists. Mine does the opposite. It is the account of a personal journey and therefore begins with a personal experience – the first encounter I had with the horror of an Ethiopian refugee camp where people were starving to death as I watched. Before long I came to learn that the individual stories of deep anguish which were told to me by those hapless refugees were repeated, on a routine basis, throughout the Third World. More than 1,000 million people[1] – about one in five of the world's entire population – experience hunger for at least part of every year as the agricultural seasons pass with their meagre fruits. They also lack clean water, elementary education and basic health care. Some 250,000 small children die from starvation or easily preventable illness *every week*.[2] For me these would now always be more than statistics. They were people, and I had looked into their eyes.

But this is not a horror story. From there the journey took me through a number of African countries, and later to Asia and Central America, where I began to discern common threads in the economic and political difficulties under which poor people laboured all over the world. My focus then shifted – to Washington, London and New York – where the decisions were taken which set the context in which the poor suffered and starved. Examination of the world's financial apparatus then led me to moral and spiritual reflection on the justice of a global system which can allow such anguish. From there I returned to the Third World to wonder at the positive approach which so many of its people are showing, even in the face of such degrading and dehumanising poverty, and to wonder how those who care in the First World can best go about helping them.

The total debt of the Third World early in 1990[3] stood at $1.319 trillion – a figure so enormous as to be meaningless even when spelled out in full: what the poor nations are said to owe to the rich is $1,319,000,000,000. Even before the ink was dry on the announcement the debt had grown again. It continues to grow exponentially.

To repay it Third World governments are being forced by the international monetary authorities to cut food subsidies to the poor and their health and education budgets. After decades of improvement in levels of child nutrition and literacy the situation in much of the Third World has begun to decline. The United Nations children's organisation, Unicef, has worked out that as a result of these budget cuts a total of one million African children have died in the last decade. Throughout the developing world an additional 500,000 children died, from this direct cause, in 1988 alone.[4]

Most people think that the rich world helps the poor world by sending it aid. The sad reality is that, even at the best of times, the amount the First World sends in aid is less than half of what we take from the Third World in terms of the tariffs and duties we impose on the raw materials they sell us.[5] In the past decade that situation has actually worsened because of the build-up of debt which has been allowed. The latest figures show that the debt and interest payments due from the Third World are three times more than all the aid they currently receive.[6] According to figures published by the World Bank in 1990 the countries of the Third World in the previous year sent to the West some $52,000,000,000 more in debt repayments than they received from us.[7]

Throughout most of the last decade the overall flow of resources has not been from rich to poor but from poor to rich.

Far from playing the Good Samaritan the rich world has developed a new role. Today we are Bad Samaritans. We do not simply pass by on the other side, as did the priest and the Levite in the parable. We cross over and announce our intention to help. We take the injured man to the inn. But we do not acknowledge that he has been injured and robbed by men who work for us. The silver we pay for his convalescence is only a small proportion of what our agents have stolen from him. We have created a new dimension to the parable. We are not just blind to his needs as were those men in the original story. We are blind to an even greater injustice. We are blind to our own role in the proceedings.

In the past there may have been some excuse for this myopia. The iniquities of the system of international trade and finance have been disguised in the jargon of macroeconomics which is remote from most people. Its proceedings seem too complex to understand and, in any case, appear irrelevant to our daily lives. But the Third World debt crisis – which has now rumbled on for almost a decade, but which is a crisis still for all that – has drawn attention to the direct relationship between poverty and high finance. It is impossible for us in this era of colour photography and television satellites to remain unaware of the misery which infests the life of so many of our fellow human beings.

This is the relationship which is examined in this book. I hope to take the reader through the shocking detail of that relationship much as I discovered it. We will look at how the complexity of finance is used, often wilfully, to disguise the degree of our exploitation of our fellow men and women – an exploitation which, if it were presented more directly, would be deemed by most people to be totally unacceptable. We will examine also the concept of structural sin and how individual acts of greed or injustice can quickly build a system whereby all participants, willing or not, are compelled to play by the same sinful rules. We will consider to what extent such structural sins may be inherent in the free market capitalist system which today dominates the world economy as never before and which even the erstwhile communist countries of Eastern Europe, after the momentous events of 1989 and 1990 which followed the opening of the Berlin Wall, now seem eager to embrace.[8] We will explore the changing response of the Church to the problems which this has thrown up. Finally we will look at some possible solutions and the role which individual Christians can play in working towards them.

I am indebted to a number of people who have assisted me in working through this process. The late Charles Douglas-Home, as editor of *The Times*, first sent me to Africa and encouraged my interest in the practice and theory of aid. His successor, Charles Wilson, allowed me to pursue the issue for a further two years, long after most other newspapers had lost interest in the aftermath of famine in Africa and its international ramifications. John Wilkins, the editor of *The Tablet*, first suggested the idea of a series of articles on The Structures of Sin. Robert Ellsberg of Orbis Books in New York suggested they should be expanded into this volume. Pat Walsh, Paddy Walsh, Michael Nazir-Ali, Richard Thomson and Stuart Vernon helped on individual points of theology, ethics, banking and law. Charles Elliott, Julian Filochowski, Patrick Fitzgerald WF, John Mitchell and Chris Sugden all read the book in manuscript form and offered a host of helpful comments. Margaret Breen gave unstinting help on a welter of details.

Most of all my wife, Heather, and daughter, Catherine, helped in countless often indirect ways. For all of which, thanks.

Notes

The British use of the word billion has long been abandoned by the banking world in favour of the American usage. Therefore in this text: billion = 1,000 million and trillion = 1,000,000 million.

I have taken quotations from whichever translation of the Bible seemed most apposite.

One of the most vexed issues in this debate is that of terminology. Long ago the expression 'under-developed' country was dropped because it was felt to be demeaning to the peoples who lived there. Similar reservations have been expressed about most of the other commonly used terms.

The phrase 'developing country' has also now fallen into disfavour. As one Third World economist has written: 'By using a term that presupposes that these very poor countries are developing, an important question is begged.'[9] Many in the Third World, as we shall see, have come even to reject the word 'development'. Others have rejected the phrase 'Third World' on the grounds that it describes most of the world's nations as if they had come last in a race, though in fact it was thought to be coined by a French demographer, Alfred Sauvy, who had in mind the 'third estate' of France before the Revolution, which constituted everyone except the privileged first and second estates, the aristocracy and the clergy.

Some Third World theorists have suggested that, as they constitute the majority of the world's population, they should be called the Two-Thirds World, which has the unfortunate odour of a bad pun about it. Others object even to the terms 'rich' and 'poor', suggesting that in spiritual terms they could, in fact, be inverted. North and South have been suggested as synonyms by the Brandt Report but these, with geographical approximations so rough that they neglect Australia, sit uneasily still in the minds of many. I rejected as perverse a suggestion that I should create new terms of my own, on the grounds that it would only cause more confusion. Instead I have therefore struggled with an uneasy mixture of all of these terms where they seem most apt. Such a struggle is a symbol in itself.

Twickenham
July 1990

Chapter One

ETHIOPIA: THE EYES OF THE DYING

'Encompassed on all sides by the enemies of their religion,
the Aethiopians slept near a thousand years, forgetful of
the world, by whom they were forgotten.'
                    Edward Gibbon, Decline and Fall

'Give a rich man less food and he becomes thin; give a
poor man less food and he dies.'
                    African proverb

It was 6 a.m. A chill dawn crept over the mountains that
glowered intimidatingly all around the vast plateau of Korem
and the camp which huddled, unprotected, in the centre of
its plains. The growing light revealed a layer of mist, white
and impenetrable and distinct as a geological stratum. The
coldness, local people called it. It hung like a judgement
over Ethiopia's largest refugee camp.
    The new day stole shamefacedly across the serried ranks
of tents, uncovering a tableau of indignity, suffering and
wretched resignation which the darkness had disguised.
There were almost one thousand tents, improvised from
sticks and large plastic sheets stretched across shallow pits
dug into the hard black earth that was once prime crop-
growing land. On average forty men, women and children

were packed into each one; the proximity helped to preserve their body warmth against the cold Ethiopian winter night. These were the lucky ones; many others had no shelter at all.

I stood and watched, with the slow incomprehension of a visitor from another world. It was the first month of 1985. A week before I had been in London, settled in the comfortable routine of life in one of the world's great metropolitan centres. And now this.

With the start of another day the refugees shook themselves into movement. In their makeshift homes, open at either end to the elements, they shivered as they removed the blankets and thick *shammas*[1] which protected them from the sub-zero temperatures of the highland night. They bared their pitiful sagging skin for a few moments as they donned the thinner white garments which later in the day would deflect some of the anger of the hostile sun.

In the distance the funeral parties could be seen. Nine people had died in the night. Only nine. There was a time when more than a hundred died every day in Korem, but that had been three months before when thousands of starving peasant farmers and their families had arrived each day, many of them beyond help. Now the flow of new arrivals had slowed to a trickle. Korem was no longer a place of crisis, but one of dogged drudgery and seemingly hopeless survival. There were no farmers here any more; they had become camp-dwellers who seemed to have forgotten everything except how to struggle through another day. Many of them had been here for ten months, some longer. Nine deaths were just part of the new reality that was camp life.

Waiting was what happened at Korem: waiting for the clinic to open, waiting for admission to the feeding programme, waiting for attention in the crowded hospital sheds, waiting for the preparation of the high-energy food for the badly malnourished children, waiting for the government distribution of grain which did not come yesterday, does not come today and probably will not come tomorrow. Everywhere there were queues or else great herds of people, penned inside black plastic fences designed to bring some order to the milling chaos of bodies. Between the corrugated-iron hospital sheds they sat and waited, sometimes glancing up with feeble curiosity as relief workers moved purposefully by. In their tents they sat and waited, their features washed by blank indifference. In desultory groups across the unsheltered plains they sat and waited for the temporary release of food or the permanent one of death.

Outside one tent, crouched with his buttocks resting on his heels, was Aberbe Gabru. There was grey in the tight curls of his dark hair and his beard was grizzled, but he did not look the seventy years he claimed. They are hardy, these mountain people, and once they have passed the age of five, below which half the children die, they can in normal times live to a good age. Before him Gabru had five scrappy bundles of wood. He squatted on his haunches on the hard ground and surveyed them.

'What are these for?' I asked. The old man looked mystified as the question was translated.

'They are firewood, he says.'

Wood was in short supply, I knew that. Months of fuelling the tiny cooking fires had denuded the surrounding landscape of trees.

'Where did he get them?'

'From the hills.'

'How long did it take him?'

'Two days. Every time he goes for firewood he says he must walk further.'

'Where did he sleep last night in the hills?'

'Between the rocks.'

'What will he do with them? Use them or sell them?'

The old man made no reply, but looked at me and then at the pathetic piles of sticks. His fellows in the camp were destitute. Only a visitor or someone from the nearby town could afford to buy firewood. What were they worth, I wondered. More than I could have carried with me, I thought, weighing up the cost in human distress of the little collection of twigs before me. I pulled two *birr*[2] notes from

the bundle in my pocket and gave them to him. Like most
of the currency in the rural areas the notes were tattered
and disgustingly soiled. They smelled of sweat and dirt and
seemed impregnated with the misery of his entire nation. He
was elated. The two *birr* would buy him enough grain, even
at the grossly inflated prices of Korem's street-market, to
last him with frugal use for a couple of weeks. In the bar of
the Addis Ababa Hilton they would not even have bought a
glass of beer.

At 9 a.m. the expatriate relief workers from the Save
the Children Fund (UK) and the medical volunteers from
Médecins Sans Frontières[3] arrived from their ramshackle
hotels in the town. They listened to the reports of the local
people whom they employed as field workers in the camp.
In the feeding areas the news was that there would, that day,
not be enough food to give their 7,520 badly malnourished
children the six daily meals they needed for recovery. Two
meals would have to be omitted, the local SCF co-ordinator,
Ato Fekadu, reported. In the hospital wards the nightwatchmen who all wore, almost as a badge of office, absurd floral
kipper-ties, fashionable imports from the time when the
Emperor Haile Selassie kept Ethiopia in communion with
the West, reported to the medics on who had died and who
had been badly ill in the night.

Dr Serge Bechet was not long out of medical school. Like
all the French medics there he was in his late twenties; the
career structure for doctors in France is such that the only
time they can easily volunteer for service in the Third World
is between college and their first job. Korem was a baptism
of blood: the patients and the problems were so many. The
young doctor shrugged. 'There is only one problem here –
starvation. People are dying of dysentery, pneumonia, typhus
and relapsing fever, but what they really die of is hunger.
The average weight of an adult here is thirty-four kilos, half
the weight of a healthy person. What we need is more food.
We are discharging people when they are better and they go
out and get no food and become ill again.'

In the SCF centre the charity's senior field worker, Kathy

Bogan, was briefing her staff before she left on a two-day journey to another SCF camp at Kobbo and on to the towns of Kombolcha and Dese, the sites of the massive provincial warehouses which stored the grain brought in from the port of Assab, where aid was unloaded. The reports were that the warehouses were full, yet grain had not been reaching Korem in sufficient quantities for the past six weeks. Kathy Bogan wanted to know why.

Save the Children had six fully-trained nutritionists in the camps, along with fifty Ethiopian auxiliaries and 120 peasant farmers recruited in a Food For Work programme, which offered grain in return for help in the camp's gigantic kitchens. As Kathy set out, her team began their daily tasks. That day in Korem there were about a hundred newcomers just arrived from the outlying countryside, most of them in a desperate condition. They had to be weighed and measured to determine the exact degree of their malnourishment and then allocated to one of three feeding programmes. After the new admissions the centre had listed in its books 742 children who were classified as 'up to 20 per cent underweight'. These would need extra high-energy food to supplement the rations which the government's official relief organisation was supposed to distribute to everyone in the camp; that meant an extra 500 grams of rice porridge and a quarter of *kitta*, a bread pancake, all cooked in massive pans in the camp kitchen, plus two high-protein biscuits. In the category of 'between 20 and 30 per cent underweight', which in the relativity of starvation is classed as 'moderately malnourished', there were now 5,815 little specimens of skin and bone who should have had intensive feeding of six high-energy drinks made up of soya wheat-flour, butter oil, dried skimmed milk, sugar and boiled water, plus two meals each of biscuits, porridge and *kitta*. In the category of more than 30 per cent underweight – 'critically malnourished' – were now 963 children who were deemed to need intensive feeding, which meant all the above plus a further six helpings of the revitalising drink.

This is what they should have received. But supplies had

been severed by the Ethiopian government, which claimed a transport shortage. Many relief workers, however, suspected that the stoppage was a deliberate attempt to starve peasants into 'volunteering' for the government's controversial resettlement scheme. The supply of food had not dried up a mile down the road at the transit camp for those who had agreed to move from the unstable self-sufficiency of the wild highlands into regimented resettlement villages in the south-west of the country, where they would work in government-controlled collectives to produce coffee for export. Either way the result was, on that one day in Korem, 6,778 starving children would receive four tiny meals instead of the six their frail bodies needed. There were some who were too ill to care; eighty-seven were being fed through the nose with gastric drips.

After being placed in one of the three categories those newcomers who were able to walk crossed to the de-lousing unit, where their clothes were steamed for twenty minutes in old oil drums above steady fires while their skin was treated for parasites and their heads were shaved. 'Many people find it shameful but it has to be done,' said the Ethiopian aid worker at the door of the rough jute screen which surrounded this area of final humiliation. Visitors were not encouraged to go in to watch.

Back at the hospital, where the bare earth was covered only with green plastic sheets, a young Belgian midwife, Ines Huberty, was busy in the maternity wards. She worked in jeans and a T-shirt, her long curly hair uncombed. She had already delivered four babies that morning. 'Life goes on, even here,' she said. 'Besides, the birth of a new child is one of their few happinesses. Most women have already lost so many.'

She worked with a matter-of-fact speed, interrupted by the occasional burst of affection as she lifted one of the shrivelled infants and pressed a kiss to its forehead. At that moment she was crouching over what looked like a new-born baby, though in fact it was eight months old.

'Her name is Hadas. She was completely malnourished

when she arrived three months ago and she had bronchial pneumonia. First she gains weight, then she gets diarrhoea and loses it. I am trying to fix an intravenous unit to rehydrate her, but I can't find a vein big enough to put the needle in. She is too small. Look.'

The little girl's bulbous head, her arms, her legs, were covered with veins raised and bruised by the nurse's attempts. Finally she shifted a silver foil package that was getting in the way and successfully fixed the drip in the child's fragile arm, which was no thicker than my index finger.

What was in the package?

'A baby.'

It had looked as if it was a pack containing her sandwiches for lunch. She opened the foil to reveal a tiny, tiny human being.

'It will die. It is too small, it came very early. In Europe it would be in an incubator, in Africa it will die.'

It was past midday now, the seventh hour as the highlanders called it, using a clock that has not changed since biblical times.[4] The sun was hot and a sickly sweet stench has risen throughout the camp – a mixture of sweat and human excrement, of decay and death. It clung inside my nostrils even after the relief workers invited me to return to their base for lunch under a canvas awning. The French medics beckoned me to a table that was spread with tins of paté and tuna fish, rice with diced salami and a salad of tinned beans and tomatoes. It was modest enough by the standards of their homeland. After the camp, with its queues of strained faces and its bowls of milky gruel, it looked like a feast. I hesitated, overcome by a feeling that to eat would be somehow inappropriate.

'Trust the French to eat well,' I said hastily, to cover my embarrassment.

'What do you expect?' demanded a young nurse, detecting an unintended accusation in the comment. 'If we ate as the people do in the camp we should weaken, catch the illnesses and be of no use to anyone. We are workers, not romantics.'

At the ninth hour, back to the camp. Ato Fekadu was organising the supplies of food for the next day's cooking. In the compounds groups of two or three thousand people were sitting in rows, waiting patiently, placidly, more from awful habit than from expectation. They knew there would not be any more food coming round that day. There had not been enough. There never was. But they had nothing more productive to do than to carry on waiting. So still they sat there, ignoring the fact that there was food in plenty on offer at the resettlement camp only a mile down the road.

In the hospital the doctors were making the rounds of the non-emergency cases, whom they had not had time to see during the hectic morning session when people had still the illnesses of the night upon them. In the children's ward a young Frenchwoman with the worried smile of an earnest sophomore was looking at a two-year-old child. Dr Valerie Schwoebel was in fact aged twenty-nine and a fully qualified paediatrician. She was talking to a nurse about the child. 'She is much better, she is doing fine.'

'This little girl is called Sege. I have to confess she is one of my favourites. When she arrived, months ago, she was badly starved and we fed her up. Then, three days ago, she developed pneumonia; weak children often do after measles. I had to use an aspirator to remove the fluid that had accumulated in her lungs but I think now she will be OK.'

She bent down and touched the sleeping child gently on the head. It was a gesture of love. The doctor smiled. She did not know that the next morning she would stare in disbelief at an empty bed. Sege was to die that night.

The chief local official of the government's Relief and Rehabilitation Commission was wandering through the camp on a tour of inspection. Yeshitila Demerraw was kind and genial, but cowed by the weasel-faced Workers' Party man who dogged his every step. These were the men who were supposed to ensure a steady supply of food from the warehouses at Kombolcha and Dese.

'There is no food. There is none in the warehouses,' Yeshitila said.

'Write that down,' the Party man said to me.

Yet United Nations officials who had just completed a food distribution survey reported that the warehouses nearest to Korem were full to the ceiling, I replied. Yeshitila seemed genuinely perplexed to hear this. 'I did not know that. I had not been told. In any case we have no transport. We have only one lorry. You will have seen it broken down on the mountain road.'

But Colonel Mengistu Haile Mariam, the chairman of Ethiopia's provisional military council, the Dergue, had promised that army trucks would be used to move food now.

The Party man stood impassively at Yeshitila's side, affecting to gaze unconcernedly across the camp. By his shoulder he held the battered portable tape-recorder he carried everywhere. Yeshitila looked worried. 'I have not been told that. People do not tell me these things. I just have to do the best I can.'

He seemed to be doing that. There was genuine concern for those he surveyed as he showed me round his unhappy domain. As we walked we came across four women and a man who sat in a half-circle, moaning as they rocked back and forth, intoning some wailing litany. 'It is a funeral,' he explained. 'They are telling of the qualities of the woman who died and was buried this morning.'

This was the reality I had been avoiding all day. I nerved myself to walk across to the woman who was obviously the chief mourner. I stood before her, a silent but brutal interruption. She was a small woman, strikingly beautiful, with the fine-sculpted features of the Abyssinian highlander. Her ears were pierced, but now they were bare of the jewellery that had been in her family for generations. It was the last thing she would part with, but it had been sold that morning to buy the swaddling bands for the burial. Later I found that such jewellery made its way to the market in Addis Ababa where we aid tourists could buy the ear-rings for five dollars a pair; for twenty dollars you could purchase the solid silver cross of a dead Ethiopian priest. The woman looked at me. There were tears in her eyes, but no accusation. Perhaps my intrusion seemed no more barbarous than all the others which had been forced upon her in recent months.

'Who has died?'

Yeshitila translated my question.

'Her sister.'

'Where was she buried?'

'In the Coptic cemetery, over the plains. We have offered them a burial ground here but still, even in this condition, they prefer to walk for two hours to the churchyard.'

All the women were looking at me now. One of them had a growth the size of a large grapefruit in her throat, the result of a simple iodine deficiency which I knew could produce cretinism in her children. The appalling goitre[5] held my gaze like a magnet.

'What did she die of?'

'The illness, in the stomach.'

'When did she last eat?'

'Not for a long time, she says.'

'When did she last receive a food ration from the government?'

Yeshitila translated the question into Amharic. He did not fudge the answer.

'Six weeks ago.'

'Thank you,' I said, inadequately, to the woman. Something else seemed called for so I bowed to her, and then to the other women, and then to the man, before turning to walk away. It was late. The sun was being swallowed by another land beyond the mountains. Dusk falls as quickly as a curtain in these tropical highlands. As the gloom descended, the rocking orisons of the mourners rose again into the air and mingled with the blue smoke of a thousand tiny fires. Soon the coldness would be on the camp once more.

TWO WORLDS IN COLLISION

I had arrived in Ethiopia less than a week before from a different world entirely. Until then all my assignments for *The Times* had been within Britain. I had travelled the world while working for other papers but my particular interest had always been in the arts. My international travels had been to interview opera singers, musicians, actors and directors. I had been to Africa only once before, to write a travel article on a safari holiday in Kenya. That had been all first class hotels and cloistered landrover drives where the least refined conditions we encountered were at the up-country safari lodge at Treetops, where Queen Elizabeth had spent her honeymoon. It had been all wild animals, graceful savannahs and smiling well-fed Kikuyu servants. Nothing could have prepared me for what I was brought to stare into the face of in Ethiopia in January 1985.

Had anyone asked me in those earlier days if I was a Christian I would have said I was. I had on a few occasions, most especially when alone on the wild and majestic moorlands of northern England, been seized by that fleeting sense of awe at the transcendence of nature and of my own insignificance which is a common precursor to religious experience. In my local church I had drawn comfort from the faith of others and from the framework which it created. But, I suppose, I had never felt challenged. It was a comfortable Christianity. Ethiopia threw all that into turmoil. I spent a month there before the government threw me out for unmalleable reporting. It was a month which threw faith into a mad kaleidoscope of influence and experience, much of it contradictory or irreconcilable.

There is a cycle of response to the awfulness of such an experience. It ranges through horror, anger, depression, guilt, indifference, determination and hope. Aid workers were later to tell me that it is, apparently, normal to shift through these emotions repeatedly, though I was not to know that at the time. The horror of the abject indignity of that first visit to Korem I think is beyond communication in words, and the pages above can only cast the palest of shadows. In those first days I stood, incredulous, face-to-face with people dying of hunger. I walked by long lines of them. Wherever I stopped there was a tragedy entire in itself – the hollow eyes, the shrunken limbs, the swollen belly spoke of an empty home, a barren field, a history of bereavement, a breakdown in something fundamental to human existence. I felt paralysed by its presence. All I had to fall back on was my instinct to write it down. Mostly I wrote of individual victims and of the immediate needs of the relief workers helping them. But after several days of harrowing observation and discussion with camp doctors I wrote this:

This is what happens when you starve to death: at first there is hunger and a craving inside which after two or three days turns to a pain. But the obsession with food does not last long. After four or five days the gnawing pains subside and the stomach wall begins to shrink. This is a process which can happen repeatedly in situations where food arrives only at rare intervals.

Even the thinnest person has just beneath the skin layers of subcutaneous fat. At the next stage the body begins to live off these reserves. How long they will last depends on how healthy you were to start with. In the affluent countries we often try to reach this stage by design; we call it slimming. If you are an African whose body has been weakened by years of poor diet and intestinal parasites this stage may last three weeks, or four perhaps. If you are getting a little food, no matter how meagre the supply, this could spin out the whole process for many months.

Eventually though your body runs out of fat and begins to live off the substance of the muscles in your thighs, buttocks and upper arms. In a desperate attempt to stay alive you are consuming your own body. As if in revolt at this unnatural act, your body erupts in all manner of warning symptoms. Your tongue begins to ache, sores appear at the corner of your mouth, your gums start to bleed or your hands and feet begin to swell. So does your stomach; in children, often aggravated by parasites, it becomes huge.

At this stage the hunger begins to eat into your brain. You have become too tired to work or make much effort to search for food. You have, by now, lost all interest in the idea of food anyway. You become irritable. Occasionally you fly into a real rage, for no reason at all. You find that you are unable to concentrate. You are becoming a different person.

About now, if you are a woman, you stop menstruating. Your body can no longer consider the possibility of reproduction. In any case you long ago lost interest in sex. There is little milk left now in your breasts for your infant.

Now your hair loses its colour and sheen. It goes soft and falls out in handfuls. Your skin begins to take on a piebald texture. A stranger could now count your every rib from ten yards away, and the TV cameras come much closer than that. Your upper arms have shrivelled to the width of your forearm, in which you can now see the two parallel bones and the ligaments which join them. Your elbows and wrists stick out like huge comic bulges in comparison. So do your knees, on legs which look like broomsticks covered in skin. Now you really know what is meant by the expression 'skin and bone'. It is all you are. Not that you care much. Your mind has gone past the stage of irritation now. You are overcome with an undefinable sadness. Your eyes have become glazed and a seductive apathy has seeped through every fibre of your body. As starvation takes its final grip you lose interest in everything, even in your own baby who is dying on your lap as you sit motionless, on the ground.

The aid workers who arrive do not seem to understand this. They keep trying to force you to eat the milky porridge they offer. They keep putting the spoon in your hand and guiding it to the baby's mouth. When they turn to the next sufferer you let it fall from your fingers. It falls to the dry soil and the flies buzz around; it does not enter your mind to wave them away. You do not even notice that they are crawling around the baby's eyes and over his face, which is shrivelled now like a little old man's. You sit and stare at nothing. All about you the world goes about its business. You watch through an impenetrable window. You will probably not actually die from malnutrition itself but the wasting has lowered your body temperature and increased your vulnerability to the most minor of infections. Death, when it comes, will be a blessed release.[6]

It does not take long however for horror to transform itself to outrage, and then the instinct is to look for someone to blame.

In Ethiopia there was an obvious target – a government which had adopted from its Soviet mentor a system of economic and social priorities which included enforced resettlement and collectivisation, implemented with the same ruthless consequences as had been produced in the Ukraine in the 1930s when similar policies had been pursued by Stalin. Its commitment to put systems before individuals was at best insensitive and at worst utterly callous. Nowhere was it more apparent than in the treatment of the cholera outbreak which gripped several of the camps at that time. The authorities were appalled not by the terrible epidemic itself but by the possibility that the news would get out. Cholera, unlike many of the other acute diarrhoeal killers, is a disease which governments are obliged to notify to the World Health Organisation in Geneva. To have done so would have jeopardised a deal which the government had signed not long before to sell, even at the height of the famine, dried meat to Egypt. It would also have meant international pressure for the cessation of the resettlement programme, which the government had hoped the Western agencies would help to fund, and which it saw as a vital element in its collectivisation of agriculture and 'villagisation' programme which sought to reorganise the population into settlements controlled by the Ethiopian Workers' Party. Hence the cholera could not be acknowledged. Ethiopian officials who reported its existence were told from above to be silent. In a police state like Ethiopia fear was one of the threads woven through the entire social fabric. The people feared the officials, the officials feared the Party men, the Party men feared the secret police, and the secret police feared the Dergue, within which there was constant wary circling around the remorseless leader, Colonel Mengistu.

There is something horribly unmistakable about cholera. Doctors who have worked with it speak of cholera eyes and cholera stench. To watch a man or woman being treated for it is an awful and haunting experience. When the patient is attached to an intravenous drip as much as 20 litres of rehydrating fluid can spew out of the bowels of a body gripped by the deadly vibrium. The Western doctors in the camps had no doubts, but the price of continuing working there was silence. In a camp like Harbo where the death rate leapt from fourteen to fifty-two a day when the cholera struck, the doctors had little option if people were to be saved. Local Ethiopian officials would admit nothing; when they contacted the Ministry of Health privately and asked for intravenous fluids their requests were turned down by mid-ranking officials who did not dare pass the news on up the line of command. Fuelled by a sense of outrage I wrote a series of articles, at the end of which I was visited by the secret police and dispatched to another part of the country. Some weeks afterwards I was to uncover the first proof that farmers, often split up from their families, were being forced at gunpoint on to trucks and Soviet air force Antanovs to be taken to the 'voluntary' resettlement areas; after my articles on that I was told that my visa would not be renewed and forced to leave Ethiopia the next day.

Locking horns like that with the politicians was, in retrospect, a way of reducing the problem to a size which I knew how to cope with; but it reduced me too. Later I realised that it had enabled me to walk through the camps looking only for evidence to support a case, almost impervious to the people around me. In its final throes starvation creates not pain but a glassy-eyed apathy whose victims sit like vacuous waxworks. In my wrath they had ceased almost to be people at all.

The next phase in the cycle of response was depression. From Addis Ababa it was possible to drive north for nine hours and see nothing but parched land, dried-out rivers and thousands of square miles of unyielding terrain. The logistical difficulties involved in distributing enough food to compensate for the vastness of the blow which nature seemed to have dealt were enormous. Even without the exacerbating problems of the Dergue's policies the people of this blighted land would have been in severe trouble. One phrase kept echoing in my mind: an act of God. The sheer size and intractability of the problem was mind-numbing. At the camp in Alomata a feeding programme and clinic were run by the evangelical agency World Vision. The relief workers were determined that the centre should not grow into a camp and insisted that people returned home after they had received their allocation of food. Only those children in need of intensive feeding were admitted to overnight care.

On most mornings there were about five hundred huddled in eight lines outside the centre. They had struggled in, those who had been able to make journeys which often involved several days' walk, and were now waiting for the arrival of Dr Hector Jalipa, a physician from the Philippines employed by World Vision. His task was to inspect each one and decide whom to admit. Some days he had as few as sixteen places to offer.

The day I joined him it took him two hours to progress through the waiting lines, which was just the prelude to his day's work. He pulled at the skin on the scrawny forearms of the children; on those he deemed most needy the skin fell back like wrinkled crepe paper, all its natural elasticity gone. He turned the worst to inspect their buttocks; where the skin hung down in folds, which he called 'its baggy pants', it showed that the child's body had exhausted all reserves of fat and had begun to live off the muscle. Dr Jalipa carried a small pad of scrap paper. On it he scribbled the name of the section the child should be admitted to: feeding or supplementary feeding, intensive or super-intensive wards, or simply the clinic where the problem was purely medical.

The anxious parents knew the value of these little scraps of paper, passports as they were to the border between life and death.

'He has no mother, he has no mother,' repeated a wild-eyed father, running behind the doctor, holding out his child who had earlier been passed over as insufficiently malnourished. The man was pushed away by the camp guards.

'He looks ill,' I ventured.

'He is, but others are more ill,' said Dr Jalipa.

The next boy was particularly thin, but the doctor spotted that beneath the ragged cloak which covered his arm was a little pink bracelet. The guards conducted a heated conversation in Amharic with the woman.

'Cut it off,' the doctor said, and moved on down the line. 'The bracelet means that the child was already in our feeding programme but his mother has sold his ration card in the market and was trying to get him readmitted to get another one. So I have thrown him out,' he explained.

For the woman it was a costly gamble to have lost. 'Yes, but she has to be taught a lesson or they would all do it, sell the ration card to buy coffee or some other thing in the market. In a few days she will reapply and we shall have forgotten all about it and readmit her.'

Dr Jalipa's daily round seemed a microcosm of the depressing enormity of the whole relief effort. There was something terribly arbitrary about who would reach him and who would not, whom he would choose and whom he would pass over, who would live and who would die. He was forced daily into making terrible decisions, and yet the wave of people continued to pour into his camp, making a mockery of what little he was able to do. I was seized with the conviction that his presence was utterly pointless.

Because the doctor professed himself a Christian I asked the question I had not found the courage to ask at Korem. How could he make these decisions, on whom to admit and whom to exclude? Was there not an awful sense of taking on a function which properly belonged only to God? 'It is because I am a Christian that I can do it. We choose the weakest and feed them because we do not want anyone to die and they are the most vulnerable. To a Christian every human life is sacred. A non-Christian might make a different judgement: we do not have enough resources to go around here so why waste them on children who are probably going to die anyway? why not give the food to those who have the best chance of surviving? That, as I understand it, is a common attitude in Africa and one that Ethiopian culture seems to share: if a woman here has two children, one weak and one strong, she will feed the strong one first. In war doctors do something similar; it is called *triage*.[7] But that does not seem to me to be a Christian approach.'

Such an approach produced the hapless situation where the doctor had to pass over a child today on the grounds that he was insufficiently malnourished to warrant treatment; tomorrow when the child had become ill he would be fed. 'Yes it is crazy; it means we feed them back to health and then release them. A few weeks later they are back because their families cannot feed them and the official rations arrive only sporadically.' There seemed no sensible response and my gloom deepened the more.

Between visits to the camps I returned to Addis Ababa to join the rest of the press corps who had ensconced themselves in the Hilton Hotel. By taking advantage of the multitude of aid planes flying daily to numerous destinations it was possible for the unadventurous journalist who did not want to overnight in the field to make day-trips to the squalor of the camps and return in the evening to the comfortable bars and cordon bleu restaurant at the Hilton. The hotel had one of the few reliable private telex machines in Addis; that, we said, was our prime motive for staying there, but few of us were unhappy at what now seemed the luxury of a hot shower and a good meal, and few of us escaped the pangs of guilt prompted by the juxtaposition of the two worlds. Some days, when I had to stay all day in the hotel to write, I found myself wallowing unashamedly in the luxury of the surroundings. I was overcome with a sense of relief that it was not me caught in the terrible tragedy of the poor Ethiopian peasants; it was a strange detachment which I found shocking even at the time.

The hotel seemed to symbolise many of the paradoxes at the heart of the strange universe in which I now found myself. It had two room rates, not because it had two different types of room but because on one side they overlooked the expansive swimming pool and had a view of the mountains on the horizon, on the other side they overlooked the shanty-town. In Addis Ababa, as in so many Third World capitals I was later to discover, there was none of the discreet propriety of the Western world where rich and poor occupy separate suburbs of the same town; here the privileged and the destitute lived cheek by jowl. Their only connection was in the surprisingly small number of beggars, the able-bodied as well as the maimed, who beseiged the foreigner as he left the sanctuary of the hotel grounds. Giving to them assuaged the guilt of not being able to do anything more about the famine than telex back stories about the need and the successes, limited though they could only be, of the relief effort. On my return to London one of my daughter's schoolfriends nailed this uneasiness with a simple question. 'What did you eat?' she asked. 'Couldn't you have taken the food from your hotel to the starving people?' There are no answers to questions so simple. In truth I had, with singular naivete, taken with me from England a two-pound bag of boiled sweets which I intended to dish out to children whenever appropriate. It never was. There were always too many children in any one place, and too few sweets. As with so much else, I had not brought enough.

There is a constructive as well as a negative side to guilt, but learning that was to prove more painful. Though it was quicker to fly around the highlands I had discovered that the long and arduous journeys overland were much more revealing. I set out in a bumpy landrover for the camp at Bati which until a few years before had been the second largest market in all Ethiopia. In the past, tens of thousands of farmers and nomads had gathered there, on the edge of the rift valley half-way between the highlands and the lowland desert plains. They had gathered again, but this time without the cereals and livestock which previously formed the basis of their trade. Both groups, some thirty thousand of them, were now destitute after a drought which had lasted almost five years.

The camp was accounted one of the successes of the region. Only around five people were dying every day. Government food supplies had been regular and the Red Cross had mounted a comprehensive medical programme. The people were in better health. Surprisingly, the effect was unnerving. In Korem people seemed to have gone beyond despair, beyond feeling even; they sat like breathing statues, drained of everything except the mechanics of being alive. At Bati the response was more devastatingly human. People smiled, cursed, begged, laughed, held out their hands or stared in silent accusation.

Between the tents a gleeful boy played with a toy made from a stick and the empty box of an anti-diarrhoea medicine. In the yard of the feeding centre the men sat on their haunches in a semi-circle; some stared pointedly at the ground, others looked with pleading expectation, others yet with forthright curiosity and others with glaring hostility. I found it hard not to avert my gaze. It did not feel right that an outsider should witness their shame, their prostrate degradation. These people were robbed of independence, initiative and privacy; they are a proud people and they resented it.

Kubra Muhammed was in the clinic watching her two children being weighed. They were the same size, though the boy Hussein was three and his sister Wela was only one year old. Hussein held his hand over his eyes; he did not want to be weighed. Wela acquiesced placidly. I asked the interpreter a list of questions which had by now become a mawkish routine and she translated the replies.

'She says she is forty, she thinks. Her husband left her six months ago to look for work. She has not seen him since. She does not know where he has gone. They have run out of the grain they stored at the last harvest. Last year was a bad harvest but this year there has been nothing at all. She has come to live here. The boy will get supplementary feeding, the girl will not.'

Then Kubra Muhammed turned and spoke to me. 'Why do you want to know all this?'

In the hospital tent the canvas walls had Christmas pictures still fastened above the beds. They had been sent by children

in Scandinavia, anachronistic reminders of a time before this
new reality. In one corner, under a picture of a snowman,
sat Fatima Muhammed. She was a beautiful woman with the
fine features of the Afar nomads. She smiled as I approached,
and yet before her was the most horrifying sight I had ever
seen.

On the bed was her eighteen-month-old child, Hadra. She
lay like a grotesque puppet, her head huge, her limbs like
insensible twigs flopped aimlessly about her. Her huge eyes
stared with such ferocity as if they had an independent life
and were straining to move back inside her head, away from
the world outside which had brought her to this. Her mouth
was open, and a fly ran around its pitiful circumference.

It seemed an inanity to ask, but I did: 'How is the child?'

'She is dying. Soon I will be able to go back to my village
to see my son. He is four years old.'

I told her I was sorry and I hoped that the boy was well.
She smiled and said something else.

'What was that?' I asked the interpreter.

'She says, thank you. She says how are you? How is your
family?'

I smiled and nodded, with no real answer to give. She
smiled too. We smiled at each other over the dying body of
the matchstick child.

It was from the guilty realisation at Bati that – until now
– I had not responded fully to the humanity of the victims
that the next phase of the cycle of reactions began. It was
one of determination that something must be done. Once
my perspective had shifted I began to notice that all over
Ethiopia were signs of hope. They lay in the acts of generosity
and devotion of individual aid workers and in the gentleness
and courtesy of women like Fatima. Small comfort perhaps,
but some comfort at least. The manifestations differed. There
was the atmosphere of beatific peace amid the material
squalor in the camp run by Indian nuns from the Sisters of
Charity for the 'hopeless cases' – the old, the lame, the blind
and the dying whom other relief organisations had turned
away. There was the feverish dedication of a young Irish

nurse, Maggie Darragh, who had come from her previous posting in Zambia to run singlehandedly a small health post in Sidamo which she kept open the day I met her despite suffering herself from a severe attack of malaria. There was the quiet bustle of the mission run by Sister Colette in the south of the country which, with its textile workshop, school, clinic, well-digging project and its peripatetic mother and child primary health programme, spoke amply of the English nun's twenty-five-year commitment to the country.

Earlier I had met a nun working at a relief camp in the northern province of Tigré. Her base was surrounded by the area which was held by the anti-government rebels of the Tigré People's Liberation Front. Because of the fighting, aid reached the people there from neither side. She told me that she could 'see the face of Christ in the suffering of the poor'. I had been mystified by the notion. All I could see there was a blank abnegation. I had given her the large bag of boiled sweets which had become as burdensome as an unkept promise.

But now, even if I could not see the face of Christ I could see his hands busy in the compassionate tasks of the relief workers, both religious and secular. The hungry were fed, the naked were clothed and the sick were comforted. Here were people, not daunted by the enormity of the problem, responding with the immediacy which characterised the unhesitating actions of the Good Samaritan. A quotation from Edmund Burke began to turn repeatedly in my mind: 'Nobody made a greater mistake than he who did nothing because he could only do a little.' It was a sentiment which found a direct correlative in the wave of generosity which swept the affluent nations when the Live Aid concert raised almost $100 million for the drought-stricken region, more than any charitable event had ever before raised. It was a start, but it was not long before I began to realise that the problem was bigger than that.

Chapter Two

AROUND AFRICA: COMMON DENOMINATORS

'All the inland parts of Africa . . . seem in all ages of the
world to have been in the same barbarous and uncivilised
state in which we find them at present.'
Adam Smith, The Wealth of Nations

'We carry within us the wonders we seek without us: there
is all Africa and her prodigies in us.'
Sir Thomas Browne, Religio Medici

Africa is not just another continent, it is another time. Most
water there is drawn still from the well or the river. Most
food is reaped with simple blades from land that was sown
by hand and turned laboriously without the aid of any beast.
Fruit still grows wild, when the weather is kind, to be plucked
in season from the bushes and trees. Wheat is ground between two stones and bread baked, unleavened, on top of a
wood fire. Men and women rise with the sun and count the
hours in single progression through the midday until dusk
when they sleep. I have travelled in Israel but it nowhere
evokes the presence of the biblical age in the way that Africa
does. The single-bladed hoes used to turn the hard land are
only slightly larger and squatter than the spears which the

hunters and warriors still carry in the more remote areas; to think of weapons being beaten into ploughshares requires a smaller leap of imagination than would be called for with the sophisticated agricultural and military technologies of the developed world. Here Christ's parables, drawn from the life of the land and from the daily realities of rural existence, have a new immediacy.

After the shock of the camps in Ethiopia I travelled widely throughout the continent for the next two years. Eventually a new perspective emerged on why Africa is the poorest area in the world, but there are a number of stages which must be charted in the process. These include questions about the political leadership of the poor world and the nature of the aid it receives. More fundamentally it raises questions on what we mean by 'natural' disasters, the type of incident which both the popular press and the insurance industry with unaccustomed piety refer to as 'acts of God', and on the complex issue of the population explosion.

About a month after leaving Ethiopia I travelled to Sudan to meet members of the Tigré People's Liberation Front, one of the rebel Ethiopian groups who had invited me to enter their country illegally by crossing the border directly into the territory they held. Reports were that no aid was reaching that area, where conditions were worse than in government-held parts of the Abyssinian plateau, and relief was urgently needed. By now it had become abundantly clear that the solution to Africa's problems was more likely to be found in protracted development work and not short-term relief, but for journalists, as for aid agencies, such thoughts were forced into the background by the sheer scale of the Ethiopian tragedy. Only later was I to discover the disproportionate nature of the developed world's response; in 1983 all the aid agencies in Britain raised between them around £1 per head of the population in response to the chronic crisis of Third World poverty which forces an incomprehensible one billion people[1] to spend at least part of each year in a state of malnourishment which annually kills 17 million people,[2] including 14 million children;[3] the appeal for aid during the famine in Ethiopia, which affected ten million people and may have killed a million men, women and children raised almost exactly the same amount.[4] By drawing the comparison I am not seeking to belittle the generosity of the reaction to the terrible famine in Ethiopia, nor the need for it; I merely note that individual donors, in common with many aid agencies and journalists, find it easier to relate to the drama of a particular event than to address the more deep-seated causes of the problem. Later we shall look at the theological tradition which has restricted the Christian response in a similar way. In early 1985, however, there was little time for such consideration.

POLITICAL CORRUPTION

I never got to Tigré. I had been in the Sudanese capital Khartoum for a week preparing for the difficult cross-border trek when it became clear that the rumours of discontent against the President of Sudan, Jaafar Nimeiri, were mounting into something more serious than mere rumblings. Like so many of the Third World's authoritarian rulers Nimeiri had come to power with a wave of popular euphoria and then, during the course of his sixteen years of increasingly capricious and dictatorial rule, had alienated one section of society after another. He had seized power as a young colonel in 1969 and within three years had brought peace to the country which had been in the grip of a civil war, with the mainly Christian South fighting against the domination of the largely Muslim North, by making major concessions to the autonomy of the South. His tactic for survival was to play off different social factions against one another. Over the years he banned trade unions, undermined the independence of the civil service and the judiciary, which had previously been run in the tradition of the former colonial power, Britain, and promoted the interests of his Sudanese Socialist Union. He borrowed heavily to pursue ruinous agricultural policies in pursuit of his dream to make Sudan the 'breadbasket of Africa' and the nation's crucial cotton industry was organised in such a way as to milk the land of quick profit from which the corrupt men of the SSU could take their ten per cent. In 1983 his heavy-handed manner towards the South provoked the civil war to begin once more. He nurtured a byzantine network of ruthless secret police and grew in megalomania as he did in age, frequently phoning junior officials to countermand the orders of their superiors or calling bank managers telling them to move money from one account to another. Towards the end he even appointed himself coach-in-chief to all the country's football teams, on the grounds that the existing coaches were incompetent.

The country was in dire financial straits. Its external debt was $9 billion dollars and it could not even afford to pay the interest on the loans. Then in September 1983 Nimeiri had undergone a sudden and unexpected conversion to Muslim fundamentalism and, in an attempt to woo cash from Saudi Arabia, had introduced *sharia* law, complete with its criminal punishments of mutilation and its distinctive fiscal codes. The economic effect had been the opposite of what was intended. The ban on alcohol among the beer-drinking Sudanese cost the treasury millions of dollars in lost taxation. His introduction of the Islamic system of alms-giving, *zakat*, to replace income tax, produced a two-thirds drop in revenue. His outlawing of usury and creation of Islamic banks with their privileged monopolies, tax exemptions and service charges which were three times the cost of the interest they prohibited under the Prophet's instructions led businessmen to withdraw money from circulation and send it abroad, invest it or simply hoard it.

His creditors were distinctly unimpressed. The United States had a history of strong support for a country which lay strategically between the adventurist Libya of Colonel Gaddafi and the Soviet-backed regime in Ethiopia. Sudan had become the largest recipient of US aid in sub-Saharan Africa, receiving $1 billion during the Reagan years. But eventually Washington decided to hold back large sums of cash. It insisted that Nimeiri lift government subsidies on food, petrol and other commodities before it would release $67 million it had already promised. Only weeks before I arrived Nimeiri changed tack yet again. He threw the fundamentalist Muslim brotherhood out of his cabinet, blaming them for the excesses of *sharia*, including the execution of a seventy-six-year-old theologian who had been deemed a heretic.[5] He reintroduced income and corporation tax. Secretly, and amply rewarded by a briefcase full of dollars from an agent of the American Central Intelligence Agency (CIA), he sanctioned the use of Sudan as an escape route, complete with clandestine dawn airlifts in the desert, for thousands of the persecuted Falasha sect, the so-called 'black Jews' of Ethiopia, who were being transported to the United States, Canada and Israel[6] – an arrangement which would have outraged the Muslim fundamentalists in his own cabinet and his financial backers in Saudi Arabia. Finally he decided also to introduce food price rises but thought it best if he was out of the country when the announcement was made. He flew to Washington soon afterwards and, while he was there, was overthrown in a bloodless coup.

Nimeiri was in many unfortunate ways typical of the second generation of African leaders in the post-independence period, who have seen their post not as one of stewardship but as an opportunity for personal aggrandisement and the accumulation of large personal Swiss bank accounts. It is important to acknowledge the faults of such men for, notwithstanding the later suggestions of this book on the issue of the global economy, there can be no real future for the people of the Third World while such leaders hold power and the undemocratic structures obtain which allow them to take it. Their behaviour only gives a specious credibility to the criticisms of those who find it convenient to lay the problems of the Third World at the door of its own leaders and thus avoid the necessity for action themselves. But we will later come to see that when it comes to villainy such men play a comparatively supporting role.

Riots immediately followed. They began in the market the day that the 33 per cent rise in the price of bread was announced. Women stoned traders. Men set fire to their stalls. The disturbance was fuelled when it was discovered that rises were due also in the cost of tea and sugar, commodities which even the poorest Sudanese consume in large quantities. Riot police quelled the protest with brutal efficiency, shooting several people dead. On the third day of the riots half of the capital's doctors voted to go on strike and called for other professions to join them in a general strike in leaflets which they distributed on the streets denouncing Nimeiri's 'regime of hunger'. On the fourth day leaflets began to circulate from the outlawed police union which declared 'the police have been a tool in the hands of the dictator Nimeiri'. A counter-demonstration could raise only around three thousand Nimeiri supporters; they could not even celebrate the news that President Reagan had agreed to unfreeze $67 million of the promised aid, though $114 million more was still being withheld, because in Sudan the US freeze had never been made public. In any case, by then it was too late. The next day the poor were joined by Khartoum's middle classes led by the professional bodies of the capital's doctors, engineers, lawyers, academics, bank workers and students. Even the judges' association lent its support to the twenty thousand people who marched the streets.

It was a quiet revolution when it occurred. On the Friday, the day of rest, and the tenth since the agitation began, the city woke to an eerie silence, with birdsong echoing down streets normally bustling, even on a holy day, with cars and street traders. At dawn roadblocks had been thrown around the capital. The boulevards were deserted and the city was holding its breath. The brown dust storm which had hung heavily in the air for the past three days had cleared. The skies were blue and empty. But the rumour was that Nimeiri had returned in the night and taken control, as he had done so many times in the past. Then, at 9.31 a.m., the official government station, Radio Omdurman, ceased its military music and introduced the head of the army, General Swar al-Dahab, who announced that in the name of God who was merciful the army had, to prevent bloodshed, taken over power, which would be handed back to the people after a transitional period.

Within seconds the city erupted into a joyous cacophony of shrieks, chants, laughter and the blowing of car horns. Khartoum's population is about four million. Suddenly it seemed as though most of them were on the streets cheering, dancing and waving branches of vermilion bougainvillea pulled from the trees along the old colonial avenues. The red- and green-bereted troops now moved from the road-blocks into the city centre. Waves of happy citizens called to them: 'The army and the people are one.' The soldiers raised their rifles in reply and grinned. There was only one negative note in the proceedings. Large sections of the crowd began chanting in English 'Down, Down USA', 'Down, Down IMF'[7] and 'We say no to World Bank policies.' It was the first time that I had heard a direct link made between the policies of the world's financial establishment and the hunger of the poor. It was not to be the last. For the time being, however, the diplomats to whom I spoke brushed the topic aside: the economic mess was due to bad management and the world recession; the happy Sudanese were chanting out of ignorance.

The truth could not be established then in Khartoum. Besides, there were more immediate stories demanding a journalist's attention. The flow of emaciated Ethiopians making the long trek from their parched highland homes into the desert fringes of eastern Sudan had suddenly swelled to a flood. There were now hundreds of thousands squatting under the fierce lowland sun in camps along the dusty plain just inside the border. I catalogued the specific plight of seven of them in a series of articles, but every refugee camp is a distillation of human misery and little would be gained from a repetition here of such massive woe. Dante summed up the vision well when he imagined the seventh circle of hell: 'A plain of arid close-packed earth, which spurns all foliage from its withered surface; where exhausting heat, reflected from the sands, redoubles pain; where great herds of naked souls most wretchedly bewail their lot, some supine on the ground, some upon their haunches squatted low, other roaming ceaselessly and resting not.'[8]

There was one experience in those camps which was to change my attitude once more, but it was two years before I felt ready to write about it and then only for a specialist magazine, Children First,[9] published by Unicef:

> Already she was too old to run, this little woman of thirteen years. Haste was the unseemly mark of a child; she would leave that to her little brother who was only six and to me, the peculiar journalist from Europe who had brought to Africa with him the pointless urgency of an alien way of life.
>
> Berhana Nagash walked slowly, as befitted the dignity of a Tigrean woman who, in the ancient culture of the Abyssinian highlands, was already two years past the marriageable age.
>
> Three days earlier her father had died of a bloody diarrhoea by the dusty roadside on the long trek from Tigré to Sudan in search of food and away from the war between the Ethiopian government and the Tigrean rebels. Berhana and her brother Kassa, whose name in Amharic means consolation,[10] were left alone five weeks' walk from their home in the Tembien Plateau. They had not seen their mother since their parents quarrelled five months before and she moved out of their home to live with their uncle's family in another village. Divorce is that easy in the highlands.[11]
>
> It was 1985. This was the other side of the Ethiopian famine which was making so many airtime minutes for television and column inches for newspapers out of Addis Ababa. The mass exodus of hundreds of thousands of peasants to Sudan was never such big news. Two years later many of those peasants who made the long trek have made the arduous journey home and now this story is no longer news at all. Yet this is the story which remains with me.
>
> For two days after the death of their father the children had walked with the straggling crowd until they reached the town of Angerab where the rebels' own relief society, REST, had established a feeding point for the migrants. There Berhana spotted a man from her uncle's village. He was one of the handful of Tigreans who were heading in the opposite direction. He had gone to Sudan some time before but found no hope there – no

work, no prospects of emigration, and no sign of any remission from the terrible oppressive heat of the malaria-ridden lowlands camps. Now he had decided to make the long journey home to where he had hidden a small supply of seed grain in the hope that he would be able to plant a crop in the season of the short rains. In the chaos of conflicting desperations in this forsaken part of the world these returnees had stopped to eat in the same transit centre used by those leaving Tigré after having finally given up hope of trying to eke out a survival from the dry impoverished soils of their homeland.

The man told Berhana that her mother Mebrahtu had been in the Sudanese reception camp at Wad Kowli and might be there still. The girl approached the REST officials at Angerab and asked to be sent to Wad Kowli. The two exhausted children were put with a group of fifteen orphans to travel there in a food lorry which was returning empty to Sudan.

They arrived at Wad Kowli in the middle of the night and Berhana had to wait until morning to tell the REST officials of her hopes. Perhaps they had too many other problems to deal with. Perhaps their priorities were different. At any rate they did nothing. Until, that is, the Western journalist arrived.

I interviewed a number of people at random. Then I came across Berhana and her story. I demanded that something be done. They said it would be, when they could find the time. No, I insisted, it must be done now. They looked at me as if I was odd but agreed and looked up her name on the camp plan.

We went in a line – the boy and I hurrying and Berhana, with quiet dignity, following behind and gazing without apparent curiosity at the haphazard collection of yellow straw shelters around her. But when we reached the mother's hut it was empty. A blank incomprehension clouded their features. Mebrahtu had been taken ill and was in the camp clinic, the people around said.

At the hospital the REST official made them wait outside as he searched the long lines of figures slumped against a mud wall, waiting for treatment.

The children moved slowly when he came to fetch them. Their mother was sitting on the hard earth in the middle of the massive gloomy ward, leaning against one of the poles which supported the straw roof. The woman was aged forty but she looked thirty years older. Her bony face was drawn with pain and her limbs were too weak to move in salutation. Berhana and Kassa moved to stand before her. Only her eyes betrayed the recognition.

There was no sudden drama to the reunion, only a tense formality. Berhana stepped forward and kissed her mother eight times on alternate cheeks. Then she stepped back and little Kassa did the same. Not a word was spoken.

The woman began a low ceaseless muttering which was painful to hear. This was not what I had expected of the situation I had engineered. I took out my camera. The newspaper would like a photograph. 'Move the children in by their mother,' I instructed the officials. The children stood beside her and looked at me, uncomprehending. They had not read 'happy family reunion' stories in Western newspapers. 'Tell them to put their arms around her,' I demanded. It still did not look right. They were stiff and unnatural. 'Tell them to kiss her cheek.'

They did as they were told. The camera flashed in the darkened hut. Then Berhana turned away. Slowly she moved out of her mother's sight and, silently, she began to weep. The little boy was shooed out of the hut by a camp official. He went without a word and only a slightly puzzled backward glance. In the corner Mebrahtu continued her whispering wail and waited for the doctor.

Outside, filled suddenly with self-disgust, I opened the camera and, under the rays of the merciless lowland sun, pulled out the film and threw it away.

Later I was to learn that the ancient culture of the highlands demanded that, from about the age of three, children should demonstrate total respect for their elders by remaining completely silent in the presence of adults, and this was rigidly enforced.[12] But even at the time, unaware of the details, I knew that I was guilty of the kind of arrogant insensitivity for which journalists are notorious. But it seemed to me more than that, it seemed a symbol of the manipulation implicit in the relationship between the developed and the developing worlds where power is used, consciously or unthinkingly, to bend the poor to the cultural requirements of the rich. I pondered the relationship. Clearly there was a Christian imperative, summed up in the Good Samaritan's action, to offer material help to those in need, and I was clear that my job, reporting the facts to those who could help, was a useful contribution. But it could not be a fully Christian response to do this in a way which robbed people of their dignity as my equals as members of the family of God. I had to use my expertise in a way which helped them to be more fully what they were, rather than to try to remake them in my own mould. It was only later that I realised this truth had economic implications too. There was intellectual baggage which needed to be left at the airport.

THE MISUSE OF AID

Not long after the fall of Nimeiri news began filtering through that the drought which had triggered the Ethiopian famine was now likely to do the same in the west of Sudan. Aid workers said that a million people were at risk and that half that number might die. It was almost 1,200 miles from Sudan's main port to some of the affected regions in the provinces of Darfour and Kordofan and the prospect of distributing food aid over an area which was the size of France and yet had almost no roads was daunting. There was a railway out to the town of Nyala but the final 300 miles of it were the narrowest gauge railway of any length in all Africa. Trains were forced to divide before they could traverse it; even then there were four or five derailments which closed the line every month because of shifting sand in the dry season and washed-away tracks in the rains.

This was a different kind of famine from that in Ethiopia and in the east of Sudan. The weeks I spent there chronicling the vagaries of the relief effort raised three new issues: how aid can become a political and ideological tool; how aid can be corrupted to benefit the middle classes and not the poor; and the extent to which natural causes are the prime cause of hunger.

One difference was apparent on arrival. It was hard to find the Darfour famine. There were no huge camps, though Save the Children and Unicef had set up two for refugees who had fled into the area from the war in neighbouring Chad. Instead there were pockets of hungry people spread over a wide area across the middle of the region, mainly living in the streets of small towns on the dusty tracks which served as arterial routes. Their deaths, singly and unnoticed in backstreets or on the desert fringes, were, I began to learn, far more typical of the normal pattern of death by starvation in the Third World than were the dramatic concentrations of the Ethiopian camps.

Migration to the area from the fringes of the Sahara in the north and the semi-desert reaches to the south was traditional. But it was usually restricted to the heads of families, who took their livestock to the central savannah for dry season grazing and then returned to their homes and families in time to plant a new crop in the rainy season. That year, however, after seventeen years of poor rains, severe drought had hit. The area had received only a quarter of its usual meagre rainfall, and entire families were on the move. In the region livestock prices fell by 400 per cent while grain prices soared: a sure indicator of the advent of famine. At the market in Nyala a cow would sell for only enough to buy bread for a couple of days. With nutritionists from Oxfam I drove past dozens of empty villages. One spoke for them all.

It stood on the crest of a hill, a collection of small houses of dry ochre grass surrounded by fences of dead thorn. Broken cooking pots with holes knocked in the bottom had been inverted and stuck on poles in the barrier of thorn, a hex against malignant spirits, we later learned. There were nine separate compounds, each containing two houses, some of which were starting to break open to the wind. Inside, low beds sprung with leather thongs stood covered in a fine brown dust. Ancient leather water skins lay in corners, shrivelled and desiccated as old fruit. Tucked neatly away behind one hut was a pack saddle for a donkey. It was hardly worn and could not have been made long. A few yards away bleached donkey bones lay half buried in the sand which between the compounds was blown into perfectly formed ribs by the Sahelian wind. No footprint had disturbed it for some time.

Even the flies seemed to have deserted it in the oppressive heat.

Then, from over a distant hill, appeared a bent figure of a woman. Under one arm she carried a massive basket. The village was called Hej el-Eja, she told us. Until a few months ago eighty people had lived there but they had long ago run out of food. They had eaten their seed. The wells were dry. Her name was Asha Abu Issak. She had once lived in a nearby village but she too had left and now lived in the streets in the town of Silaya where a little food aid was distributed by a German charity, but only a kilo a week, less than a third of what nutritionists consider the bare minimum.

She showed us her basket with its sparse layer of brittle desert dates and yellow *mokheit* berries which are poisonous but which can be eaten if they are soaked for three days. She had walked for nine hours from Silaya because all the nearby *mokheit* had now been gathered. Now it was running out there too and the season was almost over. The same story was told to me by scores of women throughout the region.

What was distinctive about this famine was that although some 95 per cent of Darfour's three million population were said to be in need of food aid there was enough food in the country to supply their needs. A massive commitment to provide food aid had been made by the United States government: Sudan was considered a strategic ally in the region and the Reagan administration was anxious to mount a copybook relief operation to prove the superiority of a private sector operation over centrally-planned relief efforts in Ethiopia, where food aid was clearly being used as a political weapon by the Marxist government to manipulate hungry peasants into participating in its collectivisation schemes. It was to cost $400 million and be the biggest single distribution of free food the world had ever seen.

The move rebounded badly on the US aid planners. This was partly because they failed sufficiently to investigate the actual capability of Sudanese Railways in comparison with its more impressive on-paper capacity; in practice it was a nightmare of bad management, restrictive practices and outright corruption. But it also failed because they placed undue faith in the abilities of the Sudanese private sector's trucking firms to outperform the state-controlled system in Ethiopia. Critics noted at the time that the Khartoum office of the United States Agency for International Development (USAID):

> . . . ignored the recommendation of every report on the railways that even with the system operating at its best lorries would also be needed; it badly underestimated the speed with which its own aid counterpart funds[13] could be recovered within Sudan; it did not look with sufficient care at the possibility of bringing in food from the Atlantic ports through Chad – as one German agency has successfully done. It handed out the contract to a single logistics firm with few lorries of its own, leaving it to the mercy of a sub-contractors' cartel. It acted with a self-confidence bordering on arrogance in not involving the Sudanese government in the operation . . .[14]

When agencies such as the Red Cross, Band Aid and Save the Children offered trucks these were turned down on the grounds that their interference would upset the market structure. When SCF turned up with empty lorries and offered to carry food one of the US employees of the major road contractor, which was half-American and half-Sudanese, told the agency: 'You're trying to cut me out of the market. I've got to make a profit, you don't. This is relief work not charity. It helps the US farmer who has excess grain. It helps the US silo man and the US shipping line. It helps a government which is a friend of the US. It helps a US company here in Sudan which then sends dollars back to the US. You want to rock the boat and upset that.'[15] Offers by UN organisations to help distribute the food aid were also turned down until it was too late. Two weeks before the rainy season was due to start there were 520,000 tons of US food in Sudan: 220,000 was being held at Port Sudan; 200,000 was said to be 'stored or in transit'; 100,000 had been distributed, of which only 29,500 had reached the worst hit province of Darfour. The rains came before much more of the food was delivered and the relief operation organised by the European Community and the United Nations was forced to turn to the much more costly option of air transport for emergency food – a bitter irony for those who set out to prove that privatising the famine would lead to a cheaper and more efficient distribution of aid.

Just how many died is hard to tell – certainly thousands and possibly tens of thousands, though probably not the huge numbers predicted. Later Oxfam and SCF officials postulated that the wild roots and berries had a higher nutrient level than had been suggested and that the hardy desert folk required lower levels of nourishment than had been realised. UN officials maintained that the original estimate of those at risk was over-estimated. The Red Cross, more pessimistically, suggested that many of those included in figures had in fact already died unheeded in the 1983–84 famine. Whatever the truth USAID was dissatisfied. It sent a senior team of analysts from Washington to discover what went wrong. Soon afterwards the US decided to pull out of food distribution in the country and handed over responsibility to the UN Emergency Office.

The whole operation also gave a graphic illustration of the abuse of aid. Mercantilism is the dominant social ethic in Sudan. Ask a class of children what they want to do when they grow up and nineteen out of twenty will reply: 'Be a merchant'. Trading has a far higher status than actually producing. It is a country of middle-men, where each expects his 10 per cent. The notion rubs off even on to those who are not entitled to it. The pilferage of food aid from the railway was notorious. An Oxfam survey of grain which arrived in Darfour showed that most of the sacks which arrived were between 10 and 20 per cent below their stated weight. Some of the deficit was caused by leakage from poor-quality sacks but most of it was attributable to theft.[16] At one point a train containing 8,000 tons of sorghum went missing. In the provinces local officials commonly took a 'commission' from food aid and then distributed it on the basis of favouritism. Truck-owners trebled their prices for

journeys carrying food aid. Dubious deals were done juggling
consignments of free US food with cash grants from the EC
to buy local seed.[17] Nationally the grain merchants used the
inflow of food aid to hoard local grain and make massive
profits from future speculation and manipulation of the market. The inescapable conclusion was that those in power –
either entrepreneurial or official – were in a position to make
more out of aid than were the very poorest for whom it was
intended.

Three of the four concerns in my mind as I left Sudan
centred around abuse. It was clear that there were dangers
to the world's hungry from corrupt, fanatical or maladroit
Third World leaders. It was clear that aid was often designed,
not to help the hungry, but for a variety of other purposes,
not the least of them to advance the political interests of the
donor. It was clear that the bourgeoisie would contrive to do
better out of aid – as they do out of everything else – than
their poor compatriots would. But all these elements seemed
to me as yet to derive from poor planning rather than
from some inherent internal weakness. What was not clear,
however, was whether such matters were of any consequence
in the face of the two great natural problems which seemed
to loom over the continent – the changing pattern of the
weather and the rapid growth in population. From the outset
the questions on the climate seemed to demand the most
immediate attention.

THE CHANGING CLIMATE

Later that year I travelled the width of Africa from Mali
to Ethiopia in search of the common denominators in the
countries which made up the Sahel, that belt of semi-desert
savannah land which runs beneath the belly of the Sahara
across the continent. The apparent shift in the climate seemed
to have triggered a similar crisis in each place and was turning
the fertile land to desert. Nowhere was the problem more
graphically illustrated than in northern Mali in the legendary

city of Timbuktu. For hundreds of years its very name has
been a synonym for the most remote place on earth but now
it was facing a new kind of extremity.

From the thirteenth century onwards this forbidden city
had carried on an impenetrable existence in the heart of
Africa, but to its inhabitants and those merchants who con-
verged on it at the crossroads of the ancient caravan routes,
the town on the fringes of the desert was a haven from the
unyielding harshness of the Sahara, a place of rich grazing
for cattle and camels, a university town, a revered centre of
worship and a market place of both commercial and cultural
exchange. During the last two decades however the desert
has been reclaiming Timbuktu. There had been drought
there for seventeen years; for the previous four it had been
increasingly severe and that year the area found its rainfall
cut again by half. The sands of the desert were moving south.
Every year the encroachment continued.

That year the desert swept around the town and surrounded it entirely. Occasionally it was possible to glimpse
beneath the dust the baked clay surface of what was once a
fertile loam, but even that was increasingly rare, the locals
said. Huge dunes of sand were creeping onwards, thousands
of tons at the rate of twenty miles a year. The fine white
dust fell constantly, almost imperceptibly, from the heavens.
Often there was so much of it in the air that it blotted out
the sun for days on end. There is an apocalyptic quality to
living with the earth above your head for so long.

In the town the streets were full of the soft sand which is
slowly swallowing the buildings. In the courtyards of the
mud-walled houses it lay ankle-deep. By the sides of the
sixteenth-century Sankore mosque it was piled in little drifts.
Only twenty years before it had been possible to arrive in
Timbuktu by boat along a canal dug from the River Niger.
But now the channel was entirely dry, its sides cracked and
crumbled, with heaps of old rubbish on its bed among which
skinny donkeys grubbed for sustenance. Of the 250-mile
canal which once stretched north into the Sahara, towards
the Taoudennit salt mines, where even today slave labour is

said to continue, there remained no sign at all. Even the mighty Niger dries up; once it carried 1,500 cubic metres of water every second; in May 1985 it was reduced to a mere two cubic metres; in a good year it now flows for only seven months.

Deserts, the ecologists say, feed upon themselves and grow. The bare soil and stone reflect more solar radiation back into the atmosphere than do grass and trees. This keeps the air hotter, disperses cloud and reduces rain. Without rain the grasses on the edges of the desert wither, a process exacerbated in these poor countries by over-grazing and felling trees for fuel. Without vegetation the wind throws more soil into the air. Increased evaporation lowers the moisture content of the earth and further suppresses rain. Aid workers in Bamako, the capital of Mali, look north and talk about grand schemes of 35,000 wells dug across the country with trees planted around them to fix the soil. But most of the development workers who lived in Timbuktu discounted such ideas as massive white elephants, doomed to failure in a drought they feel sure is caused by a permanent shift in the climate. 'The desert has advanced more than 200 miles southward in the ten years I have lived in Timbuktu,' said a Dutch water engineer, Eugene Van Camfort, who runs a large rice project irrigated by giant Archimedes screws from the river. 'The only place the desert can be halted is at the river with schemes like this.'

But was the main cause of desertification a permanent shift in weather patterns? Meteorologists, I discovered on my return to London, disagreed on this key issue. Some painted a gloomy picture. The odds of a drought lasting for seventeen years were 125,000 to 1, according to Derek Winstanley of the US National Oceanic and Atmospheric Administration. Despite fairly large fluctuations in the short-term, the rainfall during the rainy season has been declining for 200 years, he claimed.[18] But climatology is a relatively young science. Comprehensive records in the First World go back little more than 120 years and the data from the Third World is much more patchy; it is not much of a basis for considering climate

changes which need to be measured in long periods of thirty
years or so. It is true that there is growing evidence that
the emission of increasing amounts of 'greenhouse' gases –
carbon dioxide, CFCs, methane and nitrous oxide – by the
industrialised world, is warming the atmosphere by trapping
the heat which would otherwise have been radiated back into
space. Researchers at the Climatic Research Unit at the
University of East Anglia have predicted that not only will
the overall temperature rise by 2–3 degrees Centigrade during the next century[19] but that this greenhouse effect will also
increase the variability of the climate.[20] But specialists on the
Sahel are more cautious about whether the greenhouse effect
is responsible for the climatic shifts in the region over the
past two decades. Michael Dennett of the University of
Reading, who has studied the rainfall in the Sahel over a
forty-year period, points out that only a small change in
levels of rain produces drought. 'The Sahel's rainfall from
1974 to 1983 was about five per cent less than in the 1931 to
1960 period' but he nonetheless believes it is still too early
to be certain that a long-term decline is evident. In 1980 the
World Meteorological Organisation reported: 'Most analyses
imply that the droughts of the 1970s, although severe, are
normal to the climate, in the sense that they have occurred
before and presumably will occur again.'[21] Certainly the
folklore is there to support that: the years of bygone famines
are known among the nomads by peculiarly poignant names:
1903 was The Year of the Sold Children because families
were reduced to selling their offspring in the hope they would
have a better chance of survival as the slave of a rich man;
a more recent year was known as The Year of the Crushed
Calabash because the Fulani nomads powdered the gourds
they use for carrying water and ate them.

The shifting sands of the Sahara were a graphic symbol
but in fact the process of desertification is less dramatic,
though in many ways far more serious. The main threat to
the productive ability of the soil in the area comes not from
the fringes of a real desert but in lots of small deserts breaking
out like a canker in areas which have been over-cultivated,

over-grazed, badly-irrigated (which turns good cropland into salty, barren wastes) or denuded of trees by a growing population ever in search of more firewood. It is now estimated that more than 90 per cent of pasture and 85 per cent of crop lands in the nineteen sub-Saharan countries closest to the Sahara are affected by desertification.[22] I saw this in Chad, Niger and Burkina Faso; areas which a decade before had been productive farmland or good grazing were bare stretches of earth with a widening ring of impoverished fringes spreading constantly from them. At first I did not believe the chieftain in Niger who showed me a stretch of scrubby desert and told me: 'When I was a boy, forty years ago, this was a forest, full of wild animals: hyenas, lions, foxes and many birds.' But the story was repeated too often all over the Sahel to doubt it. At Agadez in Niger small boys approached me to sell tiny flint arrow heads which they hunted for among the sand – the only relics of their grandfathers' hunting days. What became clear as I travelled was that it was bad land use more than the weather which was prompting the major change. There were too many people making demands on the land.

Individual development projects sought to counter this with re-afforestation and soil conservation schemes, many of which were demonstrated to be effective and low-cost, but there does not seem to have been the commitment by donor and recipient governments and aid agencies to implement them on a large scale. Attention was drawn to the issue in 1977 by the UN Conference on Desertification (UNCOD) but the subsequent anti-erosion programmes, handled by the UN Environment Programme (UNEP) in 1984 conceded that 80 per cent of the money raised to combat desertification had been spent on 'preparatory or supportive actions', which meant 'road construction, water supplies, research, training courses and meetings'. Only 20 per cent was spent on field action and UNEP's director later confessed: 'Far too much technical and financial assistance has gone to showpiece projects and into measures aimed at appeasing the more politically advantaged urban population.'[23] Those small-scale schemes that were working well often seemed doomed to failure because they operated against the tide of economic forces in the area. In Sudan, where one agronomist told me that if trees continue to be consumed for cooking wood at the present rate, there will be none left in the entire country in eight years' time, one peasant woman summed up the immediate paradox most pointedly: 'You tell me not to cut down this tree for firewood because, alive, the tree will keep the desert at bay, and allow grass to grow for our cattle in the next season. Fine. But tell me this: What do I use to light the fire to cook tomorrow's dinner for my five children?'

What is it that confronts the poor with such a dilemma? It is not something inherent to drought, but something woven into the economic circumstances of the poorest people touched by it. There are, after all, no recorded deaths today from famine in the mid-western farming area of the United States (as there were a hundred years ago). Farmers may go bankrupt, but they do not starve to death; domestic political opinion ensures that the cost of such droughts, which still occur every twenty years or so, is spread through the whole population, via the tax and insurance systems. The Oxford economist Amartya Sen defines the key question as one of entitlement: it is not that there is no food, but that there are large numbers of people who have no claim on the available food because of their positions in society.[24]

Across the Sahel several common factors emerged. Some $14 billion in aid and cheap aid loans was received by the Sahel countries in the decade up to 1984, around 80 per cent of their external resources. Only 24 per cent of this aid was spent on agriculture and forestry and only one per cent was spent on rain-fed (as opposed to irrigated) agriculture which accounts for 95 per cent of cereal production. All this is part of a structure of policies which encourages Third World governments to favour cash crop production (which brings in the foreign currency needed to run a government and a capital city) over the production of food. In 1984, the year the famine began, Senegal, Mali, Burkina Faso, Niger, and Chad gathered in a record harvest of 154 million tons of cash crops (compared with 23 million in 1967) while the Sahel also imported via food aid a record amount of cereal – 1.77 million tons, compared with 0.2 million in the early 1960s.[25] Even in their food production policies governments seek to favour the town-dweller over the peasant farmer. The basis for this, according to one relief worker in the Sahel, is starkly simple: 'Politicians live in the capitals: if the city-dwellers starve they riot there; if the peasants starve they die quietly, out of sight. It's hardly surprising what they choose.' One of the unhappy side-effects of improved education in such countries is that most of the brightest people are attracted to the cities and the better lifestyles they afford. As a result many end up in largely unproductive government jobs. In Mali, for example, one of the five poorest countries in the world, the government is the biggest employer by a factor of ten. To keep food cheap for the urban classes governments have pursued a policy of fixing food prices at artificially low levels. The result has been to deprive farmers of the incentive to produce more than they need for self-sufficiency; often prices are lower than the costs of the seeds and the fertilisers to grow them, without taking account of the cost of labour. At the same time, according to Professor Michael Beenstock, a former World Bank adviser in the Sahel, 'grossly inefficient state-controlled organisations have taken over a large part of agricultural production. They are overly concerned with the production of cash crops rather than basic foods and are insensitive to the market-place and the needs of ordinary people.'[26] A US State Department document claimed that cereal production in Mali, Burkina Faso, Niger and Chad could be doubled if fair prices were offered to farmers and irrigation projects were better managed.[27] Badly managed food aid can make matters worse rather than better. For a start it can pervert the tastes of local people; educating them into preference for types of food, such as wheaten bread, which cannot be produced locally. More seriously it can pervert local markets. In Gao in Mali a glut of free US maize had brought about a drop in the price of locally-grown millet from 120 francs to 25 francs a kilo. Something similar happened in Tete in Mozambique. The effect both of changes in taste and of flooding the market is to destroy farmers' ability to sell enough even to buy the seeds to plant a crop the following year; it meant that food aid would be needed then too.

THE POPULATION EXPLOSION

But what of the question of population? Everywhere the problems were compounded by the fact that the population was growing rapidly. Some time in June 1987, demographers estimated, the world's five billionth inhabitant was born. In celebration of this dubious event I visited Kenya. The odds on the child being born there were sadly high for the country has the highest birth rate in the world and seems to be storing up serious economic and social problems for the next century.

The difficulties caused by a birth rate which far outstrips economic growth are common throughout the Third World but nowhere more evident than in this former British colony. In 1948 the population of 5.4 million was growing at the already phenomenal rate of 2.5 per cent a year. Today there are more than 20 million people and the rate has expanded to between 4.1 and 4.3 per cent.[28] By the year 2000 there will be more than 35 million Kenyans and the country will need six new cities each the size of present-day Nairobi. It will need to create 7.5 million new jobs. No one supposes this will happen. In the year that I visited all the funds available for investment would produce only 1.4 million extra jobs, at best. House building was only 10 per cent of existing need and the government was building no new schools. The future prospects for most people are of increased poverty, malnutrition and disease.

The magnitude of the problem was set out in 1986 in a Government report, *Economic Management for Renewed Growth*, which estimated that an annual economic growth rate of 5.6 per cent was needed over the next fourteen years. The World Bank estimated that the actual growth of Gross

Domestic Product between 1980 and 1985 was 3.1 per cent, extremely high for Africa but far short of this population-determined target.[29] 'Without rapid economic growth the provision of even the most basic services will be in jeopardy,' the Kenyan report said.

In 1971 the World Bank was called in and ambitious family planning programmes drew extensive funds from Western donors. But the schemes, which were largely addressed to the women, foundered on the prejudices of the men. According to Dr Eric Krystall of the Nairobi office of the Family Planning Private Sector (FPPS) programme, which now aims to organise through work places: 'They also made the mistake of thinking that all you had to do was provide the facilities and people would use them.' Even the scale of the AIDS pandemic has not brought about a widespread increase in the use of condoms, and although the disease is having a devastating effect in East Africa the check to the population explosion is only localised and temporary.

The Second World Population Conference in Mexico in 1984 concluded that promoting economic growth was more important than programmes to directly curb population growth, but the formula has proved inappropriate for Kenya. Although 1986 was a boom year for its principal exports, coffee and tea, the anticipated surge in private investment by foreign companies and banks did not materialise. The long-term prospects are even more questionable. Already several multinational companies have begun to scale down their investments[30] in a country which they fear will become, at the very least, less profitable and, at the worst, a powder keg.

The irony for Kenya was that in some measure these problems seemed the fruits of success. Comparative prosperity had improved the average diet and education had raised standards of hygiene and nutrition. Better diet made the population more fertile and, over the past twenty years, had halved the infant mortality rate to 72 per 1,000 births, less than half the regional average, which itself had improved by 50 per cent over the previous thirty years.[31] But such progress had less immediate impact on traditional values. The average woman still had eight children; in a life of uncertainty an amplitude of sons and daughters continued to be regarded as a kind of insurance for the parents' old age, as well as being useful in farming and tending livestock from a very early age (I have seen youngsters of only five in charge of small herds). Fertility was reckoned a blessing from God and a woman who bore no children could still be returned to her father and the dowry repaid. Islamic and Christian leaders, in particular the Catholic Church, were either against contraception completely or were certainly against it being provided to single mothers and adolescents, though more than 50 per cent of the population were already by then under the age of fifteen. Western disapproval of female circumcision had curtailed the practice which rendered some women infertile.[32]

The problems of Kenya, although more graphic, were not untypical. The world population is now growing at approximately a billion every twelve years; 90 per cent of this growth is in developing countries.[33] But rapid population growth, according to demographers, is not always a problem. In Europe at the Industrial Revolution and in the nineteenth-century United States it was welcomed. Why then should it not be in Africa? For, according to a 1983 study by the UN Food and Agriculture Organisation, the world already produces enough food to feed all its inhabitants.

The key issue clearly is one of distribution rather than production. This raises a methodological question: should the population explosion be tackled as a contributory cause of poverty and hunger? or is it merely a symptom?

Undoubtedly the present population explosion – which is more rapid than any part of the world has ever before experienced[34] – can only put more people at risk in parts of the world where poverty is already endemic. There is an obvious need to address the problem, and one for which the Catholic Church must bear a particular responsibility given the regressive nature of its official position on contraception.[35] But this does not prove a causal relationship between the two. Certainly there is no evidence of a link between density of population and hunger: famine exists in both Bolivia with 5 inhabitants per square kilometre and India with 172 – but there is no famine in the world's most densely populated country, Holland, where there are 326. Nor does the availability of cropland seem a factor: 0.63 hectares in Bolivia, 0.30 in India and only 0.06 in Holland, calculates the writer Susan George. 'Up to now, the press has not been clamouring for birth control for the Dutch,' she notes with acerbity.[36] Nigel Twose in a study for Oxfam (UK) is even more pointed: 'The world already produces enough food to feed everybody in it. So what do people mean when they talk about "too many" people? Does "too many" perhaps relate to the amount of food people eat? Are there too many Americans because they consume 35 per cent of the world's resources even though they are only 6 per cent of the world's population? The entire population of the Third World uses up only the same quantity of the world's resources as the United States.'[37]

Twose and George have different explanations for the population explosion. Twose blames the poverty which deprives people of the means of contraception: 'A comprehensive survey in 1983 showed that 68 per cent of women with four children did not want any more; 39 per cent of women with only two children did not want more.'[38] George believes that the poor *want* more children: 'Another baby for a poor family means an extra mouth to feed – a very marginal difference. But by the time that child is four or five it will make important contributions to the whole family – fetching water from the distant well, taking meals to father and brothers in the field, feeding animals. Later the child will help with more complicated tasks which would all devolve on the mother of the household if she could not count on her children.'[39] In a situation where many children die in infancy the incentive to have many, to ensure that a few survive, is very great.

Whoever is correct the conclusion is the same: if poverty is tackled then population will drop automatically. The empirical evidence seems to support such a view. Two generations ago infant mortality rates in Britain and the United States were as high as they are now in most Third World countries. Improvements came about gradually. And the move to two-child families took place only after the infant death rate fell and society shifted to an industrial from an agrarian base, which meant it no longer relied on the labour of children. Parallel with this was the development of opportunities for women to work outside the home.[40] A report by the World Bank, which studied sixty-four different countries, indicated that when the income of a nation's poorest group rises by one per cent, the general fertility rate drops by almost three percentage points.[41] More recently in countries such as Sri Lanka, China, Costa Rica, Malaysia, South Korea, Thailand and Kerala state in India, where governments have adopted preventive health programmes which amount to a 'child survival revolution', the result has eventually been some of the lowest birth rates in the developing world. This has been done by encouraging breast-feeding, which still prevents more conceptions than overt family planning programmes, and women's literacy programmes which have been found to have a direct effect on lowering both infant mortality and birth rates. A campaign has been mounted to encourage parents to leave periods of at least two years between the birth of children, a tactic which has been shown to lessen infant mortality by 25 per cent. Demonstrating a long-term decline in the death rate of children under five is the first step to changing attitudes.[42] A World Health Organisation report maintains that the death of a child, or indeed the fear of the death of a child, tends to increase the fertility of a couple, regardless of income or family size.[43] 'The bottom line is that there has never been a significant and sustained fall in birth rates which has not been preceded by a significant and sustained fall in child death rates,' Unicef maintains.[44]

The problem is that there is an interim period during which the death rates have dropped but the birth rates continue in the old patterns. 'Political revolutions can happen overnight;

technological revolutions in a few years; but social revolutions take decades. The delay, sometimes fatal, is called cultural lag . . . for those countries really caught on the treadmill . . . the population boom is the biggest single obstacle to the economic progress that is supposed to bring an end to the population boom.'[45] This Catch 22 clearly requires a simultaneous assault on several fronts, involving a shift in domestic food-producing policies within a framework of overall economic development and a parallel strategy to promote birth control programmes which, like those in Zimbabwe,[46] work with local cultures rather than against them. Such a subject is matter for a book in itself; for our purposes let us note that the population issue, like that of desertification before it, brings us back squarely to an economic perspective and to the issue of social justice which makes the matter so imperative a Christian concern. In the next chapter we shall begin the process of analysing the moral positions which lie hidden within the existing economic structures. But I will conclude this account of my direct encounter with Africa with some observations on the overt workings of the economy in three countries: Mozambique, which is dogged by war and which was just emerging from the Soviet sphere of influence and being drawn into the Western camp by a package of IMF credit; Zambia, which has one of the longest, most unhappy and most instructive histories of dealings with the IMF and other international financial bodies; and the small country of Burkina Faso, one of the few Third World countries to make an attempt at self-sufficiency, also without an entirely happy conclusion.

IN THE GRIP OF WAR

Travelling around Mozambique was like a gruelling exercise in seeing the woes of the Old and New Testament made flesh. Locked into a relationship of economic dependence and exploitation by white South Africa which takes tens of

thousands of Mozambicans in migrant labour to work the
mines of the Transvaal, they are a people in hard bondage,[47]
a people of widows, orphans and strangers,[48] a people whose
neighbour makes them serve him for nothing and does not
give just wages.[49]

In normal times Mozambique's ports would offer the region's black states access to the sea, which at present they
have only through the ports of South Africa. In an attempt
to maintain the control it can exercise through this transport
monopoly the South African government has pursued a
policy of economic manipulation, blackmail and political
destabilisation to render useless the ports of Beira and Maputo and the railways which link them to Zimbabwe and
Zambia. It has done this by supporting a vicious guerrilla
campaign by the Mozambican National Resistance (Renamo), whose forces have burned crops and homes, bombed
factories and plantations, destroyed hospitals, clinics and
schools, performed terrible mutilations upon teachers and
nurses (who have had their ears slashed off, their eyelids cut
deliberately away, and their fingers amputated) and driven
more than a million Mozambicans into refugee camps and
settlements in the comparatively small areas the government
can make safe: to progress through them is to encounter the
people among whom John the Baptist's emissaries sought
Jesus: the blind, the lame, those with the skin disorders of
malnutrition and disease, the deaf, the dead and those who
mourn for them and above all the poor and the hungry.[50]

In the new settlements I encountered those with dramatic
or ghastly tales to tell: escapees from the slave labour camps
the rebels had established in the bush or witnesses of grue-
some atrocities who had seen hospital patients systematically
hacked to death in their beds or busloads of ordinary passen-
gers callously burned alive or pregnant women whose bellies
had been split apart with machetes exposing them and their
foetuses to a lingering death. I also spoke to scores who had
suffered the less dramatic trauma of flight and homelessness.
They were indeed the people for whom Christ announced his
ministry: the afflicted, the captives, the blind, the oppressed,

those in need of the proclamation of the year of the Lord's favour.[51] Yet amidst them all, and the Mozambican and foreign aid workers who worked with them, there was an uplifting sense of hope, bravery and reconciliation.

One community of people, from Marriebe in Zambezia, once the breadbasket of Mozambique until Renamo struck with its policy of systematic mass terrorism, had been wandering like a lost tribe for six months in search of safety; every time they settled the rebels struck again. Yet the day that I met them they were building new homes of wooden poles and thatch. Another group, of 3,800 people from Mauanza also in Zambezia, had arrived naked except for the bark of trees, having had even their clothes stolen by the guerrillas; within a year they had built themselves 597 houses, a school and a health centre. They had organised foster parents from among their own number for their eighty-five orphans. They had planted 125 hectares of maize and sorghum, sixty of rice and forty of manioc to supplement the Western food aid they received and maintain the habit and dignity of cultivation until the return home they planned. One British nurse, Marion Birch of Save the Children Fund, had fled the health post at Nicuadala along with all the local people, as the rebels approached. They destroyed everything, as they had done at more than 500 other health centres and 720 schools; what they could not steal they dumped in the river to render it unusable, even equipment for sterilising instruments, 'even the speculae we use for gynaecological investigations,' the nurse said. Yet not long afterwards she was back in town and re-opened the centre in an old store-house. 'People are afraid to come to us, but gradually they will return.' In the capital, Maputo, I paid an unnerving visit to a school for thirty boys, aged between five and twelve, who had been captured from the guerrilla ranks. The pupils had been kidnapped from their villages and, with mutilations and threats of death, forced into the rebel army. Those who were not strong enough to carry a Kalashnikov were used as spies. Most of the boys in the class had killed several people. They sat there, drawing pictures and learning to read. 'We had two options,' said their teacher, Miss Ana Rita Sithole. 'Some people, particularly in the army, wanted to treat the boys as prisoners of war or criminals and lock them up, especially after the psychotic behaviour of some of them – one got hold of a machine gun recently and started to shoot up the barracks where he was held. But we have persuaded the government that the right thing to do is treat them as victims and to try to restore to them their lost childhood and innocent delights.' It was like visiting a people of the Beatitudes: the poor, the gentle, those who mourn, those who hunger and thirst for what is right, the merciful, the pure in heart, the peacemakers.[52]

It was hardly surprising that, amidst all this, the Mozambican economy was in dire straits. Its economic growth had always been meagre. In 1975 on independence from Portugal health care had been available to only 7 per cent of the population and education provision was virtually non-existent; the government made this a priority, establishing 1,222 rural clinics and over 1,200 schools, but in the economic sphere it adopted a centrally-planned system involving comprehensive nationalisation and the maintenance of low food prices which robbed farmers of the incentive of a fair price. All this, combined with the world recession and the aggressive strategies of South Africa, proved calamitous. The prices it obtained for its exports of agricultural produce fell with the world-wide drop in commodity prices; the cost of repaying its debts for imports rose as world interest rates soared. By 1987 per capita income was only 60 per cent of the 1981 level, and falling. The 1985 output of cotton was a mere 10 per cent of the 1981 level. Cashew nut and sisal production were down by 60 per cent and tea by 75 per cent. Most seriously, in a country where the UN estimated that 3.8 million people were at risk of starvation, cereal production in 1986 was calculated to be at its lowest for thirty years. But the nominally Marxist government, which has shown a remarkable propensity for pragmatic self-criticism, began a programme of reform: as early as 1980 it denationalised the retail trade, reintroduced wage incentives and appealed for foreign investment; in

1983 it introduced policies to encourage private farmers and switched its efforts from large to small-scale production; subsequently it loosened the bonds of price control, allowed private enterprises to receive foreign aid direct and guaranteed that foreign investors would be able to repatriate profits. In December 1986 it agreed a package of measures with the International Monetary Fund (IMF) which included devaluations which reduced the local currency, the *metical*, to only 6 per cent of its original value, the trebling of prices paid to farmers for maize and rice, and lay-offs in the public sector. New life was breathed into the economy: by December 1987, when the second round of negotiations with the IMF was begun, shops in the capital were full of goods (many of them imported), the markets were amply supplied with fruit and vegetables, and even petrol, once rationed, was freely available. Prices to farmers had increased tenfold and food production was up 26 per cent, textiles and food processing up 18 per cent and construction up 5 per cent.[53] That month in the second round negotiations Mozambique, in return for more credit, agreed to further measures to liberalise trade, boost exports, support industry and curb government spending. The key question was whether commercial activity was simply experiencing a surge because of the injection of the IMF cash, or whether the IMF policy reforms were really working and its loans were kick-starting the economy into life.[54] I had the opportunity to examine that issue in another context when negotiations with the IMF broke down dramatically in Zambia, which was at independence perhaps the most prosperous state in black Africa but which had a fraught history of relations with the IMF dating from 1971, when the country began borrowing after the price of its main export, copper, began to fall.

INTERNATIONAL RESCUE?

The food riots in Zambia's Copper Belt in December 1986 took everyone by surprise, not least the country's President, Kenneth Kaunda, who had authorised rises in the price of

mealie-meal, the staple maize flour, only three days before.
Fifteen people were killed and $10 million of damage was
done by rampaging mobs in the once prosperous Copper
Belt. President Kaunda, badly shaken by the rioting, appeared on television to declare that he was reversing his
decision. Within weeks he also announced the suspension of
the system, also sanctioned by the IMF, whereby the country
every week auctioned what little foreign currency it had
available to Zambian businesses at ever-increasing prices,
which ended with the Zambian *kwacha* worth only 11 per
cent of its original value against the dollar. The restoration
of the food subsidy would add an annual $50 million to public
spending. The suspension of the auction ended a strategy
designed to ration the use of foreign currency to those
industries which could use it most efficiently (and demonstrate this by paying most for it). With them the two remaining planks of the IMF platform collapsed.

Zambia had begun borrowing heavily in the 1970s, with
the hearty approval of both the IMF and the World Bank,
when the price of copper fell on the world market. Copper
alone produced 90 per cent of Zambia's national income but
its price had always gone through cycles. 'Production has
traditionally always been about 40 to 50 per cent above
demand or below it. It was always feast or famine. For
Zambia independence coincided with a boom in prices. The
new Government suddenly found itself in control of a far
greater income than in colonial times.'[55] It spent it, and not
in diversifying the economy away from copper, as would
have been prudent. Prestige buildings were erected – high-
rise office blocks, an airport, luxury hotels. Zambia became
a one-party state with a parallel Party operation which wasted
large amounts of money duplicating the efforts of government. 'When the prices plummeted in 1974 they continued
to spend, borrowing to tide themselves over until demand
increased again. The copper industry did the same thing,
using loans to maintain capital programmes and even to
subsidise running costs.' But this time the turn-around never
came. The rise in oil prices suppressed much of the industrial

activity on which copper depended, and the micro-electronics revolution reduced the demand from the electrical industry. Furthermore, because the government, out of misplaced pride and confidence, refused to allow the *kwacha* to deteriorate in relation to other currencies, Zambian copper became over-priced on the world market and sales fell. Export earnings plummeted and so did levels of re-investment and even maintenance.

But each loan was followed by a bigger loan as Zambia rescheduled the debt and then each time failed to meet the repayment terms of the new agreement. In 1985 the IMF administered its biggest dose of monetarist medicine. In return for a massive loan Zambia agreed to significant devaluations, to lift restrictions on imports, to cut government spending and to remove subsidies on food and increase prices paid to farmers as an incentive to produce more food. The similarity with the 'adjustment' demands in Mozambique is clear enough; in a later chapter we shall examine the implications. For more than a year the policies were carried through, to the delight of the IMF officials, who saw Zambia as an exemplary case.

The managers in the copper industry were less pleased. By 1987 production was a mere 60 per cent of the old levels. One said: 'We hope it is at its nadir. We produced 750,000 tons in 1971, and only 450,000 tons in 1985 and 1986. This year will be much the same. And the less we produce the less foreign exchange we earn, which reduces our activity still further, because we do not even have the money to buy spare parts. At Nchanga open mine we have 110 earth-moving lorries, each of which can shift more than 100 tons of copper-bearing load at a time; at the moment thirty-three are idle, not because there is no ore to dig but because we cannot get foreign exchange to buy the spare parts or pay the expert mechanics we need to repair them. We are now earning in real terms only half of what we did in the early years of independence. The irony is that for every dollar the government allocates to us we can earn four. With our present resources we could easily be producing 550,000 tons, but they won't make the exchange available.'[56] A similar story was told in other industries. The Dunlop factory in Ndola had the capacity to produce enough tyres to supply the needs of the entire country but it was working only at half-capacity because the government would not authorise the foreign currency it needed to buy raw materials; at the same time the government was using the same hard currency to buy tyres imported by the container load from Japan.[57] Almost all industry relied on imported inputs for around 30 per cent of materials or spares.

One other sector of society which failed to see the benefits of the IMF package was the poor. The cost of mealie-meal had risen by 70 per cent in 1980 and by another 80 per cent in the two months after the 1985 IMF package. An Oxfam report noted that some sections of the community had benefitted from the IMF package; the better off peasant farmers, for example, were enjoying improvements from the higher prices paid to food producers. But the poorest 40 per cent of the population showed a significant rise in malnutrition in urban areas because of the food price rises and a deterioration in health standards in rural areas because of cuts in the health budget. The health cuts produced a particularly absurd situation. Laying off health workers was considered politically too explosive, so instead the cuts were made in the budget for essential drugs and transport. 'After salaries had been paid . . . there was virtually no government funding left over for running costs.' It was left to Oxfam to provide the transport and the Swedish agency SIDA to buy the drugs.[58]

Agriculture ought to have provided the avenue of escape from all this. But tragically the Kaunda administration, despite the rhetoric of good intentions, had neglected to develop it during the copper-rich decade after independence, even though it was known from the outset that Zambian copper would run out just after the turn of the century. The country has vast tracts of unexploited land, good soils, plentiful water for irrigation, cheap hydro-electric power and abundant manpower. Yet only 5 per cent of all the country's class I and II arable land is under cultivation and some 40 per cent of Zambia's rural families are short of labour while, by President Kaunda's own admission, two million people are without jobs in the urban areas.[59] Moves now to alter this may be too little, too late. Agriculture too suffers from the chronic shortage of hard currency. Though a fertiliser factory was built at Kafue, for example, no attempt was made to develop the mining of the rich indigenous phosphate deposits. Instead phosphates for it were in the early years imported – a strategy favoured by World Bank experts at the time – and paid for from the surplus on the national trading account; now that these could no longer be afforded the factory was working at half capacity. Even sectors which are successful are dogged by the same problems; in 1986 Zambia had a bumper harvest, approaching self-sufficiency in maize for the first time, but as much as 25 per cent of it was left in the fields after harvesting and was ruined by the rains, because of the shortage of fuel and spare parts for tractors, and another 10 to 15 per cent was smuggled out to Zaire and Malawi where farmers secured prompt cash payment at favourable prices.

There was, then, little lamentation in the country when in May 1986 President Kaunda jettisoned the recovery plan and fell into arrears with the IMF – an unforgivable action under the Fund's rule-book. Negotiations have continued on and off since, though many wondered whether a viable alternative existed. In February 1987 Zambia owed about $160 million in arrears to the IMF, a figure which through interest has been rising by around $2 million a month ever since.[60] President Kaunda seemed to see no way out of the dilemma. 'It is a vicious circle that we're trying to break,' he told me. Cuts in subsidy were impossible without provoking further riots: 'If there's no peace there'll be no production.'[61] But he also seemed to recognise that there would be no progress without the aid money which donors like Britain and the United States continued to withhold until an agreement was reached with the IMF. In January 1989 he announced a Fourth National Development Plan which aimed at achieving 3 per cent economic growth, curbing the rate of population growth and cutting the budget deficit to less than 2 per cent of gross domestic product. But he also announced that a threefold increase in the price of mealie-meal would be postponed to enable more people to register for coupons which will allow families to continue buying it at subsidised prices.[62]

What prospects can all this hold? One commentator described the IMF's approach as that of a doctor who has one medicine for every ailment, and who saves the patient from immediate death only by putting him in a coma: such is the restrictive effect which IMF packages have on debtor nations. Why is the IMF doing this? Before we can answer we need to study the nature of the world economy in which the IMF has come to assume the role of global policeman. Before we do so, by way of an appendix to these reflections on direct experience on the ground in Africa, we should finally turn our attention to the fate of a country, or more particularly a leader, who tried to by-pass the world of international finance for which the IMF stands sentinel.

THE COST OF SELF-SUFFICIENCY

Burkina Faso, formerly known as Upper Volta, is a small landlocked country in West Africa. In the two decades after independence its government had been characterised by periods of democracy which were periodically ended by bloodless military coups leading to rule by senior army officers. But all the rulers were part of the small élite which ran the country in the interests of the privileged classes who lived in the capital, Ouagadougou. In August 1983 however a coup by junior army officers, led by Captain Thomas Sankara, established a new radical regime which showed that it intended to shift the emphasis from the capital to the rural areas. As Sankara described it: 'In Burkina 97 per cent of the people live off the land. Yet of 57 billion francs in the national budget 15 billion are spent in the capital on hotels, electricity, carpets and other things the people do not have. It is for the élite, the people I went to school with. Yet they are 3 per cent of the population. Is this fair? I say no. So I have introduced austerity measures. I make diplomats sleep on the floor in their offices instead of using hotel rooms. I make them eat sandwiches instead of expensive lunches. I make them drive in small cars. The city is no longer happy. I do not allow the import of French cheese, wines and perfumes. I diminish their wages. They are not happy. I myself am no longer happy because I too am a little bourgeois like them.'[63]

The shift was more than symbolic. The new regime abolished taxes on the peasantry and set up a network of peasant committees throughout the country in an attempt to place control of their affairs in the hands of the farmers, many of them women, themselves. These 'committees for the defence of the revolution' have organised the building of more than two hundred small-scale dams throughout the country and, with finance from foreign aid agencies, established co-operative cereal banks which go a long way to controlling the activities of the grain speculators who traditionally buy cereals at harvest time when they are cheap and then hoard them for seven months, releasing them at four times the old price just when people have run out of their own stocks. The major campaigning power of the government shifted into 'three struggles' – against deforestation, over-grazing and bush fires. It established a pyramidical structure of nation-wide training which speeded up practical education at no great cost. National experts taught courses to regional teachers who taught district teachers who taught teachers at village level. They discovered that by this method one expert's most relevant knowledge could be multiplied twenty-fold in two months, four-hundred fold in four months and eight thousand-fold in six months. The system was used to train 7,000 village health agents and 7,000 traditional midwives. It was used to vaccinate 2.8 million children over a fifteen-day period in September 1984, which was proclaimed by Unicef as a model campaign. In January 1984 1,200 women were taught how to build stoves which minimised the use of fuel; by October 1985 there were 30,000 of them in Ouagadougou alone and moves were being made to spread the stoves nationwide. It also built new motivation and self-respect among the farmers, many of whom would raise the money to send one of their number to such training exercises.

Sankara also extended the principle of self-sufficiency to a national level by refusing to deal with the IMF as his predecessors had done. He also scorned the idea of aid packages from the Soviet Union and United States alike, which inevitably came with strings attached, as 'imperialist meddling'. Inevitably the approach was less popular with the urban middle classes whose salaries he cut and whose scope for political opposition he restricted. An Amnesty International report in 1986 revealed that Sankara dealt harshly with dissenters, particularly those allegedly engaged in plots for a counter-coup. There were accusations of torture and of detention without trial, though the report the following year indicated that many of those imprisoned without trial had been released. But discontent among the urban élite continued and they began to allege that Sankara's reforms were prompting ill-feeling among the rural population whose traditional social structures had been overturned by the arrogant young men of the revolutionary committees. There was dissatisfaction in particular among the trade unions which represented only a limited number of urban workers and which had previously been able to force pay rises out of governments afraid of being toppled on the issue as the civilian government in 1967 had been.

Before I left Ouagadougou one resident UN official summed up the revolution. 'Of course, we're not supposed to have views on things like this but, although the schoolteachers and trade unionists whom Sankara has locked up would not agree, it has to be said that Sankara's revolution with its anti-bourgeoisie, anti-metropolitan policies is just what an agriculture-based economy like this needs. It encourages hard work, it discourages dependency on aid, and is not rigidly ideological but fairly pragmatic within its radical populist tradition. If Sankara is not overthrown within the next decade then Burkina Faso could turn itself into a Third World model of how even the poorest nation can pull itself up by the sandal straps into some form of self-sufficiency.' On 15 October 1987 Thomas Sankara was shot dead in a military coup. The next days thousands of ordinary Burkinabe peasants flocked to his unmarked grave on the outskirts of the city. Not long afterwards the new government began negotiations with the IMF.

My three years travelling through Africa had proved a disconcerting experience. My eyes and ears and nose had been confronted with the dirty, stinking, degrading squalor in which hundreds of millions of people passed their everyday life. It was a squalor which before I first went to Ethiopia I had never comprehended and which I knew that those who remained in the comfort of their First World homes could never fully appreciate either in terms of its scale or its abject indignity. There had grown the awareness that what aid we gave was inadequate, both in quality and in quantity, and indeed that often it was given with impure motives. There had been an acceptance, unwilling perhaps at first, that the leaders of the Third World bore a good deal of the culpability for the hunger of their people. There had been the slow comprehension that there was no refuge in fatalist notions that the problems were caused by factors beyond our control, like the weather or a wild explosion of world population. In the end everything came back to dollars and cents. It was clear that the international system of trading and finance was heavily loaded in favour of us and against them. Finally there had been the realisation that, through the IMF which acted as a kind of global debt collector, we wealthy nations were actively contriving to make life even worse for the poorest people in the world.

Again and again, however, I returned to that original inequity and to the most uncomfortable insight of all. At home my life had felt, in the spectrum of London existence, neither rich nor poor but with a pleasant comfort. In Africa I realised that in global terms I occupied no such mid-way point and returned to England with trepidation and thoughts of rich men and camels. The inescapable conclusion was that there was a duty upon those of us in the West to do something about the situation. The onus was clear enough on grounds of humanity; to a Christian it was a moral imperative. When so many people lived in such abject poverty there could be no neutral ground and there was no possibility of abstention. You are either with the poor, as Christ was, or against them. We in the West are against them, whether we know it or not.

Chapter Three

PRINCIPALITIES AND POWERS

'In their greed they will exploit you with false words.'
2 Peter 2:3 RSV

'The purpose of studying economics is not to acquire a set
of ready-made answers to economic questions, but to learn
how to avoid being deceived by economists.'
Joan Robinson, Collected Economic Papers (1960)

There is an unmistakable clarity in the call to Christians to
do something in the face of the wretched poverty in which
so much of the world exists. The question is: What should
that response be? In the year which followed the first news
of the African famine throughout the rich world individuals
responded spontaneously and with generosity. The phenomenon of Band Aid, Live Aid and Sport Aid raised a new
level of concern. Charities and aid agencies received a major
increase in donations. For a short time even, hunger in the
Third World had become a domestic political issue towards
which governments were forced momentarily to genuflect.

Such a response was in line with the ethic of personal
charity which has become well developed throughout the
history of the Church and the Western world in which its
traditions are, in part at least, extant. The model was that of

the Good Samaritan.[1] To the question 'Who is my neighbour?' Christ responded with a parable which depicts someone who acts immediately and without qualification to relieve
the urgent physical suffering of another person. Moreover
the Samaritan is a foreigner, an enemy even, whom the
normal social codes of the day would expect not to be
bound by obligations of brotherly fealty. Also significantly,
he acts on his own initiative, without waiting to be asked
by the man in need. He proves himself a neighbour. The
greatest exemplar of such an approach is, of course, the
behaviour of Christ himself who responds immediately and
directly to human need, not least when that need is
physical. Such Gospel encounters are not merely physical
symbols standing for some spiritual correlative: Jesus
refused on two separate occasions to send away the
multitudes hungry, even though his overtly spiritual teaching for the day was concluded.[2]

Parallel to that is a whole tradition of Old Testament
biblical thought stretching from the prophets of the eighth
century BC to the epistle of St James, which maintains a
deep suspicion towards wealth. This tradition continues into
modern thought via the early Church fathers and a whole
series of individuals and groups who made periodic attempts
to return to the purities of basic Christianity – from Francis
of Assisi and the Lollards, through the Anabaptists, John
Wesley and the Christian Socialists, to the rejections of
wealth among the Lifestyle movements which today urge
people to Live Simply, that Others May Simply Live.

What we have discovered from Chapter Two however is
that there is a web of influences which maintains the hungry
people of the world in their poverty and which means that
such a simple and direct response, while admirable in itself,
is not enough. There are further questions which we now
need to ask and new parables which we need to consider.

What should the Good Samaritan do if he travels the same
route every day for several years and finds another victim of
the muggers each week at the roadside? Treat each victim
with the same kindness? Give up his acts of compassion on

the grounds that his purse will not bear the demands? Or begin to ask what is wrong with this particular road or the society through which it passes?

What should he do if he arrives on the scene one day in time to witness the muggers in action? Wait until they have gone and then help the victim? Attack the muggers and compromise the purity of his response or indeed risk injury himself? Or raise the matter in another place?

What should he do if he discovers that one of the muggers is a member of the family of the victim? Or that the muggers are working a protection racket in the area? Or that they are hoods acting to collect the rents on behalf of an extortionate landlord? Or that they work on behalf of a cartel of grain merchants who seize the produce of the poor, paying a fraudulently low price, and attacking those who protest? Or that the victim is not ailing from a physical beating but from having food taken from him or denied to him?

The influences which hold people in the grip of poverty are, as we have seen, not individual acts of culpability or selfishness, although these do often play a part. 'Obstacles to development,' wrote Pope John Paul II in *Sollicitudo Rei Socialis*,[3] 'have a moral character.' They are 'influences and obstacles which go far beyond the actions and the brief lifespan of an individual'. These he described, borrowing from the vocabulary of liberation theology, as *structures of sin*. Our response must therefore be structural too. We have to analyse the existing systems and isolate within them the moments at which an unethical assumption is made or a sinful process begins to operate.

In such circumstances only to maintain the Good Samaritan's simple and direct response of succour would be wasteful in economic terms. More importantly it would mean that the Samaritan does nothing to address the attack on the dignity of the victim, who as his neighbour is his brother and his equal before God – surely in spiritual terms a consideration of greater weight, and one which seems often to have been overlooked by secular aid agencies and even by Church agencies in recent decades.

The conventional solution to such problems is to say that where they have become beyond the scope of an individual's action they become a social responsibility: the defence of the person becomes institutionalised into public security with a police force and army created to enforce it; likewise charity becomes institutionalised in the form of public welfare programmes. In the case of help to the poor overseas, this is dealt with through aid which will relieve hunger and promote the economic development which will lead eventually to self-sufficiency. Such, at any rate, is the commonly held view of aid. The reality unfortunately is somewhat different.

PRELUDE: AID – DOES IT WORK?

In February 1988 a confidential meeting was held in the heart of the Sussex countryside at the private conference centre of the British Foreign and Commonwealth Office. Gathered there were senior representatives of the governments of the United States, Britain and various European countries, along with senior officials of the key United Nations relief and refugee organisations. They were there to discuss with a top-level delegation from the government of Mozambique the operation of the emergency famine relief programme in that country. In private the participants were able to be unusually frank with one another. A number of disquieting facts emerged:

* Of 700,000 tons of food promised by donor countries only 300,000 had actually ever arrived.

* Certain donors insisted on sending food they wanted to get rid of, rather than what was needed.

* Some donors insisted that planes, ships and lorries which they had paid for could only be used to transport food provided by themselves; vehicles had to stand idle while food from other donors had no transport.

* Some emergency aid took as long as nine months to arrive and donors then insisted that it had to go to a particular province,

even though that area had become over-supplied and others were now in need.

* Donors insisted on high levels of accounting, in order to be able to satisfy any embarrassing questions from their public, at a time when an IMF austerity package was demanding that government administrative staff should be made redundant.

* Several donors would not give permission for food aid to be sold in areas where the population was hungry but could afford to buy it. The result ruined the market for local farmers and robbed them of the incentive, and the cash for seeds, to plant again next year. It also denied the government the opportunity to raise local cash for reinvestment in other relief work.

Why should such unproductive and unreasonable restraints be imposed on aid in an emergency in which 1.8 million people were homeless and some 3 million imminently at risk of starving?

The reason is that aid, all too often, is not aid but something more base in disguise.

Until now the intention of this book has been to take the reader through the same process which I went through in learning of the complexities which lay behind the horror of those scenes of naked and starving African children. From this point we will change tack. I spent the years that followed my arrival in Africa inquiring into the structures in which those hapless children were trapped, reporting on the activities of the IMF and World Bank and on the direct effects these were having in Asia and in South America, much as they were in Africa. My aim now is to present my conclusions, and the theological framework within which I arrived at them, in a more systematic form. As a prologue we will consider aid, or the convoluted activity which goes under that name.

'Who can possibly object to aid for the less fortunate?' asks the right-wing economist, Peter Bauer, now Lord Bauer since his ennoblement by Mrs Thatcher. Professor Bauer does object, strenuously, because aid, he says, is a misnomer. 'Foreign aid is the transfer annually of billions of dollars of

Western taxpayers' money to distant governments directly or through international organisations . . . To call these transfers "aid" simultaneously disarms criticism, prejudges the effects of the policy and also obscures its realities and results.'[4] Interestingly, certain critics on the Left would agree.

There are three basic types of aid: bilateral aid, multilateral aid and private aid.

Bilateral aid is the direct transfer of money, goods or services from a First World government to a Third World one. This category, which for many countries includes food aid, accounts for more than 75 per cent of all aid to developing countries.[5]

Multilateral aid refers to the contributions which rich countries make to international bodies, such as the World Bank, the largest body, and the European Development Fund. Others include regional banks, which operate like mini-versions of the World Bank, but in specific spheres, such as the Inter-American Development Bank, the African Development Bank and the Asian Development Bank. The various United Nations bodies are included under this umbrella which includes the UN Development Programme (UNDP), the World Food Programme (WFP) and the Food and Agriculture Organisation (FAO), the World Health Authority and the UN children's agency Unicef.

Private aid is that raised directly from the public through aid agencies like Cafod, Christian Aid, Oxfam, the Red Cross, Save the Children Fund, and Tear Fund and in the UK and Care, Catholic Relief Service and World Vision in the US. Often, however, governments can channel funds through the private bodies, known in Britain as Non-Governmental Organisations (NGOs) and in the United States as Private Voluntary Organisations (PVOs). This practice, which involves far larger amounts in the US than the UK, enables governments to direct aid to countries with which they might not wish to have official contacts.

The average voter has an image of aid as a series of ships full of grain and tractors leaving the rich world for the hungry nations. Cash grants are made to help with development schemes which will benefit the poor. First World technicians take short-term contracts to pass their skills on to their less advantaged colleagues in the Third World.

Such an image is quite distant from the truth.

With each of these types of aid there have been significant problems in the past. In some cases it has been seriously and extensively misused by donors anxious to use aid to influence recipients or to further the interests of the donor. In certain cases they have actually made the poor worse off.

Bilateral aid is perhaps the most abused, so we will concentrate on that here; the nature of multilateral aid is dealt with in Chapters Four and Five and private aid in Chapter Seven. To the governments of the United States and Britain bilateral aid is not primarily a way of getting help to the poorest, it is simply another tool for the furtherance of their foreign policies or commercial interests. The former US president Richard Nixon admitted as much with aggressive frankness: 'Let us remember that the main purpose of American aid is not to help other nations but to help ourselves.'[6] For a start most aid does not go to the poorest countries in the world. It goes to political allies, such as Israel, in need of support. Much of British bilateral aid seems to have been geared more to the needs of British industry than to the needs of the world's poor.

An important part of US and UK aid is food aid.[7] Food aid is divided into three categories: project aid, programme aid and emergency relief. Project aid gives food to particular development ventures such as food-for-work schemes. Programme aid gives food to a government so that it can be sold and the cash raised used by the government for some approved purpose. Taken in total about 70 per cent of the First World's food aid goes directly to governments who sell it to those who can afford to buy it – usually not the very poor – and keep the money to supplement their budgets. 'Some governments have come to rely on these food sales for a significant part of their revenue; it is not in their interests to have food policies which would stimulate greater food production and thereby lose this part of their revenue.'[8] Such aid is 'a kind of bribe to help make it worth their while to continue to co-operate with the drain of capital from their countries.'[9]

There are two main problems with emergency food aid: quite commonly it arrives ludicrously late and sometimes what arrives is grotesquely inappropriate. About 20 per cent of European Community (EC) food aid is given away[10] but the type of emergency food and the amounts given have borne far more relation to the current state of Europe's embarrassing food mountains than to the needs of the recipient country at the time. The EC emergency relief system has a history of being notoriously slow. Oxfam in Mali reported emergency food which arrived four months late – just in time to coincide with a bumper harvest.[11] There have since been some attempts to improve the EC system and to weaken the link between the food mountains and the type of aid which materialises. But the lexicon of aid anecdotes is still constantly replenished with new examples.

Different countries have different rules on food aid. About 50 per cent of the world's food aid comes from the USA, 30 per cent from the European Community with another 14 per cent from Australia, Canada and Japan together.[12] Some 25 per cent of this is disbursed through the World Food Programme. The largest food aid donor, the United States, under Public Law 480, spells out the clearly political nature of its food aid. The statute defines its purpose as:

> to expand international trade among the United States and friendly nations . . . to further international economic development, the expansion of US agricultural and commercial export markets . . . and make maximum efficient use of surplus agricultural commodities in furtherance of the foreign policy of the United States.

There are three main types of US food aid under this statute.[13] Title I sells food at a small discount to friendly governments which pay with their own coinage rather than hard currency. They then sell the food to their own people and use the money raised, which is known as counterpart funds, for some purpose approved by the USA. In the past this has included 'common defense' which usually meant buying US weapons: although PL480 is known as the Food for Peace programme, over $2,200 million raised in counterpart funds was spent on military or 'internal security' purposes before it was outlawed by Congress in 1974. Title II food provides free food for urgent famine relief, again to 'friendly nations', but such donations have for years been limited to 20 per cent of all US food which is sent abroad. Under Title III food is exchanged for strategic raw materials required by the USA, especially in the past those minerals necessary to its atomic energy programme.

The political manipulation of food aid has been quite shameless. The bulk of US food aid has never gone to the countries most in need but to the most strategically important ally of the day: Israel and Turkey in the 1950s, South Vietnam in the 1960s and 1970s; today Egypt, South Korea and Pakistan are the major recipients. In Chile during the Allende administration the US offered only small amounts of Title II food; one month after the coup which overthrew the man the US had decided was a threat a credit was offered eight times more than had been extended during the entire Allende period.[14] In Bangladesh, during the famine in 1974 in which between 27,000 and 100,000 people died, the US deliberately withheld food aid because Bangladesh had recently signed a $3 million jute deal with Cuba: 'Famine victims were dying in the streets of Dhaka . . . This grim drama was being transacted in the full view and knowledge of the United States embassy.'[15] In 1985 the USA shipped nearly four times more food aid per capita to support three of its political allies in Central America – El Salvador, Guatemala and Honduras – than it did to the entire famine region in Africa.[16]

The bulk of bilateral aid, however, is not food but cash, much of it in grants, though with some still in low interest loans.[17] Significant amounts of it are given over to general government coffers to relieve their balance of payments problems. Here political, strategic and commercial considerations are even more apparent. The lion's share of US aid in 1989 was not allocated to the poorest countries on the globe. The top six recipients were: Israel ($3,000 million), Egypt ($2,402 million), Pakistan ($581 million), Turkey ($563 million), the Philippines ($479 million), and El Salvador ($394 million). Ethiopia was allocated $4 million.[18] Strategic bases are high in British priorities; in 1985 £18 million to repair a dockyard at Gibraltar came from the aid budget; the same year each inhabitant of the Falkland Islands to which Argentina still lays claim as the Malvinas received the equivalent of £5,500 per head in aid while India received only 15 pence per capita.[19] To further US policy in Central America (to isolate and undermine the Sandinista regime in Nicaragua) the US and Britain combined to deny development aid to Nicaragua using the technique of making unusually demanding conditions for loans: when Nicaragua asked the Inter-American Development Bank for a loan to help reconstruct its fishing fleet in 1983 the US delegation demanded a guarantee that the fleet had sufficient fuel supplies; within weeks the US-backed rebels in Nicaragua, the Contras, using a US naval vessel, blew up storage tanks containing 1.6 million gallons of fuel and the loan was cancelled.[20] In 1985 a confidential memorandum was leaked in London which revealed that British policy was to 'continue to oppose proposals for Nicaragua by finding technical reasons for doing so'.[21]

Another major constraint on the aid budget is that governments often insist that money can be spent only on goods and services purchased from their own country. The system is known as *tied aid*. The United States operates such a system and in 1984 paid $159 million to US firms and universities working with the Third World – half as much as it gave to sub-Saharan Africa.[22] Some 75 per cent[23] of all British bilateral aid is tied to the purchase of British goods or the use of British personnel in this way; some 80 per cent of all Canadian aid is similarly tied. Estimates are that Third World governments find it is usually between 20 and 40 per cent more expensive[24] to buy with tied aid than to buy the same product on the open market, though of course such an option is not open to them. Another result is that the Third World is often pressed to take types of aid it does not want. In March 1986 the Indian government was forced by Britain, which was undergoing a major domestic political crisis over the future of its only helicopter firm, Westland, to take £65 million aid in the form of 21 Westland helicopters. India was told if it did not accept then £65 million would be axed from their aid allocation for the next two years even though the Indian prime minister, Rajiv Gandhi, himself a pilot, pronounced the aircraft unsuitable for Indian conditions.

The most commercial element in the British aid system is its Aid-Trade Provision (ATP). This offers aid to the Third World in individual packages of mixed credits – part loan, part grant – to buy specific British products. It is in reality not so much aid to the Third World as a disguised method of subsidising British exports. A graphic example of that is quoted in the 1986 report by the Independent Group on British Aid:

> In December 1985 George Hughes, the managing director of Willowbrook, a coach and bus body manufacturer in the Midlands (who had given a £50,000 contribution to Conservative Party funds) was awarded an ATP-financed contract to supply buses on chassis to Zambia. The grant was awarded against the advice of our own High Commission in Zambia. It appears that the buses [unsuited to the difficult roads] fell to pieces within a short space of time. UK–Zambian relations inevitably suffered. Willowbrook shortly thereafter went into receivership.[25]

But even where tied aid has not so overtly set out to assist Western industry such an effect has been built into the system. The emphasis in the Sixties and Seventies was on large-scale development programmes in prestige projects like building massive dams, airports, universities, power stations, road networks and even new capital cities. Their development value was dubious. Their rationale was that they would fuel the growth of the economy and that the beneficial effects would trickle down through an invigorated system to the poor – a theory that has now been abandoned since trickle-down has so lamentably failed.[26] As Dr Keith Griffin, the former director of the Institute of Commonwealth Studies at Oxford puts it:

> The incidence of poverty among certain groups, above all in the rural areas, has failed to decline significantly even where growth in per capita production has occurred. Hunger persists despite greater average prosperity. The persistence of inequality, poverty and hunger is due not so much to the absence of growth as to the characteristics of the growth that has occurred – rising landlessness; greater reliance on casual non-permanent employment; increased unemployment; reduction in the asset base of the rural poor; stagnation or reduction in the real daily wage rate; a fall in yearly household income; and political, economic and social discrimination. When these economic and social conditions prevail, growth in total economic output may actually increase rather than reduce poverty and hunger.[27]

What such projects undoubtedly did was gobble up huge aid budgets which were spent almost exclusively in the West buying high-tech equipment, sophisticated construction materials and the expertise of Western specialists. In the event most of these schemes were what one European development commissioner, Edgar Pisani, eloquently called 'cathedrals in the desert' or merely afforded luxuries to the Third World urban élites in their Western-style capital cities, who are often in outlook and lifestyle as far removed from the poor of their nation as are the people of the First World. In some cases such pharaonic projects actually worsened the plight of the poor, as when farm mechanisation put labourers out of work or when poor farmers found themselves landless because a new dam would flood their land[28] or were priced out of supposedly free irrigation projects.[29] Peter Bauer argues that developing countries should not receive aid when they are wasting so much of their own money:

> How do the poorest benefit from the creation at vast expense of brand new capitals such as Brasilia, Islamabad, Anuja in Nigeria, Lilongwe in Malawi or Dodoma in Tanzania? It does not help the

poor in Zaire or Ghana that these countries have international airlines with elegant offices in the West End of London . . . The huge expenditure on arms by Third World governments, intended mostly for use against other Third World governments or against their own subjects, is also pertinent. Third World governments account for about one fifth[30] of total world expenditure on armaments.[31]

Under the Reagan administration military aid became a bigger component in the overall aid package. The cash amount rose by 83 per cent, even after adjusting for inflation.[32] Military aid to Latin America grew from $21 million in 1980 to $274 million in 1985 and to sub-Saharan Africa by 40 per cent.[33] One third of the governments receiving US aid were under some form of military rule.[34] Some arms subsidies were hidden in the proceeds from the resale of food aid and other general subsidies. 'If the martial-law regime of General Zia were not the Economic Support Fund's fourth largest recipient -- $200 million in 1985 alone – could the regime afford to spend almost half of all government revenues on the military?'[35]

No wonder according to Peter Bauer who concludes, among other things, that official government-to-government aid should be abolished.[36] His argument goes too far, as do those of so many pure theorists: he argues against all aid when his conclusions are valid only for bad aid. Some of his excesses derive from his assumption that because some Third World governments are corrupt, inefficient or biased against the poor, this is necessarily true of all of them. Other conclusions are also inimical to a thoroughly Christian view of the notion of sufficiency and stewardship, as we shall see later. But many of his criticisms of the past abuses of official aid are persuasive.

Aid, therefore, as at present constituted, is a thoroughly impure system which offers far less than it promises. Often, as we see, it is not aid at all but a loan, a form of investment or a tool for manipulation. Aristotle, in his *Nicomachean Ethics*, draws a useful distinction between a genuine benefac-

tor and a mere creditor and their relationship to the poor.
'Those who have lent money have no friendly feeling to their
debtors, but only a wish that they may be kept safe with a
view to what is to be got from them . . . Those who have
done a service to others feel friendship and love for those
they have served, even if these are not of any use to them
and never will be.'[37] There is very little friendship, let alone
love, apparent in many sectors of the aid industry.

* **Here, then, is our first structure of sin: not aid itself but the
fact that there are many things which are not aid but which
masquerade as it.** The evolution of such a system has created
among the general public a sense that something is being done
when often it is not. Were this realisation more widespread there
would undoubtedly be a far greater demand that the situation
should change.

> *Woe to you, scribes and Pharisees, hypocrites! for you are like
> whitewashed tombs, which outwardly appear beautiful, but
> within they are full of dead men's bones and all uncleanness.
> So you also outwardly appear righteous to men, but within you
> are full of hypocrisy and iniquity.*[38]

The purveyors of such distorted aid are the modern equivalent
of the money-changers in the temple. *'It is written: "My house
shall be a house of prayer"; but you make it a den of robbers.'*[39]
If they cannot be cleared out at once it is, at any rate, necessary
to discomfort them by clearly identifying them and calling out
their name, which is legion. We shall consider action on this in
our epilogue (see page 333).

There are, fortunately, enough good aid projects within
the existing system to avoid the extreme conclusion at which
Keith Griffin arrives: 'In practice foreign aid is doing little
to promote growth in the Third World and even less to
alleviate poverty. In the end it appears to be doing little
more than sustain corrupt regimes in power, sometimes
deliberately (Guatemala, El Salvador) and sometimes perhaps not. In either event the time may have come to abandon
the enterprise.'[40] The positive elements are well catalogued
in the major report prepared by Robert Cassen and Associ-

ates for the Joint Ministerial Committee of the World Bank and International Monetary Fund. Entitled *Does Aid Work?*[41] it concludes that the answer is 'Yes, quite often it does . . .' This is important. There may be corruptions in the mechanisms of aid but the system is not irredeemably flawed.

Even a perfect system of aid, however, does not hold the answer to hunger in the world. Aid at the moment accounts for only 5 per cent of all the income of the Third World, as distinct from trade, which represents more than 80 per cent of all cash flows from rich to poor nations. In 1985, the total amount of emergency aid to Africa from all sources was around $3,000 million; yet in that same year Africa paid $6,000 million in debt repayments to First World institutions.[42] Around that time a staggering $19,000 million was wiped off the value of their exports by a price collapse on world markets.[43] Even a massively increased aid network cannot offer a solution to problems on that scale, no matter how well organised it was and how pure the motives of those charged with the decisions and their administration. To see why, we have to look at a much larger canvas and at the whole relationship between the economies of the First and Third Worlds.

THE COLONIAL PROCESS: DEVELOPMENT OR EXPLOITATION?

In the Middle Ages there was a broad similarity between the social and economic structures of Europe and the rest of the world. Feudalism was the shared basic order, trade was limited and all manufacture was by hand. The precise sequence of events which gave birth to the new economic order of capitalism in north-western Europe has long been a matter of debate between scholars. But whatever the causal relationship a number of factors coalesced which were to put Europe on the road to an accelerated material development. There was a small population after the ravages of the Black Death and the scarcity of labour had brought labourers a new freedom in their relations with their feudal overlords. Serfs became peasants and at the same time a significant agricultural surplus led to a blossoming of trade in foodstuffs. The class of merchants who dealt in them had not suffered undue restriction, for political reasons: kings saw them as natural allies, and sources of finance, in their attempts to contain the power of the nobility. Christendom was a fragmented body, in economic and political terms, and did not have the cohesion which characterised the great empires in the East; the constant warring between European states led to further developments in military technology and skills which more peaceful regions found unnecessary. The East nonetheless had made advances in other technologies – textiles and steel in India and China – which provided potent lures to increase trade. In the fifteenth and sixteenth centuries improved technologies in navigation, cartography and boat-building brought new dimensions to the trading relationships and offered the possibility of dealing direct with the Indies, by-passing Arab middle-men and the restrictions on the lucrative spice trade imposed by the Turks. It also led to the discovery of the New World. As the historian R. H. Tawney put it:

> It was the mastery of man over his environment which heralded the dawn of the new age, and it was in the stress of expanding economic energies that this mastery was proved and won. Like sovereignty in a feudal age, the economic efforts of the Middle Ages, except in a few favoured spots, had been fragmentary and decentralised. Now the scattered raiders were to be organised and disciplined.[44]

The result was a rapid growth in wealth, an increase in trade, and a concentration of financial power in the hands of a new class. With them the new class brought a new culture and system of ideas which swiftly conquered the creaking certainties of the *ancien régime*. It was the vastest economic crisis that Europe had experienced since the fall of Rome. It produced a new kind of empire: those in the past had been driven by dreams of power but for the new conquerors the dream was of profit. 'Their empires arose almost as a by-product of the individual pursuit of wealth.'[45] We shall consider the interaction between this and the religious changes of the time in Chapter Seven. What we must note here is that this is when the door to colonial expansion was unlocked and that, from the outset, in the trading relationship established with the Great Discoveries, the balance of advantage lay with Europe. That imbalance was only to grow with the rise of capitalism and the Industrial Revolution which eventually followed. It was to develop through three distinct phases from the early days of plunder and looting, through a systematic exploitation of resources under colonialism proper, and most recently through the indirect influence of international finance and the explicit mechanisms of multinational companies which today directly control 40 per cent of all world trade and as much as 90 per cent of all traffic in commodities,[46] and influence a good deal more.

COLONIALISM: PHASE ONE – PLUNDER

The discovery of the New World offered unprecedented opportunities for plunder using guns and horses which the indigenous peoples had never seen. Cortés subdued the Aztec capital, Tenochtitlan, with just 600 men, seventeen horses and ten cannon, and then melted down the exquisite jewellery in the Aztec treasury and turned it into gold bars. Pizarro took over the vast Inca Empire with only 102 foot soldiers and sixty-two horsemen. When the treasure houses were exhausted the Iberian *conquistadores* put the local people to work in mines such as that at Potosi, the 'mountain that gushed silver', and in the sugar plantations they established throughout the Caribbean and the Americas. Many died from overwork, European diseases or outright massacre. Estimates of the numbers killed range from 12 million to 15 million.[47] It was to replenish the workforce for the plantations of sugar, which had first been planted in the Caribbean by Columbus and soon became established throughout the Americas as the first tropical crop planted especially for export, that the slave trade began. This is not the place to catalogue the iniquities of that terrible traffic in human beings which transported anywhere between 10 million and 100 million Africans across the Atlantic, some 20 per cent of whom are said to have died on the journey.[48] But it is important to note that the slaves, often paid for only with guns and rum to West African chiefs, produced another important source of capital; three million alone were transported in British ships at a profit of £20–£30 a head.[49] 'It was in part the cash of Liverpool, centre of the triangular trade in slaves, cotton and rum between West Africa, the West Indies and Britain, that financed the mills of South Lancashire, the cradle of the industrial revolution.'[50]

The initial expansion swiftly established a new international nexus of trade, finance and population movement, but as the great proponent of free trade Adam Smith, who was later to be espoused by the apologists of Empire, observed: 'The savage injustice of the Europeans rendered an event, which ought to have been beneficial to all, ruinous and destructive to several of those unfortunate countries.'[51]

The gold and silver shipped to Europe shifted the balance of trading power between that continent and the East. Until then Europe had 'lagged behind Asia in industrial skill. In exchange for silk, cotton, sugar and spices, Europe could export only small arms . . . The superiority of commerce, handicraft and administration in China in comparison with the Italian cities was the theme of the fascinating story Marco Polo told . . . His story relates to the end of the thirteenth century, but there is no indication that Europe was catching up with China in the following century and a half.'[52] Two things altered that: military might and the Industrial Revolution.

By the sixteenth century Europe had the wealth for the first time to trade on equal terms with the East, but before long that was not considered to be enough. In the next century in India the Dutch attempted to secure by force of arms a monopoly in the spice trade. For the British too the flag followed trade. Conquest became necessary to deny access to other Europeans and guarantee the safe movement of goods in India. The British won the Battle of Plassey in India in 1757. 'The famous Bengal Plunder began to arrive in London soon after, and its arrival coincided with what is generally considered to be the beginning of the Industrial Revolution in Britain.'[53] Between 1757 and 1815 Britain is said to have extracted £1,000 million at a time when British national income was only around £125 million a year. In the nineteenth century, after the use of quinine was discovered to combat the deadly ravages of malaria, Africa too fell to the British, French, German, Belgian and Portuguese colonisers. Even the nominally independent Liberia was dependent financially and in other ways on the United States. Only the ancient Ethiopian Empire, secure in its remote mountain fastness, maintained its autonomy after defeating the Italian invader. Elsewhere European military superiority, on land and at sea, was soon able to force advantageous trade practices on the rest of the world, reaching its perverse epitome in the Opium Wars which forced the Chinese Empire to agree on import concessions to Britain, Japan, and the United States and conceded to the British the right to sell the deadly drug to the large population of China.

It was the profits from such trade which in a large degree financed the Industrial Revolution which was to foster the creation of today's enormous gap between the rich and poor worlds. The value of the gold and silver taken from Latin America up to 1660, the booty extracted from Indonesia by the Dutch East India Company from 1650 to 1780, the harvest reaped by French capital in the eighteenth-century slave trade, and the profits from slave labour in the British Antilles and from a half-century of British looting, add up, in the estimate of one economic historian, to 'more than the capital of all the industrial enterprises operating by steam which existed in Europe around 1800.'[54]

COLONIALISM: PHASE TWO – ORGANISING THE RESOURCES

The rise of industry was to add a new turn to the ratchet of development constructed from the new economic order: colonialism, militarism and yet more advanced industrialisation. Back in Europe capitalism was moving into a new phase. Throughout the seventeenth and eighteenth centuries it had revolutionised agriculture. Farms became bigger. Measures like the Enclosure Acts in Britain forced peasants off the land and into the role of wage earners on bigger farms where production was more efficient. Now the same thing happened with the growth of industry, where productivity was constantly raised by new forms of mechanisation and the breaking down of jobs into simple and repetitive elements which could be performed ever more rapidly. It was not without its social cost in England. The quality of life deteriorated in terms of dietary standards, the growing congestion and squalor of town life, the exploitation of child labour and the misery and danger of work in the new factories. The economist Peter Donaldson, quoting contemporary commentators like John Stuart Mill and Lord John Russell, describes it as 'sacrificial development' – with intolerable burdens being imposed on immediate generations in order that subsequent ones would benefit.[55] But industry grew as a result, and at such a rapid rate in Britain that, with a limited population of around six million, it needed to find new markets for its goods if its mass production methods were to continue to improve in efficiency and profitability.[56]

The colonies provided the obvious answer. A burgeoning Europe had already begun to export its population. In colonies like the United States, Australia and New Zealand the Caucasian immigrants soon outnumbered the indigenous peoples. They had developed rapidly with the aid of capital inflows from the mother country. In other colonies there had been no such development but the substantial indigenous populations had been concentrated in easily accessible units to work the mines and plantations to provide the industrialised world with raw materials. Now the aim was to turn all these colonies into markets for European industry. To secure these markets a number of protectionist measures were instituted. The Navigation Acts forbade colonies from developing their own industries which might compete with the mother country. 'For example the North American colonists were forbidden to manufacture caps, hats, woollen or iron goods. They were expected to send the raw material for these products to England to be manufactured and then to buy them back from England.'[57] The Irish were prohibited from weaving their wool into cloth and forbidden to export to anywhere but England, at prices dictated by the English. To kill competition from the well-established textile industry in India an elaborate net of prohibitive taxes and restrictions was established which put 75 per cent duties on all goods imported into Britain from the sub-continent. Many Indian peasant weavers had their little fingers deliberately broken by the colonial power so that they could no longer practise their craft. Between 1815 and 1832 the value of cotton goods India exported fell from £1.3 million to under £100,000. Tens of thousands of weavers lost their jobs. Similar policies were followed in Egypt and throughout Africa. Only in the North American colonies did the attempt fail.

* **Here then is a second structure of sin: an inequality between nations built on a series of actions which, in terms of conventional morality, were reprehensible.**

> *Woe to him who builds his house by unrighteousness,*
> *and his upper rooms by injustice;*
> *who makes his neighbour serve him for nothing,*
> *and does not give him his wages.*[58]

To maintain this inequality does not require such blatant wrongdoing. A more 'neutral' mechanism is used for that. It is in analysing that mechanism that we shall find a whole series of structures of sin.

> *For we have to struggle not just against flesh and blood human beings, but against the principalities and powers, against the world-rulers of this darkness, against the superhuman spirits.*[59]

FREE TRADE OR FAIR TRADE?

At this point in history came a crucial development, which still has major repercussions throughout the Third World. Having pursued policies which protected domestic industry – to the point of killing off actual and potential competition – Britain made a key shift in its economic policy. It abandoned protectionism and espoused the free trade theories being expounded by the 'classical' economists like Adam Smith and David Ricardo. Their thesis was simple: instead of each country being self-sufficient each should produce what it could produce most cheaply, the commodities in which it had what they called a *comparative advantage*, and then exchange their goods for what could be produced more cheaply elsewhere; thus everything would be produced more cheaply and everyone would be better off. The 'invisible hand' of market forces would direct every member of society and every nation, using the engine of the self-interest of each, to the best possible situation for the global economy. It is, crudely speaking, the theory which lies beneath the policies which the IMF and the World Bank pursue today in trying to alter the policies of Third World governments, and which have led on to the 'adjustment programmes' which have cost more than a million additional deaths in the poorest countries.[60] In theory, of course, the free market system should work to the benefit of all; in practice, when the system is imposed from a starting point where all nations are unequal, what free trade and market forces do is to magnify those inequalities.[61] It is in this that the 'development gap' between the rich and poor nations finds its genesis. When those initial inequalities are built on the policy of piracy, bullying and slaughter which Europe pursued, and the United States and Japan later acquiesced in, then free trade is no longer the neutral and value-free mechanism of neo-classical theory but an instrument to maintain and indeed increase injustice. The structure may masquerade as neutral but in fact it has a hidden immoral bias.

* **Here then is the third of our structures of sin: not the operation of market forces and free trade in themselves, but the bullying imposition of them on those who are less powerful than ourselves:** *'But you have turned justice into poison, and the fruit of righteousness into wormwood . . .'*[62]

An inequity has become inbuilt: *'Behold, this was the guilt of your sister Sodom: she and her daughters had pride, surfeit of food, and prosperous ease, but did not aid the poor and needy.'*[63] We shall return to this issue in Chapter Seven, but for the present we should note that a series of other inherently malign structures stem from the basic immorality of imposing the unfettered operation of the free market on a situation of forced inequality.

As a further complication we should note that for the theory of free trade to work properly it needs to be adopted by every nation in the world, so that all barriers and tariffs are removed; in reality this never happens – today the United States, the EC and Japan, the countries who most loudly advocate free trade for Third World countries, themselves maintain protectionist barriers. Here we have a clear hypocrisy compounding the structural evil.

COMPARATIVE ADVANTAGE: TOOL OR TRICK?

In the process of colonialism there was another crucial structural matter which, though it was unrecognised at the time, served to widen the development gap even further. The theory of comparative advantage was bound to be disproportionately disadvantageous to poor countries dependent upon agriculture or mining. Under this theory colonial administrators decided what the natural strength of a colony was and then maximised it. Existing patterns of farming were wiped away and huge plantations of single crops were developed, always with the needs of the European processing industry in mind. There was global transfer of plants to facilitate this. Maize and cassava from South America were spread world-wide. Cocoa was taken from Mexico and planted throughout West Africa. Rubber from the Amazon was taken to South-East Asia. Sugar, from Bengal, went to the Caribbean and the north-eastern coast of South America. Coffee from the Middle East was planted throughout Latin America and Africa. Tea from China was planted in India, Sri Lanka and East Africa.

In more recent times these practices have begun to take an environmental toll. The native soils, on which crop rotation or fallow systems had been previously practised, were often quickly impoverished and virgin land was constantly cleared for new plantation. Local farmers were forced to become landless labourers working for pitiful wages or had to move to marginal land to grow the national food crops; as a result began the erosion of the soil which slowly was to produce the devastating desertification evident throughout the Third World today; and with the erosion came steadily decreasing quantities of local food, and populations now increasingly dependent upon imports of basic food while at the same time exporting record amounts of more exotic foods to the West. The imported food is, in some cases, surpluses from temperate climates, such as wheat, which creates a taste for types of food which can never be grown locally. Moreover the concentration on a few major cash crops or on the extraction of a major mineral source left the countries, on independence, incredibly vulnerable to dramatic fluctuations in the prices of those commodities on the world market.

But there was an even more fundamental difficulty with the economic formula devised in the years before independence. At the time it seemed logical enough that the colonies would provide raw materials and that these would be sent back to the imperial power where a more sophisticated industrial network already existed to process it.

The problem was highlighted by Professor Raul Prebisch, economic adviser to Argentina, when the first United Nations Conference on Trade and Development (UNCTAD) was convened in 1964. He argued that the Third World's demand for manufactured goods was bound to grow more rapidly than the First World's demand for raw materials. This was because the Third World, which has two-thirds of the world's population, would need large quantities of manufactured goods as part of its development. The First World, on the other hand, had already reached a level of consumption which satisfied its basic needs and would therefore not need greatly increased quantities of raw materials. Indeed, progress in the rich countries meant that they would need *less* because technological advance meant that the First World was becoming more efficient at squeezing extra output from the same amount of raw materials. It was also inventing new synthetic materials which replaced many Third World materials. Ironically, development was enabling the Third World to produce more rather than less of these products, so that the market was over-supplied and their prices fell. The end result of all this would be that the gap between rich and poor nations would actually widen.

* **Here then is a fourth structure of sin: not the division of labour between the countries of the world but a division which systematically widens the gap between the rich and poor:**

> *Woe to those who lie upon beds of ivory,*
> *and stretch themselves upon their couches,*
> *and eat lambs from the flock,*
> *and calves from the midst of the stall . . .*[64]

> *They sell the righteous for silver,*
> *and the needy for a pair of shoes –*
> *they that trample the head of the poor into the dust of the earth,*
> *and turn aside the way of the afflicted.*[65]

BUILDING ÉLITES AND RIVALRIES

Another set of problems was built in to the structures of the colonies and the methods of administration employed. At their most fundamental these began with the very creation of the colonies which are today nation-states. In Africa, for example, national boundaries were the result of lines drawn with a ruler on a map in Berlin where the Europeans met to carve up the continent. They bore no relation to natural frontiers or to the historical boundaries of different races or tribes, storing up a legacy of constant boundary disputes between neighbouring countries after independence. It also created states with citizens who were traditional tribal enemies; to combat this many African leaders were later to institute one-party states to promote the notion of homogenous nationhood, but bringing with it all the totalitarian dangers such a system can encourage, such as the abuse of human rights. In Latin America colonialism destroyed egalitarian communal systems of landholding and replaced them with a structure of large estates and landless labourers which is still a major barrier to human development today. Many colonial capital cities were not established in the best place from which to administer the country, but in the spot which gave easiest access to the outside. In order to facilitate exports the capital was usually sited on the coast, or in a landlocked country as near to it as possible. Some twenty-eight African capitals are ports, while those in Chad, Niger and Mali are all in the extreme south-west corner of their vast countries. There was no need to build up a network of towns throughout the colony; all trade could go straight from the countryside through the metropolis, thus creating capitals which were as big as eight times the size of any other town in the country, and road networks which went nowhere but to the ports.

The development of the human resource was just as blinkered. The British ruled through existing local hierarchies, a process which unconsciously promoted the most malleable, collaborative or corrupt of local chiefs; where no such hierarchy existed, as in Bengal, they created one, turning tax collectors into a class of landowners. The French and the Portuguese tried to turn selected native people into honorary Europeans who would rule on their behalf – the French called this new breed *évolués*, the Portuguese named them *assimilados* – creating a local élite alienated from the needs and indigenous aspirations of their own people. In such a context the democracy which was bequeathed was a shallow graft; there have been forty-one military coups and takeovers in independent Africa.[66] The colonial education system was geared to building a class of unimaginative but obedient administrators and concentrated on Westernising the most able of the indigenous people. After independence these élites looked to Western models of development or more commonly to the example of the Soviet Union – a country which had accelerated its growth from a peasant economy to that of an industrial superpower. They pursued programmes of industrialisation and modernisation which involved inappropriate capital-intensive investment, uneconomic import substitution and over-valued exchange rates which disadvantaged the agricultural sector. They also looked to extravagant Western symbols as proof of their new nationhood: huge dams, power stations, high-rise capitals and state universities in countries which had no network of secondary schools. 'On reflection,' says Paul Harrison, 'it is obvious why few of the new ruling élites developed an indigenous model of development. Most were not themselves members of traditional ruling élites. If they owed their new-found power to anything, it was to their literacy, their Western education, the familiarity with Western ideas and the Western-style institutions they had inherited.'[67] The universities they built created a tertiary problem – to find jobs for the university graduates and prevent them from becoming a disaffected opposition. In Mali, for example, one of the poorest countries in the world, the essentially non-productive civil service is now, by a factor of ten, the largest employer. Members of the urban élite often see their interests as aligned with the values of the First World rather than with those of their own people. They can resent being sent out to work in the provinces. Sometimes the result is inefficiency, as in Niger where bureaucrats with no stock-rearing experience were sent out to manage government ranches. In other situations the new élites sought personal advancement outside their own society. Hundreds of thousands of university graduates emigrated from the Third World to Europe, Japan and the United States. These individuals are usually the doctors and the scientists whom their homelands can least afford to spare.

THE CHURCH IN THE COLONIES: CHRISTIAN SPIRITUALITY OR CULTURAL SUPERIORITY?

The role of the Church throughout the process of colonisation was ambivalent. Missionaries had been dispatched in 1493 with the authority of three Papal bulls which divided the New World between Spain and Portugal and authorised them to subjugate it and to dispatch thither 'wise, upright, God-fearing and virtuous men who will be capable of instructing the indigenous peoples in good morals and in the Catholic faith.'[68] For several centuries their basic approach in many countries was an attempt to stamp out local cultures, which they regarded as the work of the devil, and replace them with a religion in which Christianity and the cultural values of Western Europe were inextricably intertwined. In the early years the approach was a failure. Professor Stephen Neill in *A History of Christian Missions* wrote:

> No serious attempt seems anywhere to have been made to face all that is involved in a mission to quite primitive peoples – the needs for a deep and accurate knowledge of the language, understanding of their customs and mentality, the long and patient instruction that must precede baptism, the endlessly patient pastoral care that must follow it.[69]

Success came only when the missionaries began to move with the traders and colonial administrators who, except in a few cases, welcomed their efforts. Later writers were to cast serious doubt upon the integrity of the relationship between the Church and the process of colonisation. J. K. Galbraith commented:

> The real motives for colonialism, were they stated, would be altogether too uncouth, selfish or obscene. So where colonisation

has involved people – where it has not meant merely the appropriation and settlement of unused lands – the colonists have almost always seen themselves as purveyors of some transcendental moral, spiritual, political or social worth.[70]

Certainly a whole variety of compromising relationships developed between the two groups. Some missionaries perceived an overt relationship between the two sets of interests. 'I go back to Africa to try to make an open path for commerce and Christianity,' David Livingstone told an audience at the University of Cambridge in 1857. His logic was that the slave trade, of which he had a profound horror, could only continue because of the collaboration of Africans in it; it would only be ended when the option of legitimate commerce was offered to the local people. Archbishop Desmond Tutu recalls a harsher local judgement on those who made this connection: 'They used to say . . . "The missionaries came to Africa and they had the Bible and we had the land. And then they said, 'Let us pray.' And when we opened our eyes, we had the Bible and they had the land!"'[71] Others simply carried the cultural baggage of their world and time with them without realising it. 'Many missionaries went out with the best intentions of carrying out the declared intention of the London Missionary Society to preach the pure Gospel without tying it to any Western form of organisation or polity, but they usually ended up by producing a copy, faithful down to the minutest detail, of that form of the Christian faith to which they themselves were accustomed in their own country.'[72] Those who departed from the cultural norm were 'lucky to be considered merely wrong; far more often they have been thought unpatriotic or traitorous.'[73] Bishop de Marion Bresillac, a Catholic prelate in south India, was forced to resign for such dissent.

Missionaries tried a variety of approaches. In Uganda they involved themselves in the introduction of cotton through the Uganda Company which they controlled and which contributed greatly to the viability of the railway from Kampala to the coast which the Colonial Office in London was anxious to establish. In West Africa the Basle Mission played a key part in the introduction of cocoa-farming.[74] In East Africa in order to liberate slaves they bought them and then established them in Church-owned plantations. As an attempt to establish the Church in Africa it was a dismal failure; their offspring became Christians in decreasing rather than increasing numbers. The settlement they built as 'Bagamoyo stands like a ghost town today, with its huge and empty cathedral, its slave blockhouse . . . and its melancholy graveyard filled with the remains of so many young missionaries with the sleep of a century upon them.'[75]

Next they tried a new apostolic method: pre-mission – to prepare the people to receive the Gospel. There were two arms to this: a range of caring activities, such as running hospitals, orphanages and homes for the blind and elderly to display the love of Christ in action, and education, to enable people to read the Scriptures and raise the general intellectual level to aid their understanding. Before long education became the great missionary activity, with great competition between Catholics and Protestants to build more schools. In 1928 an Apostolic Visitor gave Rome's direct sanction to the strategy when he arrived in Dar es Salaam and told a gathering of bishops: 'Where it is impossible for you to carry on both the immediate task of evangelisation and your educational work, neglect your churches in order to perfect your schools.'[76]

It was in this area that the Church had its most important effect on the shape of colonial development. Undoubtedly there were great benefits from the spread of a basic network of primary education throughout much of Africa and Asia. But it also set up a more long-term problem in the attitudes it moulded. For a start there was the colonial theology[77] which it articulated. Doctrines of the separateness of body and soul and of earth and heaven, of the acceptance of poverty as God's will, of unquestioning obedience to both Church and State, of the importance of the individual over the community in matters of salvation and social enterprise, of the pacifying promise of a heavenly reward – all these stifled the creative communal action which was vital to genuine development. In the field of education the debilitating effect was more insidious. Occasionally there were disputes between the colonial administrators, who wanted a competent but pliant body of clerical staff, and missionary teachers who had a broader view of education, but basically the system suited both. In 1880 the *African Times* proclaimed: 'The educated élite, more or less under the influence of Christian faith, are and will be indispensable as a vanguard of the great army of civilisation that must be projected upon the ignorant barbarism of heathen Africa.'[78] The effects of this in the post-independence period were to be damaging. By alienating the brighter pupils from their own culture and often making them scorn it, the Church created a future leadership whose values were alienated from the people they would be called upon to serve. Often the process was unconscious. Pupils sought to imitate the lifestyle and attitudes of teachers they admired. The result was a colonial élite who mimicked the colonists to such a degree that, as happened most strikingly in India, they became more European than the Europeans. This process was reinforced by what the black philosopher Frantz Fanon described as a systematic social humiliation. He wrote:

> Every colonised people – in other words, every people in whose soul an inferiority complex has been created by the death and burial of its local cultural originality – finds itself face to face with the language of the civilising nation . . . The colonised [person] is elevated above his jungle status in proportion to his adoption of the mother country's cultural standards. He becomes whiter as he renounces his blackness, his jungle.[79]

This further reinforced the tendency for the black élite to assume the values of their colonial masters. Small wonder then that now, when the vision handed on to those élites has been revealed to be bankrupt, there is 'a kind of blind rage sweeping Africa, blind in that it is neither planned nor organised. Sometimes it is seen as a quiet rage against the Church. More than 5,000 independent churches, broken off from the traditional missionary churches, have sprung up in Africa in recent years. Sometimes it is rage against the political powers that be, whether black or white, for not producing the freedom and justice and peace and prosperity so loudly promised.'[80]

> * **Here then is a fifth structure of sin: the confusing of the essential values of the gospel mission with Western cultural assumptions.** These were to pervert the development of the poor and entrap them in notions of inferiority – and us in notions of superiority – which today still act as barriers to a full recognition of the people of the Third World as our equals before God.[81]

> *I hate, I despise your feasts*
> *and I take no delight in your solemn assemblies.*
> *Even though you offer me your burnt offerings, and cereal offerings,*
> *I will not accept them,*
> *and the peace offerings of your fatted beasts*
> *I will not look upon.*
> *Take away from me the noise of your songs;*
> *to the melody of your harps I will not listen.*
> *But let justice roll down like waters,*
> *and righteousness like an everflowing stream.*[82]

THE COLONIAL HERITAGE: BRINGING IN A VERDICT

What in the end will be the judgement of history on the colonial era? Undoubtedly it brought some advantages including the network of primary education and advances in medical care which have saved the lives of millions of people. Right-wing economists like Lord Bauer go much further. He maintains that however badly off the Third World is it would have been a lot worse without colonialism. Development and growth may not have been 'fair' but they have taken place just the same. Countries which were not colonised are, in absolute terms he claims, worse off than those which were. Remote areas, cut off from trade, are still the most backward and the seats of the worst famine. The Europeans invested large sums of capital in the colonies and brought with them a law and order which made those countries, previously racked by tribal warfare, safe places to trade and farm in. They brought fruitful plants from other parts of the globe. They brought clean water and sewage systems, schools and hospitals. They built roads and brought mechanical transport to areas which previously had relied on human porterage for all traffic: 'Black Africa never invented the wheel,' he says in a particularly rebarbative essay entitled 'Western Guilt and Third World Poverty'.[83] The prosperity of the West is not from colonial exploitation; some of the richest nations, like Sweden and Switzerland, never had colonies. The West does not fix the low prices for Third World commodities; they are arrived at by the neutral trading mechanisms governed by supply and demand. If the West is more highly developed that is only because the people of the Third World demonstrate a 'lack of ambition, enterprise and skill'[84] or that they insist on maintaining social systems or religious values which inhibit economic development. Those in the West who deny all this are 'exponents of guilt . . . concerned with their own emotional state and that of their fellow citizens and not with the results of the policies inspired by such sentiments.'[85]

Bauer is, however, highly selective in his data and high-lights symptoms as though they were causes. There is an unpleasantly racist assumption in his contention that those in the Third World work less hard, are less talented or less enterprising than Europeans. The ancient civilisations of the Egyptian and the Persian, the Aztec and the Inca, the Mossi and the Arab, and the Indian and the Chinese were all highly developed when Europe was still backward, in both technical, artistic, scientific, mathematical and spiritual matters. The European ascendancy when it came happened to coincide with a concatenation of influences including devastating bubonic plagues and resulting changes in agricultural production which Europeans can hardly claim demonstrate any inherent cultural superiority. There may be virtue in their enterprise in technology, exploration and trading. But where that is aided by their expertise in war and plunder it surely indicates a cultural predisposition of a more dubious kind. To argue otherwise is to fall into the trap of equating material and moral progress.

It is true that colonialism created a form of public security, but it also created countries whose boundaries are purely arbitrary and which often contain two or more groups which were traditionally enemies, thus fostering the wars, civil wars, guerrilla movements and border disputes which bedevil much of the Third World. Clean water, sewage and hospitals there may be, but only for the metropolitan élites – most of the ordinary people are still without. At the time of independence the entire continent of Africa, with a population of 200 million, produced only 8,000 secondary school graduates.[86] There is little sense to saying that famine is in remote areas cut off from trade when a good percentage of the population has been forced to farm those marginal areas, causing erosion and desertification, precisely because they have been forced off the good land to make way for cash-crop plantations. Europe may have pumped money into the colonies but most of it went to the 'kith and kin' colonies of the United States, Canada, South Africa and Australia, to which Europe had exported its excess of population in such numbers that they overwhelmed the indigenous peoples. Even countries like Switzerland and Sweden which had no colonies were, as we shall see, inextricably linked with the international financial network which was pump-primed in its early days by the wealth of the colonies and has refused to surrender its economic advantage ever since. It is true that certain social and religious values in the Third World might inhibit a Western style of economic development. But that, compared with inequities of trade, is a comparatively small factor when set against the problem, and goes no way to absolve us from the responsibility to remove first the beam in our own eye. Finally, while it may be true that, on balance, the Third World is better off after colonialism than it was before, it is wilful to ignore the structural elements which it has built into the relationship between rich and poor nations and which will ensure that, if market forces are allowed to operate in an unrestricted and 'neutral' way, the gap between them will not only be maintained but will constantly grow.

'You shall know them by their fruits.'[87] In the end colonialism failed in most areas to raise living standards to a level of basic human decency. But what is worse from a Christian standpoint, it robbed people of the dignity of their own identity and the right to participate in decision-making on the equitable footing which is the birthright of all those who stand equal before God. In his recent book *Global Economy* the German Lutheran theologian Ulrich Duchrow notes: 'If we still accept the theological notion of something in the nature of *original sin*, we cannot in reason and conscience deny such guilty associations in respect of our European colonial history or evade a structural analysis of the present neo-colonial system.'[88]

COLONIALISM: PHASE THREE – AT ARMS' LENGTH

This neo-colonial system is the third phase of the process of colonialism. It is in this way that the colonial imbalance continues to function, to the benefit of every man, woman and child living in the First World today. Under the present system there are three distinct methods by which rich countries maintain their advantage over the poor nations: the first is through the mechanism of modern international trade; the second is through multinational companies; the third is through the whole international financial system, which we shall consider in detail in a later chapter.

The trading mechanism is a complex one but there can be little doubt that its overall function is to inhibit the optimum development of poor countries. The legacy of colonisation means that today half of all Third World countries earn at least 50 per cent of their income from one or two crops or minerals; indeed nine African countries earn more than 70

per cent of their foreign exchange from a single crop.[89] Third
World countries are forced to trade with the West because
this is the only way they can obtain the money to import
those goods which are essential to break through to the next
stage of development. But the structural imbalance which,
as we have seen, constantly widens the gap between the
producers of raw materials and the producers of manufactured goods means that they constantly have to produce
more in order to buy the same amount of First World
products. In 1973 it took one Latin American cow to buy a
barrel of oil; in 1983 it took nine. In 1970 it took a ton of
bananas to buy a steel bar; in 1980 it took two tons.[90] The
economists call this process a deterioration in the 'terms of
trade'. The problem is worsened because every poor nation
is trying to produce more all the time and so the world market
in their raw materials becomes ever more over-supplied and
the prices paid for their goods fall ever lower. Such prices
fell by 18 per cent in the first five years of the 1980s,[91] cutting
an estimated $40,000 million every year from Third World
incomes, which is more than the total of aid they received.[92]

The cost of all this effort is devastating in both human and
environmental terms. Malnutrition and infant mortality are
increased as land once used for food production is turned
over to cash crops for export. As one Salvadorean wrote as
long ago as 1929: 'The conquest of territory by the coffee
industry is alarming. It has occupied the highlands and is
now descending to the valleys, displacing maize, rice and
beans. It has extended like the *conquistador*, spreading
hunger and misery . . . It is true that the cost of importing
maize is small in relation to the benefits of the export of
coffee, but is the imported grain given to the poor *campesino*
who has lost his land?'[93] Africa, which as recently as 1970
was producing enough food to feed itself, now relies on
imported grain to feed more than a quarter of its population.[94] The environment is steadily assaulted – at present
rates it is estimated that the jungles of South-East Asia will
completely disappear within fifty years[95] and a fifth of the
world's forests will be destroyed within fifteen years and

much of the land is being given over to products used only for cattle-feed in the West.

The problem is only worsened by the normal cyclic nature of modern capitalism with its constant phases of boom and recession which cause dramatic oscillations in the price of commodities. In January 1986 coffee on world markets was $2.20 a pound, by July it had fallen to $1.37.[96] This figure was only 40 per cent of what coffee had fetched a decade earlier. It takes three years for a coffee bush to produce any berries at all and five years for it to come into full production. Bushes cannot, of course, be dug up and replanted to fit in with the monthly or even annual vagaries of the international commodity market. The decision to replant an entire area with another crop would require a major investment – one which itself would bring new risks for wild price variations in most Third World crops – making sensible long-term planning a nightmare. These sharp swings in price are exacerbated by the activities of speculators in the commodities futures market, where a mere 5 per cent of the deals actually involve the delivery of goods. Speculation on this scale perverts free market trends which, as we have noted, are already biased against the poor commodity producers.

PROTECTIONISM: LOADING THE DICE

The only way the Third World can break out of the downward spiral is to export fewer raw materials and replace them with goods which are processed or manufactured. The world's fifty poorest countries could double their export earnings if they processed their commodities and exported, for example, cocoa powder rather than beans. So why do they not do this? Because the First World has instituted a system of import duties which are low for raw materials but higher for processed commodities and higher still for finished goods: the difference between the rates is what economists call the rate of effective protection. To sell fresh pineapples within the

European Community, for example, a Third World producer must pay a tariff of 9 per cent, to sell tinned pineapples it must pay 32 per cent and to sell pineapple juice 42 per cent[97] – the effective rate of protection in this instance is equivalent to a tax of more than 75 per cent. As a result only 3 per cent of all the manufactured goods which are sold in industrialised countries are made in developing countries[98] and the World Bank estimates that if the West cut its tariffs on agricultural products by only a half the Third World would gain $5,900 million a year in extra income without having to produce or sell an ounce more than at present.[99]

The harsh truth is that, for all the rhetoric of the rich nations about aid and assistance to the poor, their trading policies are not designed to alleviate the problems of the Third World but actually to worsen them. In July 1944 the Western industrial nations met at Bretton Woods in New Hampshire to agree on mechanisms for normalising post-war international economic relations. They set up the International Monetary Fund and World Bank respectively to help member countries to handle short-term cash flow problems and channel investment resources more freely through the international community; we shall deal with these more fully in the next chapters. They were also planning to set up the International Trade Organisation, a major world body to create fairer trading practices. It was designed to expand international trade and to remove taxes which had been placed on foreign imports in the years between the wars, when governments had tried to combat large-scale unemployment by protectionist policies designed to shelter their own industries from foreign competition, but which resulted in a disastrous shrinkage in world trade.

The theory behind all three organisations was that freer trade would be in everyone's best interests. But the US Congress vetoed the powerful ITO and instead a much weaker body, the General Agreement on Tariffs and Trade (GATT), was later established. But even this was not to work in the interests of the world's poor. In practice GATT deals were done on the principle of 'reciprocity'. The poor nations had little to bargain with and most of the GATT concessions were restricted to trade between the rich nations. Third World products were mostly excluded from tariff cuts. The same thing happened at subsequent meetings of GATT. In the 1960s GATT cut by half the tariffs on goods traded among the rich nations but there was virtually no reduction in products from the Third World;[100] by 1967 the rate of protection of First World goods was 19.2 per cent, against 33.4 per cent for poor nations.[101] In the 1970s taxes on First World products were reduced by 33 per cent but only by 24 per cent on Third World products – at the end of the negotiations the agreed reductions were 60 per cent on raw materials, 27 per cent on processed goods and 24 per cent on finished manufactures.[102]

In some cases restrictions have actually increased. One of the areas in which the Third World has attempted to industrialise is textiles and clothing. This vitally important trade between rich and poor countries is now covered by what is known as the Multi-Fibre Agreement which severely restricts imports of clothing from poor countries. When Bangladesh tried to export more shirts to Britain, additional import restrictions were introduced to protect the British clothing industry from competition.[103] These were only removed after a public campaign organised by a British pressure group, the World Development Movement. Under GATT arrangements countries are allowed to extend privileges to one another under 'Most Favoured Nation' status. Ironically in Britain's case its list includes South Africa, the USA and Japan but no poor countries.

In addition to such quotas and tariffs there is a whole range of 'non-tariff barriers'. These include customs regulations, packaging and labelling requirements, health and safety standards and a host of other restrictions with apparently legitimate justifications but which are often little more than protectionist devices. These can effectively raise tariffs to more than 200 per cent.[104]

Unfortunately the discrimination does not end even there. To protect their farmers the major industrial nations, most particularly the United States and the European Community, give heavy subsidies to domestic agriculture in order to maintain jobs on the land and improve the stability of Western food supplies. This means that in certain agricultural commodities, which is all the Third World has to export, the poor producers face unfair competition. To keep European farmers in work 'the EC produces about a seventh of the world's sugar crop, about three million tons per year more than it needs . . . Rather than build up an embarrassing mountain, the EC exports vast quantities of sugar usually at highly subsidised prices.'[105] The story is the same in butter and cereals. In 1985 it sold seven million tons of cut-price grain to the Soviet Union just to get rid of it; this was the year of the great African famine, yet more of this form of 'food aid' went to the Soviet Union than to Sahelian Africa. The fact that the whole grotesque edifice could ever have evolved this way gives some idea of how the West orders its priorities. In 1986 taxpayers in Europe, the USA and Japan, paid out £27,000 million to subsidise their domestic food production.[106] For every £1 given as aid £3 was spent on food mountains. As a result poor countries which could grow food to export to the First World were discouraged from doing so and the dumping of food in the Third World was artificially lowering prices there and thus making it uneconomic for local farmers to produce even for domestic consumption.

* **Here then is a sixth structure of sin: protectionism – a network of deliberate restrictions which maintains and increases the gap between the rich and the poor and inhibits them for proper self-development.**

> *Woe to those who enact unjust decrees,*
> *who compose oppressive legislation*
> *to deny justice to the weak*
> *and to cheat the humblest of my people of fair judgement,*
> *to make widows their prey*
> *and to rob the orphan . . .*[107]

THE MULTINATIONALS: PARTNERS OR PROFITEERS?

The second mechanism by which the Third World is maintained in a state of neo-colonial disadvantage is through the operations of multinational companies, or transnational corporations as the United Nations now calls them. The trade in almost every group of raw materials provided by the Third World is controlled by two or three, but rarely more, gigantic international companies. The decisions taken by the executives in these firms have as much, if not more, influence on trade between the rich and poor nations than do either First or Third World governments or any of the international financial institutions. The Brandt report, based on the findings of an international commission of senior politicians chaired by the former West German Chancellor Willy Brandt, said of multinationals:

> They are now major actors in the world's economy. They control between a quarter and a third of all world production and are particularly active in processing and marketing. The total sales of their foreign affiliates in 1976 were estimated at $830,000 million, which is about the same as the then Gross National Product of all developing countries [excluding oil exporters].[108]

The economist Gunnar Myrdal has estimated that US corporations 'now control or decisively influence between 70 and 90 per cent of the raw materials resources of Latin America, and probably much more than half of its modern manufacturing industry, banking, commerce and foreign trade.'[109] Oxfam has suggested that multinationals control as much as 40 per cent of world trade and up to 90 per cent of all commodity trade.[110]

Analysis of their exact techniques is not simple. One of the largest multinationals, Cargill Inc, which is a private company, for example, has a total turnover of $32,360 million and in 1987 was reported as having registered an annual profit of $257 million the year before. Through a host of subsidiary companies it controls 23 per cent of world trade in cereals and protein crops, 15 per cent of all oilseed trade, 10 per cent of coffee, 6 per cent of jute and sisal and is the world's largest trader in cotton. It also deals in cocoa, rubber, soya, potatoes, hard timber and fish-flour. It is also the world's largest trader in fertiliser. It is a power in the land in Nigeria, Sudan, Malawi, Pakistan, Brazil, Colombia, and Argentina. It has a shipping fleet of 1.7 million tons, much of it registered in Liberia. It has subsidiaries in Panama and Switzerland and owns processing plants in the UK and USA, where it is also the country's largest miller. If the famous list of the world's top 500 companies published by Fortune magazine were to include private companies, number 11 would be Cargill Inc. 'The leverage attendant on that economic power, real or potential, is enormous.'[111] Even where multinationals are public companies like Unilever or General Foods the published accounts are so aggregated as to make detailed analysis impossible. The individual accounts of the subsidiaries responsible for particular Third World activities are not available or are impossible to unscramble.

Their general method of operation, however, is clear – as is the reason for their attraction to the Third World with its abundant resources, cheap labour, weak or non-existent trade unions, lack of environmental laws and tax concessions[112] from desperate, manipulable or corrupt government élites. The multinationals' PR men argue that their presence aids Third World development; they bring resources of technology, capital, and research, management and marketing skills which would otherwise be unavailable to developing countries. There is some truth to this. There are some multinationals which establish symbiotic relationships with developing economies and they can bring development which at the moment would come from nowhere else. But the price the Third World pays for this expertise can be a high one.

For a start, the power and size of these companies accelerates existing unhelpful trends within Third World economies. Multinationals have played a key part in the rush to clear virgin forest land and then use it with small regard for the long-term environmental consequences. Most serious however is that on a huge scale they encourage local people to plough up land previously used to grow food for local consumption and use it for growing export crops. Brazil is now the second largest exporter of agricultural commodities in the world and yet 50 per cent of its population is malnourished. Land which once grew the peasant staple, black beans, now grows soya beans which, with World Bank and government support, have increased their acreage twenty-fold in the past two decades; most of it is exported to Western Europe as animal feed while the price of the black bean on the local market has risen by 275 per cent.[113] To add a bitter irony to the injury the country, now the world's largest producer of orange juice,[114] sells 97 per cent of its crop to companies like Coca-Cola which vigorously market large quantities of far less nutritious drinks to a people often severely deficient in vitamin C. The morality of heavy marketing and the creation of new 'needs' through advertising to people who do not have the resources to satisfy basic needs is suspect. There are dozens of other examples: in Kenya where maize grew there are now flowers, which are taken in refrigerated vans and then by air to Europe;[115] in Mali food production has fallen by 10 per cent but cotton output is up eight-fold;[116] in El Salvador beef exports have increased six-fold, pushing subsistence farmers off their land to create new grazing and resulting in 72 per cent infant malnutrition;[117] the story is repeated throughout the Third World.

Nor is the land for multinationals always acquired scrupulously. Eye-witness accounts from the Philippines, under President Ferdinand Marcos, told of troops evicting inhabitants from their subsistence farms so that pineapples and bananas could be produced for export. The farmers and their families were thrown out and their farms bulldozed. Any who resisted were arrested, tortured or killed.[118] Similar stories come from elsewhere.[119] Evicting peasants also has the added advantage of creating a class of landless labourers who are then entirely dependent upon the bare subsistence wages the multinationals can then pay them. Working conditions in many parts of Latin America and Asia are 'similar to those of the super-exploitation which existed in the earlier stages of European industrialisation. The hours worked are very long, safety legislation is minimal, the use of child labour is increasing'[120] and above all the wages are a fraction of those paid in the First World. There are indications that there may be a further structural evil inbuilt in this wage system. The economist Arghiri Emmanuel in his book *Unequal Exchange* has argued persuasively that if identical goods are produced in the North and South, but wages are substantially lower in the South, then the greater profit which will be made on the sale of the second constitutes a kind of transfer of wealth from poor to rich. Estimates are that an extra $22,000 million should have been added, if this extra wage cost were included, to the Third World's $35,000 million of exports in 1966.[121]

Another area of malign multinational influence is in changing tastes in the Third World to build demand for their products. This is not difficult given multinationals' powerful marketing and advertising skills, coupled with the bombardment of the Third World with films and television programmes impregnated with Western cultural assumptions. As a result many poor urban populations aspire to white bread made with imported wheat, rather than more nutritious local staples; they prefer expensive scented soap to more effective local scrubbing soaps; they prefer whisky to local spirit or Coca-Cola to some local brand. More and more of them are persuaded to smoke by sophisticated advertising techniques, some of them banned in the West, which link cigarettes to the image of affluent Western life, ironically at a time when smoking in the West is in decline; and they smoke the poisonous high-tar cigarettes which health-conscious First World smokers have abandoned.[122] The evidence is damning in a long line of dubious promotions: adverts in India which showed a woman receiving a prescription for Horlicks drink from a doctor; in Zambia the government eventually banned adverts for the soft drink Fanta after it was discovered that

54 per cent of the seriously malnourished children in hospital in the Copper Belt had been given Fanta by their mothers who had been convinced by adverts that this was the best drink for infants.[123]

The greatest scandal in this line was the way that Nestlé and other leading manufacturers of powdered baby food mounted a massive promotion to shift mothers to their product and away from the far more nutritious natural breast-milk. It was led by powerful advertising campaigns and even employed saleswomen dressed like nurses.[124] Not only was the product less nutritious, it was expensive and consumed a major slice of the weekly budget of the Third World mothers. Worse, it could be dangerous because of the risk of contamination from unsafe water, unhygienic conditions and the real possibility that poor and illiterate mothers who could not read the printed directions might over-dilute it to make it stretch. Reports were that many babies died unnecessarily.

Often the products promoted by multinationals are inherently unsafe. Some 38 per cent of the international trade in pesticides is with the Third World and 30 per cent of those were not approved for use within the country which exported them.[125] Birth control methods which are outlawed in the First World – unsafe IUDs, high-estrogen birth control pills and the injectable Depo-Provera, are widely promoted in the Third World.

But the multinationals' chief influence is from the sheer weight of the economic power in their particular markets. These companies are so big that they substantially affect prices simply by the timing of their announcements of their decisions to invest or contract in certain areas. Reports published by them, or by brokers linked to them, can often move prices dramatically in one direction or another.[126] The views of their observers at international commodity gatherings can often be decisive. The scale of their purchases is such that they can usually by-pass commodity auction rooms and do direct deals with Third World governments for the whole of their produce in certain items. In the 1976 report *Nestlé in Developing Countries*, that transnational, which is the world's largest trader in coffee, cocoa and milk, admitted as much: 'The volume of our purchases of coffee and cocoa is so vast that it influences the market for these commodities.' According to Susan George what this means in practice is that in 1974 Nestlé paid the Ivory Coast just a quarter of the average world price for coffee and Ghana half the going rate for cocoa.[127] Multinationals can similarly influence currency exchange rates by the sheer bulk of their currency movements; by anticipating or withholding these, the rate too can be manipulated to their advantage. Some economists have dubbed this as the 'monopoly capital' phase of capitalism, because such companies have secured for themselves a virtual monopoly; they have become so large that they no longer grow through competition with other firms but in effect set the pace of their expansion themselves in order to ensure profitable growth.

Control comes not just through purchasing power. Many of the trading companies, through other subsidiaries, also provide the seeds and fertilisers to farmers and negotiate fixed price contracts usually before the crop involved is harvested and quite often before it is even planted. Many farmers, under what is known as the *colonia* system, rent their land and sell their labour, to multinationals who provide all the seeds, fertilisers and even tools and tell the farmer what to plant, when to plant it and when to harvest. All he has to do is what he is told. By thus renting, and not owning, land the multinationals avoid the possibility that their assets might be nationalised and give themselves an added flexibility to move easily and quickly when necessary. This is why 'Nestlé owns not a single cow nor an acre of coffee or cocoa producing estates' though 50 per cent of their profits derive from such products.[128] It was such flexibility which enabled Unilever, the world's biggest food and soap company, to transfer almost all its palm oil investments from West Africa to Malaysia, causing Africa's share of the world market to drop from 57 per cent to 29 per cent during the 1970s.[129] When workers in Hawaii became unionised the big companies simply switched production to the Philippines and Thailand where labour rates were between 10 and 15 cents an hour.[130]

Claims by multinationals that they bring technology and capital need to be inspected carefully.

Much of the technology is in highly expensive machinery which can actually abolish jobs for labourers, rather than creating them, and which often is too expensive or inappropriate to serve as a pilot scheme for more widespread indigenous development use. Similarly agricultural technology may be inappropriate; many of the high yield variety seeds which have brought about the Green Revolution in Asia need high levels of fertiliser, irrigation and pesticide to survive. If farmers are wealthy enough to provide these then the harvests can be highly profitable; but most peasant farmers cannot afford them and find that the new strains are less hardy than traditional varieties and more vulnerable to weather changes. In addition, of course, a portion of the harvest cannot be kept back for replanting; the scientists employed by the agribusiness firms have engineered the hybrid seeds so that they are infertile, forcing farmers to buy another batch of seed from the multinational the following year.

Much of the capital which multinationals claim to provide is in fact not brought by them from the First World but is raised in the country of operation. It is not difficult to coax investment cash from the local rich who scent a better and safer investment in the hands of the foreigners than they do in indigenous local industries. Studies have shown that as much as 80 per cent of investment capital for multinationals is actually raised in the Third World. In one such study some 52 per cent of its profits were, on average, 'repatriated' to the First World, which was, in effect, yet another mechanism for transferring capital from the poor countries to the rich.[131]

Perhaps the most insidious characteristic of the multinational is its lack of accountability to anyone but its shareholders – to whom its only responsibility is to make as big a profit as possible. This means that many of its deals are never made public, which offers the opportunity for a host of legal and illegal transfers of cash. Some of these are blatantly immoral. Investigations by the US authorities have revealed that up until 1977 alone no fewer than 360 US companies had admitted to making 'questionable payments' in foreign countries. The 95 largest had paid out around $1 million each in bribes over a few years.[132]

Other tricks are more sophisticated but just as questionable. One device which has commonly been used is the system known as *transfer pricing*. Under this a multinational can adjust the price of goods it transfers between its subsidiaries in different countries in order to pay as little tax as possible in each place. More than half of all exports from US firms are exports from multinational parent companies to overseas subsidiaries[133] and some 30 per cent of all world trade consists of 'intra-firm trade' within multinationals.[134] So there is plenty of scope to value goods differently in different places and thus shift profits around the world without paying much tax. There are three well known ways of doing this. A firm can use tax havens like the Bahamas, Barbados, Bermuda, the Cayman Islands, the Netherlands Antilles or Panama. Goods are shipped, on paper at least, from Britain or the United States to a tax haven and then 're-exported' to their destination in the Third World at a much higher price; all the profits are thus made in an area where there is no taxation.[135] Or funds can be lent by a parent to an overseas subsidiary at an artificially high rate of interest.[136] Or a subsidiary could make generous payments to the parent for the privilege of using a well known brand-name.[137] There are other techniques too, and transfer pricing is not confined only to the Third World. It helps to explain why Nestlé's $650 million US operations (where taxes are about 40 per cent) makes a loss, as does its enormous UK subsidiary. However the Swiss subsidiary (where Nestlé on average pays a mere 5 per cent of its profits in taxes) declares over £300 million in profits.[138]

It is difficult to estimate the amount of money lost to the Third World through transfer pricing, though multinational executives have admitted that their profits from the Third

World are many times higher than from trade among industrial nations, a fact which they excuse by saying that the risk is much higher. The economist Constantine Vaitsos analysed the financial transfers of fifteen drug multinationals operating in Colombia. The average rate of money returned to their parent company was 79.1 per cent; their average declared profits in Colombia was 6.7 per cent. He then found similar disparities in the rubber industry: the real profit was 43 per cent, but only 16 per cent was declared. 'If these figures are representative then the true level of repatriated income of multinationals in the early 1970s may have ranged from $20,000 million to $90,000 million,' wrote Paul Harrison in *Inside the Third World*. Since then it is claimed that levels of repatriation have diminished. But it still remains true, as Harrison suggests, that 'the real income is almost certainly much higher than the official figures suggest. The huge global conglomerates are amoral beings. Their ethics are the minimum required for political survival.'

* **Here then, within the operating system of the multinationals, is a seventh structure of sin: not the operation of a First World company in a Third World economy, but a method of operation which is not rooted in mutual benefit and true partnership.** Instead it is rooted in an unequal power which seeks the highest possible profits based on the exploitation of the cheap labour and undefended fields in the Third World:

> *Woe to those who join house to house,*
>   *who add field to field,*
> *until there is no more room.*[139]

> *Seizing the fields that they covet,*
> *they take over houses as well,*
> *owner and house they seize alike,*
> *a man as well as his inheritance.*[140]

This system buys the work of the poor for a pittance and sells it for a profit far higher than is considered 'normal' in trade between rich nations:

Listen to this, you who crush the needy
and reduce the oppressed to nothing,
you who say: 'When will the New Moon be over
so that we can sell our corn,
and Sabbath, so that we can market our wheat?
Then, we can make the bushel-measure smaller
and the shekel-weight bigger
by fraudulently tampering with the scales.
We can buy up the weak for silver
and the poor for a pair of sandals
and even get a price for the sweepings of the wheat.'[141]

Occasionally the rich nations get embarrassed by the inconsistency of their stance, which pursues protectionism for themselves while imposing free trade upon the poor. The rhetoric in favour of changes is fine-sounding and widespread. Unfortunately our governments never actually do much about the problem.

CRUMBS FROM THE TABLE OF THE RICH

As long ago as 1964 the United Nations set up in Geneva what has become a permanent Conference on Trade and Development (UNCTAD) designed to work for the narrowing of the development gap and the promotion of growth in the Third World. Since then it has met in New Delhi (1968), Santiago (1972), Nairobi (1976), Manila (1979), Belgrade (1983) and Geneva (1987). Rich nations have been happy to say the right things but not to do them. UNCTAD approved a scheme called the General System of Preferences (GSP) designed to cut tariffs in a way which did not demand 'reciprocation' from the Third World, but when it was finally drawn up many sensitive items such as textiles were excluded and the agreement did not cover non-tariff barriers. It agreed in 1976 to set up a Common Fund to help stabilise commodity prices but it took twelve years before even a limited agreement came into operation. It discussed suggestions from developing countries for a New International Economic Order which would have combined fewer First World tariffs, more stable commodity prices, the greater transfer of technology to the South, more aid, and the creation of more short-term trading credits. But when the West created a system of annual IMF credits worth $3,000 million called Special Drawing Rights it then promptly distributed three-quarters of them among the rich nations. 'Clearly the North never had the slightest intention of making concessions, but it expertly keeps the carrot dangling in front of Southern noses for over a decade,' Susan George has written.[142] In 1987 civil servants at the beginning of the seventh UNCTAD session in Geneva could not even agree on a short-list of matters for their ministers to discuss.[143] UNCTAD, it was facetiously said, stood for Under No Circumstances Take Any Decision.

Other moves were similarly unhelpful. In 1963 the IMF agreed to create a new form of lending, the Compensatory Financing Facility, which was designed to help exporters of raw materials cope with the mad fluctuations in commodity prices; and in 1969 it created another, the Buffer Stock Financing Facility, to help countries build up reliable supplies of commodities to buffer their industries from the same market variations. But few developing nations were able to take up the loans as the terms the IMF imposed on them were onerous, though, under pressure from Third World countries, these were liberalised somewhat at the end of the 1970s. There have been other small genuflections in the direction of redressing the unfair international trading system. The European Community has developed the Lomé Convention which offers preferential import regulations to a number of African, Caribbean and Pacific countries, mainly former European colonies, but the area covered includes only 12 per cent of the Third World's total population, and in any case the existence of such regional groupings 'helps to splinter the poor primary producers into different interest groups and make it difficult for them to present a united front against rich consumer countries.'[144] One of the chief opponents to wider concessions has been the United States; its unwillingness to help has prevented action by other more sympathetic rich nations, who are reluctant to act unilaterally for fear that the real beneficiaries of their action would then be, not the poor, but their rivals, including the most powerful country in the world.

Various other Western initiatives have foundered on similar rocks. In 1980 the Brandt Commission, composed of liberal members of the First and Third World establishments, argued that improved conditions for the poor countries was the only way to build future markets for the rich nations.[145] Reforms such as those suggested in the New International Economic Order should be pursued by the North for reasons of enlightened self-interest; without a massive transfer of resources the existing world economic order would eventually be put at risk. A North–South summit was called in Cancun, in Mexico, in October 1981 to discuss these issues, but it ended in dismal failure largely as a result of the intransigence of the new US administration under Ronald Reagan.

* **Here then is an eighth structure of sin: an edifice of privilege held together by greed and by the fear which underlies self-interest.** No rich nation, however inclined it might be to make concessions to the poorer economies, can do so unilaterally without risking that it would be taken advantage of by other rich nations and lose its place in the comparative league tables.

> *Can you hear crying out against you the wages which you kept back from the labourers mowing your fields? The cries of the reapers have reached the ears of the Lord.*[146]

No national government will dare to take a lead which it fears might lose it votes at home.

> *O my people, your leaders mislead you,*
>   *and confuse the course of your paths . . .*
> *The Lord enters into judgement*
>   *with the elders and princes . . .*
> *'It is you who have devoured the vineyard,*
>   *the spoil of the poor is in your houses.*
> *What do you mean by crushing my people,*
>   *by grinding the face of the poor?'*
> *says the Lord of Hosts.*[147]

In recent years it has become apparent that there is another level at which the dice are loaded against the Third World – that of the ecological crisis. This is not the place to go into the detailed mechanics of global warming and the threat to the planet from the overload of pollution. That is the subject for another book. But it is worth noting here the disproportionate effect which global warming will have on the poorest people of the world and the disproportionate levels of culpability of rich and poor.

In brief, certain gases in the atmosphere produce a greenhouse effect which entraps heat inside the bio-sphere. Without this greenhouse effect life on earth would be impossible: the planet would be too cold. The problem today is that pollution has upset the natural balance by which the greenhouse blanket of gases traps the sun's warmth to the correct degree. The pollution is in the form of four of these greenhouse gases, carbon dioxide, methane, nitrous oxide and chlorofluorocarbons (CFCs). Some of these are produced naturally throughout the world: carbon dioxide is given off by plants, and methane is produced by the digestive processes of cattle and is given off by the anaerobic bacteria which live below the water in rice paddies. But huge additional amounts of carbon dioxide are now produced by the burning of fossil fuels in the West, mainly in power stations and in car engines. Cars are also the source of virtually all the nitrous oxides. CFCs are produced entirely by industrial processes such as the manufacture of plastic packaging and refrigerators; as well as contributing to global warming they have also been implicated in the destruction of the ozone layer which protects us from ultra-violet rays of the sun which can cause cancer. Scientists are clear that the bulk of the responsibility for all this lies in the industrial processes and high-tech lifestyle of the Western world. The most recent research shows that carbon dioxide is responsible for 80 per cent of the global warming effect.[148]

If the First World has most responsibility for the increased greenhouse effect there is little doubt that it will be the Third World which will probably suffer most from it. If the sea level rises, as scientists fear, flooding will cause most human misery in low-lying countries like Egypt and Bangladesh. Its effect on the water table in areas not actually flooded would be equally devastating; it would risk salinating one third of the area used for the cultivation of rice – the staple of Third World diets.[149] Rice is also one of the crops most susceptible to changes in temperature. Moreover any change in the climate will invariably affect most severely the poorest peoples who farm land that is already marginal and who do not have the financial resources to adapt or find alternatives.

* **Here then is a ninth structure of sin: a ruthless exploitation of the resources of the globe which fails to consider the implications of our actions for others, elsewhere in the world, or those yet to be born.**

> *Out of the ground the Lord God made to grow every tree that is pleasant to the sight and good for food, the tree of life also in the midst of the garden, and the tree of knowledge of good and evil . . . The Lord God took the man and put him in the garden of Eden to till and keep it.*[150]

What all this added up to was already by the early 1970s a fairly grim prospect for the Third World. After three decades of relatively uninterrupted world economic growth the relationship between the First and Third World had not improved. Worse than that, it was in decline; the 40 poorest nations, where the average annual income was less than $300 a head, had seen their share of world trade fall from a meagre 1.6 per cent in 1950 to only 0.5 per cent[151] today. Its peoples were stuck on a treadmill on which they had constantly to run more quickly just to stay where they were. The economic equation they had been handed on independence had proved to be inherently imbalanced. The model of development they had inherited from their colonial masters also seemed fatally flawed: they had been told to produce more exports to bring in the hard currency they needed to finance major industrial and infrastructure developments which would bring economic growth and a better standard of living for all. Yet the only advice they were getting from the World Bank was that they should do more of the same. Most aid funding was tied to producing precisely that. But the structures of international trade and finance were, as we have seen, geared against them. The situation was chronic. Then in the mid-1970s came the sequence of events which was to tip the Third World into real crisis.

Chapter Four

DEBT AND DELUSION

'The people running the major economies of the world don't know what they're doing . . . Of all the major projections we got on growth and unemployment – and we consulted a wide spectrum – not a single one turned out to be right.'
Michael Blumenthall, US Secretary to the Treasury, after his resignation

'The reader without a degree in economics probably wishes . . . that faithful discipleship in our time had less to do with such a complicated subject.'
Ronald Sider, Rich Christians in an Age of Hunger

A series of propaganda broadcasts were made to Britain during the Second World War by the German Minister for Finance who rejoiced in the name of Dr Walter Funk. The 'General Plenipotentiary for Economic Affairs' described the bright new economic order which was in prospect for a Europe under Nazi rule. Among the innovations which National Socialism would introduce was the abolition of gold as the basic standard of international finance. British propaganda chiefs chortled at this and contacted the economist John Maynard Keynes, who was then working as an unpaid adviser to the British Treasury, to ask him for material to counteract the Funk broadcasts. To their surprise Keynes replied 'about three-quarters of the German broadcasts would be quite excellent if the name of Great Britain were substituted for Germany . . .'[1] Keynes began to work on his proposals for a fresh post-war economic system, pivoted around a powerful new world bank.

Today the commonly accepted explanation for the debt crisis in which the Third World has become enmeshed, deepening still further the misery of the world's one billion poor people who live in semi-starvation, is that it was caused by the oil crisis of the 1970s. This is what is usually said: In 1973 the price of oil quadrupled because the oil producers decided at meetings of OPEC, the Organisation of Petroleum Exporting Countries, to form a cartel and increase the price. The vastly increased additional income which they earned, dubbed petro-dollars, were deposited in Western banks who then lent them at low interest to the Third World and others. The large amounts of petro-dollars swilling around the world caused a significant increase in inflation. Then the second oil price rises in 1979 pushed the world into recession because in the years that followed industry could not afford to expand fully with such high oil prices and because Western governments, most notably that of Mr Reagan and Mrs Thatcher, introduced tight monetarist policies to control the inflation. This caused a sharp rise in interest rates and the Third World debt suddenly became a problem which threatened to cause a crisis of confidence in the banks which would cause some kind of collapse of the international finance system.

The reality was somewhat different. The oil crises certainly played a part in the process, but their role was little more than to trigger a problem which was inherent in the post-war economic order. Indeed some economists would now argue that the oil crises were better understood as a symptom of that basic problem, rather than a cause. Any consideration of the structures of sin must address itself to the structural context in which the oil price rises could seemingly produce such an effect. To do that we must briefly examine how that post-war order was constructed.

The over-riding desire of the intellectual fathers of the new system was to avoid the failures of the international economy in the 1920s and 1930s. After the First World War the industrialised world had entered upon a period during which their economies adjusted against one another and in which exchange rates fluctuated chaotically. In that period the world economy had entered a phase of severe and pro-longed recession. Unemployment became rampant. Inflation rocketed. The industrialised nations had sought to mitigate its worst effects by policies designed to protect jobs in their industries from foreign competition. In effect they were trying to export unemployment. Such strict protectionism brought about an overall decline in world trade, making the slump even deeper.

Keynes' idea was to create a World Central Bank to enable the central banks of the rich countries – the US Federal Reserve, the Bank of England, the Bundesbank, the Bank of Japan and the others – to make deposits and allow over-drafts to needier nations in a controlled and orderly way. One of its great virtues would be that it would help poorer nations over the temporary crises in balancing their books which were caused by the boom-or-bust cycles which domi-nate the commodity trade. To do this it would create its own currency, which he called Bancor, which would establish a neutral pivot to the system. He wrote to the governor of Britain's central bank, the Bank of England, about his plan: 'It is the extension to the international field of the essential principle of banking by which, when one chap wants to leave his resources idle, those resources are not therefore withdrawn from circulation but are made available to another chap who is prepared to use them – and to make this possible without the former losing his . . . right to employ his own resources as soon as he chooses to do so . . . It is only by extending these same principles to the international field that we can cure the manifest evils of the international economy as it existed between the two wars.'[2]

In the US Treasury Keynes' equivalent, Harry Dexter White, was working on his own similar plans to revive the nations' economies, restore foreign trade and establish mechanisms to protect the international monetary system. He too envisaged an international currency, which he called Unitas, and a world bank – though he felt this should be under the control of governments which would allocate its funds, where Keynes had advocated a body which would have been able to expand by raising capital in the normal ways open to central banks like the Bank of England and the US Treasury. 'It was an agency for distributing money rather than, like Keynes' . . . a machinery for creating credit.'[3] White wanted two bodies, a fund to stabilise currencies and economies, and a bank to provide funds for reconstruction and development.

In July 1944 delegates from forty-four of the world's nations met at Bretton Woods in New Hampshire to agree on mechanisms for normalising post-war international economic relations. They set up the International Monetary Fund, which was to provide short-term loans to nations with balance of payment crises to prevent them from having to make constant annual adjustments to their level of imports whenever their level of exports fell temporarily. They set up the International Bank for Reconstruction and Development (IBRD), which soon became known as the World Bank, to finance and guarantee specific long-term development projects, with loans to be repaid over fifteen- to twenty-year periods. They also approved an International Trade Organisation (ITO) whose job was to organise commodity markets and reduce protectionist tariffs. It was to have done this by basing world currency not on gold but on a bundle of commodities which would have gone a long way towards creating stable commodity prices. To the developing world this was undoubtedly the most important of the three but the US Congress refused to ratify its establishment; in its place on tariffs there later came the far weaker provisions of the General Agreement on Tariffs and Trade (GATT); the issue of commodities was never to be properly tackled. This, combined with the fact that voting rights in these new international bodies were allocated in proportion to the financial strength of the member states, meant that from the outset the Third World nations and colonies were excluded from any real influence on the workings of the new system which Keynes had hoped would ensure a fairer world.

> * Here then is a more particular structure of sin: a body which has a decisive effect on the economies of every country in the world but which deliberately excludes certain countries from effective participation in its decision-making. Furthermore, by placing undue burdens on its strongest member, the United States, and placing it in a position in which it could easily manipulate the system, it exposed the American administration, as we shall see, to the temptation to place self-interest above the good of the international system.

The crucial fact, however, was that the idea for a neutral international currency was dropped. There had been fewer supporters among the politicians, central and private bankers and their international lawyers, all of whom had vested interests to defend. Gold was to remain the standard against which all currencies were to be judged and the US dollar was to remain the currency in which the world held most of its reserves and which central banks could exchange for gold on demand. Other currencies were to be pegged at a fixed exchange rate to the dollar. As the economy of Britain and the rest of Europe was in a shambles most of those countries who had held their currency reserves in sterling converted them to dollars. With American industry at that time responsible for two-thirds of total output in the capitalist world,[4] the decision to focus so heavily on the dollar seemed obvious.

But it was to prove a fatal flaw. Two things later exposed it to be so: the dramatic rise in recent times of the US trade and budget deficit and the growth of a new market-place for US dollars, outside the control of the US authorities. These two factors, as we shall see, were to allow the United States, in effect, to transmit the huge cost of this deficit to the rest of the world. For fifteen years the technique worked before the US government finally over-stretched itself and the debt crisis was born.

First let us consider the trade and budget deficit.

PRELUDE: HOW THE THIRD WORLD SUBSIDISES THE UNITED STATES

The other great lesson learned from the experience of the Great Depression which followed the First World War was that the world economy would benefit from the regrowth of the defeated nations and the depleted victors. The US government therefore decided to use its abundant reserves to this end. The Marshall Plan pumped about $13 billion into European reconstruction, partly in order to revitalise trade and restore demand, and partly to counter possible Soviet influence in the region. There were heavy aid flows too into Japan. For four years running the United States gave around 3 per cent of its gross national product to the plan, and as grants not loans – around $120 billion a year in present day prices. In doing so the US sowed the seeds of its own downfall, promoting the recovery of the very economies who were to prove its most effective competitors. Had the Marshall Plan money been given in loans the interest it would now be bringing in would be sufficient to recycle to the Third World, alleviating many of the most basic problems.

In the decades which followed the United States began to build up the equivalent of a foreign debt. The cost of development aid to Europe, of its military spending overseas and the growing foreign investments by the US-based multinational companies which increasingly saw greater profits at home than abroad, was comparatively small at first – around $1 billion a year. By the 1960s, however, the debt had become more significant; by 1960 it was $34 billion and by 1965 $70 billion.[5] The United States found its export earnings shrinking because of increasingly stiff competition from the rejuvenated economies of West Germany and Japan, which at this point were still fuelled by cheap oil – during this period it had never cost more than two cents a litre.[6] At the same time its expenditure was rising dramatically because of the war in Vietnam. By 1968 the United States, which had previously always exported more than it imported, producing a trade surplus of more than $4 billion a year, found that its trading account was almost in the red. In 1971, for the first time since the beginning of the century, the US trading account went into deficit.

The steady disappearance of the trade surplus destabilised the dollar. A series of crises hit the currency with each announcement of the latest US deficit. Some of the nations who were owed money by the USA had, for some time, been requesting that their debts should be converted into gold, as the Bretton Woods agreement allowed. The French central bank had been particularly keen on conversion[7] and had also been in the forefront of opposing any suggestion that gold should be revalued. US gold reserves, which had been worth $21.8 billion in 1960, had therefore been dwindling by around $1 billion a year.[8] In July 1971 they fell to $10 billion, their lowest level since the Great Depression. The following month, after a week of particularly violent currency fluctuations, President Richard Nixon decreed, unilaterally, that the dollar would no longer be interchangeable for gold. With the collapse of the gold standard the dollar lost about 7 per cent of its value against other leading currencies. Banks who still held their reserves in dollars thus lost 7 per cent of them against gold at $35 an ounce – they had little choice but to accept, as they showed when they agreed to an increase in the official price of gold to $38 an ounce.

No one used the word, but what the USA had done was default on a debt worth some $68 billion.[9]

Two years later President Nixon sprang another devaluation upon the rest of the world, which again found the value of its reserves diminished accordingly. This time the industrialised nations agreed to abandon the system which pegged all currencies to the dollar. Each would be allowed to float freely on the market, independent of the others.

Thus the Bretton Woods system had lost its two main pillars. Why did no one object to the unilateral devaluations? The US economist Professor Jan Kregel explains:

> By the middle to late fifties European central bankers had already started worrying that the United States gold supply was insufficient to continue supporting the gold value of the dollar. But as they had started to hold dollars as reserves they were caught in a dilemma: if they all tried to convert their dollars into gold, the value of their reserves would certainly have fallen because the United States would then have been forced to change the dollar parity. So, they were stuck. They thought it was better to keep dollars as reserves than convert them into gold, which would have almost destroyed their value. This meant the United States continued to run deficits and the central banks continued to accumulate dollars.[10]

Those who called for reform of the system, and the creation of a supra-national world currency to replace the dollar, were ignored. One such was Robert Triffin who was once simultaneously economic adviser to President John Kennedy and to the European Community. He was unable to find the powerful allies he needed in presenting his reform programme. He identified a number of vested interests pressing against reform:

> First, the United States would have lost what French President Charles de Gaulle called its exorbitant privilege to cover its balance-of-payments deficits with its own dollars. According to supporters of the dollar standard, this privilege was not only beneficial to the United States but also to the rest of the world, since in this way the United States supplies the world with the necessary international monetary reserves. So why get rid of a system which had paid off, and to which financial experts were accustomed, and replace it with a new one which had yet to prove itself?
> Second, by holding on to the dollar the United States was able to continue spending huge amounts on defence. Although this is never openly said, the Americans and most Europeans too saw the maintenance of the dollar as the reserve currency as a

way of financing their joint defence. And this is still true today, I think.

Third, West European and Japanese exporters gained by keeping the dollar as the key currency of the system. Owing to the demand for dollars the American currency remained overvalued against the European and Japanese currencies . . . If the role of the dollar had been limited [by the introduction of a new international currency] it would certainly have lost value, and the European and Japanese exporters would have faced increasing competition from American exporters.

Fourth, European central bankers were not happy with reforming the system because they feared the erosion of their power of decision. In the present system central bankers decide where to invest their countries' reserves . . . But if all this were decided through international agreements, it would obviously involve participation by the governments and central bankers would lose their absolute freedom. The central bankers have always resisted a reform of the international monetary system, and the establishment of a real European monetary system, by arguing that these measures would jeopardise the sovereignty of their countries. But in fact they are talking not of national sovereignty but rather of their own sovereignty *vis-à-vis* their governments.[11]

The central banks may not have been in favour of reform but eventually they began to lose patience with the US behaviour. According to Barclays Bank Review: 'The watershed was the intensity of the Vietnam War and the large budget deficits to which it gave rise, setting in motion an excess supply of dollars and a persistent inflationary process.'[12] In layman's language what this meant was that instead of taxing its own citizens, which would have been unpopular, the USA was passing on the cost to the rest of the international community by pushing out more and more dollars. Or as Wim Duisenberg, the head of the Dutch central bank, summed it up: 'The war in Vietnam was not in fact financed by the United States . . . but by other countries. This amazing fact is the result of the privileged financial position the United States has in the world.'[13]

Because the US dollar is the key currency of the international system, and because it is no longer linked to gold, it can virtually print and spend as much as it wishes, provided the rest of the world is willing to accept the dollar and attach a certain value to it. So long as the United States used its privilege with restraint the system functioned. Until 1965 the US government used the strategem to cover what appeared to be manageable increases in its deficit of one or two billion a year. Then came the Vietnam war. According to Professor Triffin:

President Johnson feared that if he asked for tax increases to finance the war Congress would vote against it, and he would then be forced to change his Vietnam policy. He therefore said, 'Why should I create problems for myself as long as the Bundesbank and the Bank of Japan are willing to finance the war?' Those two countries were the most important investors in dollars.

From then on, and with a clear conscience, America used its privilege to cover its balance of payments deficits, or in other words foreign debt, with its self-created dollars. Then, because of the absurd arms race between the two superpowers, the foreign debt of the United States rose from $100 billion in 1969 to more than $1,000 billion in 1984. The amount of dollars in foreign hands caused an inflationary growth of international monetary reserves, rising in this period at 13 per cent above the world's gross national product . . . A reform of the system would have prevented it. For, just like other countries with balance-of-payments deficits, the United States would have had to drastically cut its military expenditure or raise the money through stiff tax increases . . .

Ironically the richest and most capitalised country in the world is actually being financed by the poor countries through the creation of international monetary reserves. Economic logic as well as humane concerns should lead the richer and more capitalised countries to help economic development in the poorer countries. This is piously stressed again and again in United Nations resolutions. But the United States is doing exactly the opposite; it is having itself financed by poorer countries, even the poorest countries. To tell the truth, the United States is the only debtor of international reserves. The creditors – or claimants – of international reserves are: other industrialised countries for a small amount, OPEC countries for a larger amount, and other developing countries for the largest amount.[14]

As a rider Professor Triffin considered the question of culpability. Germany and Japan have continued to invest in dollars, mainly because they have too much invested now to expose the charade. 'In the end I think you can blame them more than the United States. The dollar remained the world's key currency because the central banks of West Germany and Japan have continued to buy dollars. Those who accumulate dollars, Europe and Japan, have more power to curtail the use of the dollar than those who are offering them, the United States.' Moreover as the economist and theologian Charles Elliott points out, it was countries other than the US – and in particular the French – who resisted early suggestions that gold should be revalued at a more realistic level.

Wim Duisenberg is also critical of the US government for its continued use of the same technique to finance the dramatically rising budget deficit which was produced by its doctrinaire refusal to increase taxes and its substantial increase in military spending, much of it on the Star Wars programme which is regarded even in European central banks with some scepticism: 'The United States has at once a very privileged and a very responsible position. A country which is conscious of that responsibility should not only look at the internal effects of its policy, but also look at the international repercussions. America produces tremendous shockwaves affecting the whole world – in both the industrialised and the developing countries – but continues to be strongly inwardlooking. That's why we, presidents of central banks all over the world, have been shouting "America, get your own house in order!" The situation we now find ourselves in is going to be unbearable, both for the United States and for the world.'[15]

* Here then is one of the most crucial of the modern structural sins: the system by which the United States has used its budget deficit as a kind of backdoor tax upon the rest of the world, including its poorest nations, largely to finance huge unproduc-

tive spending on defence. A deception as well as an injustice is built into this system which enables the United States to operate double standards: demanding of the powerless poor world the kind of orthodox economic probity which it is not prepared to adopt for itself.

THE EURODOLLAR: HOW MONEY BECAME ITS OWN MASTER

The second key structural factor in the development of the debt crisis had been taking place in parallel throughout the time when the US budget deficit was being built and transferred through the mechanism of international finance to the rest of the world. It was the development of the Eurodollar and the Euro-currency markets in which it could circulate without restriction.

After the Second World War the Soviet Union and China became fearful that the United States might try to confiscate the dollars they held in US banks, as the US did in fact try to do after the Korean War began.[16] As a precaution both opened accounts with European banks to hold their US currency. Dollars subsequently earned by the Soviets in international trade were also placed there. This was not a physical transaction. The dollars stayed where they were, in American banks, but instead of being held in the accounts of the Russians or the Chinese they were now held in the name of European banks. Then in Europe, in the head office of those same banks, exactly the same amounts, in dollars, were held in the names of the Chinese and the Russians. With computer technology such transfers are now the work of seconds. Once the transaction had taken place the owner-ship was perfectly disguised. Moreover the nominal dollars in the Euro-accounts were beyond the control of the US regulatory authorities and the European authorities had no interest in imposing any controls on what was still a foreign currency.

For years the existence of what later came to be called the Eurodollar was kept a remarkable secret[17] but the market for it took off in the 1960s because of legislation instituted in the USA by Presidents Kennedy and Johnson. In an attempt to bolster investment in US firms which were suffering competition from the Japanese and West Germans restrictions were introduced to prevent US citizens moving capital overseas. They had the opposite effect: those US multinationals which already had dollars abroad banked as much as $3 billion[18] of them as Eurodollars.

Towards the end of the 1960s the central banks of the major European countries, certain now that they would never be able to exchange all their dollar holdings for gold, began to off-load some of their dollars into the Eurodollar market in exchange for other currencies. To execute the transactions they used the Bank of International Settlements in Basle, which operates as the central banks' central bank. Instead they bought German marks, Swiss francs and even Japanese yen, to give their national reserves a wider base.

Motion is an essential dynamic of banking. Money which is stationary is idle and not earning interest; in a period of inflation it is actually depreciating. The banks holding these growing Euro-currency deposits therefore had to find new borrowers for the Eurodollars. They did so by offering very cheap rates of interest to customers in private Western industry, in multinational companies and in the Third World where average growth rates had not been impaired by recession to the extent of those in the First World.[19] Soon this new trade began to constitute a major component in the international financial structure. It grew from $55 billion in 1965 to $650 billion in 1975 and to more than $2,100 billion at the end of 1984[20] – a figure more than twenty times the then US budget deficit. These new markets were known as the Euro-currency markets. The bankers were delighted with them. The Citibank chief, Walter Wriston, spoke with obvious satisfaction when he said: 'National borders are no longer defensible against the invasion of knowledge, ideas or financial data . . . The Euro-currency markets are a perfect example. No one designed them, no one authorised them, no one controlled them.'[21]

The more borrowers the bankers found, the faster the money moved back to them, as Harold Lever and Christopher Huhne explained in *Debt and Danger: the World Financial Crisis*:

> In any banking system every loan creates a new deposit in the system as a whole. As fast as the borrowers spend money, the recipients bank it. The original loan can be multiplied many times as the process of lending and depositing continues. One check to the almost infinite expansion of lending and deposit-taking is the legal requirement in most countries for banks to hold a certain minimum of their deposits in liquid assets like cash or easily tradeable government bills. There are also similar rules about the ratio of lending . . . to the bank's own capital. These have the effect of dampening down each successive rise in loans and deposits.
>
> But the advantage of the Euro-market, as perceived by the banks, was the very absence of such regulation. The restrictions of national systems were lacking. The extent of credit creation was to a large degree dependent on the banks' own definitions of their capital . . . The less risk they perceived, the more the money-go-round could accelerate unchecked.[22]

And because there were no restrictions the money could move even faster, and more dangerously. In the United States, for example, if a bank took a $1 million deposit from a customer it was obliged by law to keep 3 per cent of it in an account at the Federal Reserve – where the $30,000 did not earn interest. Moreover the law required that the bank must keep a further proportion of up to 20 per cent in its own reserves, to cover any possible run on the money. In effect this means that of the $1 million the bank is able to re-lend, and earn interest on, only $770,000. But with a $1 million Eurodollar deposit the bank can re-lend every cent of it – thus making a far greater profit than it could in the US, and also taking a far higher risk.

* Here, then, is another crucial structure of sin: a system of finance has been allowed to develop which is free of moral and social constraints. But it has also been freed of all the political

controls which might otherwise have provided a mechanism to curb it. It was precisely this lack of control which was later to allow the Euro-bankers to lend with breathtaking recklessness to the Third World.

There were three other aspects of the Eurodollar markets which were significant. The first was the invention of syndicated lending under which a group of banks combined to make a single loan and spread the risk among them. This was important because it allowed for much larger loans than before and because it allowed a new recklessness to enter decision-making by the banks. They tended to take less care in assessing the risks concerned when they had the false sense of security of knowing that the rest of the herd was with them. There were fees for setting up a syndicate – usually 1 per cent of the loan's value and up to 20 per cent of the profits – so, even when big banks came to doubt the wisdom of further major commitments, they nonetheless continued to play a vital role in organising syndicates for other banks.[23]

The second innovation was that banks in the Eurodollar market changed the old system of interest. The previous system had been that loans were at a fixed rate of interest – which meant that the bank took the risk that interest rates might rise and the loan might become less profitable. Under the new system the rate of interest varied with the market rates – just as it does for domestic borrowers who have taken mortgages to buy houses. Interest was adjusted every six months on a rate which was effectively the market rate, known as the London Inter-Bank Offered Rate (LIBOR), plus a profit percentage for the lender. This meant that whatever happened to interest rates it would be the borrower who took all the risk.

The third influential development was that a key number of banks, which became known in the United States as Money-Centre Banks, began to move outside the normal banking role of lending the money which had been deposited with them. These banks, which included nine of the most prominent US banks (Bankers Trust, Bank of America, Chase Manhattan, Chemical, Citicorp, Continental Illinois, First Chicago, Manufacturers Hanover and Morgan Guaranty) and the four leading British banks (Barclays, Lloyds, the Midland and the National Westminster) began to act more like money-brokers than banks. They began to buy money, on the Eurodollar market or from other banks, and then lend it on. By the end of 1985 all the US banks and two of the British banks had actually lent more money than they had on their books.

* Do we have here a further structural sin: the treatment of money as a commodity to be bought and sold? Certainly Aristotle would have disapproved and St Thomas Aquinas would have branded it sinful. We do not want to enter here into the type of discussion which characterised Roman law and medieval theology on the subject of whether money is a fungible (something which is changed by use and cannot be returned in its exact form).[24] Some moralists have argued that there is no reason why there should not be a market for money as this does not necessarily imply that one person has lost because of another's gain. This is a thorny problem. But what is clear is that the system offers obvious temptations to abuse. There must in many such circumstances be an ethical question mark over the practice of making disproportionately large amounts of money from merely acting as a broker in this way.

THE OIL CRISIS: THE FIRST DOMINO FALLS

Thus it was that, even before the oil crisis, the structure had been established in which the Third World was being strongly encouraged to borrow heavily on the Eurodollar market which, at the time, was offering very cheap money. In some cases the banks were so anxious to re-lend the money that the rate of interest was negative – that is less than the current rate of inflation. Seduced by the banks' enthusiasm many 'less-developed countries, particularly in Latin America, failed to realise that the newly permissive financial environment was due to the accidental conjunction of favourable but transient developments in global payments flows,' said Tim Congdon, one of the City of London's leading economists, alluding to the comparatively high prices for their commodities, and very cheap Euroloans. 'They thought that instead it was a durable change in the international financial system.'[25] Countries all over the world had started borrowing money before the oil crisis, says Professor Kregel, thus explaining why two of the biggest debtors are the oil-rich countries of Mexico and Venezuela. 'It was not the oil sector which influenced what happened in the international monetary system; it was the international monetary relations that made certain policies, actions and reactions within the oil sector possible.'

Whatever the causal relationship, the Arab-Israeli War of 1973 proved the occasion for the first in a series of price rises by the OPEC cartel. In that year the price quadrupled the cost of oil to the rest of the world. The price rises earned the OPEC countries an additional $68 billion in the first year alone.[26] As they could not possibly spend it all they deposited it in the European banks, safe there from the hands of any US attempt to confiscate it. At the beginning of the 1970s the entire Eurodollar market totalled only around $100 billion[27] and so the regular influx of so much OPEC cash gave it massive new impetus. The banks had to begin to move very quickly to re-lend it, otherwise they would lose on the interest they were paying to the oil sheiks. Worse than that, banks and governments alike agreed that if the money was not recycled to pay for goods and services its withdrawal would cause a sharp contraction in demand throughout the world, triggering a rise in unemployment and a deep and protracted worldwide depression. In the circumstances the money had to be recycled somehow. But how?

At this point governments could have intervened to direct the OPEC money through official channels such as the International Monetary Fund, or even to regulate the Euromoney market. One of the few who pressed for this was Harold Lever, a financier and member of Harold Wilson's Labour

cabinet, who predicted that the system would collapse and
the bankers would lose their money. The Third World needed
money, he said, but through a more systematic distribution.
He pressed the suggestion upon Wilson and upon the US
Treasury and bankers in New York and Washington.[28] They
discussed it but decided to leave the recycling to the private
banks which were 'equipped to handle a large volume of
funds, and have the flexibility and confidentiality required
by the lenders,' said Jacques de Larosiere, then managing
director of the IMF. The consequences of this were foreseen
as early as 1975 by Otmar Emminger, president of the
OECD: 'Our latest projection suggests that, by around 1980,
there will be one group of nations with very heavy debts,
and another heavily in credit.'[29] The warning was ignored
and indeed the banks were actively encouraged by governments to continue – something which governments later
found it convenient to forget. 'The internal reports of almost
all governments and all central banks in this period congratu-
lated themselves upon the efficient operation of the international financial markets. They did everything they could
to ensure that banks lent to underdeveloped countries,'
according to Professor Kregel, who has acted as economic
adviser to the former head of the Bank of Italy.[30]

RECYCLING THE OIL CASH: THE BANKS' BIZARRE BONANZA

The US banks in particular were greedy for the chance. Since
the gold standard was abandoned and the Eurodollar had
arisen the US banks had faced increasing competition from
European and Japanese banks. As a result profits had been
eroded. Loans to the Third World offered the most lucrative
prospect because they carried a high risk premium and were
therefore more profitable than loans to the industrialised
world.[31] The money made from these loans could be used to
bolster their declining annual profits and preserve the level
of dividends they could offer to shareholders. They began to

cast their old conservatism to the winds in a wild attempt to secure more clients while the going was good.

The accelerating speed of the banks' performance quickly achieved the dimensions of farce. All that keeps it from now seeming humorous is the knowledge that, within a decade, some of the poorest people in the world would be paying for the bankers' mistakes: throughout the Third World child malnutrition rates were to soar and infant mortality rates, which had been falling most of this century, were to rise once more.

The bankers' antics have been documented from the inside in a revealing book by S. C. Gwynne called *Selling Money*.[32] S. C. Gwynne, despite his public lack of a Christian name, is not an older man. He is, or rather was, one of the young breed of international American bankers who selected his nominal persona with the care he displayed in choosing the pinstripe in his sober business suits and his button-down Brooks Brothers shirts. He was cultivating the premature *gravitas* he felt was expected of a corporate banker. In the mid-1970s Gwynne, then aged only twenty-five and with only eighteen months' experience in banking, as his book recalls with such chilling humour, travelled the world on behalf of a large mid-Western bank with $150 million in easy credits in his briefcase, peddling loans like a pecuniary drug-dealer at any Third World country which would accept them. The stuff he pushed, they found, was highly addictive: cheap money.

When the Eurodollar market exploded the banks had found that they did not have the staff to manage. They began hiring hundreds of smart young men straight from college. Gwynne was one. Educated at Princeton and Johns Hopkins University he had only a bachelor's degree in history, a master's in creative writing and two years' experience of teaching French in a private school when he was taken on to the staff of the Cleveland Trust, a medium sized regional bank with new foreign ambitions. After a month of formal training he was assigned to the Latin America department, though he spoke no Spanish or Portuguese. 'The idea of assigning a financial tyro to analyse million dollar credits in a foreign language in which he has no fluency is bizarre indeed,' he observed.

It was a bizarre world he had entered. He was made a credit analyst, technically under the supervision of an experienced analyst, but the man spoke no foreign languages and though he was expert in domestic credit had no expertise to draw on when considering the effect of matters such as currency devaluation on the balance sheet of some Latin American company. Gwynne wrote country studies, analysing the risk before the bank made loans. It was not long before he realised how unreliable was the information on which such analysis was based. The most up-to-date financial information was often two years old. Foreign companies, he later learned, would keep several sets of books, and only the most favourable would be shown to the banks. Information which he and his colleagues garnered in the countries themselves was based largely on figures from the borrower's own central bank, whose figures were often juggled for their own purposes. Information gathered about individual companies was often irrelevant; even the soundest company might eventually be forced to default on a loan taken out in dollars if, through no fault of the company, its central bank ran out of foreign exchange because of a general balance of payments crisis.

Nevertheless banks assiduously exchanged this bad information and fed it into their computers. Around the same set of faulty premises the banks wove an elaborate network of information and analyses and then all lent in the same way to the same borrowers. Moreover, because much of the lending was done on the uncontrolled Eurodollar market, there was no central clearing house for information. Some information came from the Bank of International Settlements in Basle but it was always at least four-to-seven months late. There was no way for a bank to know when it lent how much the borrower already owed elsewhere.

Gwynne's experience of the Eurodollar market underscored this. About a year after he arrived his boss, Charles

Hammel, announced that Gwynne was to get some 'offshore' experience in the Nassau branch. Visions of palm trees and warm trade winds were quickly dispelled:

> Hammel led me back to an unoccupied desk wedged tightly against a standing partition. There were a few loose papers atop the desk and a set of rubber stamps and ink pads on one corner.
> 'This,' he said, pointing, 'is our Nassau Branch.'
> 'I thought you were talking about the real Nassau,' I said. 'The Bahamas.'
> 'I am,' Hammel said. 'From the point of view of the tax and regulatory authorities, this is the real Nassau. You should think of it that way. Everything you do here is "offshore", as though you were sitting on an island in the Atlantic. The money you move in and out of here stays offshore, forever, if we want it to. The fact that you aren't on an island isn't important. The whole thing is an abstraction, a legal and fiscal invention. That's all that matters. If the Fed and the IRS think this desk is sitting on an island in some Caribbean tax haven it is. They understand it. It's like pretending when you're a kid that your garage is a pirate ship. As long as everyone agrees to pretend it is a pirate ship, the system works. Have fun. Send me a postcard.'

The real Nassau branch was nothing more than a brass plate outside a lawyer's office on the island and an agreement with a local lawyer who held several nominal meetings every year on the bank's behalf. He conducted no business but kept a nominal set of books, compiled and audited in Cleveland. The same lawyer performed the same function for hundreds of other US banks and corporations. Gwynne's job was simply to make sure that all the Nassau documents bore the logo of the offshore branch. Gwynne, who eventually left the business in horror at the dementia, gives an example in his book of a typical chain of Eurodollar transactions. Suppose, he says, the treasurer of a big US company received a $5 million payment which he would not need to spend for thirty days. Rather than leave it sitting idle in a bank account he would want a high-yield short-term investment. He would call Cleveland Trust to speak to Gwynne's Eurodollar dealing boss, John Hansen.

Hansen then calls around to various large American banks, shopping for a rate. The best he can get is 12 per cent from Bank of America's Grand Cayman office, so he knocks an eighth of a point off that for CT's spread [the bankers' term for profit], calls the treasurer back and offers him 11⅞ per cent for 30 days at Cleveland Trust's Nassau Branch. The treasurer takes it and immediately transfers his $5 million to the account of the Nassau branch, thereby creating a Eurodollar deposit. Meanwhile, Hansen has already made his deal with the Bank of America, and so he simultaneously transfers the money from his Nassau account to the account of the bank's Grand Cayman branch. The entire transaction is accomplished in a few minutes . . .

But the money does not stop there. A chain reaction has been set off which could send that $5 million around the world several times in a single day. 'The possibilities are endless, and the sheer velocity of Eurodeposits frightening.' He continues his hypothetical example:

The Bank of America Grand Cayman places it instantly with Deutsche Bank's London branch, where because of its prime name it can command a better rate than Cleveland Trust, and thus earn a spread off the original deposit. Deutsche Bank London then re-lends it to Deutsche Bank's main office, which lends it to Volkswagen to pay for aluminium from Alcoa in Pittsburgh. Volkswagen transfers the proceeds of the loan to Alcoa's account at Mellon Bank. Thus the Eurodollars are 'repatriated' to the same bank they started from, in as little an hour. Because the funds have returned to onshore accounts there is no surviving Eurodollar. But – here is the magic – Cleveland Trust's Nassau Branch, Bank of America Grand Cayman, Deutsche Bank's London and main office branches all have $5 million Eurodollar assets on their books. So in aggregate $15 million additional Eurodollars have been created by the speed and electronic efficiency of the worldwide interbank lending network, on which the sun never sets.

This, the recusant Gwynne adds, was the most basic of Cleveland Trust's transactions in the Eurodollar market.

What accelerated bank lending even further was that industry at home was in recession and therefore not interested in borrowing cash for investment. Foreign loans were the only expanding area of business. Banks began to run regular ads in financial journals like *Euromoney* and the *Institutional Investor* in which they proudly displayed their latest list of prestige loans. Moreover there was so much money and so few borrowers that the banks began to compete savagely for business. It was a borrower's market and to get their piece of the action the banks started to offer cut-price interest rates. In an increasingly frenetic atmosphere loans were made which were increasingly dubious. 'If we don't make them some other bank will,' was a common cry. Elementary precautions which any domestic bank manager would take before lending a customer the money to buy a car were thrown out of the window. Countries once regarded as risky were able to acquire loans at rates previously reserved for the major industrial nations. Suggestions that the practice was not sound were brushed aside, or countered with half-hearted attempts to ensure that Third World governments issued guarantees to cover loans to their public and private sector firms. 'Countries never go bust,' was the oft-repeated dictum of Walter Wriston, who boldly led Citicorp into the position of top lender to the Third World.

The bank representatives continued their fevered search for more borrowers. One Latin American financier told Anthony Sampson: 'I remember how the bankers tried to corner me at conferences, to offer me loans. They wouldn't leave me alone.'[33] Even in April 1981 at the Palace Hotel in Madrid, during the annual meeting of the Inter-American Development Bank, one observer 'saw bankers queuing up to offer their banks' services to Angel Gurria, the man in charge of Mexico's borrowing, who was reclining in an armchair.'[34] Within six months Mexico was to announce its intention to default on all repayments and the debt crisis would spring apparently full-grown from the womb.

But, as Lever and Huhne so succinctly put it, it takes two sides to sign a loan agreement.[35] What, then, did the Third World spend all this money on?

WHAT THE MONEY WAS SPENT ON: BUYING DEARER OIL

Later the bankers and politicians were to maintain that if the money had gone into productive investments the profits these generated would have been sufficient to cope with the interest payments. But to assume that is to make the mistaken supposition that the Third World's loans were spent on development. The real destination of the funds is difficult to determine because, unlike loans from governments or the World Bank, there were no negotiations over the nature of the projects on which it should be spent; it was simply handed over. But almost certainly it has been spent on (and in this order): interest payments, the purchase of oil, lining the pockets and Western bank accounts of the local rich, the purchase of weapons, building prestige projects of dubious value, and only finally – economic development to alleviate poverty.

We shall deal with interest payments shortly. Here it is sufficient to note that one US economist estimated that the increased cost to the Third World of the hike in interest rates was $20 billion a year in 1980 and 1981.[36] Between 1978 and 1983 Latin America's total interest payments increased by 360 per cent. By 1984 every 1 per cent rise in interest rates was in effect adding $700 million to the annual payments of Brazil alone. By 1990 Latin America's debts were four times as large as its total annual earnings from exports which meant that every 1 per cent rise in interest rates necessitated a 4 per cent increase in exports if the continent was to pay.[37] But interest rates did not become a factor immediately.

In the early years the bulk of the money seems to have gone on buying oil at its new increased price. The price rise hit the developing nations even harder than it hit the industrialised world, because a greater percentage of their income was spent buying the crude oil they needed to transport their cash crops and to keep their capital cities functioning. At the same time their income dropped because the oil price rise caused cutbacks in worldwide industrial activity and a fall in demand for those Third World commodities needed by Western manufacturing industry. To have attempted immediately to adjust their economies to this new reality would have put a severe brake on development and, with money so cheap, borrowing seemed the obvious alternative. According to calculations by Professor William Cline the extra cost of this oil was $260 billion[38] out of the overall increased debt of $482 billion between the years 1974 and 1982. It is only since then that interest payments have taken over as the major component.

WHAT THE MONEY WAS SPENT ON: STASHES IN SWISS BANKS

But there was other spending. A good proportion of the money lent to the Third World and in particular to Latin American countries has mysteriously found its way back to the US banks, but in the personal accounts of influential Latin Americans. The *Financial Times* estimates that between $150 and $200 billion disappeared in this way between 1974 and 1985.[39] Capital flight is the term economists use, and some believe it to have been the single most destructive factor in that period. The phrase describes the process whereby a wealthy individual in a country converts his local currency into dollars – either on the black market, or through the Eurodollar system, or through false pricing of imports and exports – and then exports the hard currency to a haven usually in the United States. He then holds it abroad in the form of cash, investments, or a penthouse in Miami. In 1985 it was estimated that wealthy private citizens of Latin American and Caribbean countries had $200.3 billion worth of assets in the United States.[40] Some of the worst culprits are Third World leaders. Here we are not talking about structural evil but sin of a more conventional variety. Ferdinand and Imelda Marcos are said to have been personally responsible for between $6–$10 billion of the Philippines' $26 billion national debt;[41] President Somoza of Nicaragua, who was deposed in 1979, was another. Money from loans, corruptly acquired, left in the same way.[42] The Bank of International Settlements estimates that at least $55 billion left just the Latin American countries in this form between 1977 and 1983.[43] It says this is a conservative appraisal. Another estimate is that the equivalent of a third of the total increase in debt of Argentina, Brazil, Mexico, Venezuela and Chile was siphoned into overseas bank accounts between 1974 and 1978.[44] The president of the Inter-American Development Bank, who is a Mexican, has judged capital flight from Mexico between 1979 and 1983 at $90 billion – an amount greater than the entire Mexican debt at that time.[45]

Certainly the large US banks are aware of the return of the money they had just lent out. One, Morgan Guaranty, gauged in 1986 that some 70 per cent of all its loans from 1983 to 1985 returned to the US.[46] The representative of another New York bank has privately admitted: 'There is no debate in [my] bank over the dual role of lending money to a country and accommodating capital flight. It is done by different departments. There is no moral issue. If we don't do it, the Swiss will.'[47] Often the practice was unwittingly encouraged by governments who, because of the presence of the loan money, cherished the view that their currencies were stronger than was the case and therefore over-valued them against the dollar.[48] The effect was to reduce exports, increase imports, widen the balance-of-payments gap, defer investment in export and import-substitution industries and make the country ever more dependent on external funds. It also made overseas assets relatively cheaper and therefore encouraged more capital flight. The World Bank, citing information provided by the world's central bankers, suggests that between 1979 and 1982, $19.2 billion left Argentina, $26.5 billion left Mexico and $22 billion left Venezuela: 65 per cent, 47 per cent and a staggering 137 per cent respectively of the gross capital inflows to those countries.[49]

WHAT THE MONEY WAS SPENT ON: SOARING ARMS SALES

The figures of what is spent by the Third World on arms are almost as closely guarded as the true figures on capital flight. But according to the most authoritative independent source on world arms, the Stockholm International Peace Research Institute (SIPRI), about 20 per cent of the newly acquired Third World debt was spent on the purchase of weapons[50] – a figure which does not include the provision and training of the armies to use them. The money is still being spent. In 1988, the last year for which complete figures are available, the Third World spent $145 billion on its military. It spent $178 billion on debt repayments. Together arms and debt accounted for half of the Third World's total annual expenditures.[51]

The question of how nations order their priorities with regard to spending on arms or on economic development or on health and education has obvious moral dimensions, especially when the world spends twenty times as much in military expenditure as it does on official development aid. If developing nations devoted their annual arms budget instead to the provision of basic food, water, schooling and health care, Unicef estimates in its 1990 *State of the World's Children* report, absolute poverty on the planet could be ended in ten years.

The issue of priorities is one on which Christians have exercised considerable debate. In Britain the Catholic Fund for Overseas Development (Cafod) launched a campaign in 1989 with posters which pointed out that the £14 million spent on one fighter aircraft would also provide 700 bore wells, three million sets of agricultural tools, 4,000 village pharmacies, 90 million oral rehydration packs or 1,500 classrooms.[52] Jack Nelson-Pallmeyer has calculated that the cast of one nuclear submarine is more than all the education budgets of twenty-three developing countries put together.[53] Elsewhere it has been pointed out that the cost of the twenty-year battle to eradicate smallpox was what the world spends on arms in an hour; that the cost of a single Hawk aircraft (of which Britain sold about 100 to developing countries in recent years) would provide clean water for one and a half million people; that one tenth of 1 per cent shaved from the world's arms budget would pay for the immunisation of every child in the world against the six main killer diseases.[54] On the other hand other Christians, like Henry Kuss, a church-going Lutheran who was the Pentagon's chief arms salesman during most of the 1960s, saw the priority as creating a 'decent, free world'.[55] But Christians of either camp would have to concur that in a world of mass starvation money spent on massive armouries must be occasioned by a structural evil. Locating it, however, is the task of another book.

Similar debate can be made within the priorities of individual nations. Famine-ridden Ethiopia, for example, has the largest army in black Africa which costs every Ethiopian $44 a head each year (compared with $13 on health) out of a total annual earnings of $110 per head.[56] One of the poorest countries in South America, Peru, was spending between $300–$400 million a year at the beginning of the decade, not including a deal, financed commercially, to buy twenty-six Mirage 2000 aircraft, with equipment, for $700 million; its export earnings were already limited by barter agreements it was committed to with the Soviet Union to pay for earlier arms deals. The Brandt report observed: 'The governments of developing countries like any others want weapons to strengthen their national security; but they must share the responsibility for restraint. Some of them have increased their military expenditure at a rate which bears little relationship to their security needs, at the expense of peaceful development'. Spending on arms increased faster in Latin America, Africa and East Asia than did government spending on anything else, including health and education.[57] In addition to the debts incurred by arms deals, studies have shown that defence spending also reduces economic growth by draining resources and skills which could be used more productively in other sectors.[58] This is not the place to continue the debate on priorities by asking whether the world's

1,000 million hungry people are more in danger from death by malnutrition and disease, or death by the invading army of some neighbour or superpower. But what does concern us in our attempt to discern hidden structures of sin is the extent to which the arms industry forces a choice of priorities upon Third World nations.

Few people would accept that it is a pure coincidence that the years following 1973, which saw a vast increase in borrowing by the Third World, also saw a doubling of arms imports into developing countries[59] which already bought 70 per cent of all the arms exported by the West.[60] But, in fact, the expansion was not simply because there was now more money in the hands of Third World governments, who increasingly were military governments (twenty-two were army dictatorships in 1960 and fifty-eight in 1985[61]). Arms were now being aggressively pushed there by the arms industry and Western governments. With the ending of the Vietnam War the arms industry had gone into recession. It began desperately to seek new markets elsewhere and saw them in the Middle East, Africa and Latin America. 'The drive to sell weapons to the Third World was intensified, often aimed at stimulating new demand irrespective of real defence needs,' the Brandt report noted.[62]

The salesmen found their most willing customers in the military regimes, where the latest and largest weapons systems had prestige value and the increasingly sophisticated 'repressive technology' – electric stun batons, water cannons, and crowd monitoring and torture equipment – could be put to daily use. By a cruel irony the worse their economic situation became, and the more local people protested on the streets, the more they were able to justify buying this equipment. The arms merchants, who tastelessly describe their ventures into such new markets as 'missionary activity', were unapologetic about such use: 'the word repression is, of course, a pretty subjective word. One man's repression is another man's defence of democracy. Is it really up to us to make these judgements?' asked Colin Chandler, the head of Britain's Defence Export Services Organisation in 1986[63] whose expertise helped the UK to the position of the world's third largest provider of arms that year and to that of second, overtaking the Soviet Union, in 1987.[64] The United States, of course, is top. The salesmen opened a market not just for sales, but for constant replenishment to combat the obsolescence built in to much military technology. The secrecy which, on grounds of security, surrounds orders for arms, provided ideal cover for the bribery endemic in many Third World élites. Arms bribes were reckoned in terms of millions of dollars.[65]

The behaviour of the major military powers deserves scrutiny too. Some, like the United States and Britain, have established official sales offices for their weaponry. Up until the 1970s the major powers sold arms 'mainly to suit their foreign policy or to maintain regional balances, rather than to benefit their economies'.[66] Such a strategy led the USA in the 1960s to a policy of providing arms to both Pakistan and India. War broke out in 1965. Later J. K. Galbraith, the former US Ambassador to India, observed: 'The arms we supplied under this policy caused the war' they were designed to avoid.[67] Both superpowers also gave large quantities of weaponry away. According to SIPRI the Soviet Union handed out $490 million in arms in 1972, a figure which rose to a peak of $2.5 billion in 1979 and which in 1982 was still at $1.7 billion. The United States gave away $3.4 billion in arms in 1973, the peak year of this policy. After that the policy switched to selling arms; in 1976 only $190 million was given away and only $70 million in 1980. 'When the customer is hooked, and his generals can make sure their demands are satisfied, the switch is made to cash sales,' commented Susan George.[68] In 1973 President Nixon reversed the traditional policy under which the Pentagon had tried to keep Latin America under-armed, so that the US firm Northrop could sell $120 million in Tiger fighter planes to Brazil. Sales were also made to Argentina, Chile, Colombia and Peru. Within a decade sales had multiplied fivefold.[69] One of the prime reasons why governments were anxious to allow the explosion of sales was that it helped keep prices low for their own purchases. 'The selling of the Hercules [aircraft] abroad was of special interest to the Pentagon who (as they admitted) wished to keep open the production line in Georgia, in case they should wish to order more Hercules for themselves'[70] and to keep an important part of the economy in that state in business. By selling 150 Mirage III jet fighters to overseas customers the manufacturers Dassault managed, through the extra economies of scale, to knock 25 per cent off the price to the French government who had ordered the original 200 planes.[71]

But the most significant contribution of the arms industry to Third World indebtedness is more indirect. During his first five years in office President Ronald Reagan expanded military spending by an enormous 55 per cent in real terms with almost $2 trillion ($2,000,000,000,000) pumped into the escalation,[72] mortgaging much of the future arms budget to expanding weapons programmes. He initiated programmes for the MX missile, the space weaponry of the Strategic Defence Initiative and the Stealth bomber, a plane that is literally worth its weight in gold.[73] Setting aside arguments that all military expenditure at such a level is, in a context of global poverty, questionable from a Christian standpoint, it has now emerged that much of the budgetary expansion in arms in the early Reagan years was wasted. Tony Battista, who worked for fourteen years for the US House of Representatives Armed Services Committee, said in 1989:

What happened was too many programmes got started. We went from about 600 major programme research elements in research and development in 1976 to over 810 in 1986 – and keep in mind that for every dollar you spend on research and development today, you generate a mortgage of $5 to $10. When you look at a carrier battle group and you establish that it's $65 billion per copy, per battle group, you quickly realise what we are doing in terms of mortgaging the future for defence.

There was a lot of duplication of effort . . . We had seven different radio programmes, all to do the same thing; we had four dozen discrete electronic combat systems, all to go after the same threats; we had over 40 different imaging infra-red projects;

we had 18 [separate] millimetre-wave guidance programmes; so you see we weren't getting good return on investment, we were just wasting a lot of money. And once they get into the budget, it is as hard as hell to get it out because now that it's in the budget there are contractors involved . . . Once a programme gets sorted it becomes a freight train – you jump out on the track there, and put your hand up, and you've got wheelmarks going over you because it's an economic problem now: there are jobs involved.[74]

President Reagan's refusal to increase taxes to pay for this was the major factor in the growth of the colossal budget deficit. It was to finance this that interest rates were forced up and huge quantities of foreign capital were sucked into the US markets from all over the world. To compete for capital the Europeans too raised their interest rates. Up, with them, went the interest on the Third World debt and the amounts which suddenly had to be repaid.

* Here, then, is another structure of sin: the relationship between arms-spending and starvation. This has several elements. First, money spent on arms could be better spent elsewhere. Second, the economics of the arms industry encourages it to go out and peddle its technology in an aggressive manner. Third, there is a causal relationship between the massive US arms spending, via the budget deficit it creates and its effect on the world economy, and debt and hunger in the Third World. All this must be accounted sinful.

WHAT THE MONEY WAS SPENT ON: PRESTIGE DEVELOPMENT PROJECTS

There were two other elements in the Third World's spending on debt: the building of prestige projects and genuine economic development. A good deal of the money was spent on the former. Zaire today has a world trade centre and an underground car park in its capital and an elaborate airport beside the head of state's native village.[75] Santiago is scattered with half-completed office blocks, abandoned when

Chile's borrowing boom came to an abrupt end.[76] Gabon has 'a triumphal highway linking the airport with the presidential palace, a hotel sector with occupancy rates resembling those of a seaside resort in mid-winter, a fleet of commercial jet aircraft, enlarged government buildings, and one of the world's least economic railways', built against the World Bank's planning advice.[77] Once again, however, we are not talking here so much of structural sin as of the sin of personal hubris.

Sadly, even investment which purported to be in line with the correct 'industrialisation and modernisation' development paradigms of the day was all too often badly planned and inefficiently executed. José Carrilo Penna, the Brazilian Minister of Industry and Commerce, admitted in 1984, 'We have $50 billion worth of incomplete projects with zero degree of usefulness.' Colombia's Chinguza hydro-scheme, which was completed three times over budget at $900 million, was shut down after four months' operation with major engineering problems.[78] The Philippines' nuclear power station at Morong has never operated because before it was opened it was discovered to have been built in an earthquake zone.[79]

The sad conclusion is that only a minority of the loans which made up the massive accrual of Third World debt were spent on anything of lasting value. The borrowed money was in no position to generate profits from investment to cope with the crunch when it came.

THE RISE OF MONETARISM: INTEREST RATES SPIRAL

The turning point came in 1979. Usually this is described as the result of the second oil price rise which came when the Shah of Iran was toppled and the Islamic fundamentalism of the Ayatollah Khomeini gained sway. Once more oil doubled in price. Demand in the industrial world fell again. The recession deepened. Interest rates soared. But again the causes were more complex.

Throughout the 1970s money continued to flow out of the United States, partly because of the Vietnam War and partly because US businesses, attracted by higher profits abroad, began increasingly to invest outside the country. Inflation was rising in the United States, as elsewhere, entering double figures. In 1979 it reached 13.3 per cent which was, apart from fluctuations during the two world wars, the worst in American history. Unemployment was also running at a high level – seven million. A rapid growth in the availability of credit in the private sector seemed to be fuelling inflation, in the opinion of Paul Volcker, who had that year been appointed as Chairman of the US Federal Reserve, which operates with a considerable degree of autonomy from the US government. Volcker decided that an end to inflation must be his first priority and on 6 October 1979 he threw the monetary policy of the world's richest nation into reverse – he set up a framework to prevent the monetary base from growing more than 8 per cent, increased reserves and raised the interest rate by 1 per cent.

That date was a watershed: 'It divides the low-real-interest rate, rising inflation 1970s from the high-real-interest-rate, falling inflation 1980s,' according to Tim Congdon, formerly chief UK economist with Shearson Lehman Brothers.[80]

Within six months the interest rate had risen, in leaps, to 19.5 per cent. It fluctuated throughout 1980, dropping during the summer to create a more favourable climate for the Presidential elections, but ended in December at 21.5 per cent. Volcker's task was made more complicated by the election of Ronald Reagan whose economic advisers were 'supply-side' monetarists dedicated to what George Bush at the time called the 'voodoo economics' which decreed that if tax rates were cut then overall tax revenue would rise because the economy would be stimulated by the new incentive of low taxes. In addition to his huge expansion of the military budget, Reagan took $23 billion away from the poorest families and cut tax rates to increase the income of the richest by $35 billion. All this expansion complicated Volcker's task considerably but he persisted with his policy of high interest rates. Interest rates are not so drastic an imposition on most US citizens because many forms of interest can be charged against income tax. It was not so for the deeply indebted Third World. The effect, and perhaps the intention, was to restore the hegemony of the dollar, which had been eroded by dollar crises for more than a decade. 'The only way out of the US crisis envisaged by those in power was precisely the one that hurt other countries most deeply, affecting the indebted countries of Latin America like an earthquake,' wrote two Brazilian-based financial writers.[81]

> * Here we may have detected a further structural sin: the US decision to adopt the monetarist strategy policy seems to have been taken more for selfish reasons concerned with revitalising the dollar rather than in the best interests of the global economy which required an adjustment of an entirely different direction. If this was deliberately so then it was morally dubious.

The Eurobankers, however, did not at first realise the full implication of what Volcker was doing. They launched upon a recycling of the proceeds of the second oil shock, much as they had done with the first. They did not realise that Volcker's policy would turn the large but manageable debt burden of 1980 into the unmanageable crisis of 1982. To some extent their attitude was understandable. Previous episodes of monetary restraint had been short-lived. The Federal Reserve might be expected to crumble in its resolve in the face of hostile political forces at home. This time it did not happen.

There was some realisation in the twelve months that followed that things were not quite so easy as before. Moreover, this time two factors were different.

The first was that the scale of lending in the past few years was such that by the end of the 1970s the balance of Third World debt had shifted significantly. It no longer owed much of its debt to official institutions and governments, which could postpone capital and even interest payments as political circumstances required, but to private banks which cannot accept postponement without it being seen by the world of finance as a challenge to their credibility. The proportion owed to commercial banks at the outset in 1973 was only 11.6 per cent; by 1983 it was 43 per cent.[82] In the case of the richer debtors in Latin America the percentage rose from 23.8 per cent to 62 per cent.[83] Some estimates put it as high as 80 per cent.[84] When the day of reckoning came it would come more swiftly.

The second factor was that the terms of the Euroloans had created another structural problem. Normal lending on development offered by the World Bank is long-term. Its commercial credits, known as IBRD loans after the bank's official name, are for fifteen to twenty years for most developing nations; its more favourable loans to the poorest nations, which are extended through its soft loan arm the International Development Association (IDA), are for fifty years at less than 1 per cent interest. By contrast Eurodollar loans were all due for repayment within eight years. No one involved, neither borrowers nor lenders, assumed that these debts could be repaid in that time. The presumption was that after eight years the loans would be rescheduled – that is, new loans would be taken out to repay the old ones. But, as the Commonwealth Secretariat has pointed out, no system was ever devised to regulate these reschedulings.[85]

The debt trap began to close. Frederick Clairmonte of UNCTAD and John Cavanagh of the US Institute for Policy Studies gave a succinct account of the process which was to send the Third World deeper into debt and the foreign profits of the seven biggest US banks rocketing from 22 per cent in 1970 to 60 per cent in 1982:

Assume this country borrows $1,000 for a ten year period; the loans are to be repaid over 20 years; and the rate of interest charged is 10 per cent.

In the first year the country borrows $1,000 and pays $150 in interest and amortisation, thus leaving the country with $850 to make use of. In subsequent years its debt servicing will increase progressively . . . In Year 2, debt servicing would be $295 (thus leaving $705). In year 5 debt servicing rises to $700 (leaving only $300 to use). By the end of the eighth year debt servicing ($1,060) outstrips new borrowing by $60. At this point the debtors must find new financing merely to meet payments on the old debt.

From then onwards, there would be an increasing net outflow of capital from the country. In the tenth year debt servicing would be $1,275 and there is a net outflow of $275.[86]

Three factors make the debt trap even worse. First, interest rates were not constant, as in the example above, but in reality quadrupled. Second, the model above assumes that new lending will continue to maintain the cycle of cash; but in reality the banks slashed their lending, as we shall see. Thirdly, it assumes that repayments are made on time and in full; when they are not, as happened in the international debt crisis, the shortfall was constantly added to the debt, with new interest. The total net transfer of cash from the Third World to the rich countries rose from $7 billion in 1981 to $56 billion (1983) to $74 billion (1985).[87] A further $39 billion was added in 1988.[88]

'The most powerful criticism of the banks is that they did not react to the events of 1979 by restricting credit immediately,' wrote Tim Congdon. 'On the face of it, the banks' response to the changed monetary environment was at best eccentric and at worst downright foolish. The higher level of dollar interest rates would obviously make it more difficult for the debtor nations to repay. But the banks appeared to be lending them more money not less.'[89] The explanation for this is that the banks knew that heavy lending was unsustainable at such interest rates but did not expect them to remain so high. Gradually, throughout 1981 as the realisation dawned that the rates were to stay for some considerable time, they began to try to limit their exposure.

To do this when the eight-year loans came up they insisted that they would reschedule only on a medium-term basis. Later they began to insist on a short term to each loan, hoping that in the event of serious trouble this would enable them to pull out more quickly. Each rescheduling gave the bank more profits and the debtor nation some breathing space but made the loan more difficult to service. An analysis by American Express Bank shows that in 1980 Mexico had no short-term debts but by 1981 it had $6 billion and by 1983 $23 billion. The picture in Argentina and Brazil was similar. The study shows that for twenty-four indebted countries the turning point – at which more money started to flow out of the developing country in repayments than arrived in new loans – came in 1981. Loans became shorter and shorter-term. At one point Brazil was even accepting overnight loans in a last-ditch desperate attempt to stay solvent.[90]

THE CRUNCH: MEXICO DEFAULTS

The crisis point came on Friday 13 August 1982. Mexico was being asked to repay one of the largest debts in history, at the most usurious rates in living memory, in a currency that was rapidly depreciating and with an estimated $100 million leaving the country in capital flight every day.[91] The country had borrowed more heavily than most and had been careless about its use of funds, particularly its short-time loans. It had reached the point where it could not negotiate any further loans, even short-term, to repay the $26 billion debts which fell due that day.

The Mexican Finance Minister, Jesus Siva Herzog, travelled to Washington to announce that his coffers were empty. Mexico was to suspend payments on the interest and principal on its $80 billion debt, most of it owed to US commercial banks. The international financial establishment was horrified. Nine of the largest US banks had a staggering 44 per cent of their capital tied up in loans in that one country; if Mexico stopped paying the banks could crash, throwing the international financial system into chaos.

The financial establishment acted quickly. The US Federal Reserve, the Bank of England, the US Treasury and the Bank of International Settlements quickly organised a short-term bridging loan to avert the immediate crisis. The International Monetary Fund worked out how the debt could be restructured, how much cash this would need from the commercial banks, and how severe a programme of financial austerity could be imposed upon Mexico to put the country back on the road of financial orthodoxy. The banks were at first reluctant to put up yet more money. By a judicious combination of stick and carrot the establishment brought them into line and they worked out the detail of the rescheduling which brought $8 billion in new money to the country. But the conditions which were imposed upon Mexico were extremely tough.

As the decade proceeded, one Third World country after another was brought to the brink in the same way. The package which had served to rescue Mexico was used repeatedly as a model. Each time the banks made more money from the rescheduling and, just as importantly, succeeded in demanding that Latin American governments take over responsibility for the debts contracted by private companies in their countries, which until then constituted 37 per cent of the debt.[92] Each time the key condition was that the debtor accept an IMF package of austerity measures which involved draconian cuts in the living standards of the poorest citizens of the Third World.

Chapter Five

ADJUSTMENT AND ANGER

'The profound comment of our era is that for the first time
we may have the technical capacity to free mankind from
the scourge of hunger. Therefore today we must proclaim
a bold objective: that within a decade, no child will go to
bed hungry, that no family will fear for its next day's bread
and that no human being's future and capacity will be
stunted by malnutrition.'
*Henry Kissinger, US Secretary of State, at the World Food
Conference, Rome, 1974*

'Must we starve our children to pay our debts?'
Julius Nyerere, former President of Tanzania

The wheels of the white Mercedes saloon spun uselessly in
the mud. My driver turned to me with a look, half apologetic,
half bewildered still that anyone could have asked him to do
such a strange thing. It was 1987 and I was in Zambia, once
the richest country in black Africa, to report on the economic
and political turmoil into which the country had been
plunged. Falling copper prices and rising debts had led the
government to adopt a series of austerity measures which
the International Monetary Fund demanded before they
would offer the cash Zambia needed just to pay the latest

instalments on its massive debt of $5 billion. The most recent development had been a doubling of the prices of mealie-meal, the staple maize flour, and the ordinary people had responded by a series of riots in which fifteen people died and $10 million worth of property was destroyed. I wanted to meet the rioters.

The riots had taken place, not in the capital Lusaka but in the industrialised and mining zone in the north of the country known as the Copper Belt. When I alighted from the Zambian Airways plane in Ndola I had hired a white Mercedes because I had been told that things had changed recently in Zambia. South African commandos had staged a number of raids on strategic targets within Zambia, including most recently the headquarters of the outlawed South African opposition group, the African National Congress (ANC), in Lusaka. A sense of paranoia had developed since and the population had been warned to look out for South African spies. A number of dubious characters were indeed arrested, but along with them so were a number of journalists, overland travellers and even a hapless Japanese tourist who had aroused suspicion in the streets of the capital by looking at a map. I had been advised to dress and behave like a businessman. I wore a suit and hired a white Mercedes.

The driver had been pleased at the commission but was less so when I asked him to turn off the highway just before the industrial town of Mufalira and into a ramshackle shanty town called Kawana West which sprawled beside the tarmac road. Within a few hundred yards we were stuck in the rich red mud of the cart-track which weaved its way between the small houses of baked mud with roofs of corrugated iron or reeds. Everyone stopped to watch. Women appeared from inside their homes or straightened up from where they had been bent over their small vegetable gardens. Skinny-looking children peered out from behind the maze of hedges which surrounded the houses. A youth with a battered and ancient bicycle stopped and looked on with dignified disdain. Then the children, without prompting, moved around to the back of the Mercedes and began to push it. The wheels turned and sprayed them with mud. They squealed with delight and pushed harder till it was free of the deep water-laden ruts and moved on along the bumpy little track. From the rear window I could see them all, mud-spattered and laughing as they pointed at the extravagant patterns the fine red dirt had made across their trousers, their naked chests and faces.

Kawana West township was on the front line of the conflict between the Zambian Government and the IMF. As with most battlegrounds its occupants did not choose to be there. As in most such engagements it was the poor who suffered the most.

In the language of the local Bemba people Kawana means 'small, beautiful place'. Once it may have been both. Now it was neither. The shanty town had sprung up there in 1970 when one of the mining companies moved forty families from their homes on land it wanted to exploit. They were installed in Kawana and provided with four water taps. Seventeen years later there were still only four taps in the compound, though they now served 12,000 inhabitants who lived in the sprawling complex of tiny houses. Most had arrived in the early 1970s, attracted to the booming mines from rural areas which had received little or none of the massive government revenues from copper. But from 1974 the price of copper had fallen drastically on the world market and the jobs of the people of Kawana disappeared. By the time of my visit copper was worth, in real terms, only a quarter of its value during the boom years and now 60 per cent of the people were unemployed. For those under the age of twenty-five the figure was nearer 80 per cent. Recently their numbers had been augmented by thousands of miners retired from the state-owned industry under an IMF-inspired redundancy scheme and who lost with their jobs their tied houses and eligibility for the mine's education and health facilities. Kawana itself had no school or clinic.

Ten years before there had been five townships like Kawana. Now there were thirty-eight. In a country where the poverty line was then, on the last dated figures, placed at 350 *kwacha* (about $43) a month, the people of such townships represented the very poor. Those few lucky enough to have a job made around 200 *kwacha* ($25) a month. But most people scraped together only an average of 70 or 80 *kwacha* ($9 or $10) a month from selling cigarettes by the road, making baskets or acting as nightwatchmen in the nearby town. Some tried to make charcoal to sell but supplies of wood thereabouts were very low and they had to walk ten miles every day to the nearest place where wood could be found.

The average family in Kawana had five children. Every month each family consumed about two fifty-kilo bags of mealie-meal, which cost 37 *kwacha* each. Whatever cash was left over from their meagre earnings went to buy cooking oil, charcoal and second-hand clothes imported from Zimbabwe. Even those were beyond the means of many compound dwellers. A pair of trousers cost 45 *kwacha* and shoes were 150 *kwacha*. Most children did not want shoes but they needed them. In a hangover from missionary days when white priests proclaimed proper footwear to be a sign of civilisation, shoes in Zambia are obligatory still for those who want to attend school.

From the mealie-meal is made *nshima*, a stodgy rather tasteless maize porridge. Traditionally it was eaten with what the people called 'relish', which meant a small quantity of meat, fish, vegetables, beans or peanuts to give the dish some flavour. But increasingly the *nshima* was being eaten in Kawana without relish of any kind. Normally the flour was milled into two qualities – breakfast meal and roller meal – for *nshima* was eaten at every meal. In Kawana only the inferior kind was now eaten.

'Over the past ten years the poverty has grown rapidly more extreme. Many people here now only eat once a day.' I was told by Serge Roy-Voisin, who had lived for several years in one of the mud houses in the centre of Kawana as part of an attempt by the French aid agency, *Frères des Hommes*, to encourage self-help among the shanty dwellers. He had encouraged them to form a community association to press the local town council to extend the water facilities and perhaps even introduce an electricity line. The new community association had begun to conduct surveys to monitor the health of the people. 'Malnutrition is on the rise. Infant mortality here is now 25 per cent compared with a national average of 10.5 per cent. And the situation is getting worse.'

This was the context in which the government of President Kenneth Kaunda and his IMF taskmasters decided that they could knock a third off Zambia's budget deficit by eliminating the 1 billion *kwacha* maize subsidy. They had done it before. In both 1980 and 1985 the price had almost doubled on each occasion. President Kaunda knew that the move would be unpopular. He kept promising the IMF he would do it, but kept procrastinating. He did not even dare to inch the cost up gradually in a series of small price rises. But the IMF continued to nag and President Kaunda announced an overnight increase which would take the standard bag of meal from 37 *kwacha* to 82 *kwacha*. That was when the rioting began. Standing that day in Kawana, surrounded by the rioters, it seemed to me that they had had no other choice. It took a while for news of the gravity of the situation to percolate through to Lusaka in the south. The riots escalated and on the third day President Kaunda made a television broadcast in which he announced that the price rises were cancelled.

THE IMF SOLUTION: DEVALUATION AND DEREGULATION

The day I visited Kawana a team of Zambian officials were in Washington negotiating once again with IMF officials. This time the discussions centred around whether the Fund was prepared to recommend that a commercial bank should lend Zambia the money it needed to pay off its IMF arrears, without which Fund officials refused to negotiate further on new IMF loans to the country. In Kawana the decisions were more basic. I heard one woman talking about whether her family should eat their maize porridge only on alternate days in order to buy shoes for her son to get to school. Whatever the outcome in Washington it would be the people of the shanty towns who would count the cost.

That year Zambia was one of thirty-five countries labouring under an IMF austerity programme. In each the conditions differed slightly but the aim of the IMF approach was the same. If a country was to pay its debts it needed more money. The way to raise this was to earn more, by increasing exports, and to spend less by reducing imports and cutting government spending. A number of mechanisms were employed.

* Regulations covering foreign exchange and tariffs and duties on imported goods were 'liberalised' – that is, made more favourable to First World importers. Measures to encourage foreign investment were instituted; these included guarantees that all profits could be taken out of the country by the investor.

* To encourage exports the local currency was devalued, sometimes more than once and by large amounts; this had the effect of making Third World products cheaper and therefore more attractive to foreign buyers and it also made imports more expensive, thus discouraging consumption.

* An anti-inflation policy was introduced. (This was necessary because currency devaluations – as above – tend to stimulate inflation). This commonly included measures to reduce the amount of credit available by raising interest rates and demanding that banks hold greater reserves and lend less. Government spending was cut by sacking large numbers of people employed directly by the public sector. Wages were frozen.

* Free market principles were introduced, in everything except wage bargaining. Controls to keep prices down were abolished. Taxes were raised and charges were introduced for public services, such as clean water, electricity, health and schooling. If social services could not pay for themselves they were to be axed. If they could, they were to be privatised. Subsidies on basic foodstuffs were scrapped.

A whole raft of questionable ideological assumptions support these mechanisms, as we shall see later. But there was no doubt that, on one level, Zambia needed desperately to adjust. The price of copper had plunged on the world market and the attractiveness of Zambian copper over that of other Third World producers was reduced because the exchange rate for the *kwacha* was ludicrously high; the thriving black market in dollars in Lusaka was clear proof that it needed to be devalued to reconcile it with its true value against other currencies. The huge state organisations created to organise the production and marketing of food were hopelessly inefficient and, in a mistaken attempt to keep the price of food down, they paid low prices to Zambian farmers, robbing them of the incentive to produce more. Government bureaucracy was bloated and so was the apparatus of the ruling party which, as in so many one-party states, was funded from the public purse and even in 1987, after nine years of IMF austerity programmes, was having a grandiose new headquarters built on the edge of Lusaka. The IMF told Zambia that it needed to make better use of its scant foreign exchange reserves – the black market was burgeoning, supplies of imported goods were erratic, exports were discouraged and the servicing of debts was falling behind. The formula agreed by the men from Washington and Dr Kaunda was a weekly auction of the limited supply of foreign exchange that was available so that market prices would determine the exchange rate and the most dynamic companies would get the hard currency, which previously had been distributed through a corrupt allocation system. The theory was appealing enough when the auction began in October 1985.

In practice, however, what happened was that firms which dealt in those goods which made most profit got the dollars. Within a few months it was still possible to buy Scotch whisky and Japanese electronics in the shops along Lusaka's golden shopping mile. Other things became scarce. As the *kwacha* fell to only 10 per cent of its pre-auction price essential drugs became almost impossible to get; pharmaceutical imports of $400,000 in 1982 fell to only $20,000 in 1986. Immunisation programmes were suspended for lack of syringes and because there was not enough kerosene to keep the field refrigerators working which are necessary to keep the vaccines stable in hot climates. Some 75 per cent of rural health centres had run out of chloroquine and deaths from malaria were rising markedly. Those who needed an operation in Lusaka's university hospital were required to provide the surgeon with the necessary surgical gloves. Fertiliser rose in price by 200 per cent. Veterinary drugs and the chemical preparations for livestock dips ran out causing enormous destruction to the national herds. Ploughs and other basic farm tools soared in price, way beyond the reach of peasant farmers. Even household soap became a luxury. Prices rose particularly in the rural areas because the shortage of petrol increased distribution costs. The auction system, according to the governor of the Bank of Zambia was actually contracting rather than reviving the economy.[1]

'If a liner is sinking would you hold an auction to sell off places in the lifeboats? Humanity demands that priority be given to the weakest – to those who have the least chance of keeping themselves afloat until rescue comes,' wrote John Clark in one of a series of reports by the UK aid agency Oxfam which painted a comprehensive and depressing picture. Although there were supposed to be advantages for the farming sector built into 'adjustment' policies Oxfam surveys showed that 'benefits largely accrue to the larger farmer and local political leaders and the small farmers are worse off.'[2] As many as 40 per cent of the rural poor 'tend to be female-headed households, disabled people, small farmers who are cultivating less than one and a half hectares of land, and particularly farmers in the remoter regions of the country.'[3] All these were worse off under 'adjustment', as was another growing category – the young urban unemployed who numbered almost one million, a serious source of potential political instability. 'In our experience the situation for both categories has been deteriorating for several years, but the very rapid and far-reaching "adjustment" measures enforced, particularly during 1985, have greatly exacerbated

the situation.'[4] Surveys by Unicef chronicled the end results
of all this and the cuts in government spending which by 1986
had left 400 of the nation's established posts for doctors
unfilled[5] and in 1987 introduced fees for medical services.[6]
Malnutrition had risen by as much as 20 per cent. One third
of all the children under five were underweight, and 17 per
cent of them were still losing weight. Increases in deaths
from malnutrition were dramatic and alarming: before 'adjustment' 23 per cent of all those who died were killed by
hunger; after 'adjustment' the figure was 43 per cent.

In May 1986, unable to reconcile the contradictions any
longer, President Kaunda broke with the IMF. Immediately
the British government told Zambia that it was withholding
the £30 million in programme aid which it had already
promised the country. The United States and other Western
governments did the same. Dr Kaunda continued with a
series of less drastic reforms, culminating early in 1989 with
a fourth national development plan which aimed to achieve
3 per cent economic growth, to reduce population growth,
and cut the budget deficit to less than 2 per cent of the
gross domestic product. A threefold increase in the price of
mealie-meal was postponed to enable more people to register
for coupons which would allow families to continue buying it
at subsidised prices.[7] The position of the British government
remained unchanged: 'We do not believe there is any sign
of commitment to fundamental economic reform.'

That was one country. During the 1980s there were ninety-
four IMF programmes in operation all over the Third World.[8]
In 1989 some seventy countries were struggling under the
burden of IMF demands.[9]

Only the details differed from country to country. In Santo
Domingo women found cooking oil had doubled in price
overnight.[10] In Manila a bus driver had to greet his customers
one morning with the news that fares had risen in one leap
by 30 per cent. In the north-east of Brazil a peasant farmer
arrived to collect his credit payments to pay for essential
fertiliser, and found that these had been abolished in an IMF
programme.[11] In Santiago hundreds of small businessmen

closed their workshops because their home-made products could not compete in price with mass-produced foreign imports, now that tariffs and duties had been scrapped at the behest of the IMF. In Mexico accidents and injuries increased substantially as the oil industry was put into overdrive to produce record exports to pay. Even in the developed world, in Europe and the United States, more than a million workers[12] found themselves caught in the wake of the IMF-created Third World recession when they were laid off after orders from developing countries fell and left their firms without customers. Countless personal tragedies were repeated throughout the world. Each one was nothing more than a statistic to the macro-economists who devised the 'adjustment' strategies. But each one brought trauma, heartbreak and misery to an individual or a family.

Food prices rocketed everywhere. In Bolivia the cost of bread increased four-fold, bottled gas went up twenty times, and petrol seven times;[13] soon half of Bolivia's children were malnourished.[14] In Brazil prices for beans went up 769 per cent and for rice 188 per cent in one year[15] while the number of hours of work needed to earn a subsistence income rose by one fifth;[16] in parts of the north-east of the country every fifth child died before the age of one[17] and a million children throughout the nation starved to death – a number equivalent to the entire population of Liverpool or Pittsburgh.[18] Brazil is the world's largest debtor, owing $114.5 billion in 1987 and, according to the World Bank, was scheduled to pay over $60 billion to its creditors between 1987 and 1989, about 90 per cent of its anticipated export earnings.[19]

The huge increases in food prices, combined with cuts to medical services, meant that health was the area worst hit by the austerity programmes imposed to ensure the continuing flow of money to the Western banks. In Senegal, which had one doctor for every 20,000 people, newly qualified medical students had to waste four or five years while waiting for a job because the state had axed its health budget.[20] In Chile typhoid and hepatitis began to increase because of cutbacks in state provision of clean drinking water and sanitation systems.[21] In Mexico child deaths were up by 10 per cent.[22]

Education was badly hit too. In Zaire 7,000 teachers and in Ghana another 4,000 were sacked to save money.[23] In Chile, where secondary education was available for all until the CIA-backed coup in 1973, schooling became a privilege for those who could afford to pay for the maintenance of buildings as well as for books and pencils.[24] The banks regard Chile as a model debtor for, by its cuts in health and education, its severe restriction of imports and its willingness to exchange its debt for shares in Chilean companies, it has kept up payments on its massive $20 billion debt.

Prostitution increased in Thailand where tourism had been developed as the main industry to service a debt which had risen from $125 million to $9.9 billion in the first half of the decade; there are now thought to be as many as a million prostitutes in the country's infamous sex industry.[25] Taxes rose steeply in the Philippines, where the Aquino government continued the policy of encouraging Filipino workers to emigrate to lowly-paid jobs in the West, from which they can repatriate small amounts of hard currency to their families at home where moneylenders milk the poor with interest rates as high as 400 per cent.[26] In the Dominican Republic suicide rates, attributed by researchers almost entirely to economic hardship, rose to harrowing levels.[27]

Some of the poor of the Third World responded by taking to the streets in strikes and demonstrations. The IMF food riot came almost as part of the standard IMF package, it seemed. Riots took place in which hundreds of people were killed in Egypt, Liberia, Jamaica, Morocco, Tunisia, Brazil, Sudan, Peru, Bolivia, Ghana and the Dominican Republic. IMF negotiations were also the precursor to the overthrow of several civilian governments by military dictatorships which subsequently came to swift agreements with the Fund in Chile, Uruguay and Turkey.[28]

In 1987 Unicef, after three years of behind-the-scenes negotiation with the IMF, assembled a 600-page report on the effects of IMF 'adjustment' programmes. Entitled

Adjustment with a Human Face[29] it constituted a damning indictment of the policies which the Fund prosecuted on behalf of the Western governments which controlled it:

> Unicef's study of the impact of these policies confirms that deteriorating health and nutrition is widespread . . . Malnutrition during the 1980s is increasing in many parts of the developing world. Evidence of rising malnutrition exists in ten African countries, Belize, Bolivia, Brazil, Chile, Jamaica, Uruguay and parts of the Philippines and Sri Lanka. Infant mortality has been rising in some areas – including Barbados, Brazil, Ghana and Uruguay – after decades of decline, while the trend towards improvement has been halted in at least 21 countries. The proportion of low birth-weight babies increased in at least ten countries between 1979 and 1982, including Barbados, Cameroon, Guinea-Bissau, Jamaica, Malaysia, Rwanda and Tanzania. Diseases thought to have been eliminated have reappeared – yaws and yellow fever in Ghana, for example, and malaria in Peru.
>
> And these are just the countries for which information is available. Because nutrition and health statistics are weak or often non-existent there are undoubtedly many areas where rising malnutrition has gone unrecorded and perhaps unnoticed.[30]

Economic growth per capita fell throughout the Third World, disproportionately hitting the poor. 'It is not uncommon that a 2–3 per cent decline in national incomes in the developing countries results in at least a 10–15 per cent decline in the incomes of the poorest classes,' Unicef said. A further report in 1990 revealed that in the world's thirty-seven poorest countries spending on education had been cut by 25 per cent in the past decade.[31]

Moreover the malign effect of the IMF was not restricted to the health, nutrition and education sectors. In Jamaica unemployment had soared because of the IMF strategy; but far from helping to balance the budget this increased the debt from $2.3 billion to $3.2 billion in two years.[32] In Tanzania increased taxes and the inflated price of imported animal vaccines under IMF 'liberalisation' policies caused the collapse of a project run by Christian Aid and the Lutheran Church who had established a revolving credit fund to supply the poorest farmers with a cow each, which they repaid as soon as it calved. In Malawi the abolition of the state-controlled agricultural marketing board led to food profiteering. One standard element of the IMF packages is an increase in food prices in order to encourage farmers to grow more. In addition to removing subsidies, standard policy was to reform the state-owned marketing organisations which, in Africa, were usually inefficient. It became a point of IMF ideology that private sector operations were better run. In Malawi the agricultural marketing board played a vital role in buying grain from farmers just after the harvest, storing it, and then selling it back to them, at a small profit, during lean times. 'It was a buffer against hunger for the poor,' according to Oxfam's development policy adviser, John Clark.[33] But because the para-statal body made a small loss, though not on this crucial food security operation, the IMF insisted that it be privatised. After this happened most of the rural food depots were closed because they were 'uneconomic' and the price of food soared. Traders moved in to sell food to peasants during the lean periods – at seven times the original price of the food.

A moving personal testimony to the full horror of the situation was given to a special sub-committee on international debt set up by the US Senate's Finance Committee. It came from Father Tom Burns, a Maryknoll priest, who has worked in Latin America for seventeen years, who at the beginning of the debt crisis noticed an increase in emergency baptisms in his parish in Peru:

We discovered we were baptising two to three children a day in danger of death . . .

At present 50 per cent of those who die in Peru are under five years of age; 40 per cent of the children are seriously malnourished. Peru's incidence of tuberculosis (TB) is the highest in the hemisphere. When I arrived in the parish in 1974 I rarely heard of a case of TB. Today, hardly a day goes by without a new case being reported. It is an epidemic. To be poor in Peru today is to expect to come down with TB.

Just before I left Peru, I visited with Felicita, a 22-year-old polio victim who is the sole supporter of her four younger brothers and sisters, one of whom is mute. Felicita lost her two older brothers in 1982 to TB. They were 19 and 20 years old. Her parents, who were alive then, asked me to celebrate a mass for them. I buried her mother in 1985, and her father died in 1986 . . . They, too, were victims of TB. There is no doubt in my mind that the debt is the cause of their deaths, because money spent by the government to pay interest to foreign banks is money not invested in the health and well-being of the poor.

The poor, who did not borrow the money, have yet to benefit from it but are the ones who are burdened most severely with its payment – often paying with their lives. The Peruvian Bishops' Commission of Social Action estimates that the debt has cost about 20,000 victims a year – mostly children.

This combination of joblessness and malnutrition has resulted in a culture of survival . . . Education has suffered tremendously . . . Teachers often complained to me that it was impossible for them to teach children so hungry that they could not keep their eyes open. Over the past five years I've seen the older brothers and sisters of these children graduate into frustration. As one priest friend of mine said: The only choices they have are to become a thief, a cocaine trafficker or a member of the Shining Path – a terrorist group.[34]

Father Burns also told of meeting a woman in the local market-place who asked him to 'bless her empty hands, so that she would not need to eat that day'.

HOW THE IMF WORKS

How then does the IMF itself react to this grotesque accumulation of evidence? To understand that it is necessary to look more closely at the nature of the IMF and its sister the World Bank. As we have seen they were set up after the Second World War to promote the growth of free trade on an international scale. Each had a distinct function: the Fund was to make short-term loans to countries which were having temporary problems in balancing their import and export books while the Bank was to make longer-term loans to under-developed countries so that they could raise their level of exports and participate more fully in the world trade market.

To borrow, countries had to join the Fund and pay a membership fee called a 'quota' in proportion to their economic strength. The value of these quotas is increased from time to time to add to the Fund's reserves. Nations were allocated voting rights in proportion to their contributions to the IMF and World Bank coffers. As former colonies gained their independence they joined, paying in tiny quotas and receiving back a tiny number of votes. One dollar, one vote, was the rule of thumb. The whole of black Africa received fewer votes than the United Kingdom. Developing nations saw the IMF as a rich man's club; one Third World writer, lamenting the omission of the world's poor from the origination of the system, complained that the IMF had been born in a state of 'original sin'.[35] Because the Soviet Union refused to join, the United States paid by far the biggest contribution and took the most votes, giving it an effective veto over all Fund policies. 'The IMF is essentially a non-political institution,' said Donald Regan when he was US Treasury Secretary, 'but that does not mean that United States political and security interests are not served by the IMF.'[36] Although the managing director of the IMF is traditionally a European, to counter-balance the fact that the World Bank always has a US president, the real power does not lie in his office but in that of the US member of its board of Executive Directors.

At the outset only forty-five nations were members but in recent years, as more have found no option but to borrow, membership has risen to 148 countries. Loans from the IMF have conditions attached to them and the more a nation borrows the stricter are the conditions. Each member can borrow automatically a First or Reserve Tranche[37] credit, which is 25 per cent of the borrowing country's quota, but after that it has to negotiate a Stand-By Agreement for further Tranches, on which conditions become gradually more rigorous. Stand-By Agreements usually run for a year. In 1974 the Fund created the Extended Fund Facility, which provided for slightly longer-term loans of up to 140 per cent of a nation's quota, over three years instead of one, and bringing with it even stricter conditions in an attempt to get the borrower back to financial solvency as soon as possible. After the second oil crisis in 1979 this was extended further into a Supplementary Financing Facility which allows much bigger sums to be borrowed. The conditions imposed varied only slightly from one borrower to another; in broad outline they all included the measures outlined above,[38] leading to devaluation and deflation in theory, which meant inflation and stagnation in practice for the country concerned. Later, in response to the growing difficulties of the Third World, the IMF established a Structural Adjustment Facility, which offered loans at only one half per cent interest over periods of between five and a half and ten years,[39] but which had the most stringent conditionality of all.

For three decades the World Bank pursued a straightforward role lending money to developing nations. Under its official name, the International Bank for Reconstruction and Development, it lent for specific projects from funds provided by First World nations or from borrowing on the open market. Its terms were normal interest rates, prompt repayment and no rescheduling of the debts. But most of the poorest nations were considered too uncreditworthy for its loans. This became a problem when the US Senate decided that loans were a useful device to save the Third World from communism. In order to lend, primarily to India and Pakistan, the World Bank in 1960 set up a new division, the International Development Association, to offer 'soft' loans, at only three-quarters of one per cent interest, repayable over fifty years. It was, and is, however, a much more frail creature than its sister, for its long-term level of funding is uncertain – dependent upon a 'replenishment' of its coffers every three years by a vote of member nations who often exercise political considerations in the amounts they allocate. But in 1980 the Bank too entered into the arena of enforcing austerity on the Third World. It introduced Structural Adjustment Loans and Sector Adjustment Loans, which differed little from the IMF variety. Increasing amounts of World Bank money are being allocated in this way. In 1987 less than 20 per cent of World Bank lending was in 'adjustment' packages;[40] in 1989 it was reported that the figure had risen to around one third.[41]

The basic attitude, which the Fund and Bank now share, is that most Third World economies are badly managed and need to be 'adjusted' to the harsh realities of life in the modern era. Inflation and balance-of-payments problems are proof that Third World economies consume more than they produce, they say. There is some truth in this analysis but it is not, as we have seen, the whole truth, and the nature of the 'adjustment' which follows is far from self-evident. Pure monetarism would require cuts all round, but to encourage private enterprise the IMF and Bank insist that most cuts come in the public sector. They accept that their programmes are 'unlikely to be distributionally neutral' which is jargon for saying that their measures will probably hit the poor more than anyone else. But, they say, their 'shock treatment' is the only answer because by the time countries approach the IMF their problems are too serious for anything else. They argue that the new policies will make the structural changes from which new growth will spring when the recession in the industrialised world ends and international demand grows again; the costs, they say, will be short-lived, and they will be lower than the costs of any alternative.

There is no doubt that this bitter medicine can, in some circumstances, quickly bring about an improvement in the balance of payments. Despite the failure of most of the Fund's programmes in the world's poorest countries in Africa, where balance-of-payments situations showed no improvement at all and inflation continued apace, the general Third World trade deficit was reduced from $110 billion in 1981 to $56 billion by 1984.[42] And in Latin America a total trade deficit of $1.6 billion was transformed into a surplus of $31.2 billion by 1983[43] and a huge balance of payments deficit was reversed into surplus within two years.[44] But this short-term achievement is laying up a terrible long-term problem for the future. Though trade and payments balances looked good, economic growth – the measure of future prosperity – fell drastically.

THE FLAWS IN THE IMF APPROACH

There are a number of serious objections to the standard IMF analysis. For a start, if Third World economies have been badly managed the IMF and World Bank, in particular, cannot escape some of the blame for the fact. During the 1950s and 1960s the Bank advocated a series of policies which it is now clear were ill-advised. Many of the Bank's mammoth Agricultural Development Projects involving huge dams or massive plantations proved to be white elephants: to tour Africa is to stumble constantly upon the overgrown grave-yards of these curious beasts. They were expensive to run with much of the cost being consumed by expatriate staff and expensive equipment which needed constant supplies of costly imported items to maintain them.[45] They did not have the intended effect of stimulating the economy so that wealth would trickle down to the very poor, but instead the poor often found that their land or jobs were stolen by the mega-projects. Projects to help the poor directly were few and far between.

Worse still, most Bank schemes perpetuated and re-inforced the international division of labour of poor and rich countries into extractors of raw materials and industrial manufacturers, which as we have seen leads to an ever-widening gap between the First and Third Worlds. They promoted import-substitution which relied too heavily on the import of foreign components, putting industries like the Zambian fertiliser factory[46] at the mercy of future foreign exchange shortages.

Their powers of prediction were as bad as those of the Third World leaders. Both the Bank and the Fund encouraged Zambia to borrow heavily in the 1970s, through the IMF's Commodity Compensation Fund, on the assumption that copper prices would rise, which they have never done since. The World Bank's commodity price forecasts were usually considerably higher than the actual price movements in the 1980s: the Bank forecast that rubber would be 391.8 Malaysian cents in 1985, when the average price later proved to be only 187.5 cents a kilo.[47] Forecasts were so far out that some commentators suggested that they were deliberately fraudulent, 'designed to boost the over-supply of commodities and thus lower prices'.[48] There were countless other examples, but most serious was the fact that both anticipated that the recession in the industrialised world, which dampened demand for Third World goods, would be over soon. They geared their adjustment packages to the hope of early recovery which would create the growth within which adjustment would be less painful. There was no early recovery. Nor was their advice always consistent. One senior executive in the Zambian copper industry told me that at one point the government was being advised by the Fund to close production down while the Bank was advising it should be expanded.

Another flaw in the IMF formula is the assumption that most Third World economies run a balance-of-payments deficit because domestic demand is too high, that is the government and people spend too much. Many of those in the Third World find the suggestion insulting: 'the wholesale blaming of excess domestic . . . demand in a continent where some of the poorest people on earth are to be found is quite positively offensive,'[49] wrote one Nigerian economist. In fact it is clear, as we saw in Chapter Three, that the major problem for the Third World is that the world's unfair trading system consistently under-values its commodities, by as much as $100 billion a year. The reality is not that the Third World spends too much but that it does not earn enough, or more precisely it is cheated of what it ought to earn.

A further flaw is that a number of elements in the 'adjustment' packages do not seem to work even within their own terms.

* The IMF strategy of 'import strangulation' does not just cut consumption, it also cuts the imports needed for re-investment in the agricultural and industrial sectors which are essential to the recovery which the IMF says it hopes to stimulate. The other deflationary effects create large-scale unemployment and at the same time gross under-use of industry, resulting in an unnecessary loss of output. In medical terms it is the equivalent of putting a man with a high fever into a coma; the fever disappears but he cannot eat to gain the strength to recover. In the words of Dr Henry Kissinger, the IMF had produced 'a cure that is worse than the disease'.[50]

* Where countries have successfully implemented IMF programmes the influxes of private foreign investors, which the IMF said would follow, have failed to materialise.

* Increasing interest rates is a two-edged weapon. They may persuade the rich to bring back some capital from abroad, because they can now earn more interest at home than in New York. But they can also force out of business those local manufacturers who need to borrow to invest in their factories. They also force the government to continue to borrow abroad because the cost of borrowing is now so high at home.

* Reducing the barriers to foreign investment more often than not leads to a flood of imports – which can be brought in swiftly – rather than to foreign investment in local agriculture or industry – which runs the risk that capital might be trapped in the Third World country if controls were re-imposed. All this can completely counteract the package's other measures to curb imports.

* The amount of money which, under the IMF system, would annually flow from poor to rich nations would gradually increase to absurd proportions: 'The IMF's view of the scale of the negative transfers which the debtors will be prepared to make also seems extraordinary, since it implies that they will be pre-

pared to forgo *ad infinitum* the growth of living standards for which their populations are pressing.'[51]

Most seriously the global impact of such widely pursued policies is counter-productive. A few Third World countries might be able to produce and export more and raise their incomes. But if dozens of developing nations do it, who will buy all the extra exports? With the industrial world still working within the narrower framework established by recession the answer is: no one. The result is a glut on the market and falling prices for everyone. By producing more they earn the same and sometimes even less. Raw materials are now at their lowest price for thirty years.[52] The World Bank solution is to recommend diversification into manufactured exports. But with present levels of investment by First World financiers this is easier said than done.

Some economists believe that these inconsistencies reveal more than a dogged adherence to the theories of monetarism. Professor Laurence Harris of the Financial Studies Group at Britain's Open University maintains that the Bank and the Fund are really not concerned with the health of the economies of individual nations:

> The main role of the IMF and the World Bank is the construction, regulation and support of a world system where multinational corporations trade and move capital without restrictions from nation states . . .
> This . . . is in contrast to the common perception of the Fund and Bank, and to their stated aims which are to assist individual member countries . . . Their policies for individual borrowers are wholly subordinate to their prior responsibility for constructing a world system along these lines . . . Their power comes from operating on a country-by-country basis. Therefore assisting individual countries appears as if it were their principal objective . . . however their main aim is global and national growth is quite secondary to it.[53]

Professor Harris argues that the institutions' two fundamental characteristics have remained unchanged since their character was first determined under heavy US influence in

1944. 'First . . . the system they operate is subject to US hegemony and dominated by the interests voiced by the US government. Second, they are fundamentally committed to an ideology of freedom for international trade and capital movements.'[54] This is an approach they maintained throughout the 1950s and 1960s when Third World countries were adopting import-substitution strategies behind protective tariffs and import and exchange controls in an attempt to build up their native industries. The IMF response was to formulate conditions to attach to loans to counter this tendency (they were first required of Chile in 1947 and extended to a general principle in 1955).[55] The World Bank tactic was to lend to projects which fostered export promotion as an alternative to import restrictions. There was some sense to this: the possibilities for import substitution in many African countries, for example, were severely limited. But with 'adjustment' the approach was extended to lengths where it took precedence over plans to meet the local need for food. Knowing that governments and private banks would refuse loans to any country which did not have the IMF 'seal of approval' they used their unprecedented leverage over the Third World in the late 1970s and 1980s, in direct opposition to the anti-poverty rhetoric the Bank was using at the time, to press this strategy even harder. The process, according to the Nigerian economist Professor Bade Onimode, increased the structural dependence of poor countries and integrated them more tightly into the international capitalist system.[56]

This explains the curious fact that the Fund and Bank often offer the same medicine, almost without alteration, to every country, regardless of its circumstances and regardless of whether its balance-of-payments deficit has been accumulated through gross mismanagement or through factors entirely beyond its control.

It also explains why they simultaneously pursue policies which would be contradictory if their aim was real development: they call for countries to establish an equilibrium between imports and exports to achieve an acceptable balance of payments but at the same time they demand an end to all import duties and tariffs which will undermine the attempt to balance the books, even insisting that no tariffs should be imposed on grossly subsidised items like US wheat.

According to Professor Harris those who suggest that the solution is merely to temper the unacceptable harshness of IMF austerity programmes fail to understand the basic problem – the commitment to free trade between unequal partners. Many, like Unicef, have called for a new style of 'adjustment' programme over longer periods and with more flexible policies to promote economic growth and protect the most vulnerable groups in society. 'All such reform proposals assume that the institutions' main concern is the individual national economy and their concern is, as a result, only with a small change of the trade-off within that: some greater emphasis on growth and less on balance-of-payments equilibrium; some greater social protection for the poor to give a stronger humanitarian and political underpinning to structural adjustment programmes.' Such reforms can never address the fundamental problem.

What then is the fundamental problem?

The chief characteristic of the IMF approach lies in its assumption that the existing system is unalterable and that therefore Third World countries just have to adapt to it. Hence their approach is to enter a country, often as a joint mission, and for the IMF team to look at the balance of payments and exchange problems while a Bank team discusses export promotion policies and appropriate tariff structures.[57] A leading IMF official has told the *Financial Times* how they begin: 'First you look at what the capital account can be over the next few years, then you derive the current account.'[58] In other words the IMF looks at the level of debt first and then works out how the national income can be channelled and redistributed to pay for what is due. It does not even consider the reverse strategy: to see how much a debtor can reasonably be expected to pay from his current account, even assuming it is purged first of inefficiencies, and then pay off the debt in amounts which do not cause hardship or inhibit future economic growth.

It is within this philosophy that the term 'adjustment' has been coined, with its overtones of proper and harmonious equilibrium. The phrase clearly implies the need for a return to some golden norm when, as we have seen, the previous norm was seriously biased against any developing country. 'If the previous conditions and economic structures in these countries were satisfactory then they should not have given rise to adjustment problems and periodic crises in the first place,'[59] argues Professor Onimode.

The IMF seems fixed in its view that most of the blame for all this belongs primarily with Third World governments.[60] But as we have seen so far in this survey there is a clear order of culpability. It begins with an unfair order, established through violence and exploitation. It proceeds through a series of mechanisms of trade and finance which purport to be neutral but which, as we have seen, are inherently loaded against the poor. It continues through the wilful refusal of the rich nations to make any serious concessions on the reform of that order. It extends through the responsibility of the oil-producing nations which sought maximum profit from the money they squeezed from the industrialised world without proper thought for the consequence to the poorest. It persists through the banks which sought to make, and are still making, large profits from the oil bonanza in a bout of reckless lending. It touches the governments of the Western world which abdicated the responsibility to control this cash surge for the general good. It ends with the élites of the Third World who borrowed irresponsibly and used the money inefficiently and even corruptly. The one group this chain of culpability does not include is the group of people who have been left to shoulder the actual burden – the poorest men, women and children in the poorest countries in the world. All of this the IMF approach conveniently ignores. There is never any suggestion that the debt crisis is a responsibility to be shared and that therefore its cost should be shared too.

Nor is there any hint that an alternative approach might offer any solution. There are a number of IMF premises which cannot be accepted uncritically. 'Is a search for balance of payments equilibrium so critical and desirable as it is being emphasised by the IMF and the World Bank? In any case should stability and equilibrium be the basic national goals in underdeveloped countries?'[61] asks Professor Onimode. Even the great guru of the free trade movement, Adam Smith, concedes in *The Wealth of Nations* that exceptions need to be made for 'infant industries' which can benefit from protection in their early years, until they are capable of coping with competition from mature foreign rivals. Countries like Britain and the United States protected heavily early in their development. As Arthur Schlesinger, the former Special Assistant to President Kennedy, put it:

> If the criteria of the International Monetary Fund had governed the United States in the nineteenth century, our own economic development would have taken a good deal longer. In preaching fiscal orthodoxy to developing nations, we were somewhat in the position of the prostitute who, having retired on her earnings, believes that public virtue requires the closing down of the red-light district.[62]

Such questions are rarely raised by IMF and World Bank fundamentalists and the Third World nations themselves are still deprived of the votes they would need to bring about the necessary reforms within the existing structures. But there is clearly a moral dilemma at the heart of the issue of whether the well-being of individuals comes before matters of ideology, however well-intentioned that ideology might be.

Aid agencies, in particular Unicef, have done their best to keep this factor before the public eye. In the 1988 *State of the World's Children* report it said:

> The ones who have suffered the most from this recession are the young children of the poor communities in affected areas. They are the ones whose families have the least scope for making economies and have therefore had to cut back on necessities. And they are the ones who are most dependent on the govern-

ment services and subsidies which so many governments have felt obliged to cut back as a way of adjusting to economic recession.

It cannot be stressed too often that the young child cannot just 'ride out' such periods of austerity. Ninety per cent of the growth of a human brain and much of the growth of the human body is completed in the first five years of life. A child who has to go without adequate food or health care in those years will not grow to his or her physical or mental potential. There is no second chance.

It returned to the theme in the 1989 report:

For almost nine hundred million people, approximately one sixth of mankind, the march of human progress has now become a retreat. In many nations development is being thrown into reverse. And after decades of steady economic advance, large areas of the world are sliding backwards into poverty . . .

It is children who are bearing the heaviest burden of debt. And, in tragic summary, it can be estimated that at least half a million young children have died in the last twelve months as a result of the slowing down or reversal of progress in the developing world.

The IMF and World Bank began to adjust their rhetoric in response to the political unease which followed the publication of a preview of Unicef's first report in 1986. Some commentators detect a distinct, albeit very slow, change in attitude among some members of the Bank's staff, though others say it is cosmetic. But the Fund, the unflinching policeman of international capital, has remained unmoved in all essentials of policy.

THE BANKS BEGIN TO WRIGGLE

Throughout all this the private banks, which under the aegis of IMF 'adjustment' packages continued reluctantly to lend to the Third World, so that it has the money to pay the old debts, were raking in constantly increasing profits from the process. Ironically, from the moment that it became clear that the debts might never be repaid, the banks began to make even more money from them. When Mexico first threatened to default the banks were able to insist that 'exceptional risk premiums' should be charged on new loans to that country: they added an extra half per cent to the interest rates which brought them an additional $500 million. In Brazil, where the new risk premium was a full 1 per cent, the banks earned an extra $1 billion.[63] Overall in those early years of crisis the cost to Latin American countries doubled, and these figures do not include the extra charges banks made for arranging the loans. Each year in the early 1980s, as living standards among the world's poor fell, the banks made huge amounts of money. Profits among the big US banks each rose between 39 per cent (Citicorp) and 84 per cent (Chase Manhattan). Dividends paid to shareholders increased by one third. The banks' value on the stock market shot up by between 83 and 174 per cent.[64] In 1986 the big four British banks declared record profits. It was not to last.

Feeling growing concern about the stability of the situation and increasing discomfort from the complaints of aid agency pressure groups and bodies like Unicef, the political leaders of the West began to make tentative proposals to ameliorate the situation. The common factor to them all was a concern with symptoms rather than causes, as we shall see in Chapter Eight. But here we should note that the opposition of the banks was a key factor in the failure of them all, even though, as the chairman of the Federal Reserve Board, Arthur Salomon, calculated in 1984, to have abandoned their additional profits on all Latin American debt by 1986 and simply charged the basic current market rate would have cost the twenty-four largest US banks a mere 6 per cent of their pre-tax earnings.[65]

The banks knew that their situation was unstable, though publicly they pretended it was not. Their plan was gradually to maintain the fiction that the debts would at some point be repaid while at the same time making Third World lending a smaller part of their business. They began to develop domestic opportunities, moving into the credit card, home loan, stockbroking and insurance sectors. At the same time they withdrew from all Third World lending which was not essential to maintain the flow of interest payments back to them, which was vital if the charade of stability were to be maintained. Suggested solutions from politicians, which as we shall see helped to forestall the threat of a mass default by Third World countries acting in concert,[66] gave them the cover they needed for their long, slow retreat.

Then in February 1987 Brazil, with its foreign reserves almost depleted after a daring attempt to combat inflation and preserve economic growth, announced that it too could no longer pay. Its debt in 1978 had been $35 billion. The high interest rates took it to $82 billion by 1982. In 1987 it was $110 billion, and still rising. This was despite the fact that, between 1979 and 1985, it had paid back $79 billion – far more than the original sum it owed. The debt was what one Brazilian economist[67] at the time called 'fictitious dollars' which represented nothing more than a series of book-keeping entries in New York. Brazil was the world's largest debtor (unless you count the United States, which nobody does) and its moratorium on repayments of both interest and capital on the $60 billion of its debt which was owed to commercial banks, sent shock-waves through the financial world. The value of several major banks fell on the stock market, raising some of the first public doubts about the over-inflated nature of the US stock market. Behind the scenes the banks began to accelerate the process of refusing to lend new money to debtor nations to help them to pay the interest on the first loans.

Before the moratorium had reached the crucial point ninety days after the announcement when, under US law, the loans would have had to be declared non-performing, the world's biggest bank, Citicorp, suddenly announced that it was to register a $2.5 billion loss in its second quarter accounts in order to raise its provision against bad debts to $5 billion. It was the first public confession from the private banks that some of the debts would never be repaid. The move took the banking community by surprise but other banks were obliged to follow its lead. Within two months all the major US and British banks had increased their loan loss reserves by 25 to 30 per cent. The British banks alone set aside £3.4 billion.[68] Two of them, Lloyds and Barclays, declared losses for the first time in their history. Another, the Midland, was forced to sell off two subsidiaries and raise more money on the stock market. After the ninety-day mark was reached the Federal Reserve Board had to bail out Texas's largest bank, First City Bank Corporation, which had assets of only $480 million against $1.1 billion of bad debts.[69] The dollar weakened and nervousness increased during the summer. Finally, on 19 October 1987, came Black Monday when the New York Stock Exchange fell by a record 22.6 per cent and $1 trillion – an amount then more than the entire Third World debt – was wiped off the value of shares in a single day.[70] One commentator observed:

'On that Black Monday the world's stock markets suddenly woke up to the fact that nothing was holding them in place . . . The US economy was no longer able to export enough to pay for its own consumption, or to earn enough on its overseas investment to plug its growing trade deficits. Essentially, it was now dependent on a continuous flow of funds into the US economy, some of them from Latin American interest payments, much more from loans and direct investment in the US economy on the part of the British, West Germans and Japanese . . . Black Monday showed the sacrifice of the poor for what it was: economically irrelevant, because the solution did nothing to restrain the madness of an integrated world economy tying its future growth to the unearned consumption of a single country, and unnecessary, because the total debt in whose name the poor had been sacrificed amounted to the gains made by speculators on the world's stock market in a single year.[71]

But despite the banks' sudden acknowledgement that the enormous Third World debt might never be repaid in full the debtor nations did not benefit. No reduction was made in the level of debt actually owed by Third World countries. The money which had been set aside by the banks was not wiped off the value of the debts. It was simply set aside in the banks' reserve vaults for when it might be needed. The amount of the debt, and the repayments expected from the Third World, remained the same.

Officially the governments of the Western world took a hard line with the banks following their belated acknowledgement that the huge debts might never be repaid. Britain's then Chancellor of the Exchequer, Nigel Lawson, said:

> The banks embarked on sovereign lending [lending to governments] because it looked like a profitable business. For some years, it was. But the banks knew all along that . . . they were in the risk business. If they did not know that, they should have done. And there is certainly no case for taxpayers to pick up a disproportionate share of the bill for commercial misjudgments.[72]

The political attitude in the United States was even harder. The folk memory was strong that once – in the Great Crash of 1929 – the public had had to bear the cost of banks' imprudence. No politician wanted to be seen publicly to advocate bailing out the banks with tax-payers' money. But in private few politicians could face the consequences of not doing so. This is why, when Mexico first defaulted, it was the governments, through the IMF, which stepped in to sort out the mess. It was why, during the early years of rescheduling, Latin American governments were pressed to accept responsibility for foreign bank debts incurred by private companies in their countries. It was why, despite his firm words, Mr Lawson granted the banks 35 per cent tax relief on 80 to 90 per cent of the losses they declared, even though they actually wrote off no debts and the Third World did not benefit. Indeed a proportion of the debts have since been sold on the secondary debt market – a market on which creditors who have lost faith that a debt will ever be repaid sell it, at a hefty discount, to speculators who are gambling that one day it might be honoured. Debts were sold mainly by banks from Europe which did not hold huge amounts of Latin American debt and had little to lose by getting rid of it while they could (bigger banks cannot afford to sell at this rate for to do so would be like a public admission that their balance sheets are far weaker than they look). Bolivian debts, for example, have been sold at only 8 per cent of their face value;[73] if one day Bolivia honours them, at 20 cents to the dollar, the speculator will make a killing. Most Latin American debts were, at the end of 1988, valued at only half their face value on the secondary market.[74] They can only continue to fall. Between March 1987 and 1989 the value of Argentinian debt fell from 65 per cent of its face value to a mere 18 per cent, those of Brazil from 66 to 27 per cent, and of Mexico from 58 to 33 per cent.[75]

Clearly many bankers have given up hope that many of these debts will ever be repaid. Yet despite this the discounts are only for fellow financiers; debtors are still expected to pay interest as if the debt was worth its face value.

Brazil held out for almost a year of debt rebellion under three different finance ministers before capitulating and beginning talks with the IMF once more in February 1988. The banks, meanwhile, found that their value actually rose on the stock markets because of the provision they had made against potential default on Third World debt. In February 1989 the British banks were once again announcing good profits. Barclays declared a record result, tripling its profits to £1.39 billion,[76] despite increasing its reserves to meet possible bad Third World debts to what one commentator described as a 'macho' 38 per cent.[77] National Westminster increased its bad debt provision by another 4 per cent and still managed to double the previous year's profits with £1.4 billion.[78] Lloyds, after a loss of £248 million the year before, declared profits of just under £1 billion and described the result as disappointing.[79] Even the Midland, after its undignified scramblings the year before, raised £693 million despite upping its provisions against Third World debt to 32.5 per cent.[80]

But this time the British banks were more cautious. The large profits were declared to maintain confidence and cover their slow withdrawal from Third World liability: six months later further large sums, totalling £1.9 billion,[81] were set aside against the day when it is openly acknowledged that the

Third World will never pay. In February 1990 this process was continued. Again huge sums were removed from the annual profits and put into loan loss provision. National Westminster set aside £990 million, Lloyds £1,763 million, Barclays £983 million, and the Midland, with its huge £4,240 million portfolio of Third World debt, set aside £846 million.[82] The move meant that the banks, whose very existence had once been threatened by perilously high levels of Third World debt, had now set aside enough cash to survive even if 70 per cent of the debts were never paid.[83] While all this had been going on they had also been selling off significant amounts of the debt on the secondary market – at prices as low as 15 per cent of its face value.[84] By early in 1990 the British banks had sold off 25 per cent of the debt, taking a loss of around 60 per cent.[85]

Similar provision was being made by banks in the United States and Canada. In the third quarter of 1989 US banks raised debt cover at levels ranging from 44 per cent (Chase Manhattan) to 100 per cent (J. P. Morgan). The biggest lender, Citicorp, stubbornly resisted, only to fall into line in January 1990 when it had to set aside $1,000 million after it became clear that interest payments from Brazil, which had dried up in 1989, were not going to resume substantially after the Brazilian general election. In July 1990 the US federal agency responsible for assessing the credit-worthiness of foreign loans told institutions to raise provision against default for both Brazil and Argentina.

The banks were paying the cost of their reckless lending – and getting tax relief on it – and slowly recovering their position. But the Third World did not benefit in the slightest from all this. A World Bank report noted:

> The threat to the international banking system has abated. Some progress has been made by the debtor countries in restructuring and reforming their economies. But most of the indebted countries are still no better off than in 1982 – when the debt crisis erupted.
> Debt disbursed and outstanding has doubled, and debt-service

payments on a cash basis are one-third higher . . . New money commitments from commercial banks were a modest $7.5 billion in 1988 (including $5.2 billion to Brazil) and only partially refinanced interest payments.

Despite adjustment measures, growth rates in the highly in-debted, middle-income countries [mainly Latin America] and in low-income Africa are still low and investment levels well below those reached in the 1970s.[86]

In December 1988 the World Bank's chief economist, Stanley Fischer, was forced to concede: 'Despite remarkably rapid growth in the industrialised world in 1988, growth in the debtor nations has not resumed.'[87]

Only weeks afterwards the people of Venezuela pro-nounced their verdict on IMF strategy. In February 1989, one month after taking office, President Carlos Andres Perez, after swift negotiations with Fund officials, imposed a series of austerity measures which included a 90 per cent rise in petrol, a 30 per cent rise in bus fares and a wage freeze. His aim was to borrow $4.3 billion from the IMF over the next three years to pay the $700 million due on a total foreign debt which, despite the fact that Venezuela is an oil-producer, has reached a massive $31 billion and which in 1988 cost the country 47 per cent of its foreign earnings in debt servicing. These came on top of weeks of shortages of bread, coffee, sugar, salt and cooking oil which had been artificially created by retailers awaiting official price in-creases. Thousands of Venezuelans took to the streets, led initially by schoolchildren protesting against the fact that their half-price bus passes were not being honoured. Wide-spread looting began and street barricades were thrown up. Four days of rioting left more than 200 people dead, with hundreds wounded and thousands arrested. Gun battles took place in the shanty towns of Caracas where the poor, who make up the vast majority of the capital's population, live in the shadow of the splendid homes of the wealthy minority. On the third day President Perez declared a state of emer-gency and suspended freedom of speech, movement and assembly and imposed a curfew. He also decreed that the security forces would henceforth have the right to raid homes without a warrant. Almost immediately the global financial establishment began work behind the scenes on a rescue package. The hand-to-mouth cycle continues. The process, in the IMF's neutral vocabulary, is called 'adjustment'.

Chapter Six

THE BIBLE ON WEALTH AND DEBT

'Take heed . . . lest when you have eaten and are full, and
have built goodly houses and live in them, and when your
herds and flocks multiply, and your silver and gold is
multiplied, and all that you have is multiplied, then your
heart be lifted up and you forget the Lord your God.'

Deuteronomy 8:11–14 RSV

What standards are we to use to disentangle the skein of
truths, half-truths and deliberate obfuscations in which the
people of the Third World are now so thoroughly enmeshed?
It is to the Bible that the Christian will turn for moral
guidance. We have already seen the aptness of many biblical
references to the subjects we have analysed. There is, however, a danger in searching for textual references which
seem appropriate to such individual circumstances. As Brian
Griffiths, the evangelical Christian who has for the past
decade acted as an economic adviser to the British Prime
Minister, Margaret Thatcher, has put it: 'The temptation
facing each one of us is to interpret Jesus's teaching to fit our
preconceived ideas . . . or else simply to justify our present
lifestyle and interests.'[1] History has shown too clearly how
selective biblical quotation can be used to bolster all manner
of questionable positions including advocacy for slavery,[2] for
apartheid and for the oppression of women.

On the issues of wealth and debt there are two distinct traditions within both Old and New Testaments: one sees wealth as a sign of God's favour, while the other sees it as a sign of blindness in the face of poverty and injustice: one sees debt as a symptom of lack of application and prudence, while the other sees it as a symbol of oppression. Within the traditions there are a number of biblical standpoints, some of them apparently contradictory. As with so many problematic biblical references some of them deal with matters of principle while others treat of specific situations, the circumstances of which are not always clear to us today. The Christian injunction on this is clear enough; the principle must come before the specific, for the sabbath was made for man and not man for the sabbath.[3] The difficulty on occasion is knowing the one from the other. To do this it is necessary to examine the historical context within which the various injunctions were made. Wealth and debt, we will find, are inextricably bound together.

THE PENTATEUCH: THE SOCIAL ORDER OF THE FIRST ISRAELITES

It was in the early Iron Age that the Israelites arrived in the land of the Canaanites to lay claim to the land which they believed God had promised them. They had been a generation in the wilderness. It was the same wilderness through which their forefathers had, before they were enslaved in Egypt, wandered since the late Bronze Age, living the life of nomadic shepherds. It was an existence which kept them in tune with the natural rhythms of the land. Echoes of this are present in the Pentateuch, the first five books of the Bible: 'If, when out walking, you come across a bird's nest in a tree, or on the ground, with chicks or eggs and the mother sitting on the chicks . . . let the mother go; the young you may take for yourself. So shall you prosper and have a long life.'[4] It was a lifestyle which produced a particular attitude to wealth. The whole clan prospered or declined together, according to what nature provided. If the rains were good and their journeying brought them to rich pasture-land the cattle and sheep of each family would grow fat as did those of his neighbour. The surplus was shared or used to provide to guests the hospitality of the desert which each family knew they might need themselves in some future year when the weather was uncharitable or if some enemy staged a successful raid. It fostered also an ethic of sufficiency – of having enough but no more – which is reflected in their account of God's provision of manna in the desert: there was enough for everyone's needs but those who tried to hoard more than they needed found it bred maggots and smelled foul.

This sense of community, of equality and of sufficiency, dominated still when the Israelites came to settle in their Promised Land. Leaving the coastal plains to the Canaanites, the tribes divided the hilly land amongst themselves, not in accordance with their relative power or strength but by casting lots. Individual parcels were then allocated according to the needs of each family, we are told in the Book of Numbers.[5] Archaeological evidence confirms that the settlers did establish small towns of between 150 to 1,000 people in settlements dispersed evenly throughout the land.[6] From the outset too the concept was established that the land belonged to God and that each individual merely held it as a trustee. According to Leviticus: 'The land shall not be sold in perpetuity, for the land is mine; for you are strangers and sojourners with me.'[7] The land was not held communally or owned by the new state for, as Professor Griffiths has pointed out,[8] to so nationalise it would be to deprive individuals of their responsibility as stewards. Land could be sold, or at least a leasehold on it could be sold to enable a purchaser to buy a certain number of harvests from it.[9] Such a sale might occur after a number of dry winters when land failed to produce an adequate crop. A farmer then might borrow to survive and, if the harvest failed again the next year and he could not repay his debt, be forced to sell the land to obtain further food. But the original owner, or a member of his family, had the right to redeem it at any time that he was able to raise the appropriate price.[10] Most radically, every forty-nine years – a sabbath of sabbath years which was given the name of Jubilee after the word *yobel* for the ram's horn which was blown to announce its arrival – the land had to be returned to the family who had originally been allocated it.[11] Wage labour was regarded only as a temporary phenomenon, what the Oxford economist Donald Hay has called a kind of social insurance for those who lost possession of their land until the next Jubilee.[12] This, and the fact that inheritance law required that provision be made for all sons and not just the eldest as European laws of primogeniture require, meant that a stop was placed on the accumulation of property in a few hands.

Such a provision had particular significance. In such a primitive agricultural community land was the basis of all economic relationships. Land was capital. Without it an individual was unable to participate in the most basic of social activities. To deprive someone of their land was thus to deprive them of social status and rob them of their power within the community of the people of God. It was to break faith with the Covenant under which God had delivered the people of Israel from slavery in Egypt. There is some debate among historians as to how widely the Jubilee principle was ever enforced but whatever the actual practice the principle towered, symbolic and educative, over the conduct of those early years, articulating the communal aspirations of the people and a vision of a future governed by the Covenant.

The same philosophy underlay the first laws laid down in the Book of Exodus and the further provisions of the Holiness Code of Leviticus and of Deuteronomy which are thought to have been written at various times during the first centuries of settlement: land was to lie fallow every seventh year during which the crops it produced could be gathered by the poor;[13] during the harvest farmers were conjoined to leave generous gleanings, at least one sixtieth of the harvest, for the poor to gather for themselves;[14] land could only be sold for a fixed price and not according to supply and demand;[15] if an Israelite who had sold his land was eventually forced to sell himself into slavery to another Jew he was to be freed at the sabbath year;[16] slaves were also to be freed in the Jubilee year;[17] when a slave was freed he had to be given an endowment to help him set up on his own;[18] all debts were to be cancelled every seven years;[19] it was sinful to refuse to lend to a poor man simply because the sabbatical year was near when all debts must be discharged;[20] a tax was to be paid every three years to relieve the destitute;[21] the taking of interest on any loan to a fellow Israelite was forbidden;[22] and if a pledge, such as a man's cloak or millstone, was taken it had to be returned when needed.[23]

In total these measures represented a mechanism for righting the social imbalance which threatened to disenfranchise members of the community by robbing them of the basic element of their membership of the people of God – the land which he had promised and given to them. It was not a soft option. The primary emphasis in the Law was on every family having access to land; the provisions for wage labour and for the poor to share in the harvest were secondary.[24] Moreover the poor were expected to work for their living: they had to glean from the fields, not simply receive charity; they had to sell themselves as bondsmen to the rich to pay their debts. But a mechanism was established which placed limits on their enslavement. It was a mechanism to secure justice for the poor, rather than leaving them to the mercy of the charitable impulses of the rich and ensure that they could never become trapped in a permanent cycle of deprivation. It was a mechanism which placed social justice above the ability to maximise profit. It was a mechanism which enshrined 'equal opportunity' into social values ensuring that in this way society could never become permanently imbalanced by disparities of wealth.

WEALTH AS A SIGN OF GOD'S BLESSING

Parallel to this tradition we also find in these early books of the Bible the seeds of the notion that God will bring material prosperity to those who do his will. Later these two traditions were to be brought into conflict by those seeking to justify the maintenance of privilege, but at this stage there is no inherent contradiction. In Genesis it is said that Abraham, after obeying God's instruction to leave his home, became 'very rich in cattle and in silver and gold'.[25] Of Isaac it is said, 'The Lord blessed him, and the man became rich,'[26] and of Jacob, 'thus the man grew exceedingly rich and had large flocks.'[27] More significantly Deuteronomy announces that blessings will come 'if you obey the voice of the Lord your God . . .'[28] and then lists in great detail various kinds of material prosperity; conversely it warns at length of all manner of curses and grievous afflictions which will befall those who fail to obey. It is on the isolated use of texts such as these that there has grown 'The Gospel of Prosperity' which has for many years been a feature of North American fundamentalism but has in recent years begun to gain ground in parts of Africa and Asia. The theologian Paul Gifford has commented on the methodological error which promotes such an approach:

There is little effort to discover any context. For example, the linking of virtue with prosperity and sin with loss in Deuteronomy was part of an attempt to explain how disaster had come upon God's people. The explanation had the merit of avoiding the conclusion that disaster had occurred through God's weakness or lack of concern; it taught that the reason was Israel's own faithlessness. This 'solution' was part of the whole debate on the question of retribution which is found throughout Old Testament Wisdom books. Fundamentalists do not appreciate that the Bible contains such 'debates' – that biblical texts in themselves can lead in all sorts of different directions.[29]

But if prosperity was once seen as a sign of God's favour the Israelites were under no illusions that it would come without effort, both individual and collective. In the early years after the settlement they remained a collection of small, self-sufficient, co-operative and egalitarian communities. The pattern of life followed the agricultural cycle of the year.

A calendar found in the ruins of the ancient city of Gezer illustrates the degree of social co-ordination required of the community in a succession of annual duties beginning with the olive harvest in September and October, then the sowing of cereals, then lentils, then between February and March the hoeing of weeds and collecting of grasses for hay, then the harvest of barley, then in May that of wheat, and finally the harvesting of grapes in July and August and of figs in September.[30] Communal effort was particularly required in ploughing with the few oxen the village could sustain and in constructing and maintaining farm terraces in the hilly areas.

Such was the order of existence for at least two hundred years. Archaeological evidence bears witness to this. The example of the community at Tirzah is clear on this, as one historian has pointed out:

> The houses of the tenth century BC are all of the same size and arrangement. Each represents the dwelling of a family which lived in the same way as its neighbours. The contrast is striking when we pass to the eighth-century houses on the same site. The rich houses are bigger and better built and in a different quarter from that where the poor houses are huddled together. Between these two centuries a social revolution had taken place.[31]

What brought about such a radical change? The crucial factor was war – and the change in social organisation it prompted.

THE HISTORICAL BOOKS: THE RISE OF A NATION STATE

In the early days, although villages were self-sufficient they were often bonded by marriage ties and would come together to face common enemies. There was no central government or regular army, however, and no central taxation to support one. During the period of the Judges this began to change.

The term Judges is something of a misnomer, for although these Jewish leaders had some judicial role they were really more of a cross between a sage, a chieftain and a general.

Judges 3 records that a coalition of Moabites, Ammonites and Amalekites captured Jericho and forced the tribe of Benjamin to pay tribute for eighteen years. In Judges 6 the Midianites are reported to have staged raids at harvest time for seven years. But most serious were the predations of the largest group of Canaanites, the Philistines, who began to dominate first the tribe of Dan and then that of Judah and after the battle of Aphek established garrisons throughout the Israelite territory and tried to prevent the Israelites from holding military weapons. In such a situation the Jews needed a regular army to fight back. This meant that men had to be taken out of agricultural production while at the same time agricultural surpluses were needed to feed the troops. But after the Philistines were defeated social structures did not move back to the pattern which Moses had ordained for the first settlement. 'A permanent change had occurred, and this would develop to the point where the independence and self-sufficiency of the Israelite towns and villages would vanish.'[32] The foundation was laid for the establishment of a Judaic monarchy.

From the outset the Old Testament was ambiguous about the virtues of monarchy. The Israelites clamoured for a king to give them the status and strength of neighbouring nations and asked the last of the Judges, Samuel, to appoint one. Samuel was reluctant and warned:

> These will be the ways of the king who will reign over you: he will take your sons and appoint them to his chariots and to be his horsemen . . . and some to plough his ground and reap his harvest . . . He will take your daughters to be perfumers and cooks and bakers. He will take the best of your fields and vineyards and olive orchards and give them to his servants. He will take the tenth of your grain and of your vineyards and give it to his officers and to his servants. He will take your menservants and maidservants, and the best of your cattle and your asses . . . He will take the tenth of your flocks, and you shall be his slaves. And in that day you will cry out because of your king, whom you have chosen for yourselves; but the Lord will not answer you in that day.[33]

It was an accurate summary of the burden of a centralised state. By the reign of the third king, Solomon, the implications of such centralised power were fulfilled. He put twelve officials in charge of the twelve regions, each of which was required to support his court in considerable luxury for one month a year. He conscripted 30,000 workers for the construction of his great buildings;[34] such conscription was to be one of the major causes of the revolt of the northern tribes under Jeroboam. He incurred substantial debts, which required that twenty cities in Galilee be ceded to a foreign king in repayment.[35] Vacant lands, which under the Mosaic code should have reverted to their original clan for re-allocation, now were deemed to be the property of the crown so that the king had land with which to reward his officers. Any operation of the Jubilee principle was thus against the interests of the king and, as the years went by, the waxing monarchy began to buy land[36] and, as is recorded in the story of Naboth's vineyard, even to steal it; when Naboth declined to sell 'the inheritance of my fathers'[37] Queen Jezebel made a false accusation against him and had him put to death so that his land became the king's.

As the monarchy grew in strength it absorbed the Canaanite cities in the coastal plain; from them it absorbed a new attitude towards land. 'The Israelites were taught to understand the land as a gift for whose use they were responsible and whose distribution was ordered by moral principles. The Canaanites in their fertility religions were much more interested in the land as an asset whose fruits were to be maximised by religious ritual. Land was a marketable commodity and economic growth was the goal.'[38] With this justification the more enterprising families were able to increase their estates on a more permanent basis, taking into employment as labourers those who had been forced by poor harvests and increasing debt to sell their land. The growth of this landless class was accelerated by the high rates of interest which were now charged on loans, commonly 30 per cent and sometimes as high as 60 per cent. Another historian wrote: 'A movement of dispossession, of slow impoverishment of former free land owners started on the one hand, together on the other hand with the rise of a new rich land-owning class created by the king's grace and favour and built upon the fief system.'[39]

But if the poor increased, the national economy prospered under the system. With the region's imperial superpowers undergoing internal crises, Israel at this point was the strongest nation between the Nile and the Euphrates. The climate was right for economic growth.

THE WISDOM BOOKS: THE GROWTH OF INEQUALITY

It was small wonder that the vision of God's design and approbation among these new powerful groups shifted considerably. It was the scribes and sages of this new class who produced, in the section of the Bible known as the Wisdom books, the next major strand of biblical writing on the subject of wealth. As the commentary of the New Jerusalem Bible puts it:

> With the exception of the latest books, Ecclesiasticus and Wisdom, this group of biblical literature does not touch on the great themes of the Old Testament: Law, Covenant, Election, Salvation. The sages of Israel show no concern for the past and future fortunes of their nation: like their gentile counterparts they are absorbed in the individual and his destiny . . . Wisdom (which is to say, uprightness) is sure to bring happiness, and folly (or vice) ruin. Thus God rewards the good and punishes the wicked.[40]

Hence Wisdom literature demands respect for the king and for authority and opposes the idea of change.[41] It approves wealth as a sign of God's favour,[42] sanctions the power of the rich,[43] and links respect and honour to riches. As Professor Robert Wall wrote:

> The theological contour of Wisdom retains an élitist, nationalist view of God and society . . . Israel's kings, and the wise men

who advised them, were primarily concerned with the nation's survival, given the possibility of military defeat and the grim memory of slavery. Wisdom, understood against this *realpolitik*, teaches how to survive and even prosper as a nation. In this sense, its theology is not for transformation but for the preservation of the national status quo.[44]

Although it also carries warnings about the duty of the rich to the poor there is small indication that this is expected to go much beyond ameliorating some of the more rank iniquities without seriously disturbing that status quo. From such a position it was not a great step to assert that those who are rich are, therefore, clearly favoured by God who has blessed them, while those who are poor must be so because they are wicked. In other words: the existing order is so because God has ordained it; there is no need for major change, indeed to change radically would be to go against God's wishes.

Corruption set in. Some landowners began to exploit the poor by hiring them only for very low wages, by selling them food at inflated prices and by lending at extortionate rates of interest. The increasing wealth of the landed was spent on items of high luxury. One historian has coined the phrase 'rent capitalism' to describe the phenomenon.[45] A theologian has preferred the idea that the poor of Israel somehow absorbed in themselves and in their affliction, the sin of the whole society: 'That's a very much wider and more demanding approach to sin than the privatised and spiritualised idea of sin that most of us have been brought up on . . . but it's a very scriptural idea that a nation or society embodies its sin in the whole way it operates and deals with people and that the poor absorb that sin.'[46]

THE PROPHETS: WEALTH AS A SYMPTOM OF OPPRESSION

In response there arose in the eighth and then the seventh centuries BC a succession of prophets who confronted the new corruption in strong language. Their detailed condemnations reveal the extent of the new oppressive materialism. The rich paid ludicrously low wages, or even refused to pay once the work was done.[47] They employed the poor to tread grapes but gave them nothing to drink themselves.[48] They exacted high taxes on what little crops the poor produced for themselves.[49] They used violence against the poor or cheated them by using false weights in selling corn.[50] They took vital goods, such as oxen, in pledge[51] and seized houses and fields.[52] They passed laws which discriminated against the poor.[53] With their ill-gotten wealth they lived in conspicuous luxury. They owned two houses, one for summer and one for winter,[54] which were filled with the spoil of the poor.[55] Their houses were of stone (not the usual mud brick)[56] and furnished with cedar panelling[57] and ivory couches.[58] They did not work but passed their days in feasting, drinking and singing songs.[59] The women, whom the prophet Amos called 'cows' because they were as sleek and fat as prime beasts,[60] paraded with stiff-necked haughtiness, with jewellery even on their ankles and with perfumed hair.[61] Hypocritically they present themselves as righteous. Yet they abide only by the letter of the law, not the spirit, when it comes to observing religious feasts.[62] As judges they pretend to be fair but they are biased against the poor[63] and can be bribed.[64]

The prophets were violent in their condemnation, in particular of wilful oppression, wanton blindness and sanctimonious hypocrisy. But despite the power of their invective, the situation was not to change significantly.

In 587 BC Jerusalem fell to the Babylonian emperor Nebuchadnezzar and the Israelite king and many prominent nobles were taken to live in exile in Babylon for some fifty years. The religious allegorists saw in this a divine punishment because the Chosen People had revoked their Covenant with God by abandoning its social requirements. But for the poor the Babylonian conquest probably meant little more than the substitution of a foreign oppressor for a Jewish one. When the Jewish aristocracy returned they changed nothing. Early in the fifth century BC groups of Israelites were complaining to the Jewish leader Nehemiah about their own rich relatives. One group complained that they had been forced to pledge their children to obtain cereals. Others had had to pledge fields, vineyards and houses. Others complained that the rent they paid, in grain, was too high and that loan and mortgage repayments were so steep that it was impossible to escape bankruptcy and therefore slavery.[65] One group was even selling fellow Jews to become the slaves of foreigners.[66] In the centuries that followed up to the birth of Christ the land of the Jews fell under the domination of one foreign power after another: after Babylon came Persia, then Macedonia, the Seleucids and the Ptolemaic hegemony in Egypt, and then finally Rome. In each case the power of the Jewish aristocracy grew as it collected the taxes on behalf of the new overlord. For the poor only the name of their landlords altered.

THE OLD TESTAMENT ON WEALTH AND DEBT

What general conclusions, then, can we make about the attitude of the Old Testament to wealth and to debt? There are nine key areas:

* Men and women are social creatures and not individuals whose relationship to God is to be seen in isolation. In the beginning God said: 'It is not good that man should be alone.'[67] The Old Testament is the history of a people, in its social relations, and not of a series of pietistic individuals. The Covenant was with Israel, not with individual Israelites.

* Part of the Covenant between God and his Chosen People was clearly concerned with establishing a harmonious social order – what the Israelites called *shalom*, which we translate, somewhat inadequately, as 'peace' but which also encompasses harmony, health, well-being, prosperity and justice. It saw the need to deal with structural matters. It acknowledged that as social and economic relationships are dynamic there must be a permanent self-righting mechanism built into that structure.

* Justice and not charity was the main motor for this mechanism. The stress is laid upon sharing with fairness rather than simply the absolute relief of poverty.

* The private ownership of property is clearly sanctioned, in the Ten Commandments and elsewhere.[68] But an owner is a trustee who must use his possessions for the general good and not for selfish indulgence. The right to property is clearly subordinated to the obligation to care for others.

* Prosperity must be worked for. It is wrong to deny anyone the right to work for that themselves. Self-help and self-development are encouraged because that is the only way for an individual to participate fully in society.

* Loans must be given in a way which respects the dignity and integrity of both borrower and lender.

* The 'option for the poor' is clearly evident in the Old Testament. That is to say that at pivotal moments in history God, right from the story of Cain and Abel, as the liberation theologians have observed, is seen clearly to be on the side of the poor, the weak and the abused. The liberation of the oppressed Israelites from slavery in Egypt is another clear example. The voices of the Prophets is another. The Incarnation will be its supreme expression.

* The right to food and clothing is God-given. In Genesis he provides them for Adam and Eve. In the desert he provides manna. But there is a sufficient level in such matters; those who try to take more than they need will find no satisfaction in the superfluity. Stress is laid upon the need for the poor to share the harvest in the laws of the Pentateuch.[69] The prophets rail against the oppressive rich with particular force where they deny these basics to the poor.

* But poverty is not defined simply by a lack of food and clothing. It is a spiritual and psychological dispossession. In Hebrew there are a whole range of words which we translate as 'the poor'; one theologian who analysed the relative use of them found that in thirty-six Old Testament passages the Hebrew word meant 'those who lack', in thirty-one 'those who are dispossessed', in fifty-seven 'those who are frail', in sixty-one 'those in need' and in eighty 'those who are oppressed'.[70] The

Old Testament refers constantly to those people who are on the fringes – the widow, the orphan and the stranger. People are poor if they are deprived of anything which prevents them from full participation in society. Poverty destroys the mind as well as the body.

Such, then, was the social legacy inherited by the first-century Jewish community into which Jesus Christ was born. He was to refine it significantly.

JESUS CHRIST: A PERSONAL OR SOCIAL ETHIC?

For almost two thousand years it has been a common view – and still is among some fundamentalists – that Christ reversed or overrode many of the traditional Old Testament preoccupations. The social dimension of Old Testament theology was clear enough, whatever view one took of it, but, many theologians argued, Christ dispensed with this entirely and constructed an exclusively personal moral code where the core relationship was a private one, between the individual and God, and into which society entered only peripherally. 'Prosperity is the blessing of the Old Testament; adversity is the blessing of the New,' wrote Sir Francis Bacon[71] as if in support of the thesis that the agenda had been changed quite entirely. In this century the eminent philosopher and sociologist of religion Ernst Troeltsch summed up a long tradition when he wrote of Jesus's teaching as 'the entire renunciation of the material social ideal of all political and economic values, and the turning towards the religious treasures of peace of heart, love of humanity, fellowship with God, which are open to all because they are not subject to any difficulties of leadership or organisation.'[72] In this the issues of equity and justice were only tangential; Jesus had no programme of social reform, he argued, but summoned people to prepare for the coming of the Kingdom 'quietly within the framework of the present world-order, in a purely religious fellowship of love, with an earnest endeavour to conquer self and cultivate the Christian virtues.'[73] Such an interpretative tradition was continued by scholars like Rudolf Bultmann and Henry Cadbury who claimed that Christ provided no framework of ethical norms to support his teaching of love. 'Jesus teaches no ethics at all, in the sense of an intelligible theory valid for all men concerning what should be done and left undone.'[74]

Certainly Christ's call for personal change is clear. *Nothing will change unless I change first*: that imperative is primary. But does it follow from this that Christ had nothing to say about the mechanics by which society operates or the man-made structures which constrain it? To decide we will need to examine not only what Jesus said but also who he was and what he did. We will find that the links between the Old Testament social tradition and the teachings of Jesus are greater and more deliberate than the Troeltsch tradition would allow.

The most obvious example of this is that Christ himself made a point of beginning his public ministry in such a way that made it unmistakably clear that he saw his mission not as a reversal but as a fulfilment of Old Testament social values:

. . . he came to Nazareth, where he had been brought up, and went into the synagogue on the Sabbath day as he usually did. He stood up to read, and they handed him the scroll of the prophet Isaiah. Unrolling the scroll he found the place where it is written:
The spirit of the Lord is upon me,
for he has anointed me
to bring the good news to the poor.
he has sent me to proclaim liberty to captives,
sight to the blind,
to let the oppressed go free,
to proclaim a year of favour from the Lord.
He then rolled up the scroll, gave it back to the assistant and sat down. And all eyes in the synagogue were fixed on him. Then

he began to speak to them: 'This text is being fulfilled today even as you are listening' . . .[75]

It was a clear manifesto, and there are good grounds for thinking that by 'a year of favour from the Lord' Jesus meant the Jubilee Year.[76] Even before that he had publicly linked himself with the tradition of the prophets by associating with John the Baptist, a man who taught vividly in the same prophetic style, as indeed did Christ himself: the rhetoric of the Beatitudes as recounted in Luke, with its contrast between the blessings of the poor and the woes of the rich,[77] is firmly in this tradition. Later he explicitly states that he has not come to do away with the old Law and the Prophets but to fulfil them[78] and when the rich man who has neglected poor Lazarus at his gate dies and asks if God will send the poor man to warn the brothers of the rich man he is told that they have Moses and the Prophets who are sufficient.[79]

Many of Jesus's themes harked repeatedly back to the important social themes of the Old Testament. He explicitly referred in the Sermon on the Mount to the idea that food and clothing are God-given[80] and made a point of first telling his disciples to feed the five thousand[81] and then doing so himself, showing that he regarded it as important to feed men and women's bodies as well as their souls. He reinforced, in the parable of the Talents[82] the idea that wealth was a virtue so long as it was used for the benefit of others and the idea that property is held in stewardship for the good of all and not for the unlimited consumption of the owner. He rebuked the rich not so much for the personal sin of malice as much as for the more social sin of blindness to the needs of others[83] and extended the Old Testament notion of retributive justice into a wider context of natural justice: the Good Samaritan had no implication in the crime against the man he went to help – just as he had no bonds of obligation beyond those of common humanity. He emphasised the criterion of sufficiency in pronouncing that covetousness is as loathsome as murder or adultery.[84] In the parable of the Labourers in the Vineyard[85] in which the Master returns to the market-place throughout the day to find ever more unemployed people in need of work, and then pays them all the same at the end of the day, he stressed that the need of each person is the proper yardstick for setting wages, not the amount of work the structures of society allow them to do: 'From each according to his abilities, to each according to his needs'[86] is as much a Christian precept as a Marxist one. He echoed, again and again in his parables, the virtue of the kind of sharing required by the codes of Deuteronomy and Leviticus: the Good Samaritan, the Prodigal Son, the Widow's Mite, the Labourers in the Vineyard all are powerful demonstrations of a Kingdom which comes through sharing; and those who refuse to share, like the Prodigal's brother, are reproved. And he took even further the Old Testament traditions of alms-giving by announcing that those who gave to the poor, gave to him:[87] every life was a further realisation of the Incarnation. Undoubtedly many of the examples he used were metaphors with deep spiritual resonances but their relationship to so many of the Old Testament social values cannot be purely coincidental.

It is in his attitude to the poor that Jesus forges his strongest links with the social teachings of the Old Testament. That Jesus demonstrated what the liberation theologians call a 'preferential option for the poor' is without doubt. He lived among them. If the focus of the Old Testament had been the Covenant with the Chosen People, that of the New was to be Bringing the Good News to the Poor. Not just bringing the good news, but almost always Jesus specified to whom he was bringing it: 'Go and tell John what you have seen and heard: the blind receive their sight, the lame walk, lepers are cleansed and the deaf hear, the dead are raised up and the poor have good news preached to them.'[88] The poor are the only group specifically singled out as recipients of the gospel.

There have been attempts, of course, to conclude that Jesus was speaking here only in metaphor and that his subject was spiritual rather than material poverty. Matthew's use of the phrase 'Blessed are the *poor in spirit*, for theirs is the kingdom of heaven'[89] is cited in evidence. To be poor in spirit, it is said, is to acknowledge, as the poor are regularly forced to do, that no man or woman can survive by their own efforts without help from outside. Undoubtedly that meaning is present – there was a tradition among the Jews, built up after centuries of occupation by foreign powers who imposed alien laws, that to adhere scrupulously to the Jewish law and refuse to compromise with the laws of the foreign masters would eventually bring even the richest man to poverty. Hence piety and poverty were, in some senses, synonymous. But those who choose to 'spiritualise' Jesus's idea of the poor are all too often, as René Padilla has pointed out,[90] people who already have all their material needs met; similarly those who quote the words 'The poor you will always have with you'[91] as a fatalistic excuse for a lack of remedial action, more often than not mean 'the rich you will always have with you and I intend to remain one of them.' Jesus's repeated references to the poor on other occasions in Matthew[92] leave little room for doubt that the poverty of which he spoke was material and degradingly so. His approach and his imagery were directed at the understanding of those whose life was hard. His parables drew vividly on the cycles of simple agricultural life. His stories like that of a poor woman who must sweep out her entire house rather than lose a single coin and his images of cloth which must be patched have now become alien to the experience of the affluent Western world. But they speak directly to the poor of the Third World today as they did to the poor of Palestine then.

In any case what we can learn of Christ's social teaching is not limited to consideration of what the Gospels report him as saying. He spoke eloquently through his background and actions.

CAN ANYTHING GOOD COME OUT OF NAZARETH?

Jesus was born into a poor family in a rural backwater, far from the centres of regional and imperial power. His birth was in uncomfortable circumstances. His cradle was an animals' feeding trough.[93] His first visitors were shepherds, a group of particularly low status in Jewish society.[94] At his ritual presentation in the Temple soon after his birth his parents could not afford the customary offering of a lamb but only the one stipulated in the Old Testament for poor people, two pigeons.[95] In the first years of his life he was a refugee in a foreign land[96] and then spent most of his life in a region treated with contempt by the rest of the nation: 'Can anything good come out of Nazareth?'[97] and 'Surely the Messiah is not to come from Galilee?'[98]

Galilee was cut off from the southern area of Judaea because it was surrounded by non-Jewish lands. Samaria lay between and as the Samaritans shared only the first five books of the Bible with the rest of Israel they were therefore regarded with the particular dislike accorded to apostates. To the north and west were the gentile lands of Ptolemais and Syro-Phoenician Tyre. To the east lay other heathen territories. The Jews of Galilee were therefore, in the eyes of the élite of Jerusalem, inevitably tainted with alien contacts and practices and were therefore ritually unclean for many religious purposes. It even had a different system of government: Judaea was ruled direct from Rome whereas Galilee was left in the hands of a native tetrarch, and later king, and tribute was paid only indirectly to Rome. It was fertile and economically self-sufficient in all that was needed for its simple and unsophisticated life. All this, notes the eminent Jewish historian Geza Vermes, 'cannot have failed to reinforce Galilean self-awareness',[99] nurturing the sense of independence and rebelliousness for which it became notorious after a succession of revolts against Roman domination. But it also served to fortify the sense in cosmopolitan Jerusalem that Galilee was a province of country bumpkins. Galileans spoke a strange dialect of Aramaic. Vermes reports a contemporary anecdote from the post-Christian Jewish scriptures of the Talmud in which a Northerner was ridiculed in the market in Jerusalem:

'You stupid Galilean, do you want something to ride on (a donkey = *hamār*)? Or something to drink (wine = *hamar*)? Or something for clothing (wool = *'amar*)? Or something for sacrifice (lamb = *immar*)?'[100]

In other words they dropped their aitches: the name Lazarus is Galilean pronunciation of the correct form Eleazar. Their speech was considered so sloppy that people from certain northern towns were not allowed to read the Bible in public when they were away from home. The word used to describe them in the Talmud is *'am ha-arez* which means peasant, but which carries derogatory connotations of a religiously uneducated and ritually unclean person:

> No man may marry the daughter of the *'am ha-arez*, for they are like unclean animals, and their wives are like reptiles, and it is concerning their daughters that Scripture says: Cursed be he who lies with any kind of beast.[101]

The second class status of his homeland placed Jesus in a particular relationship to ordinary people and to the Jewish leadership.

Materially Jesus was not one of the poorest of Galileans. He was the son of a carpenter and therefore a tradesman of some, if restricted, means. Vermes has asserted that in contemporary speech the word for carpenter (*naggar*) was often used as a metaphor for scholar or learned man. Either way the significant thing is that at some point Christ abandoned a position of some, albeit limited, social status and opted for a life of poverty. He chose the life of an itinerant[102] and threw himself upon the generosity of his followers, including a group of women, who provided for his daily needs.[103]

EMBRACING TAXMEN, TAILORS, TANNERS – AND WOMEN

But Jesus went further than embracing poverty, he embraced a whole class of people who were even more marginalised than the poor – the sinners.

In Judaic tradition the word 'sinner' (*hamartolos*) was not a moral description so much as a technical term. It was used to identify a particular group and to segregate them from the rest. It was used to describe anyone who, for any reason, could not comply with the complex and detailed prescriptions of the Rabbinic law on matters such as tithing, fasting and even hand-washing, areas in which Jesus came into conflict with them.[104] This group of sinners was far bigger than might have been supposed. Traditionally the provisions of the law applied only to the priests of the Levite tribe but from the time of the Pharisees they were extended to everyone. The Pharisees were originally a group of religious radicals who in the century before Christ set out to bring the people of Israel back to God. They believed that if all God's people kept the law for one day the nation would be delivered. In their early years they were opposed by the rulers of Israel and were at one point persecuted; eventually however they were assimilated into the establishment in uneasy alliance with the aristocratic party of the Sadducees, who were the main Jewish collaborators with Rome and who as landowners and chief tax collectors controlled administration, agriculture, employment and business. From this point the Pharisees became a kind of spiritual police force, enforcing submission to their web of rules and condemning any who refused to concur.

Among those whom the fastidious Pharisees designated as sinners were anyone with a job which meant he could not rest on the sabbath day, such as shepherds and boatmen. Other groups in the category included tailors, who were suspected of immorality because their job brought them into contact with women, and anyone whose job made them smell unpleasantly or required them to handle things defined as impure (leather-makers, coppersmiths, and butchers): once alienated they could not participate in worship. Anyone who was too ill or poor to fulfil the precise requirements of the law was also designated a sinner. The idea that sickness was a manifestation of a sinful past was commonplace in first-century Judaism. In particular lepers, haemophiliacs and the mentally ill were regarded as unclean. From the Gospel stories it is clear that many of the people in these categories had been forced by their illness to leave their homes and become wandering beggars.

There were many other groups who were ostracised or denied full civil and religious rights. The group most commonly referred to in the Gospels are the tax-collectors. Some of these were wealthy (others were merely employees of senior collectors, or even part-time collectors) but all were despised. They were denied the right to make offerings for the poor and they were not permitted as witnesses in court. They were often referred to as if they were Gentiles[105] and not true Israelites at all. Such racial discrimination, as Vinay Kumar Samuel notes in his admirable essay *The Meaning and Cost of Discipleship*, was the basis of the Rabbinic law: 'The only full Israelites were pure-bred sons of Abraham. Pure ancestry had to be carefully proven for a man to exercise any civic rights or marry his daughter to a priest. Only those with pure ancestry could share in the benefits accruing from the merit of Abraham or have a share in the messianic salvation.'[106] But sexual discrimination also alienated a large section of the population:

In Jesus's time the Jews believed that sexual desire was uncontrollable, and therefore set out to protect women, and public morality, by secluding them. Women took no part in public life and were preferably kept indoors. Religiously they were classed with Gentile slaves and minors and could only listen to worship. It was thought better to burn a copy of the Torah than read it to a woman. They were regarded as unreliable witnesses and could not give evidence in court. They had few rights in marriage. It was regarded as unfitting to address a woman in the street.[107]

Who then was not a sinner? The question is not facetious. According to the Pharisaical calculation only around 20 per cent of the entire population – 18,000 priests and Levites, 6,000 Pharisees and 4,000 Essenes, and their families – could be accounted not to be. This effectively excluded most of the population of Palestine from membership of the people of God. But those excluded, according to the Korean theologian Ahn Byung Mu, did not have a common destiny. All they shared was the fact that they were alienated, dispossessed and powerless. 'They are never represented as a class which has a power base. They yearn for something. Jesus sides with (them) and accepts them as they are without making any conditions.'[108]

SOCIAL STATUS IN THE NEW TESTAMENT

If class was the central social issue in the Old Testament then, as Professor Stephen Mott puts it,[109] status is the social theme of the New. By deliberately associating with those whose status was dubious – and saying that the Kingdom of God was to be found among them – Jesus called into question the whole social order of his time. He did not reject the honest interest of the establishment: he accepted the invitation to eat at the home of a Pharisee[110] and healed the daughter of the president of the synagogue.[111] But he spent most of his time among the poor whose status was low.[112] Most significantly he also associated with prostitutes and drunkards and told them that their sins were forgiven.[113] He entered the home of the tax-collector Zacchaeus and described him as 'the son of Abraham'.[114] He healed lepers[115] and Gentiles.[116]

He made special time for women and for children, who had no status in the community at all.[117] By the standards of the time he was particularly attentive to women. To his contemporaries even to talk to a woman in public provoked disapproval. More than that he listened to what they said; Jesus it seems was a good listener. His disciples 'marvelled'

when they found him in conversation with the Samaritan
woman at the well, yet Christ chose to use her as the method
of access to the Samaritan city where he remained for two
days, teaching. Indeed it seems possible that she and the
Syro-Phoenecian woman were the first non-Jews to become
followers of Christ, manifesting 'the historical leadership
women had in opening up Jesus's movement and community'[118] among the Gentiles, a factor which was to become
lost along with so many other elements in the early Church
after the faction of Paul, with its deeply Graeco-Roman
intellectual forms and social attitudes, gained the ascendancy
in the Church and edited the Scriptures in accordance with
its prejudices, which included the subjugation of women.
Jesus healed women, taught them and numbered them
among his disciples. He prohibited divorce and pronounced
that adultery by a man is as much a sin as by a woman, thus
giving women a new status in marriage. It was the women
who remained faithful to him in his moment of greatest crisis
when the men ran away, though even this great sign of their
fidelity reflects their low status in contemporary society, for
the male authorities would have regarded the presence of
women at the Cross as of no practical or symbolic threat. It
was the women too, whom society regarded as too unreliable
to act as witnesses in court, that Jesus chose to be the first
witnesses of his resurrection. He placed a new stress on the
virtues and importance of children who in contemporary
society had no status: 'Whoever receives one such child in
my name receives me.'[119] Later, when the disciples tried to
shoo children from him, he said that the Kingdom of Heaven
is theirs and that adults have to take on some of their qualities
to enter it.[120]
    On many such occasions Jesus added significant gestures
to underscore the social aspect of his act. He pointedly sent
the sick back to their homes after curing them – a metaphor
for returning them back into the community and thus restor-
ing their rights.[121] When he cured the woman with the
haemorrhage – she was doubly cursed, both a woman and
sick – who had touched him in a crowd, he drew the fact to

the attention of the people about him to show his disregard of the law that a man who touches a woman who is bleeding is defiled.[122] In a study of twenty-seven of the miracles in the synoptic gospels the French scholar Jean-Thierry Maertens concluded that in every case the person who was cured had, in some way, been excluded from full expression of the Jewish identity.[123]

Even as he did all this, Jesus attacked the established religious leaders who were prepared to countenance such rank injustice and at the same time maintain that true piety lay elsewhere. It was their laws, with their stultifying effect on the building of new social relations characterised by righteousness, which were the chief target of Jesus's attack. 'Woe to you, scribes and Pharisees, hypocrites! For you tithe mint and dill and cummin, and have neglected the weightier matters of the law, justice and mercy and faith.'[124] The essence of his criticism was that the Pharisees had turned the law into an ideology, fossilising its provisions irrespective of changing circumstances: 'The sabbath was made for man, not man for the sabbath,'[125] was his response. Jesus himself adopted an altogether more dynamic approach. He was not afraid to change his mind when the situation required it: as when he reversed his instructions to the disciples as he sent them out for a second time to preach the gospel.[126] He attacked in similar vein those scribes 'who devour widows' houses and for a pretence make long prayers.'[127] He overturned the money-changers' tables in the Temple not simply because they brought money into the House of God but because, as François Houtart has explained, in those days the Temple combined the roles of Stock Exchange, Central Bank and the Government Treasury in the Jerusalem economy: it was in reality a temple of financial manipulation and economic exploitation.[128] He told the rich young man not simply to give to the poor but to sell what he had and give to the poor.[129] This was the other side to Jesus's assault on accepted norms of social status. If he was prepared to include those who traditionally had been excluded he was also prepared to judge those who were normally the judges, to see a poverty in those who were wealthy, and to show contempt for those who demanded respect.[130]

This takes us some way from the argument that Jesus was concerned only that individuals should forge a new transcendent relationship with God. It undermines quite thoroughly the argument that Christ had no interest in social institutions and only a simplified understanding of society and inter-personal relationships. As Stephen Mott concludes: 'To those who claim that Jesus's ministry was merely personal, we reply that he could not have done anything more basic to challenge institutions and social structures.'[131] He did not offer analysis; he proceeded straight to action.

It was the radical direct effect of what Jesus said on the society around him which prompted such a series of dramatic reactions. The people of his home town tried to push him over a cliff.[132] His own family came to the conclusion that he had gone mad and came to take him home.[133] Huge crowds flocked to hear his powerful message of transformation.[134] And the authorities decided that he must die.[135] Had he been preaching a message only about the need for inner personal change, would there ever have been a Crucifixion?

The truth is that Jesus did not have a message with no social implications. He did not even have a message which had peripheral social consequences. His whole call was for people to follow him in new social relationships. It was a challenge to every vested interest in the land – a challenge not merely political or economic but, far more radically, a moral challenge at the most fundamental level of societal relationships. So radical, indeed, that even with the benefit of centuries of study we have yet to grasp its full ramifications.

PROVOKING CONFRONTATION

But one thing is certain: it was a deliberate and calculated challenge. Jesus did not shy away from confrontation. He courted it in full knowledge of its consequences. The Indian theologian Vishal Mangalwadi notes three key occasions on which this is plain: in them Jesus first challenges, then judges and finally offers an alternative vision.

In the first incident Jesus, at the pool of Bethesda in Jerusalem, met a lame man who had waited beside the healing waters for thirty-eight years because no one was sufficiently caring to help him into the pool when the waters stirred therapeutically. Jesus told him to pick up his bed and walk. It was the sabbath, and carrying a bed broke the sabbath proscriptions for which the authorities would undoubtedly have fined him. Afterwards they vowed to kill Jesus.[136]

> It was not by mistake that Jesus asked this powerless man to challenge an inhuman society by a deliberate act of defiance of its rules. God had provided the stirred-up pool to heal this man, and he might have been healed long before with the help of others. It was really the social pool of stagnant, selfish society that needed to be stirred . . . Christ's mercy did not touch an individual alone. It also sought to touch the heart of a society and to awaken its sleeping conscience. It troubled the stagnant waters which brought a torrent of retaliation from the vested interests.[137]

In the second Jesus, again on the sabbath day, made a blind man see. But he did not do it simply by words or touch. He spat on the ground, made mud with the spit, and then placed it on the eyes of the blind man.[138] This constituted 'work' under the sabbath code. It was a deliberate act of defiance. Then he told the blind man to break the law too, by going to wash in the pool of Siloam. The authorities interrogated the man, and his parents, and then excommunicated him – after which Jesus told him 'For judgement I came into this world, that those who do not see may see, and that those who see may become blind.' Mangalwadi comments:

> Jesus made the blind man pay a heavy price for his healing . . . Yet his excommunication must have helped many sincere Jews make up their mind against their own rulers whose blindness had been exposed and judged . . . Jesus's mercy did not touch a blind beggar alone. How many blind could he heal in three

years anyway? . . . Our mercy must not merely open the eyes
of the blind man but must also reach out to restore the sight of
a blind society. True compassion calls for dealing with the social
context that makes human beings miserable.[139]

In the third, just before his triumphal entry into Jerusalem,
Jesus waited for two days outside Bethany as his friend Lazarus
died. He made no attempt to arrive before the death. He
waited for a crowd of mourners to arrive and then, before them
all, with a loud prayer he raised Lazarus from the dead: 'I have
said this on account of the people standing by, that they may
believe that thou didst send me.'[140] Mangalwadi writes:

> It is not enough to stir a society or judge a blind establishment.
> If the leadership does not repent, if it does not decide to fulfil
> its responsibility, then it becomes our task to seek to provide an
> alternative. Servanthood is the biblical means of acquiring power
> to lead . . .
>   The miracle had the intended effect: many people came to
> believe . . . Jesus carefully built a large following that was not
> just another religious sect but an alternative centre of power in
> Israel. As a result the Jews decided to kill both Jesus and
> Lazarus.[141] Christ knew that this would be the consequence of
> what he was doing but he had no choice. The establishment had
> refused to repent . . . either Jesus had to give up his call for
> repentance and change or he had to precipitate a confrontation
> . . . Jesus was prepared to pay the price of such a confron-
> tation.[142]

JESUS CHRIST ON WEALTH AND DEBT

What general conclusions, then, can we make about the
approach of Jesus to wealth and to debt? He reiterated, and
indeed reinforced, Old Testament attitudes in many areas.
Again we see:

* that food and clothing are a God-given right.

* that the ownership and use of property is subordinate to the
responsibility to care for others.

* that men and women have both the right and the duty to work, exercising the stewardship of talents given to them, that the goods produced are to be put at the service of the community and that wages should reflect the needs of the worker.

* that because God has a desire for justice he has a compensating preference for the poor.

But he also brought a series of new injunctions:

* that personal change is the prerequisite of all progress.

* that no-one is to be excluded from the people of God and this means it is unacceptable to rob people of their ability to participate fully and equally in society – whether by economic, social, class, sexual, racial or other discrimination.

* that on some occasions the good things of life are to be consumed with joy in celebration – and that joy is increased through sharing – while on other occasions they are to be consumed only with restraint.

* that the blindness of affluence can be as great a sin as malice.

* that sharing is one of the key signs of the Kingdom of God.

* that it is not sufficient to give from our surplus but that we must give up part of what we already have to give to the poor.

* that it is not enough to aid the victims of injustice without challenging the structures which keep injustice in train.

* that judgements must be made and confrontation must sometimes be sought even though the price of it will be heavy, or even sacrificial.

Some of these principles are familiar enough; others are less so. This is because throughout the centuries the more unpalatable aspects have been buried discreetly in the background. As Professor Ronald Preston has put it: 'The Christian Church had not found it easy to live with the really radical elements in the ethical teaching of Jesus.'[143] It still does not.

Chapter Seven

TOWARDS A THEOLOGY OF DEBT

'We have been the recipients of the choicest bounties of
heaven; we have been preserved these many years in peace
and prosperity; we have grown in numbers, wealth and
power as no other nation has ever grown. But we have
forgotten God . . . Intoxicated with unbroken success, we
have become too self-sufficient to feel the necessity of
redeeming and preserving grace.'

Abraham Lincoln, 30 March 1863

'The bread in your cupboard belongs to the hungry man;
the coat hanging unused in your closet belongs to the man
who needs it; the shoes rotting in your closet belong to the
man who has no shoes; the money which you put in the
bank belongs to the poor. You do wrong to everyone you
could help but fail to help.'

St Basil the Great, 330–379

The response to the corpus of Christ's teaching has varied
with the changing economic and political circumstances of
each era. Theologies and theological trends have burgeoned
and withered. Some offered profound insights while others
merely provided justification for courses of action whose real
motivations were more base.

In the early years of the Church there was agreement on

issues of wealth, if not on all other subjects. The split that was to occur in the Church between the factions of Paul and James had no roots in this area, although in later centuries their disagreement was to have profound consequences on Christian attitudes to the poor. James maintained that faith was dead unless it showed itself in social actions. Paul insisted that God's grace brought the personal transformation which produced better social relationships. The two emphases were not incompatible, although post-Reformation history tried to make them so.

The 'communism of love'[1] of the early Church in Jerusalem, according to the Acts of the Apostles, was striking, though in terms of present-day political ideology it was a fairly muddled affair: some sold property to fill the common purse,[2] others retained theirs but threw it open to common use.[3] There was, as Peter pointed out to Ananias and Sapphira,[4] no obligation to sell, but there was clearly an expectation that whatever anyone owned was made available unreservedly to the community – it was this in which Ananias and Sapphira were found wanting when they tried to hold back a proportion of the money for themselves.

The leaders all had similar attitudes. Peter pronounced that Christians should use whatever they had received 'in service to one another, as good stewards, dispensing the grace of God in its various forms.'[5] John warned that anyone who spiritualised or intellectualised Jesus's message of love was taking an unsustainable path: 'If he does not love the brother whom he has seen, it cannot be that he loves God whom he has not seen.'[6] Paul emphasised strongly that the greedy would not be among those to inherit the Kingdom of God,[7] that material covetousness is a form of idolatry[8] and that the love of money is the root of all evils.[9] In a letter to the Corinthians he devised the first Christian formula for economic sharing: Christians should give as much as each can spare[10] which can mean more than their resources would seem to allow;[11] giving should be voluntary (and not fixed by rule);[12] and – perhaps most significantly – that the aim of the process was to achieve economic equality (something which

Christian apologists for capitalism have maintained Christianity does not require): 'I do not mean that others should be eased and you burdened, but that as a matter of equality your abundance at the present time should supply their want, so that their abundance may supply your want, that there may be equality.'[13]

Clearly the concept of economic altruism was not easily and universally adopted among the early Church: the epistles are full of passages in which the Church leaders are trying to correct half-formed ideas of what Christianity should be and check any slippage back into old ways: James railed against the rich at times like an Old Testament prophet[14] and Paul expressed his disgust at those rich Christians in Corinth who feasted at the Eucharist meal while their poor fellow believers were hungry.[15] Such people eat and drink judgement upon themselves, he said. But even if the behaviour of the people was not consistent, the teaching of the first leaders was and there was evidence that many of the people responded positively to the lead.[16]

One important precedent is worth particular note. There was within the Church at Jerusalem a minority of Greek-speaking Jews. Chapter 6 of the Acts of the Apostles recounts how they complained that in the daily distribution of food to the needy the Greek widows were overlooked. The apostles called a full meeting of the Church which elected seven men to carry out the distribution in a fair manner. The names of the seven who were elected are all Greek and their functions to some extent overlapped with those of the twelve apostles, for as well as overseeing the distribution of the dole they both preached and baptised. The significance of this was that they turned over the administration of the whole programme to the group which had been discriminated against. Here the Church responded with Christ's revolutionary attitude to status clearly in mind. To empower the group which had been discriminated against was a deliberate attempt to give them the status of full participation in the community.

WEALTH IN THE EARLY CHURCH

In the first centuries of the Church these principles seem to
have been adhered to with surprising fastness. The philosopher Aristides, writing early in the second century says of
the Christian community:

> He that hath, distributeth liberally to him that hath not. If they
> see a stranger, they bring him under their roof, and rejoice over
> him, as it were their own brother . . . And if there is among
> them a man that is poor and needy, and they have not an
> abundance of necessaries, they fast two or three days that they
> may supply the need with their necessary food.[17]

And still in the fourth century the Roman emperor, Julian
the Apostate, who temporarily withdrew the official approval
given to Christianity by his predecessor, Constantine, complained to a fellow pagan that 'the godless Galileans feed not
only their own poor but ours also.'[18]

But Julian was an exception. Christianity was accepted by
his imperial fellows and the change was to alter Christian
views on wealth considerably. Until AD 313 when Constantine
issued the Edict of Milan establishing tolerance for the faith,
Christianity had been a religion of outsiders. Now it became
the religion of the insiders – the religion of those in power.
Constantine entrusted the distribution of the corn dole,
which was the main form of public charitable relief, to the
Christian clergy. He exempted the churches and clergy from
tax. He allocated a proportion of state revenues which previously had gone to pagan temples to Christian charities.[19]

But imperial recognition was to bring with it problems.
Many now joined the new official religion for reasons of
opportunism, and part of the Church's original motivation
was diluted. With wealth and privilege crept in a new theology. Its arrival was facilitated by the distance which was
slowly being placed between Christianity and its Jewish roots.
Contact with the Empire had brought contact with the ideas
of the classical philosophers. Indeed their influence was felt
long before the Roman Empire conferred its official blessing.

Later, Augustine read the Gospels and in particular Paul's epistles, through the prism of his classical philosophy, taking Paul's writings on flesh and spirit as if they were meant to convey Platonic notions about the separation of the body and soul. This was to prove a point of particular significance, for two reasons.

Firstly, the idea that the soul was the centre of a person's true identity while the body was a mere shell opened the way for the spiritualisation of Christ's message. It was a process which ended with the absolute position, quoted from Troeltsch, in the chapter above, that Jesus has nothing to offer but a new transcendent personal relationship with God. Such a position is, as we have seen, deeply unbiblical, but it well suits those who are wealthy and do not want to abjure that way of life. As Christianity became the insider's religion it found more and more adherents for this perspective; for if a Christian is to ignore the worldly sphere and concentrate on God that usually involves, conveniently, acquiescing in the prevailing values of the culture in which he or she lives (and this was seen in medieval Europe just as it was a millennium later in Nazi Germany or in modern South Africa).

Secondly, once the Church began to categorise man in two distinct spheres it was not long before the concept came to be applied to the whole of creation: there was a realm of the spirit, which belonged to God, and a realm of the flesh, which was base and treacherous and of this world, and belonged to Mammon: for all Augustine's fierce rejection of the contemporary Manichaean heresy (that God created the spiritual world and all goodness and the Devil created the physical world and all evil), there remained elements of it in his theology. There were likewise two cities on earth, the Church and the secular world, and the way to enter the domain of the spirit was by rejecting the latter and entering the former. Over the years which followed the Church's position hardened. The Kingdom of God could only be found in the Church: *extra ecclesiam nulla salus est*, wrote Cyprian: outside the Church there is no salvation. It could be entered only through obedience to God and the Church. Care for the poor, in obedience to God, thus came to be seen as a way to win salvation. Obviously it was not practical for the whole of the community to reject the world and enter the Church in the sense in which 'Church' was understood in the early Middle Ages. What resulted was the growth of monasticism. Those who felt called to dedicate their lives completely to Christ entered a clerical or religious order; the rest were allowed to pursue a watered-down version. As Professor Ronald Preston puts it:

> Jesus's ethic was split into two; the precepts (*praecepta evangelica*) which applied to all Christians and the counsels of perfection (*consilia evangelica*) which applied only to a small minority specially called to follow them . . . The effect of this division was neatly to siphon off the radical element in Jesus's ethical teaching into a channel designed for a small minority of believers. It was like an Honours and a Pass course in Christian living.[20]

MONASTERIES AND MONEY

The discipline inside monasteries, in the early days at least, was harsh, as this extract from The Rule of St Benedict shows: 'The vice of private ownership is above all to be cut off from the Monastery by the roots. Let none presume to give or receive anything without the leave of the Abbot, nor to keep anything as their own, either book or writing tablet or pen, or anything whatsoever . . .'[21] But as the new theological world view encouraged the notion that salvation could be bought by good works, the monasteries attracted all manner of gifts and endowments from rich benefactors anxious to incur favour. Over the years the gifts began to stimulate a sense of materialism within the monasteries and decadence and corruption grew there too. Every so often a zealous reformer would break away and found a new order. 'As one phase of it succumbed to ease and affluence, another rose to restore the primitive austerity, and the return to evangelical poverty,'[22] R. H. Tawney wrote. But the cycle was unbroken.

In the world outside the monasteries things developed rather differently. The spiritualisation of religion inevitably led to the growth of the view that it was the inner and not the outer realm which was important. The notion that the Kingdom was something which should grow, through the grace of God, in human society had been lost. The material world was bad and any change in it could only make it worse. The Middle Ages was the time, *par excellence*, when the status quo was seen to be divinely ordained: 'an ordered universe arranged in a fixed system of hierarchies but modified by man's sin and the hope of his redemption'.[23] 'Take but degree away, untune that string, and hark what discord follows,' said Shakespeare's Ulysses in *Troilus and Cressida* in a lengthy defence of the same medieval world picture. But too late; the string was untuned already. It was the rising force of capital which was the culprit.

The medieval cosmic hierarchy was, as Tawney has written, at once repressive and protective. It was repressive because the society which it ordered kept most of the population in a state of feudal servitude. It protected because, in theory, its theology governed every aspect of life, including the economic. Prices were to be set at a 'just' level, which meant the value of the labour added to the value of the raw material. It was designed to prevent exploitation. 'To ensure that no-one gained an advantage over anyone else commercial law prohibited innovation in tools or techniques, underselling below a fixed price, working late by artificial light, employing extra apprentices or wife or under-age children and advertising of wares.'[24] In reality, although the theology and the social architecture were fixed, the economy was dynamic. Nowhere was this more clear than on the issue of the payment of interest on loans.

Usury was the single most consuming issue to the practitioners of medieval ethics. The Old Testament contains a number of passages which forbid lending at interest to a fellow Israelite.[25] The New Testament contains no specific

instruction: the parable of the Talents, in which the lazy
steward is reprimanded for not putting his coin with the
moneylenders to at least get interest on it, seems to endorse
the idea; but Luke 6:35 also says: 'Lend, expecting nothing in
return.' It was on this latter slim foundation that the schoolmen
of the Roman Catholic Church erected a massive edifice of law
on the sin of usury. For centuries it forbade interest on the
grounds that time is a free gift of God so it is sinful to make a
charge for money borrowed over time when it is to be returned
at the end. But over those centuries it struggled, with increasingly tortuous casuistry, to find a theological excuse for a practice which it was clear was basic to the functioning of trade and
commerce. Nowhere was it more clear than in the Papacy
itself, which in the Middle Ages was perhaps the most advanced and powerful money centre in the world: although
schoolmen denounced the practice, Pope Innocent IV blessed
the practitioners in 1248 when he gave the helpful Cahorsine
bankers the title of 'favoured sons of the Roman church';[26]
while in Avignon in 1327 the papacy had no less than forty-
three branches of Italian banking houses in its train.[27] But
because usury was, in theory, forbidden, it became furtive
and interest rates were often as high as 50 per cent since the
transaction was illegal.[28]

The central problem was that the Church's doctrinal view
was based on an unchanging view of society. In Old Testament times and at the period of Christ's ministry most loans
were those made to individuals at a time of crisis; when a
harvest failed a farmer needed to borrow food to survive
until the next season. Loans were almost exclusively for
consumption. By the end of the Middle Ages, merchant
capitalism had developed to such an extent that many loans
were now quite different: they were monies borrowed by
traders bent on expanding their business or opening up new
trade routes, and lent by investors hoping for a profit but
risking a loss. This was borrowing for production not consumption, but the Church was unable to make a distinction.
'The social teaching of the Church had ceased to count,
because the Church itself had ceased to think,' said Tawney.[29]

In doing so the Church lost the opportunity henceforward to pronounce that, although market rates of interest can be quite proper in some circumstances, in others those same rates can be sinful.

PROTESTANTISM AND THE RISE OF INDIVIDUALISM

With the Reformation, Protestantism had the opportunity to create such a distinction. Martin Luther preached two sermons on usury. In the first in 1520 he was more rigorous than the Catholic moral theologians, dispensing with many of the qualifications they had used to soften the law over the years. Indeed he even condemned rent as contrary to Luke 6:35. But by 1524, taken aback by the ferocity of the Peasants' Revolt, he changed his mind and said that interest was lawful and that the rate should be fixed by the state. Later still in 1539 he actually went so far as to pronounce that the rate ought to be fixed at 8 per cent. The lack of consistency in Luther's thought on economic matters prompted Tawney to describe his verdicts as 'the occasional explosions of a capricious volcano'.[30] His later statements were part of his thesis that God had Two Kingdoms and not one. The kingdoms were the Church and the world. This took Augustine's notion a stage further.

> God has ordained two governments: the spiritual, by which the Holy Spirit produces Christians and righteous people under Christ; and the temporal, which restrains the un-Christian and the wicked so that they are obliged to keep still and to maintain an outward peace.[31]

The first kingdom was ruled over by Christ and in it a Christian's behaviour would be ruled over by God's law. The second was the society in which Christians lived as ordinary citizens, and in this they were subject to whoever was in authority. The thesis destroyed the omnicompetence of the

Church in matters spiritual and temporal, which had a purgative effect on the corrupt edifice of medieval Christendom, but it also introduced a dangerous schizophrenia giving authority to a secular world run independently of the rule of the Gospels. Eventually such an approach was to lead to an apparent theological justification for those Christians who chose to collude with the Nazis.

The attitude of the other great Protestant reformer, John Calvin, was more focused. The chief end of man was to glorify God and in the everyday world this meant good disciplined work. Any diversion from this was idolatry, as was conspicuous consumption and luxury. This was what he meant by responsible stewardship. The result was an emphasis on thrift. 'Thrift meant saving. Saving led to accumulation, and then to investment; exactly what the burgeoning merchant capitalism required.'[32] This was what Max Weber meant when he formulated the concept of the Protestant Work Ethic and concluded that there was an 'elective affinity' between the disposition induced by Calvinism and the motivation needed to make the new capitalist system work. Calvin argued that in the Old Testament land and capital were the same thing. In his day money had taken over as the main base form of capital. If it was legitimate in Old Testament times to charge rent, then it was legitimate now to charge interest.

He set certain conditions. Interest must not exceed an official maximum. Loans must be made to the poor without charge. The borrower must reap as much advantage as the lender. Excessive security must not be taken. No man may snatch economic gain for himself at the expense of his neighbour. Calvin hedged his acceptance of interest with a fierce array of disciplines and controls which had the power of law in his own city of Geneva. As the years passed, long after the regulations were long past, the new principle remained intact. Calvin had rejected the idea that the ethics of finance was a matter of absolute dogma and decided that the ethics would vary according to the particular circumstances of each Christian community. He had taken the first step on the road to an autonomous secular money market.

This was an era of unprecedented change. The insinuations of the infant capitalism were making themselves felt throughout the economies of the Western world. A new political philosophy, which had its roots in Machiavelli and Hobbes, and was later refined by Locke and enshrined in the American dream by Thomas Jefferson, was arriving to explain, justify and encourage it. Luther's two separated kingdoms and Calvin's puritanical pragmatism offered theological correlatives. The old bonds which held man firmly in his relationship with society were dissolving. The era of individualism had begun. It is an era which is with us still today.

There can be no doubt of the benefits it brought the Western world. By liberating industry – both intellectual and economic – from the institutional stranglehold of medieval Christendom it opened up a number of avenues which previously had been closed. Independent inquiry began with new vigour in both the sciences and philosophy. Important new notions of tolerance began slowly to enter the religious and political forum as the Age of the Enlightenment ushered in its belief that Reason and not Faith should be the final arbiter of all thought. Technical innovations, long suppressed by the restrictive practices of the medieval guilds, came in a whole range of manufacture. New areas of trade were continually opened by a new breed of merchant capitalists. New commercial relationships and new structures of investment and partnership spread through Europe. The exploitation of the resources of the New World and other colonies accelerated. Everywhere the engine of economic growth was started and the wheels of capitalism began swiftly to turn. The industrial followed the agrarian revolution and a period of unparalleled prosperity began. It was proof indeed that the world economy is not what the economists call a 'zero sum game' – that the global manufacturing and trading system is not closed in such a way that one person can benefit only at the expense of another. Over the past three hundred years in the West new technology and ingenious innovative systems of organisation and finance have provided a vastly improved standard of living for most ordinary people.

But the economic miracle was not without its cost, both to the peoples of the Third World whose native economies were distorted by it, and to the peoples of Europe who were to realise only much later that the engine of capitalism had no brakes.

The new individualism was seen at its clearest in the field of theology where Protestantism placed the direct relationship of each individual with God at the heart of its method. Its outline was clear, too, in the field of political philosophy where a number of thinkers adumbrated the altogether more indirect relationship between that individual and the rest of society. Gone was the medieval world view of a comprehensive if hierarchical inter-relationship of a society in which, though individuals had different roles, they shared a common goal. The philosophers who shared this stance shared a number of assumptions which are helpfully summarised by Professor C. B. Macpherson:[33]

* What makes a man human is freedom from dependence on the wills of others.

* Freedom from dependence on others means freedom from any relations with others except those relations which an individual enters voluntarily with a view to his own interests.

* The individual is essentially the proprietor of his own person and capacities, for which he owes nothing to society.

* Although the individual cannot alienate the whole of his property in his own person, he may alienate his capacity to labour.

* Human society consists of a series of market relations.

* Since freedom from the wills of others is what makes a man human, each individual's freedom can rightly be limited only by such obligations and rules as are necessary to secure the same freedom for others.

* Political society is a human contrivance for the protection of an individual's property in his person and goods, and (therefore) for the maintenance of orderly relations of exchange between individuals.

Even without detailed analysis it is clear that many of these assumptions diverge significantly from the principles outlined in the Old and New Testaments, in which man is seen clearly as bound in a divinely ordained relationship to the rest of the society in which he exists.

Similar individualist premises pervaded the approach of the new breed of political thinkers who brought quasi-scientific techniques to bear in the field of economic relations. Adam Smith, in his classic statement of 'liberal' economics, made vague obeisance in the direction of a universe governed by the wisdom of a divine omnipotence but in essentials his ideas were grounded in an idea of man as an individual and a world which is purely mechanical. He advocated a system of *laissez-faire* in which governments refuse to interfere in the 'free' workings of a market in which each individual is allowed to buy and sell according to the dictates only of his or her own self-interest. This will not lead to vicious chaos, he said, because in some mysterious way the actions of all these individuals will be guided by an 'invisible hand'. This will ensure that so many million individuals, each pulling in their own direction to maximise their self-interest, will somehow lead to a common good which none of them had in mind. Such thinking betrays so many of the characteristics of the Enlightenment with its apotheosis of Reason as the supreme virtue, its sense of the unfailingly positive nature of progress, its idea that the present order is the best possible one, and its rather embarrassed concession that if there is a God then he has wound up the world like a giant clock and is now watching it tick. God was relegated to a place outside the workings of the world.

An institution which possesses no philosophy of its own inevitably accepts the dominant ideology of the culture in which it exists. This is what now happened to the Church. The new individualism drew an individualistic response from Christianity.

The new economic system took a terrible toll. The agricultural revolution dispossessed a whole class of peasant farmers while its industrial counterpart led to a new evil – a degrading alienation of the workforce from the old satisfactions and dignities which physical labour, however arduous, had previously produced. Of course, the physical conditions in which the industrial working class lived and laboured were in themselves horrifying, but the effects of the new system had an influence which was in the long term even more pernicious. The drift from the country to the town began and with it came shifts in values and behaviour. The compacting of the extended community into the isolation of the nuclear family became evident on a large scale. The processes of production, distribution and consumption became separated, reducing many of the natural mechanisms which previously prevented economic systems from becoming completely divorced from social and moral values. It was a tendency noted even by capitalist apologists: 'In virtue of its "impersonal" character, the capitalist economic system cannot be regulated by ethics . . . It is impossible to tell who the "ruler" really is or to confront him with ethical demands,' noted Weber.[34]

Christianity could only respond in kind. A new individualist conscience arose. It was articulated by men like John Wesley who preached private benevolence as a solution to the structural changes which were generating widespread injustice and misery. Wesley was, in many senses, firmly in the tradition of the Old Testament prophets. He had an unswerving sense of the horror of owning riches in the midst of deprivation. But he was in other ways a child of his individualist time. In his sermon on *The Use of Money* in 1744 he baldly articulated the new imperatives for his congregations of small businessmen, artisans and traders. This was the theory: 'It is the bounden duty of all who are engaged in worldly business to observe that first and great rule of Christian wisdom with respect to money: Get all you can.'[35] This was to be done 'by common sense, by using in your business all the understanding which God has given you'. Anyone who gave all his time to his work could have no time for 'silly improfitable diversions', for gluttony or drunkenness, nor for any 'regular, reputable kind of sensuality' or 'elegant epicurism'. Instead the Christian should:

'Cut off all this expense. Despise delicacy and variety and
be content with what plain nature requires.' Money should
not even be given or bequeathed to children but 'having first
gained all you can and secondly, saved all you can, then give
all you can.'

Wesley practised what he preached. When he was a student
at Oxford his income was £30 a year. He spent £28 on his
own needs and gave the rest away. As his income rose he
continued, in a non-inflationary time, to spend £28 on himself
and give the rest away,[36] even though by the end of his life
he was earning £1,400 a year from the sale of his books.[37] 'If
I leave behind me ten pounds,' he once wrote to a friend,
'you and all mankind bear witness against me that I lived
and died a thief and a robber.'[38]

But it is the fate of radicals that their message is heard
only incompletely. Many of Wesley's congregation were
happy enough to obey the first and second of his injunctions
but were less eager to observe the third. The actual legacy
of Calvin was not the strict discipline his pragmatism produced but the pragmatism itself; the social legacy of Wesley
was not his admirable individual dedication but its emphasis
of the force of individualism within the Christian faith. Wesley leaves decisions on social ethics entirely to the individual
conscience of each Christian. As Ronald Preston has pointed
out: 'There is no sense of the corporate structures within
which the getting and saving takes place, or of corporate
responsibility in distributing wealth.'[39]

In essence the nature of our charitable response has not
altered since. Admirable though it was, the vast outpouring
of money from a new generation to the appeals of Bob
Geldof's Band Aid and Live Aid in 1985 was rooted still in
the individualist notion of charitable generosity rather than
a realisation of the need for structural change to usher in
a more just system. Such emotional compassion actually
distracts us from the need to ask questions about the underly-
ing causes of such terrible starvation. This is not to belittle
his effort or the public response, which were both substantial,
but in the end it left the situation no further on. Hence when

five years later in 1989 the unchanged situation necessitated
new appeals for Ethiopia the media began to talk, as if with
exasperation, of donor fatigue: 'We gave them the cash
before: so why should we have to give again?' The question
was rhetorical, for most of the media had no desire to address
the structural problems at a more serious level. Geldof, for
all his skill as a populist, found no way of moving the issue
on from one of charity to one of justice. Just as monastic
doctrines of poverty created in the Middle Ages the very
response which corrupted the monastic impulse, so the Protestant notion of personal responsibility and trusteeship
created a concept of absolute private property which ultimately was to subvert the very idea of stewardship with which
it had begun. As one historian wrote:

> The requirement was that a man should be a good steward of
> his innate talents and external endowments, so that he was to
> work tirelessly and industriously, measuring his stewardship by
> his profits . . . A Christian's profits were a reward for virtue. He
> was required to be charitable to the poor, but outside certain
> categories there was a presumption that the poor were lazy,
> corrupt, even debauched; poverty could be imputed to many of
> them as just retribution. The effect of this doctrine on an emerg-
> ent and ambitious bourgeoisie, who were at the same time
> indoctrinated by a non-interventionist economic doctrine of self-
> sufficiency, was to encourage the creation of a system which
> sanctified profits and transformed labour and the unemployed
> into the talents available for exploitation.[40]

MARX AND CHRISTIAN SOCIALISM

A counterpart to this Protestant position developed in the
Roman Catholic Church, as was revealed in the papal encyclical *Rerum Novarum* in 1891 which, though it was later hailed
as a Magna Carta for a new humane economic and social
order, based its call on an uncritical acceptance of the existing
patterns of property ownerships and capitalist economic
structures. It failed to comprehend that the appalling poverty

and squalor which it condemned were directly linked to those structures and continued to treat them as if they were in some way errors of personal conduct or the workings out of some natural mechanism in whose creation man had had no hand.

All of this is not to say that the parallel biblical tradition in which man is seen primarily as a social being had withered. It was present as a sub-plot throughout and manifested itself in various forms. In the Middle Ages sects like the Waldensians and the Lollards struggled to find again the simplicity of the ancient Church in the face of the institutional decadence of the Papacy. After the Reformation similar Protestant groups such as the Anabaptists, the Evangelical Rationalists and the Anti-Trinitarians[41] traced the Fall of the Church back to its official recognition by Constantine and felt that in the Protestant Reformation Luther, Zwingli and Calvin had fallen prey to the same temptation to affiliate to the mechanism of the State. Many nineteenth-century Christians in the tradition of Wesley saw the need for structural and political change. Evangelicals like John Howard and Lord Shaftesbury played a major part in the reform of prisons, housing, working conditions as well as more specific measures on the treatment of the insane and child labour abuses. In Britain William Wilberforce and in the United States Charles Finney led campaigns which brought about the abolition of slavery. But for all this the dominance of the ideology of individualism was never shaken.

The most serious challenge, when it came, did not issue from a religious source but from the pen of the atheist Karl Marx. Despite the rigorous secularism of his thought Marx's views on society and justice were profoundly influenced by the Jewish tradition of his forefathers. As the Dutch economist Professor Robert Goudzwaard has noted, there are striking parallels between the Jewish and Marxian world-views: 'The labour class within capitalism is like the oppressed people of Israel in Egypt. They all suffer, they are all exploited; but justice, and therefore history, is on their side.' The suffering saviour becomes the labour class. Sin becomes exploitation. Value becomes labour value. The promised land is the golden age of Communism. 'No Pharaoh could stop the people of Israel taking the gold and silver of Egypt with them when they left. Similarly, for Marx, due to the dialectical laws of history, the oppressed class inherits inevitably the treasure of capitalism – its enormous capacity to produce – as soon as capitalism has fulfilled its historical mission.'[42]

Marx, though avowedly anti-religious, provided powerful analytical tools which were taken up by Christians of various persuasions who shared little more than a conviction that a Christian perspective must be a social one. Marx's insights into the nature of capitalism and the revealing historical context into which he placed it provided new impetus, even to those who did not share the solutions he offered or the sense of historical inevitability which he conferred upon communism. In Britain many of Wesley's Methodists became influential within the Labour Movement which tried to restore a more collectivist vision to society. In the United States Walter Rauschenbusch, the pastor to a largely German congregation of Baptists in a poor part of New York City, became the prophet of the emerging social gospel movement with his claim that 'the social gospel is a vital part of the Christian conception of sin and salvation, and that any teaching on the sinful condition of the race and on its redemption from evil which fails to do justice to the social factors and processes in sin and redemption must be incomplete, unreal and misleading.'[43] The new workers' movements then played an important part in nurturing a new sense of corporate responsibility in societies which were becoming increasingly prosperous. Other influences were pressing in the same direction. The threat of epidemic diseases in the new ever-growing cities had already prompted the development of some social thinking; indeed cholera was undoubtedly more effective than Christianity in pressing the argument that there were some forms of social provision, such as that of sewage systems, which could not be left to market forces. The foundations of a Welfare State system began to be laid. But the fragility of the demands which large-scale corporate provision makes on the philosophy of individualism has been all too evident in Britain and the United States in recent years when, under Margaret Thatcher and Ronald Reagan, the political establishment has begun systematically to attack the Welfare State on the general grounds that, in the climate of recession which has followed the oil crises, society can no longer afford it. The ideology of individualism remains dominant.

For more than two hundred years the Church, in its various denominations, has acquiesced in this indulgence of individualism. It has been only in the past three decades that the position has begun to shift significantly. Ecumenism has played a significant role in this. In the Protestant communion the admission of a number of 'younger Churches' from Asia, Africa and Latin America to the Third Assembly of the World Council of Churches in New Delhi in 1961 brought a new dimension to the deliberations of the ecumenical movement. The tendency was furthered in 1966 when the Church and Society Conference in Geneva drew attention to the need for radical 'structural changes' and in 1968 when the Fourth Assembly of the Council 'replaced the traditional emphasis on charitable appeals by an insistence on the question of justice and root causes of injustice'.[44] In the Roman Catholic Church the seeds of the change were sown, as were so many others, with the summoning in 1962 of the remarkable Second Vatican Council which, as if in symbolic gesture of the thoroughness of its revolution, with its first public document ended the Latin mass which had been the norm for fifteen centuries. The powerful institutional mechanisms which for so long had been placed at the disposal of the status quo – in the nineteenth century some popes had even condemned the concept of democracy – were thrown into reverse with an almighty jerk. It was as if the two world wars earlier in the century had finally put paid to the certainties of the Enlightenment and its belief that unending progress could be secured by the exercise of human reason unaided by the moral imperatives which brotherhood in Christ demanded. The Church, too, now began to reassess the truths of religious belief which in the face of the contempt of the rationalistic era had retreated into the cloisters of a privatised and individualised religion. Gradually a new sense of confidence re-emerged which is well expressed in the words of the theologian David Jenkins: 'If worshippers of God do not really believe that he is to be encountered in and through the actualities of daily living and contemporary history, then he is indeed merely a cultic object sustained by a "myth" which works effectively only so long as the myth dominates culture, but which is simply a mere story maintained by "believers" against the realities of the world, once culture changes.'[45]

From this point the Church was once again to see its role in the world instead of outside it. What the Bible had integrated and the Enlightenment had separated the Church now sought to bring back together. A key document was the encyclical *Populorum Progressio* (the Development of Peoples) in 1967 in which Pope Paul VI abandoned the Euro-centric perspective of his predecessors in favour of a global approach, focusing on issues of Third World development. More significantly it addressed for the first time the structural issues which lie beneath global injustice. Its rejection of the economics of individualism for those of a richer and more biblical social appreciation was, despite its moderate tone, described by the Wall Street Journal as 'warmed-over Marxism', indicating, however unsympathetic the comment, a realisation that at last the Church had returned to the analysis which attempted to deal with the structures of society and not just the morality of the individual.

THE ROLE OF LIBERATION THEOLOGY

The following year more than a hundred Catholic bishops from throughout Latin America met in Medellín in Colombia to work out how to apply Vatican II to their continent. The statement they produced was one of prophetic outrage. They denounced 'institutionalised violence', by which they meant the activity of those governments whose policies permanently violated the dignity of their citizens, and referred to the rule of such corrupt élites as a 'situation of sin' thus expanding the traditional notion of sin as a personal act or omission and establishing the idea of sin being inherent in systems which broke the provisions of divine law. They committed the Church to share the condition of the poor out of solidarity – an approach which at their next meeting, at Puebla, they characterised as 'a preferential option for the poor'. At the same time a number of theologians in South America including Gustavo Gutierrez, Leonardo Boff, Juan Luis Segundo, and Jon Sobrino were developing a new approach to their subject and to its implications for the rich and the poor in the debtor societies to which they belonged. It has been given the name of liberation theology because its advocates commonly take the release of the Jews from their slavery in Egypt as a paradigm for God's intention for the liberation of the oppressed poor in the modern world.

Much of it was an unexceptional if timely restatement of the biblical imperatives on wealth and society. The father of the movement, Gutierrez, treats for example the Good Samaritan question of 'who is my neighbour?' in much the same way that Calvin did. Calvin explained that 'neighbour' can mean a stranger and that this could mean approaching the needy with an offer of help which was not directly solicited; Gutierrez expands the same insight: 'So long as I define my neighbour as the person next door, the one I must meet on *my* way, the one who comes to me for help, my world will remain the same . . . if I define my neighbour as the one I must go out to look for, on the highways and the byways, in the factories and slums, on the farms and in the mines – then my world changes.'[46]

But elsewhere its exponents go much further. Using Marx's tools of analysis they point out that the 'universal theology' of the Church is in fact a Western theology which has jumbled universal truths together with European cultural norms. Inevitably so, for no theology can be formed outside the influence of the culture in which it was made. Its ideology is embedded in it as in its very language. Even Jesus Christ, states Segundo, in taking on the human condition also took on the ideological patterns of a particular time and place, and these are reflected in the New Testament.[47] 'Let him who is without ideology cast the first stone.'[48] Therefore, they maintained, it is incumbent upon the people of Latin America to develop their own way of 'doing theology'.

What was, and still is, revolutionary about this was their insistence that it was not enough to transfer the realm of theology from Europe to Latin America. That was only part of the process. Theology had to be transferred to the poor themselves, to the people who Christ said repeatedly were the ones to whom he brought the Good News. Theology had to cease to be something handed down from intellectuals at the top; it had to spring from the realities of ordinary life. In this they were deeply influenced by the work of the Brazilian teacher and educational theorist Paulo Freire who had spent decades working with the poor in the north-east of that country. Freire's thesis was simple,[49] and it accorded well with the new notions about the dignity of each man and woman: The poor are not stupid, or simple or primitive. They are perfectly intelligent but what they lack is education and even literacy. They are aware of the injustices of life around them but lack a wider perspective which enables them to see the relationship between the different component parts. Give them that and you give them the power they need to change things. Freire called the process *conscientisation*, which Charles Elliott translates more elegantly as the providing of critical awareness. 'It was critical in that it looked for explanations and subjected those explanations to ethical critique: was it right that (my landlord should) put up my rent when he already had great wealth and my child is malnourished? It was awareness because it invited the participants to a deeper knowledge of their whole environment.'[50]

Theology 'rises only at sundown' said Gutierrez.[51] The first book is life; the second book is the Bible, he said. 'Theology is an understanding of the faith'[52] and that understanding must be found by the poor themselves. If expert guidance is needed to provide support from Scripture or the tradition of the Church it should come from theologians who live and work amongst the poor, as Christ did.

Given the nature of the lives of the poor such reflection will have political, social and economic components which may well be revolutionary for existing economic and social institutions. The only way to bring about change may be through joining the Marxists in their class war. 'Attempts to bring about changes within the existing order have proven futile . . . Only a radical break from the status quo, that is, a profound transformation of the private property system, access to power of the exploited classes, and a social revolution that would break this dependence would allow for the change to a new society.'[53] Conscientisation might provoke confrontation if those in power are not prepared to accommodate the growing awareness of the poor as it increases. But Christ did not shy away from confrontation. Indeed he often created situations which provoked it and was prepared to pay the cost of doing so.

The reaction of Rome to all this was instinctively hostile, and even some progressive Western theologians have found fault with the liberation methodology, particularly where it pursues the Marxist path most steadfastly. None of the opposition came as a surprise to the liberation theologians; to them it represents European ideology on the defensive. But when Cardinal Joseph Ratzinger, head of the Vatican's protectorate of doctrinal orthodoxy, the Congregation for the Doctrine of the Faith, issued Rome's reprimand to certain strands within liberation theology, he conceded that Catholic social teaching did emphasise the need for structural transformation to achieve social justice. And when Pope John Paul II came to write his encyclical on development *Sollicitudo Rei Socialis*, he borrowed extensively from the thinking of the liberation theologians in denouncing the superpowers of East and West between whose strong desires for power and profit the Third World is presently trapped. Unashamedly he used their terminology and reiterated the notion that 'structures of sin' were the moral obstacle to the development of the peoples of the Third World who are at present so mired in debt.

THE ETHICS OF ECONOMICS

What then are these structures? Must we look to capitalism? to the market? to the phenomenon of interest? to the philosophy of individualism? to the notion of economic growth? Or are these merely morally neutral mechanisms caught up in structures of sin from which they might be liberated? How do these facts of modern economic life sit with the principles which the Old Testament established and Christ refined and with which the Church has so unsuccessfully struggled? To decide we must ask what are the basic organisational issues which confront any modern economy.

Economists state the problem in these terms:[54] In any society there are only ever a certain amount of resources available for human consumption. Some of these are natural – the land and its minerals, the climate and the crops it will produce. Others are inherited – techniques, technologies and tools. A third group are the abilities inherent in women and men which they use in conjunction with the other resources to create wealth. But such is the nature of people's aspirations that these resources, however plentiful, are always limited by comparison with the number of uses to which they could be put.

The first problem of economics therefore is: how is society to choose from the possible uses? In terms of simple household economics this boils down to questions such as whether a family should allocate a certain part of its budget to buying a car or a foreign holiday. On a social scale the corresponding questions might be how to decide what to spend on health compared to education. Traditionally economists, in an attempt to refine the essence of their discipline and separate it from moral or social considerations, have tended to maintain that there is only one strictly economic criterion to be applied in this: the avoidance of waste so that, whatever the desired outcome, it may be achieved with a minimum use of resources and nothing be squandered in poor organisation. Economists, with politicians in their trail, are therefore habitually preoccupied with the question of efficiency. But there is a value judgement already implicit in this, as we shall see when we come to consider the question of efficiency. For the time being let us extend the family options to a new car, a foreign holiday, or a donation to Oxfam, and expand the social ones to spending on health, education or paying a fairer amount to Third World countries for produce on which the market places an unfairly low price.

The second key problem confronting economists is: how should the relative levels of consumption of these resources be decided? Should everyone in the family receive the same? Do some need more than others? Can some put an unequally large share to a better use, for the common good? For example, should the father be allowed to consume most because he earns most? Is it justifiable for him to spend more on clothes than the rest of the family because that improves his social standing and the family's income is dependent upon his status in the world of work? In social terms, should some groups receive more than others? Are there international parallels? The problem of relative levels of consumption is usually referred to by economists as a question of the distribution of income.

In essence, then, first wealth is created by man adding his skill and labour to natural and inherited resources. In the process decisions are made about how the wealth will be used and how it will be distributed. On a social level there are two classic systems for managing this process. Politically they are called capitalism and socialism. Economically they are called a market and a planned economy. We will deal with the issue of socialism and planning shortly, but must first give our attention to an examination of the basis of the 'free' market capitalist system which has dominated the growth of a global economy in which First World prosperity and Third World squalor have become possible, and ask whether the problem is inherent within the system or merely

a coincidental by-product. The debate on acceptable solutions to the debt crisis will clearly be affected by this.
But to establish a firm context for the discussion we may
summarise biblical teaching on the economic order by quoting the economist Donald Hay, a fellow of Jesus College,
Oxford:

> The basic concept is of man as a steward or trustee of God's
> creation. It is an abundant creation over which man is given
> dominion, and from which he may derive the means of material
> life and existence. He exercises his dominion as a worker, using
> the resources efficiently and carefully. In that work there is
> division of labour, each one contributing the particular skills
> with which he is endowed. Within the process of production
> some have larger responsibilities than others. Some may have
> stewardship responsibility over much and others over little. But
> the proceeds of production are for mankind as a whole, to
> meet material needs. Consequently there is a minimum level of
> provision to which each man is entitled. There is also a maximum
> level, particularly in those situations where others have too little.
> There is no necessary connection between a large stewardship
> responsibility and a large consumption. Ideally the two should
> be quite distinct. We note that the Fall has had serious conse-
> quences in each of these areas . . . Fallen man desires more and
> more, and has no wish to share the fruits of production. As a
> consequence a fully just human society is beyond our grasp.
> There is no Christian hope of Utopia. But that should not allow
> us, as Christians, to acquiesce in evil and injustice. Insofar as
> human society, at its international level, falls short of God's
> creation ordinance, we shall strive to get justice done.[55]

THE CHRISTIAN CASE FOR CAPITALISM

There are four main elements to a market economy. First,
that in it individuals are free to operate independently,
motivated by their own self-interest. In doing so they sometimes co-operate with others to form economic units, such
as businesses, but more often they regard other members of
society as rivals. Second, that this rivalry is used as the

mechanism for allocating scarce resources. They go to those individuals who bid most for them. In this way those things which are most wanted in society (the things people will pay the most for) are made and the things which are least wanted are not made. Prices are used to measure the levels of such demand; the pricing system conveys information about demand and simultaneously provides an incentive for producers to adjust to that demand. Competition is of the essence in this. Those individuals who are most successful in providing what is wanted by their fellows will make profits. The inefficient will make losses. Thus what is most wanted in society is automatically provided and the more satisfied society is, the more will be the profits of those who best satisfy it. 'The result of economic competition, conducted within the framework of fair and settled law, will be that everyone will end up in the job that he is best fitted to do and that the economic needs of the community will be precisely identified and swiftly and efficiently satisfied.'[56] Third, that each individual has the right to dispose of what he owns to his best advantage. Implicit in this is the notion that the market accepts the existing levels of wealth each individual has, however justly or unjustly it was arrived at, and works with that. Those who own little therefore have little economic power in the market-place. Things are accepted as they are. There is no mechanism within the market for social justice and no moral imperative that it should be achieved, for these are factors in which the market sees no economic value. Fourth, that the smooth running of this system will be best ensured if nothing is allowed to distort its natural system of balance and if governments do not interfere with it – this is the sense in which the instruction is to *laissez-faire*.[57]

The philosophical justification for the free market was laid by Adam Smith in the second half of the eighteenth century and the similarity between the principles above and those of the philosophy of individualism[58] are plain enough. His conclusion in *The Wealth of Nations* in 1776 was that: 'Every individual is continually exerting himself to find the most advantageous employment for whatever capital he can command. It is his own advantage, indeed, and not that of society, which he has in view. But the study of his own advantage naturally, or rather necessarily, leads him to prefer that employment which is most advantageous to the society.'[59] This was his idea of the 'invisible hand' with its hints of a divine ordering.

But the connection with religion, tenuous at the outset, was soon dispensed with. By early this century apologists such as Professor Frederick von Hayek had boiled down the justification for the market to the need of man, once tribalism had been left behind, for an abstract system which with justice and neutrality regulated individual economic actions. This cannot be done through politics and planning, he argues,[60] because men's sense of politics is too theoretical; often they do not understand the actual implications of an abstract political idea which may sound admirable in principle. Their sense of economics, however, is much more reliable and accurate because it deals with matters which are more immediately before them. Good intentions are no guarantee of good results: a man may set out to create good and do harm; a man may set out to make money for himself and do good for society, as Lord Harris, director of the right-wing think-tank, the Institute of Economic Affairs, puts it.[61] The role of government is only to preserve the framework or order in which this impersonal mechanism can freely operate. Under this system, he acknowledges, the inefficient and the obsolete will suffer. It may be necessary to prop them up, in the interest of social justice, but it should be understood that to do so will lessen the efficiency of the system in its overall aim of creating the maximum possible amount of wealth. This approach received its purest expression in practical politics in the monetarist policies advocated by one of Hayek's disciples, the Chicago economist Milton Friedman, whose rhetoric was adopted by the Reagan and Thatcher administrations in the late 1970s and early 1980s. The theory was that inflation could not be reduced by overtly political wage or price controls but only by controlling the supply of money within society.[62] But the notion proved too pure for the realm of practical politics – the problem was finding a comprehensive measurable concept of money – and was abandoned after a few years in favour of more covert policies aimed at maintaining the same economic hegemony.

The essence of the case for capitalism, however, remains unchanged. As recently as 1980 a contemporary Conservative political theorist, T. E. Utley, wrote: 'Capitalism relies largely for its defence on one of the oldest maxims of state-craft – that the way to social peace and prosperity is by harnessing the natural instincts and affections of men to useful social objects.'[63] There can be no doubt that in many respects the capitalist system is extraordinarily effective, as Donald Hay concedes in his succinct *A Christian Critique of Capitalism*: the price system 'is able to co-ordinate the supply and demand of thousands of commodities and services arising from thousands of firms and millions of households in an economy. And it does it with remarkable precision, and with the minimum of information passing between consumer and firms. That is an amazing achievement. However we must not allow our admiration to obscure the deficiencies which lie beneath it.'[64]

Over the years capitalism has come under increasing attack from Christian social theorists. Their case has been that capitalism is a flawed system from a Christian standpoint for six main reasons:

* It presupposes that the entire sphere of economic behaviour is regulated by an impersonal mechanism which is beyond the authority of morals.

* Co-operation and not competition is the natural basis of a Christian approach.

* Its reliance on self-interest elevates the moral vice of selfish greed into a supposed social virtue and its stress on striving for wealth and accumulation of goods and capital fosters material-ism.

* Profit is a dubious concept; production should be geared

to match the needs of society and not to make profits for a comparatively few individuals.

* It ignores the fact that many individuals – such as the one billion people who live in absolute poverty in the Third World – lack the basic resources even to enter the 'free' market: 'the questions of power, domination and injustice are simply ignored.'[65]

* The market offers no ideal of distributive justice, like that of the Jubilee, to redress imbalances in society, and thus thwarts God's clear intention that men and women should live in a state of community with others.

Christian advocates of capitalism with an even 'freer' market respond by continuing to maintain that the market is a neutral mechanism. They argue that any apparent failings are not due to the market but to the corrupt moral and social framework within which it operates. 'How can the fat man in a restaurant blame his own obesity on the waiter?' asks Ralph Harris.[66] T. E. Utley goes further and disclaims the notion that all economic activity is based entirely on self-interest.[67] Motives are more varied: they include family affection, the wish to support good causes and the 'sheer exhilaration in the production of wealth'. Each of these motives is obviously capable of corruption but all, kept within proper bounds, tend towards the common good. He rejects the claim of an inherent tendency towards materialism: 'No-one is obliged to get rich in a capitalist society; no-one is forced to extort the highest price for his labour or forbidden to embrace apostolic poverty,' he adds somewhat disingenuously, side-stepping the real charge that the system has a general tendency to promote materialist behaviour by virtue of its general ethos. However, he argues, 'the world is largely wicked and much though not all economic activity in a capitalist society will spring from motives which are not wholly pure.' Nigel Lawson, later the British Chancellor of the Exchequer, went so far in 1980 as to claim that the true Christian defence of capitalism lay in the concept of Original Sin: in a fallen world economic systems had to take account of man's sinful nature[68] and that therefore capitalism – the politics of imperfection – was preferable to socialism which was based on the idea of the perfectibility of man in society which took no account of the reality of sin or of man's need of God's grace and forgiveness. And another Thatcherite economist, Brian Griffiths, has recently written: 'An attempt to legislate the ideals of the Kingdom of God into practice immediately comes up against the fact that the real world is made up of fallen human beings and is not a community of saints. To cope with this reality we need stronger social and economic disciplines than those that would be appropriate for a community radically and inwardly transformed by the presence of the Holy Spirit.'[69]

The way to help the poor, these apologists argue, is not to redistribute the wealth of the rich. It is to encourage the rich to make more so that there is more to be shared and the poor in getting their slice of the cake will thus automatically get more. Thus one US Christian economist, Peter Hill, writes: 'For instance, in the United States from 1790–1980 the bottom 20 per cent of the income distribution (that is, those ordinarily considered poor) raised their standard of living by 750 per cent. This was because of substantial economic growth rather than because of income distribution programmes . . . This is not to say that greater equality has always resulted but we must be careful not to ignore very substantial benefits that have accrued to the poor from this process . . . Indeed only the envious would penalise the rich (by preventing healthy growth, for example) if doing so would hurt the poor.'[70]

Professor Griffiths' defence is altogether more subtle. He too believes that it is not the market which governs behaviour but rather it is determined by the morality of the individuals who work within it. To argue otherwise would imply that people can live in two worlds: 'a world of the market place in which the profit motive reduces all behaviour to the low pursuit of self-interest, and the world of the family, local community and voluntary service in which caring attitudes and a spirit of service prevail. Such a division would be

impossible to justify either logically or empirically.'[71] Interestingly, however, many clergymen maintain they are able
to detect just such a dichotomy within the attitudes of many
of their parishioners. They discern a kind of schizophrenia
in attitudes to business during the week and attitudes to the
community at weekends. David Sheppard, the Bishop of
Liverpool, has written:

> Businessmen say to me, 'Bishop, you won't agree with this . . .'
> and proceed to describe their everyday business practice. They
> assume that the ideals a bishop might believe in would not work
> in their secular world. So they do not even attempt to apply
> them. They tell me they wish it were possible to practise the
> faith and the ideals they half believe in; but the pressures of
> reality, of market forces and industrial relations seem to make
> it impossible.[72]

Griffiths goes on to deny that conflict is implicit in competition. 'In thinking about competition it is important to define
it in as neutral a way as possible, by saying that it is essentially
a way of resolving conflicts of interest and judgement that
result from trying to make the best use of scarce resources
. . . Competition is to be distinguished sharply from low
rivalry and criminal behaviour.' Moreover profits are not
necessarily corrupting; profits are what a charity must make
to undertake its good works. Self-interest is not the same as
selfishness: the command to love our neighbour *as ourselves*
shows that self-interest 'can be characteristic of the highest
as well as the lowest forms of human behaviour. Self-interest
is not a consequence of the fall, although its distortion,
selfishness, is. The Christian should accept that self-interest
as well as selfishness are hallmarks of the world in which we
live. There is no point therefore in designing an economic
system, based on an unrealistic view of man and expecting
governments to manipulate that system for the common
good.' This is a significant distinction, for indeed there must
be in a Christian economic world view a right and a responsibility for each individual to work and to achieve the self-
fulfilment which comes from realising the potential of the

talents with which each is endowed. This is why the structural unemployment so characteristic of late capitalism must be counted a structure of sin. But then Griffiths goes on to argue that inequality is an expression of basic differences which exist in creation:

> Within this framework, there is no problem in defending the morality of economic inequalities that result from differences in skills, energy, ambition, and the freedom to work, innovate, invest and trade. Whilst we cannot justify every kind of inequality thrown up by a market economy, within a fallen world inequality of income is an essential aspect of Christian justice . . . a certain degree of inequality is necessary in society if human dignity and freedom are to be preserved and if basic standards of justice are to be achieved (it is important that people receive a just reward for their work).

Another Conservative theorist, Geoffrey Dawson, amplifies: 'Inequality is not the same thing as injustice. If some people make better use than others of their skills, and do so for the general well-being, it would be unjust if everyone were to receive the same rewards. Just deserts are not the same as equal shares. The Parable of the Talents is, of course, an illustration of this point . . . There can be no moral objection to rewarding the conspicuously able and energetic with a proportionately larger share of the wealth they have helped to create . . . the lack of such an incentive will certainly inhibit some workers and entrepreneurs from wealth-creation and so further depress the living standards of the worst-off.'[73] Griffiths concludes:

> The basic argument for a market economy is that, for all its imperfections, it is a system that pays respect to human dignity because it allows human freedom. It permits individuals the freedom to buy and sell, save and invest, choose their preferred form of employment and develop the skills they feel appropriate. It allows minorities the same rights too. Socialism does not: it pays scant respect to human dignity because it denies human freedom and forever restricts economic choices.

Revealingly, those who maintain that capitalism is not un-Christian turn again and again to an attack on socialism as a means of defending the moral basis of the market economy. It is as if capitalism were defined in opposition to Marxist socialism, although historically the opposite is the case. Professor Griffiths analyses the economic systems of the Old Testament and concludes that, while the Mosaic law contains strong elements of social injustice, it also evidently approves of private property rights and therefore cannot be said to endorse socialism.[74] According to Utley: 'Roughly speaking, there is a choice to be made between the kind of community which is ruled primarily by fear and the kind which is ruled primarily by offering inducements to the performance of socially useful actions. It is at least arguable that greed is less objectionable than fear.'[75]

For a Christian the choice cannot come down to that. But can socialism offer a system compatible with the Christian vision, and can central planning offer a solution to the Third World debt crisis?

THE CHRISTIAN CASE FOR SOCIALISM

In terms of shaping the social policy of a country the system known as the command economy has some distinct advantages. Under it scarce resources are allocated by state planning. The application of this approach in industrially backward countries has produced significant advances in certain spheres. The system enables rapid industrialisation, financed, as it were, by the forced savings of a population which is unable to spend freely on consumer goods. In practice such a system only works because the authorities who enforce the saving cannot be removed at the polls. This also enables the authorities to develop a broader view of the 'general interest' than the vision of material progress in which capitalism is in fact entrapped. It enables greater long-term planning than the market does: markets tend to discount the future at around 10 per cent per annum which means they look no further ahead than a decade – and today we in the West are coming to realise the long-term environmental consequences of that. Some price stability can be achieved, inflation can be contained, unemployment can be eliminated (or at least disguised) and cyclical movements within the economy can be controlled. It can promote greater equality of incomes, abolish the disparities of wealth caused by inheritance, and give priority to fulfilling basic needs for all rather than creating luxury goods for the few.[76]

In theory many of the ideals embraced by socialism correspond closely to those Christian ideals which we have found explicit and implicit within the Scriptures. Moreover as Donald Hay has shown[77] they stand in contradistinction to the ideals of individualism and 'free' market capitalism. Christian and socialist principles both see in the state a mechanism for redressing social injustice, whereas free-marketeers see it in more negative terms as the body which establishes the very minimum framework within which the market can operate. They see property, and in particular the type of property which is the basis for wealth creation, as held on behalf of a higher authority, whereas the marketeers see it as the absolute property of an individual who may consume or dispose of it without reference to the needs of anyone else. They define economic efficiency in terms of the social results it achieves, whereas marketeers see it simply in terms of the efficient satisfaction of the desires of individuals regardless of the social or environmental impact of that short-term efficiency. They emphasise that a full concept of freedom includes a realisation of the needs of others to have the freedom to eat, be housed, work and live free from the predations of right-wing death squads, whereas marketeers see freedom more in terms of rights than responsibilities and emphasise an individual's right to be free from more state coercion than is necessary to safeguard the minimum rights of others.[78] They see work as a purposeful activity which is 'a good to be enjoyed by every person according to his ability and divorced from the need to earn a living'[79] and regard it as a social activity intimately connected to notions of stewardship, whereas the definition for a 'liberal' economist is that work is a necessary activity to obtain purchasing power over goods and services. They see consumption as unrelated to production, with the biblical insistence that a man's life does not consist in the abundance of his possessions paralleled by Marx's criticisms of commodity fetishism, whereas the economic libertarian sees it as his right to consume everything he owns or produces.

But do the theories of central planning hold good? The fact that at the beginning of the 1990s the policy makers of Eastern Europe are, after decades of implementing this system of command economy, now shifting towards the introduction of market forces, must give pause for thought. It seems they are now acknowledging that, as Hayek argued, the degree of far-sightedness, flexibility and sheer breadth of intellectual grasp needed to co-ordinate such massive economies are beyond the capacities of existing systems of bureaucracy. It seems easy for the system to get out of line with what the majority of people actually want; because prices are fixed by the government and the price mechanism is no longer a barometer of whether public needs are being met, a much cruder yardstick emerges – the food queue.[80] The Soviet Union has as bad a record on pollution as does much of the West: Lake Baikal is dead, the region around Chernobyl is devastated and the Volga River is heavily polluted. Unemployment is largely eliminated by employing individuals to make goods for which there is no effective demand.

There is an argument for saying that creating unproductive employment is a more Christian option than affronting the dignity of working people by telling them that society has no use for their labour, as the structural unemployment of modern capitalism does (before then supporting them from the public purse through the welfare state). But where the Christian vision is unable to compromise with the implications of a full-blown command economy is on the issue of personal freedom. Some limitations to individual freedom are inevitable in a planned economy and it may be that some of them – such as a reduction in the freedom to choose, to produce, to own or to live where one wants to live – take on a significance which is more symbolic than realistic to those of us in the West who accept with equanimity that such restrictions are placed upon us by the diktats of the market rather than by those of government: the Ritz, after all, is open to all, but how many have the wherewithal to exercise that liberty? But certain other socialist restrictions to freedom have, from a Christian perspective, to be considered entirely unacceptable.

Any command system must concentrate all political and economic power in the same hands. In practice this means the emergence of a large class of bureaucrats controlled by a powerful élite of policy makers who have evolved their own entirely independent criteria for decision-making. This fosters the strength of the institution before the welfare of those they are allegedly there to serve.

The means have become the end. And where this economic power is exercised by those who also hold the reins of political power, Lord Acton's dictum that power corrupts and absolute power corrupts absolutely has more recently been augmented by the insights of Reinhold Niebuhr who has argued persuasively[81] that all human institutions have an inbuilt tendency to act with an ever-increasing immorality.

The lessons of history bear out such judgements. In reality a command economy seems inevitably to be synonymous with a totalitarianism which most Western socialists find unacceptable when it is clothed in the mantle of European fascism or South American military dictatorship. In the words of the Polish philosopher Kolakowski: 'Every leftist movement in a Western country misleads the population so long as it is not prepared to declare openly that the Soviet communism is one of the biggest centres of social oppression which have ever existed in world history.'[82]

Some theorists maintain that the links are coincidental and claim that a total command economy is possible without totalitarian government[83] but others have argued forcefully that there is an inherent tendency to totalitarianism in the command economy. As Marcuse has said: 'The end recedes, the means become everything; and the sum total of the means is the "movement" itself . . . Within this syndrome the oppressive elements are predominant.'[84] Walter Wink deals with the same dynamic in more theological terms: the governing values in any body bent on exercising power over others will be what St Paul refers to as the 'principalities and powers' and these, Wink says, are demons which reside in the psychic or spiritual power emanated by the organisation and the individuals in it.[85] Charles Elliott comments: 'The New Testament therefore reminds us that what is *ultimately* significant is less the power of an institution or system in an outward sense – what it can do to others – but more its inner wells of motivation and consciousness which make it use its power in a given (egocentric) way.'[86]

The means which are the real governing values are, as we have seen, determined less and less by the ideology and increasingly by the desire of the bureaucracy and the élite to strengthen its own position. The ideology is now used to give automatic legitimacy to whatever means the élite sanctions. This is exactly the kind of ideological ossification in which the Pharisees had entrapped themselves and which Jesus time and again attacked. In the end ideology is always the enemy of truth and of the kingdom of right relationships which Jesus sought to establish.

BETWEEN TWO STOOLS: THE THIRD WORLD AND DEPENDENCY THEORY

Even so it is of no use for the Christian defenders of capitalism to return constantly to attacking the full-blown socialist command economy as a way of justifying continued support for the 'free' market. Nor can they assume that because that type of socialism is ultimately unacceptable it will therefore be acceptable to allow the market to operate even more freely – which is what proponents of the system usually do advocate. 'Beware of false prophets, who come to you in sheep's clothing but inwardly are ravenous wolves. You will know them by their fruits.'[87] If the lessons of history speak against totalitarian socialism they also speak strongly against the workings of modern capitalism. There are today some one billion people living in degrading poverty throughout a world dominated by the free market system. Capitalism may have increased the prosperity of many, indeed of most of the people in the Western world, but it has yet to answer adequately the arguments of economists like André Gunder Frank who maintain that capitalism has not eradicated poverty in the West but merely exported it.[88] The questions asked within Europe and North America by the Christian socialists and the social gospel movement at the beginning of this century are now being asked in a more fundamental form by Christians in the Third World:

> They see capitalism in the legacy of the Western world on their own countries, in industries and in multinational corporations. They see firms employing people under exploitative conditions, producing goods for a small minority in their own country and for export, in order to gain foreign exchange to purchase luxury goods for the same small minority, or at best to purchase food for survival from the Western food mountains. They see the dichotomy of the labour practices of the multinational between their factories in the West and their factories in the Third World. They begin to wonder whether the success of capitalism in the West in combining welfare with self-interest has not been bought at the price of poverty in the Third World.[89]

There are for a Christian some serious deficiencies within the 'free' market philosophy and these must be made good if a solution to the problem of Third World debt and the iniquities in which it is rooted is to be found within the framework of capitalism. Undoubtedly free marketeers will protest that capitalism and socialism are pole opposites and cannot be mixed. This is the argument which has been used with increasing success in the corridors of power against the strengthening of the welfare state. But even if we accept that capitalism can never work at its maximum efficiency in

creating wealth within the context of a welfare state, that is
not a sufficient argument against such provision for social
justice. Maximum efficiency cannot be a Christian virtue if
it is achieved at the expense of the full humanity of a billion
people. To borrow some of the redistributive mechanisms
from the socialist armoury and apply them within, around
and underneath the market may lack ideological purity but
it does respond to the biblical precedents that a balance must
be struck between the creation of wealth and a just society.
There are seven main areas where accommodations must be
made by the 'free' market philosophy if it is to prove acceptable to a truly Christian vision.

MARKET FLAWS: THE IMBALANCE OF SELF-INTEREST

Firstly, for all the protestations of the apologists there is a
need to acknowledge the unhealthy extent of the reliance of
the market system on self-interest as a motivating force.
Admittedly this is not inevitably a corrupting influence, but
it has a well-observed tendency to be so. It creates temptation
and what the Catholic Church used to call an occasion of
sin. Undoubtedly it produces wealth but it also produces a
reluctance to see a fair distribution of it. There is no evidence,
as Professor Griffiths acknowledges, that an overall rise in
the gross national product of a country produces a fair
distribution of the increase in wealth. The theory of trickledown – that scraps from the rich man's table fall to the poor
and that, therefore, the more the rich man has, the better
the poor man will be – is now soundly discredited.[90] Often,
indeed, the poor are found to be actually worse off afterwards.[91] The idea that capitalism is 'the politics of imperfection' which merely takes realistic account of the fact of
original sin is ultimately unacceptable; it is not unlike saying
that the way to combat crime is to place an extra tax on
criminals: the Christian's mission is to combat sin and not to
acquiesce in it. Moreover it reduces men and women to

mere economic units for whom everything except material
prosperity becomes a mere peripheral issue. It turns into an
absolute a single aspect of human life, which is a dangerous
ideological distortion.

This is not to argue against self-interest entirely. A measure
of it is plainly necessary to a Christian view of human dignity.
In any human situation there are choices to be made. Many
of these are morally neutral, such as whether people would
rather eat cabbages or lettuces. The market offers a good
mechanism for organising such choices and there is no reason
why exercising self-interest over cabbages and lettuce is at all
undesirable. As William Temple pronounced: 'A statesman
who supposes that a mass of citizens can be governed without
appealing to their self-interest is living in a dreamland and
is a public menace. The art of Government in fact is the art
of so ordering public life that self-interest prompts what
justice demands.'[92] But when the choice is 'a fifth generation
computer game for me or bread for you' all such neutrality
disappears for the Christian. This is when self-interest begins
to corrupt: then it needs not to be harnessed but curbed.
Patently there is a need for distributive social mechanisms to
intervene long before this point is reached. As Professor
Preston puts it: 'Human beings are capable of universalism
and altruism as well as a concern for self-interest. The latter
is usually the stronger . . . so the former needs more encour-
agement. It is degrading to their humanity for men and
women to be involved in institutions which foster only the
stronger motive and deny the weaker. They need to live
in over-all structures which call upon both, but foster the
weaker.'[93]

Such a recognition would have several practical consequences. It would necessitate the construction of a range of
social and political mechanisms to compensate for various
aspects of the market. In certain cases the adjustment mechanisms would actually compensate for those aspects of modern capitalism which constitute perversions of the pure
concept of a truly 'free' market: stricter monopoly regulations
are needed to combat those situations where a few big firms

control prices in such a way that they no longer reflect the cost of the goods they make and instead maintain prices at artificially high levels by using cartel policies or by the manipulations of marketing and demand created by advertising. This is most evidently the case with the giant multinational corporations which, as we implied in Chapter Three, need to be subjected to restraints for other reasons – in particular because their relationship with Third World countries is often directly exploitative. More controls are needed over firms which transmit certain 'external costs' of their production process to society in general – factories whose processes pollute rivers, airlines whose flights impose noise on suburban residents, firms whose cars and lorries inflict congestion and pollution for which they do not pay. The 'free' market system has found no way of creating markets 'for those "bads" (as opposed to "goods") where firms could buy the right to cause a nuisance from those affected by it, thus effecting some compensation for their discomfort.'[94]

Other mechanisms must be created to foster those 'public goods' for which a market cannot be engendered because once the service is created everyone benefits whether they have paid or not. Advocates of the market are generally in favour of these for services such as defence or the police force but a Christian case can be made for extending the range of national and international 'public goods' where they can act as mechanisms of social adjustment.

MARKET FLAWS: THE MYOPIA OF PROFIT

Another area in which the market – motivated by the search for fairly immediate profit – is notoriously unreliable, is in its short-sighted perspective on investment. On empirical evidence Robert Goudzwaard concludes: 'Markets usually have no longer time-horizon than about five years: long run predictions do not have any influence on present price movements.'[95] But many social activities, particularly in the realm of justice, have much longer-term horizons. There is also a need to foster mechanisms to counter the impersonal nature of the market which conveys information about the desires, resources and abilities of its participants in an impersonal way which makes it easy for participants to lose sight of human values.

In terms of relations between the First and Third Worlds such mechanisms might, in the short term, have to take the form initially of redistribution in the form of a carefully selected package of aid. But the medium-term aim should be to ensure that the poor are no longer denied access to the resources which they need to create wealth for themselves and to participate with dignity in shaping the world in which they live. In the process any form of economic, social, class, sexual, racial or other discrimination is to be countered. The chief plank in this will, of course, have to be the dismantling of existing protectionist structures in world trade and a move towards more just trading relations. There can be no doubt that this will involve sacrificial action on the part of the First World.

MARKET FLAWS: THE DOMINANCE OF INDIVIDUALISM

There is also a need to shift away from the primacy of the philosophy of individualism and restore the biblical balance between it and a sense of corporate responsibility. Individualism is not an unalloyed bad. It brings a directness to our relationship with God and nurtures a sense of tolerance of dissent and even eccentricity. But as the Archbishop of York, Dr John Habgood has pointed out in an interesting essay on individualism,[96] there are a number of distinct and irreconcilable species of the outlook. In some cases it provides an inner gyro-compass which keeps the individual turned towards a moral goal. But in others 'the emptiness of a life not centred on some transcendent reality outside itself, or not fed from some other resource, can induce desperate efforts of both self-assertion and self-expression.' The inner goal, if it is defined at all, is then likely to be personal success. Often then conspicuous consumption becomes the mark of self-fulfilment and individualism becomes egotism. 'Self-assertive individualists without moral roots seek a brittle kind of success with no thought for the casualties.'

MARKET FLAWS: THE MYTH OF EFFICIENCY

There is, furthermore, a need to revise our definition of efficiency. A system cannot be deemed efficient if it merely improves the lot of a particular section of global society. A particularly ghastly example of such partial efficiency was quoted by Amartya Sen who made detailed studies of the Great Bengal Famine in 1943 and those in Ethiopia in 1973 and 1974.[97] In these famines there was plenty of food available in the countries concerned but the poor had suffered a sudden dramatic reduction in their buying power. Because they could not afford to buy, the market shipped the food away to other areas where purchasers did have the necessary cash. The markets worked efficiently: the resources were automatically transferred to an area where demand was backed by the ability to pay. As a result three million people died in Bengal alone. Clearly the efficiency of the market here is working in direct opposition to the creation ordinance that God has provided food and clothing as a right to all people.

    Efficiency therefore cannot be the primary concern for the Christian. There can, indeed, be evils in efficiency. War, theft, murder, and colonialism can all be efficient for the ruthless, but for the rest of us there is a moral code in which such efficiency is set. Slavery was efficient for those who were not subjugated but in the end the true Christian option was not for us to become kinder slave masters but rather to abolish slavery. Manufacturing processes which endanger the health of those who produce them – using asbestos or carcinogenic paints – may be cheaper than safe alternatives but civilised societies have quite rightly legislated against them. As Tawney said: 'To convert efficiency from an instrument to a primary object is to destroy efficiency itself.'[98]

Other aspects of 'efficiency' need also to be questioned. Even today, when ecological awareness is increasing, some manufacturing processes are counted as 'efficient' even though they have hidden costs which are borne by the rest of society – and its yet unborn children – in the form of environmental pollution. But to do this, particularly in situations where the pollution is irremediable, clearly violates the biblical notion of stewardship implicit in the revelation that the land was given to men and women 'to till and keep it'. Many of the more extreme ecologists have suggested that the only way to save the planet from man's predations is to adopt a 'no-growth' policy. This seems hard to justify in Christian terms, especially when the alleviation of dehumanising poverty throughout the world is dependent upon providing the people of the Third World with the resources to create their own wealth. So long as men and women's stewardship of creation is ecologically responsible there is no reason why economic growth should not be regarded as wholly desirable. It is part of the process by which men and women share in God's continuing creation – forging new things out of the natural resources of the earth using the skills and abilities with which they have been blessed.

MARKET FLAWS: THE FALLACIES OF GROWTH

Certainly there is a critical need to examine what we mean by 'growth'. Any expansion of production at a rate greater than the natural resources of the planet can sustain and replenish is in fact not true growth at all. The US economist Herbert Daly noted this as long ago as 1973 when he pointed out the fallacy of including increasing expenditure on military hardware in the national accounts as if it added to gross national product instead of subtracting from it:

We count the real costs as benefits – this is hyper-growthmania. Since the net benefit of growth can never be negative in this Alice-in-Wonderland accounting system, the rule becomes 'grow forever' or at least until it kills you – and then count your funeral expenses as further growth. This is terminal hyper-growthmania. Is the water-table falling? Dig deeper wells, build bigger pumps, and up goes GNP! Mines depleted? Build more expensive refineries to process lower grade ores, and up goes GNP! Soil depleted? Produce more fertiliser, etc. . . As we press against the carrying capacity of our physical environment, these 'extra effort' and 'defensive' expenditures (which are really costs masquerading as benefits) will loom larger and larger. As more and more of the finite physical world is converted into wealth less and less is left over as non-wealth – i.e., the non-wealth physical world becomes scarce, and in becoming scarce it gets a price and thereby becomes wealth. This creates the illusion of becoming better off, when in actuality we are becoming worse off.[99]

The difficulty now comes in discovering what level of growth is ecologically responsible and in discerning what types of growth are in fact disguised extra costs. Good stewardship must mean handing on to future generations a world which is as good as, if not better than, the one we inherited ourselves.

MARKET FLAWS: STRUCTURAL UNEMPLOYMENT AND THE RIGHT TO WORK

There is also a need to work for an understanding in society that the right and duty to work is fundamental and inalienable. It is part of the creation provision in Genesis *before* the fall where it is set in a context where work is fulfilling. To rob men and women of the resources they need to work effectively is to rob them of part of their creation gift. Equally for a Christian the fruits of men and women's labour are not automatically theirs to consume. Graham Dawson pointed out earlier that in the parable of the Talents the most productive steward is rewarded most greatly. But his reward is not increased consumption, it is that he is given even greater stewardship. Jesus also breaks what we perceive as the natural link between effort and 'just deserts' in the parable of the Labourers in the Vineyard who each receive what they need and not some pro-rata amount for the hours they worked. This will have radical implications when we come to consider the wealth gap between the world's rich and poor.

MARKET FLAWS: THE ILLUSION OF NEUTRALITY

Most fundamentally there is a need for an acknowledgement that the market can only operate within a proper moral framework, to which its operations must be subordinated. Capitalism is at present in danger of sawing through the bough on which it sits. The smooth operation of the market depends on a shared moral order. All involved must value truth, honesty and trust. All must repudiate deception, collusion, bribery, fraud, theft and breach of promise. All must acknowledge the sanctity of contract. All must have respect for the law and feel able to rely on the probity of judges, officials and legislators. The market assumes a complex web of custom, taboo and moral bonds which were established in a previous era and are now held in place by the less vital forces of inertia and the law which is now more often seen as the rules of a game than a vehicle for moral truths.

The crucial problem is this: the capitalist qualities of thrift and accumulation foster a materialism and consumerism which the Bible – from Deuteronomy and the Prophets to Christ himself and the epistles of Paul – warned are spiritual traps and delusions. The economist Professor Fred Hirsch has highlighted one such chimera: he argues in *The Social Limits to Growth*[100] that the thirst which consumerism creates can never be satisfied for, even if the whole world were to attain material affluence, there would still be competition for what he calls 'positional goods' which by definition are limited in number: there can only be one President of the

United States, so many luxury apartments overlooking Central Park or the River Thames, so many tickets for a Royal Opera House performance, or a limited number of people able to enjoy the tranquillity of a rural beauty spot before the peace is destroyed by the very number of people in search of it. The result is not unlike the situation at a rock concert where everybody stands to get a better view and ends up seeing the same as they would if everyone had remained seated – everyone makes an extra effort and no one benefits.

Materialism is a powerful dissolver of morality. Though those Christians who defend capitalism maintain that the religion and the market are complementary systems which require each other, the fact is that materialism has sprung into independent life like a Frankenstein monster which is now stalking across the landscape regardless of the private morality of its creators. Without a firm social, legal and religious network to counter this tendency, and a firm awareness of the insidious nature of the process which is under way, a steady deterioration seems inevitable. As this moral and social web dissolves, and as Christianity becomes more and more a minority sect within a secular culture, we may expect to see capitalism become more rapacious and ruthless.

A THEOLOGY OF THIRD WORLD DEBT?

At the end of this long survey of the history of Christian attitudes to wealth and debt, is it, then, possible to distil out some principles which can usefully be applied to the great financial problems and inequities which confront our world today?

The Old Testament depicts men and women as individuals called into a relationship with God, but it also insists that the context in which that happens is a social one. A balance is to be struck between the two. It endorses the notion of private ownership and depicts men and women as having a right to the basic resources they need in order to work. But it sees that men and women hold goods in trust and are therefore obliged to use them in a way which reflects the divine purpose. It sets out mechanisms for maintaining social harmony. These include legal mechanisms to ensure that the basic creation provisions of adequate food and clothing are available to all and that the environment be treated with respect so that it is exploited in a way which the land can sustain and continue to provide those basics. It requires that loans should be made and handled in a way which respects the dignity of the participant. It also insists on mechanisms to redistribute wealth so that the poor do not become marginalised, alienated and disenfranchised from the rest of society: most specific to this, and most far-reaching, was the principle of forgiveness known as Jubilee. In the New Testament Jesus confirms that vision. He insists that personal transformation is an indispensable part of the arrival of God's kingdom on earth. He extends the 'option for the poor' beyond those who are materially poor to all the outcasts of orthodox society. He maintains that the good things of creation are to be enjoyed and celebrated but he emphasises that the joy of sharing is a vital part of that celebration. He views need as the first criterion of justice and regards blindness to injustice as a sin as grievous as malice or oppression. He demonstrates that unjust social structures, such as those of low status, should be challenged – for the ability of each and every individual to participate and to have control of their lives is essential to the idea that women and men are created in the image of God. He shows that judgements must be made and confrontations sought, even if the cost to us is heavy.

The Church has found it difficult to live with the demanding breadth of this vision. The history of men and women's struggle to do so has met with a number of serious setbacks and diversions but it has also revealed some useful applications to human society. The early Church did more than offer justice to the disadvantaged; it placed them in positions of power to ensure justice. Paul insisted that the notion of equality should play an important part in giving and saw the state as an institution under God which must be used to divine purpose. Calvin perceived that as society changes it is important to seek for the spirit rather than the letter of biblical injunction and inaugurated within the capitalist framework the notion of concessional interest rates for the poor. Capitalism has arisen as an efficient steward, in some ways, but an unfair one; to restore a biblical sense of balance society must create a legislative and moral framework to control market imbalances. Liberation theology has shown that it is the voice of the poor themselves, and not that of the élite, which must shape our vision of the way forward.

What are to be the implications of all this for Third World debt? It would be utopian to suggest that what is required is a literal application of the Jubilee rule: that all debts should be wiped away at a stroke of the clock. In its pure form it was a mechanism appropriate to an agrarian peasant society. The society of today is enormously different from that. But the principles behind it should still be with us and mechanisms of social fairness and forgiveness appropriate to our day should be applied. It is up to us now to discern what those are. Unless capitalism is prepared to make these concessions, unless the members of society – Christian and non-Christian – are prepared to make some attempts to repair the moral fabric, then all its claims to biblical legitimacy will be void. Increasingly the peoples of the Third World might be expected to turn to other solutions.

Chapter Eight

REMISSION OR DEFAULT?

'You take what isn't yours, but you are doomed! How long will you go on getting rich by forcing your debtors to pay up? But before you know it, you that have conquered others will be in debt yourselves and be forced to pay interest! Enemies will come and make you tremble. They will plunder you! You have plundered the people of many nations, but now those who have survived will plunder you because of the murders you have committed and because of your violence against the people of the world.'

Habakkuk 2:6–8 GNB

On all sides the baked white desert stretched endlessly into the distance. Within me I could feel a suppressed sense of panic at the utter desolation of the place. We were more than three days' drive from Khartoum. All around, the landscape was utterly featureless except for the occasional euphorbia bush. Its leaves were poisonous, I had been told, as if to underline the relentless hostility of the landscape. There were no roads. Our Sudanese driver had no map. It seemed that he was driving by the sun. One of my companions from time to time furtively checked his direction with a compass. It seemed hopelessly haphazard.

'Surely we are lost,' we said to him, one word at a time as

if we were speaking to an uncomprehending child, though it was in fact he who could speak a little of our language and we none of his.

'No, no,' he said, and completed his sentence with a short burst of Arabic. He drove on, gripping the wheel with a constant effort as the land-rover bumped and bucked across the unyielding terrain. And sure enough about an hour later we arrived at Tendelti. I wondered that the place could have had a name at all, for there seemed to be little there to distinguish it from the surrounding desert, little anyone would have felt necessary to dignify with a name. In fact it was what, well into the fringes of the Sahara desert, constituted a major landmark. Beyond the primitive refugee camp which had been set up there was a dried up wadi which, on those rare occasions when it rained, turned for a few hours into one of the mightiest rivers on the edge of the Sahara. It flowed from nowhere to nowhere, appearing suddenly and then running into the insatiable sands or evaporating in the desiccating air almost as quickly as it arrived. It also marked the boundary between Sudan and Chad. The ten thousand people in the camp were mainly refugees from that neighbouring country which was troubled by civil war. Of all those registered at Tendelti only two hundred were men. They were old or crippled. All the able-bodied had either died in the fighting or had left their women here at the border while they continued on eastward towards the Sudanese capital where they hoped to find work.

Life in Tendelti was unimaginably hard by Western standards. The water was nauseously turbid and foul-smelling. The food was insubstantial and unappetising. The straw hovels they lived in were little more than raffia mats propped up by sticks, no protection against the torrential rain storms which just at that time were falling every other day. But the women of Tendelti were finding ways to live with the four thousand children under the age of seven.

Women in any case do most of the work in Africa. Almost 80 per cent of the continent's food is produced by women, it is estimated. The men, unlike their counterparts in other parts of the Third World, restrict themselves to a little cash cropping and a lot of sitting around talking politics beneath the broad branches of the baobab trees. It is the women who are responsible for the food crops – which means the hoeing, the planting, and the weeding. As well as being responsible for the children they are also in charge of the livestock. They gather the firewood, grind the corn, prepare the food and fetch the water, which alone can take up several hours of the day. In Tendelti they had also taken over the organisational and administrative work which normally would have been the prerogative of the men. Fourteen of them had been elected by the camp's seven tribes to run the centre and its feeding programme with foreign aid which trickled in unreliably from Port Sudan more than a thousand miles away.

'We have found that they are making a much better job of it than do the men,' said Mhboba Ab-Rahel Ali, a local woman who had once been a teacher but who was then employed by Oxfam to supervise work at the camp. 'Other camps are run by local sheikhs, all men, of course, and traditional leaders, and yet we have found they do not run as smoothly as this camp. It is not just that the women manage the children better in the feeding centre. They are more willing to work at problems than the men.'

That day in the camp little boys could be seen with their baby siblings strapped to their backs. In normal times this job would have been done by their big sisters and mothers but now the women were busy with men's work. Older girls were baking bricks. Mothers were building more permanent homes with walls of mud bricks and strong thatches. Grandmothers were preparing thatches of twigs from the scrubby desert bushes for the new roofs. The elected women were talking to foreign water engineers about where the wells should be drilled.

One of the recent changes at Tendelti had been a decision to end the futile attempt to distribute to everybody a share of what little food arrived. The women had devised a new system to concentrate most on those children who were most in need. Everyone else would live off *mokheit* and the other scant famine foods to which the desert people turned at times of desperation. Slowly the condition of the children, which Oxfam nurses had described as 'appalling' when the camp was first established, was beginning to improve. 'We have organised a special sitting for children who will not eat on their own so that we can make sure that they do take some food,' said Aleem Hassan Mamadan, who had been elected by more than two thousand members of the Asangor tribe, one of the hardest-hit groups of these cross-border peoples. Her husband and four of her children had died in the famine. She and four other children survived. She was finding time to look after them as well as take part in the organisation of the camp. Other women were equally impressive. Fatuma Mohammed, although aged only twenty-five, was the chosen leader of a group of a thousand Arap tribeswomen who had trekked *en masse* across the desert from Chad to Tendelti seven months before; in addition to her own two children she had adopted a third, a child whose mother had died in the drought and whose father had been killed in the war. Halima Mohammed Hassam, though only aged twenty-two, was the leader of 1,200 Marareet tribespeople and had similarly adopted two children of a murdered family.

'It is not difficult to manage without men,' said Matka Mohammed, a handsome woman who led the 1,300 Zagawe tribeswomen in the camp. Her cheeks bore the ritual scars of a warrior family – when there were Zagawe men around the camp they startled Sudanese aid workers from the capital by threatening them with long swords when the workers suggested that the Zagawe should queue for food. Now the food was distributed with a careful eye to the most needy and a methodical fairness alien to local male leaders who would commonly wheel and deal with the food aid in their trust in the small communities throughout the famine-affected region.

'We needed men to help cultivate, but the women already did most of the work and can easily take over the men's share. We needed men to dig wells, but at present there is no water in the ground. We needed men to ride horses, but now all the horses have died in the drought.'

Was there anything they could not do without men? At this point my interpreter, who was also Sudanese but a man, stopped translating and began, instead, to answer indignantly himself. Matka Mohammed looked on with eyes twinkling as he turned to me and blustered. Then she confronted him and insisted that he put the question, laughed and said: 'We are not happy without men. There is one thing they are good for . . .' she said, and broke off with a deep mischievous laugh.

There were many terrible and miserable sights to see in Africa in those years. But occasionally there was an experience like Tendelti which cracked the stereotypes and forced a new humility on any foreign observer from the developed world. There in the desert, when deep in my stomach I knew we were hopelessly lost, our driver brought us unerringly to our destination. There amid the starvation were tens of thousands of people surviving, as their mothers and fathers had done for generations, off a meagre diet of desert fruits and withered roots which the Western nutrition experts said could not sustain life. There where normal life seemed to have shrivelled in the heat were a people taking a new control of their lives with new initiative, new senses of priority and even a continuing sense of humour.

Tendelti was the first book. In it were incarnate the truths which we have seen are spelled out in that second book, the Bible. Here groups of neighbours had come together to act as a society. What little resources they shared had been allocated with justice and, it had been decided, with a disproportionate preference to those who were most in need. The sharing was not out of the surplus of the controlling élite, but came out of their sacrifice. Those who were normally marginalised by their status, the women, had been enabled to participate in the social process and in doing so had discovered a sense of control which brought them dignity despite their material deprivation. Out of it they were prepared to confront those who challenged them. It had also brought new insights on the ordering of social relations; the structures had been changed. It would be romantic to stretch the parallels any further. So destitute were these people that it was clear that they were not in possession of the resources to provide their basic means on food, clothing and adequate shelter. They certainly were denied any share in the pro-ductive resources which the creation ordinances allow is the basis for sharing in stewardship of the planet's resources: there were seeds, tools, and water pumping equipment in the regional capital – but only for those who had the cash to enter the 'free' market of which Sudanese mercantilism offers such a raw exemplar. The empowerment of the marginalised group, the women, had come about only because the men were gone, not because there had been some transformation of social relations resulting from personal or spiritual change within individuals in the group.

But it is, nevertheless, an interesting indication that a number of the crucial changes which a Christian vision of development requires are not tied directly to material im-provements in the standard of living of those it seeks to help.

This is not how the Church has always viewed the problem. Before we seek to bring a Christian analysis to the specific problem of debt it is necessary to consider how the Church tackled the wider issue of Third World development. For there have been mistakes made on development which must be avoided in dealing with the debt problem.

There have been four distinct stages in Church thinking on help to those in need and it will be useful to look briefly at them because although they have developed one after the other there are still groups of vocal opinion-makers who espouse each one. Each one has a distinct attitude to the problems of development and debt in the Third World. None of them is to be denigrated in itself, although we should be clear that some are unlikely to produce the kind of change which is so necessary within the relationship between the First and Third Worlds. Interestingly each has a parallel in the secular field of development work and, indeed, it can be argued that much of the difficulty here arises from the fact that in each case the Church has adopted a secular model and simply dressed it up in religious vestments. It is important that we do not get sucked into the same trap in seeking a Christian solution to the issue of Third World debt.

FOUR RESPONSES TO NEED: RELIEF, DEVELOPMENT, JUSTICE, OR EMPOWERMENT

The first we are now well familiar with. Rooted in the philosophy of individualism it maintains that charitable generosity is the correct response to Third World misery. It does not concern itself with what makes the North rich and keeps the South poor but says simply that the response of rich Christians to the sight of poverty should be simple and direct: to give to relieve those immediate needs. The response of the Church to this in the years after the Second World War was to set up a variety of bodies to encourage and administer this charitable response. Such an approach has been abandoned in institutional terms – relief agencies have turned into development bodies – but the attitude does persist subconsciously among many members of the public and, with deliberate calculation, among right-wing ideologists who see it as the only response compatible with arguing that 'free' market capitalism can be legitimated by Christianity.

In the second stage it becomes clear that relief is not enough and that action is needed to attack the root problems which cause the acute need to surface in crises from time to time. Its solution was summed up in the Chinese proverb: Give a man a fish and he will have food for today; teach him to fish and he will have food for the rest of his life. Philosophically and theologically its base did not differ significantly from the first stage. In institutional terms we saw the international community pursuing a variety of attempts to modernise the Third World so that the industry and technology which had produced such wealth for the West could do the same for those countries which were now considered to be 'developing'.

This was the era of huge dams, wide highways and a host of other projects for which the Third World had, conveniently, spent its aid grants and loans on buying Western technology, but which later came to be seen as grandiose and inappropriate. It was the era of trickledown: the best way to eradicate poverty was to stimulate the higher reaches of the economy, develop industry and raise the gross national product. Development was seen as synonymous with productivity: this too was a view with its roots in the Enlightenment notion that progress was linear and that moral and material progress went hand in hand. It assumed that all traditional societies were alike and that progress was only possible if they could be purged of their 'primitive' attitudes. Large amounts of aid were given; much of it was spent on high-tech projects which soon broke down for lack of high-cost maintenance once the aid money was spent or for lack of commitment to an alien technology once the expatriate aid workers had returned home.

It is now evident that the concept of modernisation had a number of undesirable by-products. It promoted the drift from the countryside to the towns and the growth of great sinks of aimless poverty in the huge shanty towns which have sprung up on the edge of major cities populated by those in the hope of getting one of the few jobs which industrialisation has brought to their country. The capital-intensive high-technology production it encouraged has not only created large debts, it has also helped to destroy many smaller local companies which had provided employment, and removed many of the traditional jobs in agriculture. Its promotion of multinational corporations has had many adverse effects including loss of control, manipulation of local tastes, exploitative wage rates (if they rise the company simply moves to another Third World country where they are cheaper) and pollution. Indeed pollution is a by-product of modernisation in many other spheres. This disrespect for the environment extends to any groups which it deems primitive. Estimates are that as many as 200 million hunter-gatherer tribal peoples have their way of life threatened still by the advocates of unfettered modernisation. When they occupy land which the modernisers want, as in the Amazon rainforest, their very lives are threatened too.

The response of the Church to the philosophy of modernisation was essentially to tag along with its approach on a smaller scale. It set up official bodies to administer this development activity; they specialised, as did the secular non-governmental agencies, in much smaller projects but their aim, in all essentials, was to foster the same world view. The projects were to improve the material conditions for a specific community of people in a local area. But the Church gave little thought to the question of whether it was promoting Christianity or Western materialism, which prompted one astute African bishop to ask: 'Is that what you think of the Kingdom of God – that it is a kind of universal Marks and Spencers?'[1]

The third stage involves making a journey from the perspective of charity to that of justice. Those who have made this journey are liable to get rather cross with those who have remained at the first stages. It comes with the realisation that the poor do not exist in poverty simply because of the size of the problem; rather they are kept in poverty by the very structures of international trade and finance, the structures of sin. It had a number of secular correlatives. As we have seen, Raul Prebish, who played a prominent role in the foundation of the UN 'justice' organisation UNCTAD, explained how it was inbuilt into the relationship of the First and Third Worlds that the rich nations increasingly would want fewer of the others' basic products, while the poor nations would increasingly want more of the high technology of the West: such a structural imbalance makes the eradication of poverty impossible. A second hypothesis goes even further: the Dependency Theory argues that the fruits of capitalism can never arrive in the Third World. Capitalism was nurtured in its early stages in Europe and America at a time when global economic conditions were entirely different from those which now confront the Third World. Through the insidious fingers of the multinational corporations and a variety of other mechanisms the wealthy West maintains its prosperity precisely by keeping the majority of the world's population in poverty.

The response to this has been a call for justice. It is based on one of two premises. The first is retributive: the wealth of the First World is based to a significant extent on the exploitation of the Third and justice demands that we now make retribution. The second is based on an appeal to natural law: it is irrelevant whether or not the West is culpable: it has a surfeit where others have a gross deficiency: common decency, or the belief that all men and women are brothers and sisters in Christ, requires that those who are in need are treated with justice and that the balance is redressed.

The response of some sections of the international community, including many of the Third World governing élites, has been to call for what the United Nations dubbed a New International Economic Order. It called for new fair trade agreements in an attempt to redistribute global wealth but it concentrated on relations between countries and largely ignored relations within nations. Many of the detailed measures it advocated were sound[2] but its overall philosophy was still to rely on a form of trickledown, albeit speeded up by new, fairer international relations. It continued many of the modernisation assumptions that the Third World needed more technology, more consumer goods and more trade with the West. It was designed, many felt,[3] to promote the desire of Third World élites to adopt Western ways of life rather than to foster a true development among their peoples. 'Can there be a new international economic order without a new international social order?' asked Dom Helder Camara.[4] The practical response of the Church in the West to this third stage was a perplexed one: it continued to maintain its development agencies, devoted to the old-style projects, but added new kinds concerned with issues like land reform or the establishment of alternative local structures, such as co-operatives. The Church agencies also increased their education programmes in their home countries.

Charles Elliott, a former director of the British Council of

Churches' development agency Christian Aid, maintains that the Church agencies in the developed world have created a structural trap for themselves which he calls 'the project dance'. In the past two decades their income from the general public and, in some countries like the United States, from the government, had become substantial and their staff began to grow. 'They needed those bureaucracies if they were to identify enough neatly packaged projects to spend their growing budgets. By the mid-1970s, however, bureaucracies were becoming adept at producing such projects – and knew they had to in order to survive. A kind of symbiotic relationship emerged between the metropolitan development agencies (which needed to spend money) and the recipient organisations (which had to play the game by the rules of the metropolitan agencies).'[5] The relationship was like a parody of that between the rich and poor world.

Many others in the Church agencies felt that Elliott's view was somewhat overstated but, what was clear was that the Western Churches, which were anxious to scrutinise most carefully every practical detail of their attempt to relieve material poverty, were failing to submit the structures they were creating to the same degree of theological reflection. Tom Sine, an evangelical theologian, has recently suggested a number of questions which should also be asked about each project by church agencies.[6] Are we unconsciously trying to help the poor climb aboard the escalator of Western material progress? Is the better future we are trying to help people attain essentially economic? Does it reflect Western values of materialism, consumerism and individualism? Do our projects show concern for the spiritual and cultural dimensions of life? Do they help build better relationships between people? Do we make any attempt to see how the values of the Kingdom of God are active in a culture before we begin projects there which might actually have an adverse effect on this? Does each project arise out of the needs and desires of the people or out of an agency blueprint? Do we treat nature as nothing but a passive, malleable resource or do we act as if we are holding it in stewardship for future generations? In our areas of practical strength are we all practising atheists?

It was from the Third World, according to Chris Sugden of the Oxford Centre for Mission Studies, that the challenge to all this came. This is where the fourth stage begins. Many of the better educated Church workers in Africa, Asia and Latin America came to the West to complete their education and then went home to work in the agencies established there by European and American Church fund-raisers. Gradually they came to realise that, for all the rhetoric about helping the Third World to self-reliance, the agenda for these agencies was set in the rich countries. Often decisions were made there on inadequate information or out of some inbuilt prejudice. At worst, the advice of the Third World leaders was ignored; at best they were forced to live from hand to mouth on budgets which were not allocated for much more than a year in advance:

> They felt themselves demeaned and ignored. This opened the eyes of the middle class leaders to the reality of the situation of the poor. It was a turning point. They realised that reform was not a question of trying to pull the levers of the existing machine your way: they won't go, they've not been built that way. Psychologically they were in the same position as the poor.[7]

Back at head office the agency chiefs justified their stance with the defence that they could not simply hand over cash to the Third World agencies without monitoring that it was spent sensibly. They had a responsibility to the public who had donated the money. In the First World the argument sounded reasonable enough. In the Third World it was seen as another case of 'he who pays the piper calls the tune.' It was of the ethos of capitalism rather than of Christianity.

The peoples of the Third World have developed a variety of approaches to these problems. Many now even regard the word 'development' with suspicion. 'Liberation not Development' has been the cry in Latin America. In Asia there have been calls for 'Identity' or 'Transformation' rather than development. What these calls have in common is the two major insights of liberation theology: that any response must demonstrate a preferential option for the poor and that the nature of that response must be shaped by the poor themselves. This in itself would require something entirely different from trickledown either in its economic or theological forms. It would also give a new perspective on arguments about means and ends which seem inevitably to boil down to the fact that it is the very poor who are penalised once sacrifices are demanded of society, global or national. Any system which creates an ideology out of the means it pursues, however laudable the ideological end, must be rejected, for that way lies the brutality of Stalinism or present-day Ethiopian Marxism in which the present is sacrificed on the altar of the future. Inhuman treatment of the population by governments intent on building better structures for future populations can never be an acceptable option for, as the Christian historian Herbert Butterfield observed: 'Each generation is . . . an end in itself, a world of people existing in their own right . . . Every generation is equidistant from eternity.'[8]

In this fourth stage of 'development' the role of Christians in the First World must be to enable the people of the Third World to assume control of their own lives. The jargon word for this is 'empowerment'. It sees the relationship between the poor and the rich as, quintessentially, one of power, much as it is between women and men, and between blacks and whites. The response at the third stage, the Justice stage, was: 'We'll give you justice'; it had overtones still of paternalism. The response now has to be: 'We will help you in your struggle to achieve justice.' For the First World this will mean talking less and listening more. This will be hard, for many of the things the Third World will say will be unpalatable, though that is all the more reason that they should be heard. The First World may even find it shocking, as did an affluent parish in the west of London when it invited a Third World speaker to address parishioners on the subject of Development and the Environment. They may have been expecting a talk on technical measures to repair environmental degradation in Africa. Instead the speaker Bernard Guri, the co-ordinator of agriculture and development for the Catholic Church in Ghana who had been in Europe for a year doing research, seemed to speak on behalf of all Third World peoples:

When I first went to a supermarket in Europe they gave me two plastic carrier bags to carry home my groceries. I folded them carefully and put them under my bed to take the next time I went. But when I did they gave me two more. I took the first two bags again, the next time. They gave me two more. It was only then that I realised I was supposed to throw them away. But I couldn't bear to . . . By the time I came to go home at the end of the year I had a whole pile of bags under my bed to take with me.

This is the way you live . . . a throw-away life. In the Third World we use something until it is destroyed. We use old oil cans to carry water; when they get a hole – we patch it. You create waste. You make rubbish and pollute the environment. You are rich: your rivers are black. We are poor; in ours there is clear water.

One day I went to a rubbish tip here in England; I saw all kinds of things which at home I could have fixed and used to furnish my house. Many of them were not even broken. They were just out of fashion. You have created adverts to tempt yourselves to buy things you don't need. Then you throw away good things to make room for them. You give farmers subsidies to grow crops; then you destroy mountains of them because you cannot get a good price for them, while in Africa we cannot get enough to eat. You talk about the environment. You talk about the ozone layer and the greenhouse effect. You talk after you have had your fill of chocolate biscuits.

My village is in the north of Ghana. You had better redraw your maps because they say the land around my village is savannah. But it is desert. Every year the desert creeps forward. There are many reasons. But one important one is that my people cut down the trees. This allows the soil to erode and so the desert creeps. There are fewer trees, so they do not give off the moisture which helps precipitate rain. So the desert grows.

We in the Third World are destroying our environment. We cut the wood to make fuel to cook. We cut the wood to sell to the cities to make our living. In fifteen years' time there will be no trees left in Ghana. It will all be a desert. All this helps towards the greenhouse effect which will melt the ice-caps and flood cities like London. We are helping to destroy the global environment.

But wouldn't you cut down a tree to cook your next meal if there was no other option?

The environment is a luxury; only those who have enough food already have the time to worry about it. You eat the chocolate biscuits – you people who have never seen a cocoa tree. We pick the cocoa beans – we people who have never tasted chocolate biscuits. You worry about the environment. We cut down trees.

I tell you: there is only one way to solve the threat to the environment. Poverty must be eliminated. How? You must have less. We must have more. You must not give of your surplus. You must sacrifice to give. You must not give out of pity or guilt. You must give out of love. We need your help. But we want to be treated like fellow children of God, not animals on whom you dump food. If you will listen, I will tell you how to do it . . .[9]

How, then, do the various solutions which have been offered to the problem of international debt measure up to the criteria we have now established that there should be a bias towards the poor who should be enabled by it to take control of their own lives? What are the harsh truths on debt which we need to hear from the peoples of the Third World?

TOP DOWN SOLUTIONS: 1985, THE BAKER PLAN

The first major attempt to take a systematic international approach to the debt problem was made by James Baker, the Secretary to the US Treasury under Ronald Reagan. By 1985 it was clear that a crisis was once again imminent. Lending by the banks to Latin America had fallen to a mere third of what it had been in the 1979–81 period. The danger was that the debtors were soon not going to be able to borrow enough even to pay the interest on their old debts. With their income from trade falling because of the effect of the world recession on commodity prices there was nowhere else they could get the cash to pay. At the 1985 annual meeting of the IMF in Seoul he outlined what came to be known as the Baker Plan. Its aim was to encourage the commercial banks to begin again to make new loans to debtor nations. The logic behind the banks' approach, particularly that of those banks who were not dangerously over-committed to Third World loans, was simple: why throw good money after bad? Baker's logic was that if lending did not continue at a certain minimum level the debtors would not even have the ready cash to pay interest on what they already owed and the whole international banking system would collapse. The Baker Plan had three main requirements. Over three years:

* the banks would lend another $20 billion dollars to the fifteen largest debtors, who in return would pursue standard IMF monetarist adjustment policies.

* the World Bank, and other multilateral finance bodies, would increase their lending by 50 per cent to $9 billion.

* $2.7 billion of IMF money would be used to provide new borrowing to the poorest countries, mainly in Africa.

But there was to be no global remedy which would apply to every country. They would be taken on a 'case by case' basis.

The plan foundered for two reasons. The debtor nations were not keen to submit to the even stricter adjustment conditions which were implied, especially as the total amount on offer – around $9.3 billion a year for three years – was tiny by comparison with the debts they had. But more significantly, some of the banks simply would not come up with the cash.

But the Baker Plan was important because it set several policy precedents. It was the first acknowledgement by the US Government that finding a solution to the crisis could not be left entirely to the market and the private sector banks, as they had previously staunchly maintained. (This was a useful development for, as we have seen, in the Christian vision the state is an institution under God and has a duty to act positively. Our review of the build-up to the debt crisis has made it quite clear that action by states is essential if a solution to the debt problem is to be found.) But by insisting that assistance would only be given to those who adhered to IMF strategies Baker also set another, more disturbing, precedent – he reinforced and legitimised the kind of policies which, as we have seen, place the greatest burden on the poor. Clearly from a Christian perspective this is entirely unacceptable. Economic adjustment often is necessary, particularly where the governing Third World élites have followed inappropriate policies. But, as Unicef pointed out, there can be more than one type of adjustment and what is needed is adjustment which discriminates in favour of the very poor instead of placing on their shoulders the heaviest burden.

From a political point of view, however, the plan was a success. It took some time for it to emerge that the strategy was not going to work, and the case by case approach forestalled any threat of collective action by the debtors. The threat that Third World nations might form some kind of debtors' cartel and refuse to pay, or place a ceiling on their repayments, was the great nightmare of both bankers and politicians throughout the First World in the early 1980s. Under cover of the plan the banks continued their strategic withdrawal by building up investments elsewhere and refusing to renew loans in Latin America. At the end of 1986 they had provided just a quarter of the amount they were giving in 1985.[10] To tread water the debtor nations were forced to raise the amounts they owed in short-term trade credits which are designed not for long-term borrowing but to provide instant cash flow to clinch trade deals. They did this to the point where, for the poorest, they now constitute in some cases 50 per cent of the total foreign debt.[11] And short-term credits carried much higher interest rates. The net flow of money from the Third to the First World continued.

The central point about the Baker Plan however was that

it failed to address the key problem of reducing the debt and the interest rates which were continuing to build it. At its heart was a contradiction: it wanted to reduce debt by lending more. In fact, its aim was not to address structural unfairness, but to maintain it and simply make it a little easier for the debtors to keep paying. This was a crucial failing.

A number of other suggested solutions followed. All came from politicians in opposition or politicians whose influence on the international stage was limited. But the principles on which they were based reveal to a Christian observer interesting parallels with the principles on which biblical precedents rested. Two came in direct reaction to the Baker Plan from Democrat politicians in the United States. Senator Bill Bradley attacked the Baker strategy of more loans as a recipe for more debt, not less. It would simply prolong the policies which caused the crisis instead of replacing them with something better. As an alternative he proposed that banks and creditor governments should knock 3 per cent off the value of the debts and, as a one-off concession for a single year, reduce interest rates by 3 per cent. For those countries prepared to adopt IMF austerity there should be a further 9 per cent knocked off the debt. Bradley and Baker in many respects shared the same approach: they were 'growth with austerity' programmes designed to enable Latin America to carry on paying and to open up its markets even more to US products. Bradley, of course, was an opposition politician but he was an orthodox member of the US financial establishment and he had established two other important precedents: concessional interest rates must be part of any solution and part of the losses would have to be taken by the banks. In other words there did have to be a bias in favour of the poor, and those who have profited from them must offer restitution.

More radical was the suggestion of another Democrat, US Congressman Charles Schumer who, in combination with the economist Alfred Watkins, calculated that 70–80 per cent of the existing debt was not money which had ever been borrowed but was simply accrued interest. In order to prevent this happening again they suggested that banking law should be changed. At present a bank is allowed in its annual report to describe as profits money which comes in as repayment on an existing loan. Schumer and Watkins proposed that this should not be allowed if the interest had been paid back with money which had itself been borrowed from that same bank. 'This will not only reduce the rewards for loaning money to pay back loans; it will also give banks an incentive to lower their interest rates to levels that debtor nations can pay without taking out new loans.'[12] Here we have the notion of a mechanism being created which prevents the social problem of an ever-increasing accumulation of debt. We will recall the numerous Old Testament parallels which aimed at similar ends.

The plan outlined by President Mitterand of France in 1986 took things a stage further. He took up the type of suggestion outlined in the Brandt Report with its call for the establishment of powerful global institutions to rectify the existing imbalances. His proposal was for a kind of Marshall Plan for the Third World which envisaged major redistributions. It called on the rich nations to raise their commitments to aid from levels below 0.35 per cent of their gross national product to 0.5 per cent and eventually to 1 per cent. The net effect would be to transfer between \$35 and \$70 billion a year from the rich world to the poor. Here we have a significantly far-reaching attempt at global redistribution on a steady and continuing scale. It creates a structure of continuing revision which, in a far more sophisticated manner, performs a similar function to that which operated every seven years in the Leviticus and Deuteronomy provisions.

In 1987, at a round of IMF-World Bank meetings, came a surprising suggestion by the British Chancellor of the Exchequer, Nigel Lawson. His plan was limited to the poorest countries of all, those of sub-Saharan Africa, but it too made important concessions. For eighteen months he tried unsuccessfully to persuade the richer nations:

*   that government-to-government aid loans should be converted, retrospectively, into grants.

*   that longer periods should be allowed in the repayment of other official debts, such as export credits.

* that interest rates should be cut for these debtors, perhaps to a figure 3 per cent below the market rate.

'We have a moral responsibility, as well as an economic one, to some of the poorest countries in the world,' he said.[13] In any case 'since there is no realistic prospect of actually securing anything like full repayment if rates are not reduced, we have to regard the cost as one that has been incurred already.'[14]

Once again there were to be conditions. Recipient countries would only be those who were pursuing 'satisfactory' IMF –style economic reform programmes. Giving debt relief to nations who refused to put their economies in order was 'just like throwing money down the drain', he said.[15] Lawson was at pains to insist that his plan could only apply to the very poor nations of Africa whose plight in the years of the Sahelian famine had been far more prominently in the public eye than had the larger problem of Latin America. It was, therefore, no precedent for cut-price interest rates for the bigger debtors. Patently, however, it was – which is why the United States and Germany refused to endorse the plan. Nonetheless the proposal had entered the debate, and from the lips of one of the system's pillars of financial probity. It was an acceptance of the distinction which the first books of the Bible had made, and which Calvin had translated into a modern economic framework: that different responses were appropriate in different situations, that what might be an acceptable rate of interest for loans concerned with production might not be acceptable for those concerned with simply keeping alive, that there should be concessional interest rates for those in need. Most of all it enshrined the notion of a bias towards the poor.

There were a number of other plans, including several by

the Japanese which were designed mainly to deflect criticism of Japan's massive trade surplus and did not offer any major new thoughts on the structure of a comprehensive rescue plan. They, like all the others, fell by the wayside because they did not secure the approval of the United States which to all intents and purposes continues to exercise a complete veto on such matters. The US Treasury was determined in any case to stick by the Baker Plan even though by 1987 it was clear that the plan had not worked. When it became clear that the banks had no intention of coming up with substantial amounts of new lending to help debtors pay the interest on the old loans it tried a new tack, though still within the basic Baker blueprint. If the banks would not offer new money then ways had to be found to reduce the debtors' need for it. Baker threw his support behind a new gambit: a menu of options. This new piece of jargon covered a range of possibilities which were presented to debtors and creditors when they met in the seemingly endless rounds of renegotiations and reschedulings. Baker's favourite option was the debt-equity swap, but the menu soon came also to include exit bonds, buy-backs and debt-for-debt swaps. This fierce phalanx of finance-speak disguised an array of attempts to persuade the banks to wipe away part of the debt in return for some other compensation. As these techniques are still the basic building blocks with which a variety of proposed solutions have been constructed it is worth looking at them in a little detail.

SHUFFLING THE DECK: DEBT-EQUITY SWAPS, BUY-BACKS AND EXIT BONDS

In debt-equity swaps the bank sells its debt for US dollars, usually at a generous discount, on the secondary debt market to an investor who wants to buy or invest in a business in the debtor country. The businessman then sells the debt to the debtor government, which pays in local currency. The businessman then uses the local currency to buy the business or shares in it. Thus the debt has been swapped for equity in the local company. A typical example was when in 1986 the Japanese car company Nissan wanted to expand its holdings in Mexico. It went to the secondary debt market and paid $40 million for $60 million's worth of Mexican debt. It then sold these to the government for $54 million worth of *pesos* which it then invested in its Mexican subsidiary.

Debt-equity swaps have been the principal devices used in attempts at debt reduction. By 1988 some $10 billion had been swapped. The banks and investors liked them. But the Third World debtors were not so keen. They did not benefit at all from the discount. What was worse, they had to find large amounts of local currency to swap for the debts and this added to the problem of inflation locally, because the basic options were simply to print more or to borrow it on the local market where, because of inflation, rates could be very high. In Brazil, where the swaps proceeded at a tremendous pace in 1988, some observers believe that the process was instrumental in cranking the country towards hyperinflation. Worse still, the process did not make a major impact in reducing the overall debt; one economist estimates that the $10 billion swapped brought real benefits of as little as $2 or $3 billion, only about 1 per cent of the debt to the banks.[16] There was just too little in the way of attractive companies and too much in the way of bank debt; where companies were attractive, foreign investors might well have come anyway, and paid in dollars, not a mere swap. Worst of all it meant that the Third World was exchanging good businesses for debt which everyone now concedes is unlikely ever to be paid in full. It is this last aspect which must raise questions from a Christian standpoint. Debt-equity swaps, which the left decry as a form of back-door colonialism, remove part of the resource base which Christians see as part of the creation provision in which the dignity of men and women as workers is invested. Swaps can sell birthrights for a mess of pottage.

Popular feeling began to grow in Latin America against the swaps. In January 1989 Brazil suspended all debt-equity auctions and resumed them on a much more limited scale in March. Mexico had already suspended them entirely. Its finance minister, Pedro Aspe, raised objections to the technique at the annual meeting of the Inter-American Development Bank in 1989. Was it right, he asked, for his government to 'subsidise direct foreign investment and the international banks' when resources were scarce and his people were suffering hardship?[17] The military dictatorship in Chile had no such qualms; over the past four years it has reduced its total debt by 36 per cent through such swap mechanisms.

Once the principle of the swap had been established a whole range of variations on the theme were heard. In 1987 the US pressure group Conservation International inaugurated the 'debt-for-nature' deal by paying $100,000 for $650,000-worth of Bolivian debt on the secondary market and wrote off the debt in exchange for the government's creation of a 1.6 million hectare conservation zone in the Beni rainforest. The following year the Midland Bank and the Sudanese government struck the first 'debt-for-development' deal; the bank wrote off a $800,000 debt and Sudan paid the equivalent in local currency to Unicef for a health, water and reafforestation programme in Kordofan. A Dutch football team, PSV Eindhoven, bought $5 million of discounted Brazilian debt, exchanged it for *cruzados* and bought Romario Farias, one of Rio de Janeiro's most talented football players. The Peruvian government even suggested to the US government a 'debt-for-drugs' swap in which debt would be written off in return for the creation of an anti-drugs fund to combat the cocaine trade. Such schemes raise all manner of ethical considerations. They are, however, small beer in the overall picture of Third World debt and not therefore worth further digression.

It was also in 1987 that the exit bond became a popular notion. This was a device offered by debtors to banks who decided they had had enough. When short-term loans come to be renegotiated the banks who form part of the lending consortium exert a good deal of pressure on one another. All would rather not be there. But all know that a certain

amount of new money must be lent to enable the debtor to
pay the interest on his old loans, for his flagging economy
will provide no other income. All are chary of 'free riders' –
banks who try to duck their obligation to their peers by
refusing to lend again. When everyone else comes up with
the money and the debtor hands out the interest the 'free
riders' then insist on their share too. Exit bonds are a device
to enable reluctant banks to quit the process: they cash in
their debt in return for the bonds, which pay much less than
the former debt but which pay at once. From a Christian
viewpoint the device has the attraction of implicitly acknowledging a shared responsibility but in practice it has only
limited use. Only banks with small debts can afford to cut
and run with the exit bonds; banks which are owed a lot
could not afford the discount which would reveal in their
annual accounts how fragile their general position is. They
have to maintain the pretence on which the system is erected.

The buy-back is a system whereby a debtor nation raises
the cash to purchase its own debt, at a discount, on the
secondary market. In principle this is an admirable solution
for it enables the debtors to deal with their debt at the
value which the market recognises as their true worth. The
discounts of the secondary market go to the debtor, not to
some Western investor, and the hypocrisy of the double
standard is removed. In practical terms, of course, it is
very limited. Few countries so deeply in debt can raise the
necessary cash in normal circumstances. Chile financed such
a deal in 1988 after windfall earnings from high copper prices
enabled it to ask banks to bid for buy-back at reduced rates
(it got a 44.7 per cent discount this way) and Bolivia was given
the cash to negotiate a buy-back by Western governments in
a deal to suppress the country's most lucrative export – its
traffic in cocaine. In practice buy-backs, like debt-equity
swaps, can only help to reduce the debt very slowly.

Debt-for-debt swaps were at one point hailed as the apparatus which would solve the debt crisis. In this banks swap
debt at a discount for long-term bonds issued by the debtor
at a lower face value or a lower rate of interest. The theory

is that the new bonds, though worth less, will be a safer investment. In February 1988 Mexico tried to organise this in a big way. The attempt was hailed as an inspired solution to the debt crisis. It set up a programme of debt-for-debt swaps which was intended to bring significant relief to its $103 billion foreign debt in return for twenty-year bonds.

But the new bonds will only be more attractive to the creditor if they are in some way safer. Sometimes, to ensure this, the debtor will guarantee the amount loaned by covering the bond with some secure collateral, such as US Treasury notes. The problem is that the debtor cannot, of course, afford to buy the full collateral. In the case of the Mexico deal the guarantees, zero-coupon US Treasury notes, covered only 17 per cent of the bonds. Of 500 banks eligible to bid for the bonds only 139 bothered to enter the auction. Only £3.7 billion of the debt was cashed in and, according to calculations by the International Mexican Bank, it saved the country only $29.1 million on its annual debt service bill. 'The debt swap is so insignificant that a mere one-thirty-second of a per cent rise in London interest rates would wipe out the gain,' according to Christopher Huhne.[18] In fact in the year up to March 1989 the interest rates which governed Mexico's annual payments rose from around 7 per cent to almost 10.5 per cent.[19]

TOP DOWN SOLUTIONS: 1989, THE BRADY PLAN

The piecemeal techniques of the various swaps, bonds and buy-backs continued to be applied. Then in 1989, came another comprehensive strategy. The Brady Plan, named after the new US Treasury Secretary, Nicholas Brady, was important for two reasons. It was proposed by the new US government of President George Bush and therefore had the power behind it which the other proposals since Baker have lacked. It made concrete the proposal, which had seemed inevitable to many observers of the scene for some time, that

the debts were no longer worth what the banks pretended
and that therefore the face value of the debts had to be
reduced. Debt forgiveness had arrived on the scene at last,
although everyone was at pains not to describe it as that.

The Brady Plan came about because of the growing awareness within the US administration that the 'case by case'
approach did little except to take the heat out of crises in
individual countries when they flared up. In the background
the overall situation was deteriorating still. The economies
of Latin America were stagnating. Some displayed very
minimal growth, others none at all. The fifteen top debtors
averaged growth of less than 1 per cent in 1988.[20] Commodity
prices were still low. Debt repayments were at their highest
level ever. The net flow of money was still from the poor to
the rich: in 1988 the fifteen largest debtor nations paid $31
billion to their creditors and national income per head had
dropped to 7 per cent below what it was in 1980.[21] The
reductions in buying power meant that the market for US
goods in the debtor countries was constantly shrinking.
Worse still the debtors were now falling seriously into arrears
on their repayments. Peru had arrears dating back to 1985.
Ecuador had been behind with payment since 1987: its debt
was comparatively small but though it owed only $6 billion
to the banks it was $1 billion in arrears. Argentina, its
economy in a shambles, went into arrears at the beginning
of 1989. It seemed likely that by the autumn of 1989 the
largest debtor Brazil would fall into arrears too.[22] The closest
election in Mexican history and the riots in Venezuela, in
which hundreds died, crystallised President Bush's fears for
the fragile nature of democracy in Latin America – he was
particularly worried for the future of his immediate neighbour, Mexico – and the Brady Plan was announced.

Some of the main elements in the proposals outlined by
the new US Treasury Secretary, Mr Nicholas Brady, to a
conference of the Bretton Woods Committee in March 1989,
were familiar enough. The strict conditions approved by the
IMF were to be required of all debtors. The approach was
to be 'case by case' and not an attempt at a universal solution.

But there were several new elements. Brady proposed that:

* the overall level of debt had to be reduced, and implicit in this was the premise that the cost had to be borne by the banks.

* public money – via the funds of the IMF and World Bank – should be used to encourage the banks to accept a reduction in the face value of the debt. This was an important concession – for it means that part of the burden is being switched from the private banks to public institutions. It was an admission that eventually governments will have to take a hand in bringing about the forgiveness which the banks have been unable to bring themselves to concede.

* changes must be made in US banking regulations to remove existing disincentives to debt reduction.

* a country's ability to pay must be reflected in new negotiations on debt. Brady made reference to the role of the market in deciding a proper level of discount on the debt.

* large amounts of Japanese aid were to be encouraged and accepted into the process of bolstering the plan.

The basic idea was that the banks would agree to write off a proportion of the high-risk debt, which it was now generally acknowledged would never be fully paid, in return for lower-value bonds issued by the debtor which were safer because they were guaranteed by the Fund and the Bank. However it was dressed up, what was being recommended was what horrified bankers called the 'F-word' – forgiveness. Here at last an echo of the Jubilee principle had been heard.

What I have been leading up to suggesting here is that there is nothing outlandish or disingenuous about suggesting that biblical principles can be applied to the current economic system. As we have seen, many of the proposals which have been made so far conform structurally to the scriptural ordinances and injunctions. They are not suggestions which have been made by utopian Christian idealists. Rather they have been made by individuals whose voices are considered sound and respectable in the orthodoxy of international finance. The techniques for the solution to the debt crisis are already available and are within the existing political vocabulary.

But what is also now clear is that many of these proposals have been linked with the kind of austerity programmes which actively discriminate against the very poorest, and which cannot be acceptable parts of any Christian solution to the debt problem. What is also lacking is a comprehensive framework for debt reduction which responds to the various balances implicit in a scriptural world view. If the Christian vision can provide that, then all the tools necessary to do the job have been fashioned and presented to us by the financial experts.

A DEBTORS' CARTEL: CAN'T PAY, WON'T PAY?

The most obvious solution to the debt crisis, it might be thought, is that the debtors should simply refuse to pay on the grounds that the debt is disproportionate and therefore unjust. 'If this debt is paid in full at high interest rates, many in the Third World will die or have their health seriously damaged. But if we don't pay back at these high interest rates no one is going to die in the United States, Germany, France or Britain,' said Cardinal Arns of Brazil.[23] The logic of this is easily extended to ask: why pay at all?

The response of the bankers is to speak of the sanctity of law and the paramount need to maintain trust in the fundamental principles of contract. Without those conventions, they say, the very basis of all human commerce, trade and banking is called into question. Charles Elliott, in a study of the ethics of international debt,[24] implies that such fundamentals may already have been breached by the bankers themselves. He identifies four basic ethical principles which underlie the nature of the contract of loan:

  * The first is mutuality: the debt is freely entered into by both parties and neither is free to renege on it. The lender cannot

demand repayment before the stated time and the borrower cannot refuse to repay.

* The second is efficiency: Elliott perceives that the contract assumes that the borrower will use the loan efficiently so that it is put to use in a way which produces a surplus out of which eventually to repay. To lend or borrow without assuming this is either foolish or wicked.

* The third condition is appropriateness: can the conditions which surround the contract be said to be appropriate to other ethical considerations: 'If the only way a country can increase the availability of foreign exchange in the very short run is by reducing the level of living of those who are already poor, those of us who base our ethics on biblical insights of the value of the poor, would have to express strong reservations about the appropriateness of such a step.'[25]

* The fourth is sustainability: it is neither ethical nor rational to produce a solution to any problems concerning debt which creates worse problems than are solved. In its widest context this means that if adhering to the letter of contract incurs unacceptable costs to democracy or the environment then the contract is questionable. Similar reservations obtain if the terms of repayment are so onerous that the debtor in paying is deprived of the resources he or she needs to earn a living and continue the repayment.

Doubts over the last two principles are self-evident in the case of the international debt problem. Elliott feels they are apparent, too, on the principle of efficiency which was breached wholesale in the period up to 1982 by banks which lent recklessly and governments which borrowed thoughtlessly. He has more reservations over the issue of mutuality, which he feels still binds the Third World even in a situation where circumstances have deteriorated significantly. Others, however, have raised questions on this point too. Cardinal Arns quotes Pope Paul VI: 'If the position of the contracting parties is too unequal, the consent of the parties does not suffice to guarantee the justice of their contract.'[26] Certainly there are ample biblical precedents of the need for moral principles to take precedence over the law, and we may conclude that the banks' concerns over the possibility of default are as much based in anxiety to protect the huge level of profits which they have taken from the Third World as in concern for the ethics of contract.

The arguments against Third World default are in fact more practical than ethical. Financial institutions would cut off a defector from the short-term trade credits which any nation needs to buy the essential products it must import, such as oil and crucial machinery spare parts to fuel the economy. This is exactly what happened to Brazil when it announced not a total repudiation but a mere moratorium. Had it taken the precaution of building substantial reserves of foreign currency to pay its immediate trade debts during this period, its default might have been more permanent; on the other hand, had it had such reserves it probably would not have felt the need to call a moratorium in the first place and would have continued paying up. Other countries have been too afraid even to try. 'Have you ever contemplated what would happen to the president of a country if the government couldn't get insulin for its diabetics?' asked one US Treasury official, revealing the ugly nature of this international financial blackmail.[27] In addition a whole barrage of crippling economic and political reprisals could be directed against any defaulter. The brutal efficacy of these is evident enough from the hapless example of Nicaragua.

A powerful case, however, has been made by Anatole Kaletsky in his book *The Costs of Default*[28] for what he calls 'conciliatory default'. In this debtors will cease to pay the full amounts required but do so with an air of apology rather than of defiance. They would take care to announce that they did intend to pay as soon as they could afford it and, as a sign of that intention, would continue to pay smaller amounts, either by fixing an upper limit on what their economy could stand that year, or by unilaterally reducing the rate of interest they were prepared to pay, or by skilfully electing to pay more to certain key creditors. In such circumstances the full weight of the creditor governments would not be thrown against them because, although the Western banks would be angry, the firms which traded with them – including the powerful multinationals – would have an interest in ensuring behind the scenes that a negotiated settlement was reached which protected their investments in the defaulting country. Such divide and rule tactics would turn the tables on the First World which has, for the past decade, used the same strategem on debtor nations to keep them from uniting to form a debtors' cartel which would have formed a far more serious opponent.

Conciliatory default 'would be like a slow leak in the banks' balance sheets . . . A repudiation, by contrast, would be like an explosion below decks; it would blow a hole right through the centre of the banks' capital structure, which could sink some of the banks before there was even a chance to begin emergency measures,' says Kaletsky.[29] As such it would be a useful mechanism for allowing the banks to take their share of responsibility for the debt problem in which their recklessness played such a key part. This, or the threat of it, could therefore well form another useful weapon in the armoury which is available in working towards a comprehensive solution to the global problem. If the First World continues to dodge the need for a solution, this may have to be the one which the Third World forces upon them. The retreat into enforced self-sufficiency, however, would not be a good thing: the cost of tightening belts would inevitably fall most heavily on the poorest people in the defaulting nation. This has been the experience of Peru, the only country to try conciliatory default in a major way. In the early years the consequences were disguised by its government's strategy to let inflation rip; more recently however the burden of its spiralling prices has begun to hit the poor hard.

Outright default, then, does not seem a solution to the debt crisis. It is plain therefore that what is needed is a resolution which involves a sharing of responsibility between the Third World élites who incurred the debt, the banks who lent it, the Western governments who encouraged the lending, and the multilateral institutions like the IMF and

the World Bank, whose officials advised the Third World in
its ill-conceived response.

TWO FUNDAMENTALS: PARTICIPATION AND BIAS TO THE POOR

There are two prime elements which any solution must
contain if it is to be compatible with the Christian vision.
The exact balance between the components which stem from
them will be a matter for those expert in the fine detail of
international finance but there are two fundamentals which
it must contain.[30] The first of these is that there must be a
series of mechanisms for ensuring the fullest participation of
the Third World poor. This may seem an odd first priority,
but if we do not accept it then we fall into the same trap in
which the Church was ensnared for decades. We begin with
charity and then move to justice but finally we must arrive
at participation. Anything other than an acceptance of the
full humanity of the poorest is a delusion. We must first take
on board that we are dealing with equals – sisters and brothers
made, as we are, in the image of God – and that they must
be accorded a spiritual and moral equality, not simply a
paternalistic attempt to offer help towards a material
equality. People can only truly be developed when they have
the dignity which comes from controlling their own lives.
Ultimately it is a question of power. At present the relationship is between unequals. We cannot even give the poor that
power. We must, rather, help them as they discover it within
themselves.

The practical implications of this are wide-ranging. At the
level of international institutions it means that a Christian
vision will include the full and equal participation of the
Third World in the major financial bodies. That requires a
campaign for the poor nations to have a proper voice at
bodies like the International Monetary Fund where at present
they are accorded risible voting rights which allow them no
real say in shaping the destiny of the global financial system.

When dealing with Third World governments it means supporting those characterised by full, participatory democracy and encouraging, cajoling or even opposing military or totalitarian regimes or those characterised by a disrespect for human rights. Susan George suggests a national development fund, parallel to the state, or even a regional one which would cross the boundaries of several states in an area, which would be managed by directly elected representatives from all sections of society,[31] and although the suggestion may be queried on grounds of *realpolitik* it does enshrine the Christian aspiration on such matters. At more local levels it means supporting development projects which bring material benefits but also raise consciousness and critical awareness such as literacy and workers' rights campaigns, some of which might in conventional terms be decried as 'political'. For First World governments it means assigning money more to small-scale projects which directly help the poor; rather than building one power station for a capital city, it means building many basic rural health centres. For aid agencies it means changing emphases in the relationship between 'donor' and 'recipient' so that the North responds to the needs as perceived by the people of the South; he who pays the piper must no longer call the tune.[32] It also means selecting projects which foster alternative structures which allow power to be assumed by those normally denied it – the women, the landless, and those like the rubbish-pickers in Delhi who, reflecting society's view of them, call themselves the *konjars* – the nobodies.

Only with the fullest participation of the poor, and with the benefit of the direct knowledge and experience they bring, can we ever develop a complete understanding of the second Christian fundamental – the bias towards the poor. Everything else in the final resolution of the debt problem stems from this foundation. Before all else, any solution must make clear provision for that which is denied to one billion people throughout the planet: the basic right to food and clothing which are part of the creation *fiat*. The sacrifice of these basics cannot be part of any acceptable solution to the debt crisis. In international terms this means that the needs of the very poorest countries, largely in Africa as Nigel Lawson suggested, must be addressed with the most urgency, before those of the Latin American countries known as the 'middle-income' debtors which, because of the sums of money involved, tend most to occupy the minds of those attempting to disentangle the complexities of the debt conundrum. Inside individual countries it means specific national and international programmes targeted on the most vulnerable groups – children, the infirm, pregnant women and the unemployed. But the most basic need of the poor is, as the prophets of eighth-century BC in Israel saw only too clearly, the need for justice.

The search for true justice does not mean retribution but the restoration of a natural balance. That does not require denunciations of the guilty. But it does mean that we must apportion responsibility where that helps us towards finding a solution.

SHARING THE BURDEN: TACKLING THE US BUDGET DEFICIT

It takes borrower and lender to create a debt crisis. Yet for the past decade the borrower has borne the entire cost. There has been adjustment of the most painful kind in the Third World. But among the First World there has been none. As we have seen, the ultimate cause of the crisis has not been rash lending and foolish borrowing. It has been the structure of sin which precipitated those events. That structure is the US budget deficit. Through it the United States has been living beyond its means and sending the bill to the rest of the world. Much of the burden has fallen on that billion people who spend part, if not the whole, of each year in hunger.

It is, in truth, the United States which needs more than any other nation, a rigorous programme of adjustment. It is because of the gigantic budget deficit – which is twice the size of the entire debt of all Third World nations put together – that the United States has had to keep interest rates so high, to attract in the money it needs to finance the deficit. It is borrowing to consume. This is even a short-sighted policy for the US national self-interest: it means that the potential customers for US goods are in no position to buy because 30 to 50 per cent of their foreign exchange earnings now goes in servicing debts. 'It is therefore American and European manufacturers, rather than . . . bankers, who are suffering the consequences of the developing world's indebtedness. Conversely, a resolution of the debt crisis could reduce the US trade deficit by up to $30 billion a year. In total the debt crisis and the consequent cutbacks in imports by the developing nations are estimated to have cost Europe, North America and Australasia approximately six million jobs during the 1980s.'[33]

It is, according to Tim Congdon, who was formerly the chief economist of Shearson Lehman Brothers, a monetarist problem which requires a monetarist solution, without which any other debt proposals will go for nothing:

> The debt crisis was caused by the sharp rise in real dollar interest rates between 1979 and 1981 and is insoluble unless real interest rates return to a level closer to the underlying growth rate of real incomes . . . [any solution] is highly conditional on fiscal policy in the USA, because a return to responsible government finances in the world's largest economy would reduce real interest rates there, which would induce a sympathetic downward movement in borrowing costs elsewhere.[34]

In practice what that means is spending cuts in the area where President Reagan most boosted expenditure – the military budget – and increased taxes on corporations and wealthier individuals. The process will have to be skilfully managed over an extended period to ensure that the resulting deflation does not cause a slump in the world economy. But if this key issue continues to be dodged then the extravagant consumption which is typical of the US lifestyle will continue to be subsidised at the end of a long indirect chain by people who suffer from malnutrition. The choice is as stark as that.

SHARING THE BURDEN; THE RESPONSIBILITY OF THE BANKS

The immediate alleviation of the problems of the debtor nations however requires more specific redress. Debt forgiveness must play a part in this. The central question is, who should fund it?

At present the cost is borne by the Third World alone, which is manifestly unfair. Between 1976 and the end of 1981 Latin America borrowed some $272.9 billion dollars. According to one estimate 91.6 per cent of this money went straight back to the banks: 62.2 per cent went in interest and other debt service charges, 20.5 per cent went to them in other outflows, particularly capital flight, and 8.9 per cent for the build-up of international reserves. Only 8.4 per cent ($22.9 billion) ever actually arrived in the continent for use, possibly, but not always, in development work.[35] This might be dubbed the 'legitimate debt'. There are a number of assumptions in this analysis we should want to examine before we accept its detail but let us accept the general point: a large share of responsibility for the size of the debt must lie at the door of the banks and the multilateral institutions who later began to make loans to the increasingly desperate debtors, packaged with demands for economic reforms, some elements of which proved ill-advised. Moreover, as Cardinal Arns points out, there must be question marks over who within the Third World are the real debtors. The archbishop adds another dimension in describing Brazil's debt as the fruit of a military dictatorship:

> In 1964 the dictatorship inherited a foreign debt of $3.2 billion. Between 1964 and 1974 the debt grew to $14 billion. Between 1974 and 1979, under General Geisel, it rose to $50 billion. Between 1979 and 1985, under General Figueiredo, it rose to $104 billion . . . Our foreign debt is a dictatorial decision imposed on a whole nation. How, where and why the money was spent was never explained. However, when it was time to pay the debt, it then became the debt of the Brazilian people and especially of the workers.

In seeking to work out a just co-responsibility and a fair sharing of the burden we must, then, look to the banks, the Western governments and their multilateral institutions and to the Third World leaders.

The Western banks, although they have expanded in other areas to reduce their perilous over-exposure on Third World debt, have in no sense made any significant contribution to its solution. No adjustment has been forced on them in the sense that it has on the Third World. They have all declared losses after setting aside funds as a contingency against Third World default; but they have not actually used those funds to write off selected parts of the debt where that would most alleviate the burdens of the poor. Commonly it has been said that it would be too dangerous to allow the banks to bear the cost of their recklessness. The consequences for a system of international commerce which depends above all else on confidence would have been disastrous for the entire world. For a time that may have been true. But under cover of the Baker Plan the British and US banks have slowly retreated from their position of terrible vulnerability by growing in other areas and at the same time refusing to make many new loans to the debtor nations. Slowly they have set aside amounts to cover default. The big British banks in February 1990 declared losses after setting aside funds to cover around 70 per cent of the debt.[36] Earlier provision had meant they were already covered for at least 48 per cent of their risk, which put them on a par with their French and Spanish counterparts. The German banks, thanks to more generous tax laws, already had 70 per cent provision. Even the major US creditors have slowly improved their position; most are now covered for between 22 per cent and 50 per cent of possible losses.[37] According to the former British Chancellor of the Exchequer, Nigel Lawson, 'there is no longer a serious risk of a systemic breakdown of world banking.'[38]

There is no reason now, therefore, why the banks should not begin to shoulder their share of the burden. Determining what should be their fair share is a difficult matter. There are sound arguments for saying that they should be obliged to write the value of the debts down to the prices at which the debts are traded on the secondary market, as this, advocates of the market system would maintain, is their true worth. Other possibilities include fixing a figure for 'legitimate' debt, as above. But we shall look at this matter in a moment.

The Western governments cannot escape culpability either. Acting directly and through the IMF and World Bank they encouraged the banks to recycle the OPEC petrodollars, without any public sector control, and they then encouraged the Third World governments to borrow the money. The advice the World Bank and IMF gave debtors about commodity prices and about fiscal management was at best confused and at times contradictory. For all this they have tended to disclaim liability. The debt problem belonged to the Third World and to the private banks. Throughout they have 'reiterated their opposition to transferring risks from the private to the public sector'. No tax-payers' bail-out for the banks, was the cry, most strident of all from the United States, where memories of the banks' role in the 1929 crash are kept alive as an article of faith. There is no role for the state in private sector, 'free' market matters, was the more ideological response from the Thatcher government in Britain.

SHARING THE BURDEN: THE TASK OF WESTERN GOVERNMENTS

All this is disingenuous. The state is already playing an important behind-the-scenes role in the debt crisis. As the banks have backed out of new lending in Latin America the state has had to take on this role, acting through the multilateral institutions, as Nigel Lawson has acknowledged: 'The proportion of total debt of the fifteen largest debtors outstanding to official institutions has risen from about one-fifth in 1982 to one-third today.'[39] The banks already have a tacit underwriting by the state. In the United States the

Comptroller of the Currency announced as long ago as 1984 that the government would not allow the top eleven US banks to collapse.[40] In Britain 'it is clear that the major banks enjoy an implicit public sector guarantee . . . The balance sheets, provisions, profits and even the dividend policies of the major banks are determined as never before by the guidelines set by their financial authorities.'[41] City insiders claim that the latest round of losses announced by the British banks, prompted by increased provisioning against Third World default, were declared at the insistence of the Bank of England. And for all the talk about 'no bail-out' the fact is that tax-payers in most countries are already contributing to the banks' 'adjustment' because they receive tax relief on what they set aside against future losses. It is thus a delusion to say that the state is not bailing out the banks. The anticipated tax relief on the latest provision announced by Lloyds Bank, for example, will bring the total paid by tax-payers to this one bank alone to around $500 million. 'If that isn't a bail-out, what is?' asked one acerbic debt expert.[42] The only sadness is that the tax-payers' money goes to the banks who, at present, are doing nothing more than stashing away money in case the Third World one day defaults. To prevent that from happening that money ought to be going to the debtor nations to wipe away part of their debt burden. It should not be a question of bailing out the banks as much as bailing out the Third World. If the evidence was clearly and fairly presented, many tax-payers of the First World would not object.

There is no reason why all this intervention by sovereign states should not be happening. What is needed now is that the Western governments should acknowledge it publicly and then extend it. They can even find justification in their gospel, *The Wealth of Nations*. In Book Five, Adam Smith says:

The . . . duty of the sovereign or commonwealth is that of erecting and maintaining those public institutions and those public works, which, though they may be in the highest degree advantageous to a great society, are, however, of such a nature that the profit could never repay the expense to any individual or small number of individuals, and which it therefore cannot be expected that any individuals or small number of individuals should erect or maintain.

There is a strong case, as we shall see, for the erection of such an institution, at an international level, to deal specifically with the current debt crisis and the structural changes which underlie it.

There is cause too for more state activity at the national level. There can be many options here within a Christian framework, so we will simply sketch out a few examples. The regulations and laws which govern banking activity need to be revised in ways which would encourage banks to offer more debt relief. The provisions under West German law could profitably be studied by others, and indeed there would be much to gain by some international co-ordination on these matters so that the banks of particular nations are not disadvantaged in relation to the others.

In the United States it could usefully become a tax deductible expense for banks to create new general reserves to cushion them against the loan losses which are almost inevitably to come. Or the US regulators could force banks truly to write off loans on which they have already been given tax relief, so that the Third World would actually benefit. They might alter regulations to allow write-downs to be spread over a number of years. They could alter the status of the low-interest bonds (offered in many debt-for-debt swaps) which at present would have to be declared as a loss. They could require US banks to identify money from capital flight so that the authorities in the Third World can initiate any appropriate action in the courts.

In Britain the government could take similar steps and could refuse to give banks tax relief on their declared losses unless the debts were actually written off and the Third World country benefited. A small step in this direction was taken in the House of Commons in July 1990 when a government spokesman indicated it was prepared to review its tax treatment of certain categories of Third World debt. There could be a number of mechanisms devised to this end. In place of tax relief the government could allocate an equivalent sum actually to buy the debt from the bank. The debt could then be written off, or used in a debt-for-development swap, or where appropriate the interest on the debt capped so that the debtor nation would continue paying but at a concessional rate.[43]

States also have a role to play at the multilateral level through bodies like the IMF, the World Bank and the European Community. A first step was taken towards recognising this in July 1990 at the Houston summit when Western leaders had presented to them a debt review which looked at how Third World debts to Western governments could be reduced. Many aid loans had already been converted to grants. The proposal was that the same should happen with export credits on the grounds that, without this, even if all debt to commercial banks was eliminated the Third World would still be in difficulty. World Bank projections were that by the end of 1990 debt rescheduling countries will owe $522bn to private creditors – almost exactly what they owe to governments. Six years previously the official debts were only half of the private ones.[44]

Once the principle that it is proper for states to interfere has been acknowledged there are many options. Again we will choose a few obvious examples. These bodies could be used as guarantors for exit bonds to make them more attractive to banks in debt-for-debt swaps. Governments which have already written off official debts to the poorest countries could insist that a similar approach be taken with the loans of the European Development Fund and the International Development Association, the soft-loans department of the World Bank. In future money from these funds should be given in the form of grants, not loans. Much if not all of the IMF arrears to the poor countries of Africa could be written off, enabling its hard-pressed governments to make a clean start. Governments could use the multilateral bodies to provide cheap loans to debtors with which they could purchase their old debts at discount on the secondary market; they could, in particular, coax the swiftly growing Japanese aid budget to be used in this way. These various measures would need to be co-ordinated to ensure that the cost of the debt fiasco is borne in due proportion by the banks, the tax-payers of the rich countries, and the Third World nations.

Here again we see the need for some central body along the lines of the one outlined by the banking division of American Express, which has made a detailed proposal for such a body on the grounds that a slowly drifting debt problem will cost all nations more over a ten-year period than an organised solution would now. Amex have dubbed it the Institute for International Debt and Development. 'The creditor countries must manage the problem; if not, the problem will manage them.'[45]

SHARING THE BURDEN: MAKING THIRD WORLD LEADERS ACCOUNTABLE

The fourth party with clear culpability in the debt crisis is the Third World leadership. Undoubtedly many of the leaders of debtor nations found themselves enmeshed in systems beyond their control once the debt machine was set in motion. But others exacerbated its workings by incompetence, while others collaborated with it to line their own pockets. Many of the leaders of African countries which had been independent for less than two decades, did not have the economic expertise to understand exactly what was happening and struggled on, persisting in applying the formulae they had been taught before world recession, oil shock and the new monetarist orthodoxy. Others did not have the economic or technical infrastructure to pursue alternatives. It was easier to talk of transferring the initiative to the private sector than it was to find a competent African bourgeoisie to hand anything to; they had little option but to plough on, trying to make the huge state plantations or mining operations work as they had before. Many, like their counterparts in Latin America, insisted out of a misplaced sense of national pride on preserving exchange rates at old levels which did not reflect the dynamics of the changing economic relationship. Others persisted out of sheer hubris with the prestige modernisation projects which they had come to feel were their due. There can be no doubt that for many of these, policies of adjustment are appropriate, though what kind of adjustment we shall consider shortly.

Those Third World leaders who were guilty of corruption, however, provoke the need to distinguish between different kinds of debt. In the Philippines Citibank lent $2.1 billion for the construction of a nuclear power station at Bataan. Much of this went back to an American company, Westinghouse, to build the plant, it having secured, at the last minute, a contract which had previously been going to its great rival, General Electric. The *New York Times* reported that President Marcos received $80 million in commissions from the firm via a third party.[46] The scheme is alleged to have cost double the price of comparable reactors elsewhere in the world. Westinghouse claimed that allegations of illicitly inflated costs were 'completely without merit' but acknowledged paying a commission to a Marcos associate.[47] Servicing the debt now costs the Philippines $355,000 a day in interest[48] and, to add insult to injury, the Aquino government has found that the plant can never be used after discovering it has been built within the earthquake zone of a nearby volcano.

REPUDIATING DEBT: AN INTERNATIONAL TRIBUNAL

Incidents like this raise the issue of whether certain selected debts should be repudiated. Such a notion bristles with legal and constitutional difficulties. Conventional notions about national sovereignty assume that the debts of one government become the debts of its successor. The idea of repudiation is not without precedent – the USSR, Cuba and China have done so, as did Japan after the Meiji restoration. But the risk of alienating the international community is great – so great that Nicaragua did not attempt it after the fall of Somoza who fled the country taking huge amounts of money with him.[49] The process of taking to the courts every dubious debt would be a complex and exacting one. A number of non-governmental development agencies have suggested[50] that an international tribunal should be established to adjudicate on such matters. A simpler mechanism might be for such decisions to be negotiated through arbitration at the new multilateral debt body.

The argument for such a new body is that:

> A ten-year solution to the crisis means less jobs and economic activity in all the affected countries,[51] increased risk of instability, and all the downside risks and aspects of lack of social and economic development. The cost, in terms of lost economic activity, of a delayed solution may, in dollar terms, be hundreds of times greater than the present dollar cost of the solution.[52]

But it is not enough simply to set up a Debt and Development Institute. There are distinct Christian priorities which it would need to adopt. Again participation would be a *sine qua non*, and this would mean a spread of representatives from the Third World as well as those from the West, along with statutory advisers from the IMF, World Bank, Unicef, environment groups and non-governmental development agencies. Again the bias to the poor should be its dominant perspective, within which it would safeguard other valuable insights about the need to preserve the dignity of the poor by according them proper access to the use of resources. It would also foster the notion of effective and careful stewardship, which would range from discouraging the wasteful nature of much Third World public spending to ensuring that future development did not draw on the natural environment in a way which was unsustainable.

Within this framework such an Institute could perform a number of functions which at present are haphazard or go by default. Again, we give just a few examples. It could structure and balance the mechanisms for debt reduction by disconnecting the debt solution from the free market demands of the international monetary system; it could organise rescheduling and could, where appropriate, fix interest rates at concessional levels or allow them to float but only up to a certain level, or it might place acceptable ceilings on the percentage of a country's export earnings which would go in any given year on debt servicing; it might link repayments to fluctuate with the world price of a country's main commodity or make arrangements for certain debts to be repaid in local currency to prevent certain nations from continuing to battle with the mighty dollar. It could also offer a channel through which the loans and arrears of the IMF and World Bank could be converted, retrospectively, to grants without damaging the AAA credit rating which allows them to borrow most effectively in the normal money markets. It could find ways of differentiating between debtors and adjust its financial tools appropriately to discourage those Third World governments who are profligate in their spending or who pursue political, social or military policies which are anti-development, such as those in Chile or South Africa. It could initiate the exchange of financial and fiscal expertise between different Third World nations of differing degrees of efficiency.

Such a body could also house the tribunal to consider selective repudiation of debts like the Philippines power station and would declare null and void those debts which were tainted with corrupt dealings, with the illegitimate export of flight capital or the promotion of bogus development schemes. It could also search out those individuals who profited exorbitantly from corrupt debts and pursue legal remedy through the normal legal system; such a move might not yield up all the stashed cash but the psychological benefit for Third World peoples might justify the effort. By pursuing once-and-for-all solutions in many areas it would also bring to a close the endless rounds of renegotiating which absorb so much of the energies of the Third World ministries of finance, taking time which should be devoted to running their economies.

ADJUSTING TO THE NEEDS OF THE POOR

The new Institute would also offer a more just basis upon which to structure the adjustment which would still be necessary for those Third World economies dogged by policies which are unsound economically or unfair socially. But adjustment now would mean that the emphasis was upon righting the balance of the economy so that it could grow and, most importantly, grow in such a way as to benefit the mass of the poor. This would reverse the thought processes of the IMF. When it arrives on the scene it looks first at the level of debt and then works out how the national income can be channelled and redistributed to pay for what is due. What is needed is the opposite strategy: to see how an economy needs to be restructured to promote economic growth and true development and then work out what will be left over in the current account to make debt service repayments without causing hardship to the people or inhibiting future growth.

Within that restructuring new priorities must be evident. Statistics on the health and education of the people must be compiled and consulted as carefully as are the usual economic indicators about inflation and balance of payments. Production needs to be restructured so that more food is produced locally using more local manpower. Programmes must specifically target a fair share of foreign exchange, credit, land, water, skills and fertilisers to the poor.[53] Schemes of positive discrimination must be set up for women, the landless and other disenfranchised groups. Mechanisms must be created to draw the productive sectors of the 'black economy' which operates on city streets into the conventional economy to revitalise it.[54] Spending must be re-ordered from a small number of high-cost, high-tech areas to provide low-cost basic services for a far greater number; so that, in health for example, budgets are diverted from neo-Western hospitals in the capital to establishing rural health centres and widespread immunisation and health education. Cuts must be made in prestige projects: does Delhi need a new fly-over and improved traffic light system before rural areas have a primitive road to the local hospital? The concept of 'conditionality' developed by the IMF need not, necessarily, be abandoned. New assistance, through adjustment programmes, could be made conditional on cuts by Third World governments in their prestige projects, of which military spending must rank as the most extravagant.

A new Institute would need to be financed by grants from the wealthy governments of the world. It would be unrealistic to assume that there would be any new money from the commercial banks. They will continue to withdraw and spread their capital elsewhere for the conceivable future. Indeed it may well turn out that the involvement of the commercial sector in sovereign lending was an aberration and is never to be repeated. On that point we shall simply have to wait the judgement of history.

In setting out these options I have deliberately not dwelt on detail and must apologise if the tone has been peremptory. Such cursory treatment may seem unsatisfactory but in the world of international finance circumstances change and the details of such measures will perforce change with them. But what will not shift in such a way is our perception of how changing economic events must constantly be subjected to the scrutiny of the Christian vision. My hope is that, by now, the reader will feel equipped to evaluate those events as they arise. For if we do not do that, we will quickly be swept along by the swift tide of those events and will be lost in the current.

In the end, however, the debt crisis is not so much a problem as the symptom of a problem. It springs from a much more deep-rooted system of injustice which is woven into the structure of international trade and monetary control. At present the First World demands free trade policies from the poorest nations, and free trade, as we have seen is a mechanism which makes the gap between rich and poor nations ever wider. To compound the problem the First World refuses to practise free trade itself and imposes a wall of protectionist measures to safeguard its own industries. As Nigel Lawson has observed: 'World Bank figures suggest that protection by industrialised countries cost the developing countries more than twice the amount of official development aid they receive.'[55] There are powerful voices within the US establishment who are even now attempting to lure the world's most powerful economy into greatly increased 'trade management'. All of this runs quite contrary even to the view of the free trade guru Adam Smith who acknowledged that, although free trade was best for the developed world, it was necessary for developing industry to be accorded some protection from direct competition until it was sufficiently well established to obtain significant economies of scale. In this Smith's philosophy of 'infant industries' accords exactly with the Christian notion of an option for the poor. The peoples of the Third World are like those Labourers in the Vineyard who were hired at the eleventh hour: irrespective of their contribution they must be accorded the essentials of life which are accorded to those of us in the West. What is needed is the erosion of all First World tariffs and barriers whilst allowing the Third World to maintain some protection for its tender industries, to control the excessive import of luxury items, and to protect itself from the current practice of 'dumping' whereby the United States and Europe grow food at subsidised prices to keep their farmers in business and then dump the huge surpluses on poor countries, thus stifling their attempts to develop their own agriculture. Mechanisms to stabilise commodity prices within this free market are also essential to a fair treatment of the poorest nations. But to begin to discuss the detail of this would require another book.

There is one other crucial ingredient needed to bring about the necessary transformations in all these matters: political will. The Bank of England, it is said, has almost a hundred plans drawn up for different solutions to the debt crisis.[56]

But they are only so many pieces of paper without the willingness of politicians to adopt them. Bankers and their apologists expressed widespread public and private doubts when the Brady Plan was first mooted. When Mexico was selected as the test case the banks showed a reluctance to co-operate which was said, privately, to have shocked even the director of the IMF, Michel Camdessus.[57] But for four months Nicholas Brady and his staff worked intensively behind the scenes, persuading, cajoling and apparently even threatening the banks with new laws if they did not co-operate.[58] Eventually an agreement was reached which wiped 35 per cent off the burden of medium and long-term debt which had been worth $52.6 billion, around half its total foreign debt. Within days John Reed, the president of Citicorp, which leads the commercial banks in their attitude to Third World debt, was announcing that the Mexican deal was a one-off which could not be extended to other countries. His remarks were billed as 'an obituary for the Brady plan';[59] the Third World would, he said, have to rely on its own resources. Without political pressure that will remain the case. And political pressure will only come about in response to the spur of public opinion.

PRACTICAL ACTION

'Why do you live as if you still belonged to the world?'
Colossians 2:20

'Is not this the fast that I choose:
to loose the bonds of wickedness,
to undo the thongs of the yoke,
to let the oppressed go free . . .?'
Isaiah 58:6 RSV

'No ray of sunshine is ever lost. But the green that it awakes into existence needs time to sprout. All work that is worth anything is done in faith.'
Albert Schweitzer

What is to be done? As a child at school I can recall being given a pink card covered in small squares which made up the shape of a cross. One square could be coloured with crayon every time a coin was brought in to be donated to the missions. When the cross was filled a black baby would have been saved. It all seemed so straightforward then.

Today it all seems so complex. It is now all too easy for a terrible spiritual and mental paralysis to descend upon those who set out with a determination to make some personal contribution to improving the lot of the poorest people of the world. The more detailed information we accumulate, the more intractable the problem seems.

The sheer enormity of the problems facing the Third World is indeed daunting. But we should not allow ourselves to be snared in the delusion that the problem is too big and that there is nothing which mere individuals can do. Practical action is possible on three levels: personal, communal and structural.

PERSONAL CHANGE

One of the most basic prerequisites for social action is personal change. The extent of this will be a matter for each individual but there is a whole range of possibilities open to those determined to transform indignation into action. The most through-going example of this is evidenced by programmes like those advocated by the Life Style Movement. These give priority to demonstrating a dedication to the Christian world view, laying particular stress on the ethics of sufficiency, just stewardship and the option for the poor. In varying degrees its adherents commit themselves to a modest way of living. They consider the food they eat (and grow), the clothes they wear, the transport they use, the way they feed their pets, the way they consume energy – all with the aim of freeing more of their income to help those in need. Live simply that others may simply live, is their motto.

Jorgen Lissner, a Danish Lutheran, has put forward a number of reasons why such a commitment is important: some change in the way we live is an act of faith performed for the sake of personal integrity, an act of self-defence against the mind-polluting effects of over-consumption, an act of withdrawal from the high-pressure aspects of society, an act of solidarity with the poor, an act of redistributing what we have usurped through the unjust economic structure from which we all benefit, an act of anticipation of the time when the poor will assert their rights and there will be less prodigal luxury available to us, and an act of witness in that deliberate underconsumption will provoke the questions of others.[1]

The movement is not without its critics: 'In an individualistic bourgeois society, the life-style movement tends to get mixed up with other considerations (the slimming courses of an affluent society) and dwindles into the merely banal. It can also become a substitute for action, much as charitable work does when it makes the assistance it offers an excuse for evading the basic structural questions.'[2] Perhaps so; or perhaps such a harsh response reveals how uncomfortably close to home the Life Style message comes in a world which houses both video games and malnutrition. There should, of course, be balance in this, as the balanced scriptural tradition indicates: celebration and sharing are not divisble. The exact balance will be different for each individual but there are potent reasons for not excluding it from our response.

If we are to move beyond what Teilhard de Chardin called 'gentle philanthropism'[3] we must expect that our commitment should manifest itself in our daily lifestyle in some way – even in ways which seem tiny by comparison with the Life Style pledge. At its simplest it can mean monthly financial contributions to development agencies whose work goes beyond charitable relief and tackles issues of justice and participation; the more sizeable the contributions as a proportion of income, the greater the weaning process from the snare of materialism. It can mean shifting the daily routine of the family household to ecologically sound practices which are more aware of the responsibility to act as good stewards of the finite resources of the planet. It can mean switching consumption of products like tea and coffee – whose pickers are among the most exploited of any Third World industry – away from the big brand names to those which are marketed by fair trading bodies like Traidcraft or Oxfam, even if they do cost a little more. (To stop drinking them altogether, however, could on a large scale lead to a drop in production which might cause more hardship than it would relieve.) It can mean altering the way we shop.

This last is a particularly interesting option. In the past those concerned for Third World justice have always appealed to society and its politicians for action which compensates for the injustices created by market forces. 'Shopping for a better world', on the contrary, seeks to manipulate those market forces to moral ends. Its thesis is that every time we shop we cast an economic vote. In Britain in 1988 three million people gave £1.8 billion to aid agencies dedicated to bringing about fairer trading relationships with the Third World. But as consumers they spent £280 billion – 155 times as much. At present those charitable donations and the shopping behaviour have tended to occupy separate spheres of consciousness. If they can be brought together and shopping can become a justice activity then the influence this would exert over supermarket chains and others could be significant.

The approach was devised in the United States by a pressure group, the Council on Economic Priorities, which has for some years produced a heavy tome entitled *Rating America's Corporate Consciousness*. It reviews the social and charitable policies of the largest US companies. Until 1988 it was a minority publication but then in November it produced a spin-off booklet, *Shopping for a Better World*, which listed 1,200 of the nation's best known groceries and then rated them for the ethics which lay behind the label. Within six months it sold 300,000 copies and market research showed that 80 per cent of those who bought it claimed it had changed the way they shopped. In Britain two new groups, centred around magazines, were launched in 1989 to foster the same approach: the *New Consumer*, based in Newcastle-upon-Tyne and *The Ethical Consumer* based in Manchester. Of the two the first is probably the more significant for it has received a grant from the Rowntree Trust (which severed its links with its parent company when Rowntree was taken over by the notorious Nestlé) with which it is building up a substantial database on British firms. By contrast *The Ethical Consumer* depends largely on second-hand sources. *New Consumer* is compiling data on companies in fifteen broad areas and asks, do they:

* willingly disclose non-commercially sensitive information to the public?

* participate in international cartels?

* pollute or exploit non-renewable resources inefficiently?

* promote equal opportunities for women, black and disabled employees?

* respond with sensitivity to local community interests?

* have an attitude of partnership or of confrontation to their workers?

* have progressive social and personnel policies?

* contribute to political parties or quasi-political bodies?

* promote tobacco, alcohol, gambling or conspicuous consumption?

* test products on animals?

* have subsidiaries in countries with poor human rights records?

* have an exploitative attitude to the Third World?

* sell arms or military equipment?

* manufacture components for nuclear power stations?

* have an irresponsible marketing policy?

If the three million people who support development agencies were to go shopping with such guidebooks in hand the impact could be serious.

COMMUNAL CHANGE

At the communal level the scope for action is significant. Does the organisation of our local church reflect the Christian vision of participation or is it caught up still in the old fallacies of hierarchy and bogus authority? Has it taken on board the bias towards the poor as something which is central to Christ's incarnation as a poor Asian villager or does it still look on the poor as mere candidates for the gentle philanthropism which is the by-product of pietistic spirituality? Does it still believe that the Kingdom is to be found in the Church rather than realising that the Church should be found in the Kingdom? How do our parochial committees work? How are their finances structured? Are financial and economic practices regarded as issues for theological reflection or are they still kept in a separate secular strongbox? Similar questions should be asked at a national level and, for Roman Catholics, of the finances of the Vatican which are still today shrouded in scandalous secrecy. Investment portfolios should be scrutinised and purged of dubious companies. They should be replaced by investments which might be less profitable, but which are more consonant with Kingdom values – when the Capuchin Order in the Netherlands analysed their portfolio they redirected a large amount into a fund to protect and stimulate socially useful employment.[4] They should also be particularly debated in the churches' development agencies, along with the analysis of what kind of development it is that we truly want to foster.[5]

The local church is a key forum in which to raise many of the structural issues for debate. This can be done through practical measures. The church, after the Sunday service, can offer a platform on which the fair trading organisations can operate far more efficiently than they can when dealing direct with mere individuals. It offers a shop window not simply for the products themselves but for the issues of fair trade and just commodity prices which they symbolise. Every packet of tea or sugar sold raises still further the awareness of the local community of Third World justice issues. Annual projects, perhaps through Lent, can be adopted not simply to raise money within the parish but – in consultation with agencies who look to structural solutions – to develop awareness of the range of problems confronting the poor. In addition, direct links can be made with Christians in the Third World so that communication becomes two-way and we are offered new insights into Christian community in return for our material assistance.

The parish also offers the perfect base for educational campaigns. Meetings can be held to give church members direct access to the experiences of visiting Third World speakers. In public meetings the complex issues of international wealth gaps and debt can be raised. In smaller study groups parishioners can work out for themselves how to apply such global matters to the daily life of the community. In the end politicians will initiate changes in the international economic order only in response to public opinion. It is in the local churches that public opinion can be truly informed. The first step in the process of such social healing is acknowledging the need for change.

There will, of course, be setbacks. There may be resistance from those still trapped in a dualist view of the sacred and the secular. There may be a refusal to see by those afflicted by the psychic numbness which we develop in order to survive in modern society. There may be outright hostility from the new religious Right who are seeking once again to harness religion to the forces of reaction.

The warnings of Jesus are clear on this: following his path of prophetic resistance will not be easy and will involve the scorn and opposition of those who are still enslaved to false ideologies. It will sometimes involve us, as it did Jesus, in confrontation with established status and structures. The role of the prophetic minority is to be separate and distinct, as is the yeast and salt which Christ said should transform the dough of society into living bread. As Pope John Paul II said: 'Anyone wishing to renounce the difficult yet noble task of improving the lot of . . . all people, with the excuse that the struggle is difficult and that constant effort is required, or simply because of the experience of defeat and the need to begin again, that person would be betraying the will of God the Creator.[6] Therefore the job must be returned to constantly, with patience, diligence and, above all, with good humour and a sense of the joy of sharing the wonder of what has been created. Working for justice and peace is not a po-faced activity; in the company of others, it can be a positive, affirming and fun experience.

Similar initiatives can be pursued at a national level. In 1988 in Holland churches of various denominations joined with aid agencies and the government development ministry to launch a new brand of coffee. The consortium is concerned primarily with paying a price for coffee beans which results directly in better wages for the impoverished peasants who actually pick them. To invite people to pay 10 per cent more for their coffee might not seem the most adroit of marketing devices. Yet within the first five months of its launch the brand had taken 2 per cent of the annual £450 million national market. The big roasters are concerned. For them to lose even one half per cent of the substantial market had significant financial consequences for their profitability. Demand for the new brand is continuing to grow and the big firms are now thinking of looking at what their coffee pickers are paid. There is no reason why educational campaigns, orientated towards direct political action, should not be intensified along similar lines.

POLITICAL CHANGE

At the structural level there are dozens of avenues for action. In addition to the church agencies and secular development agencies there are a number of pressure groups which do not involve themselves in fund-raising and restrict themselves to campaigning for systemic change. In Britain the most authoritative and best-informed of these is the World Development Movement. In the United States there are the Institute for Food and Development Policy and the Institute for Policy Studies. In Germany there is Food First Information and Action Network. In Holland there is the Transnational Institute.

These, and a number of others, produce magazines which give regular updates on a spectrum of issues including GATT, UNCTAD and Lomé negotiations, the activities of the World Bank and International Monetary Fund, and changes (or lack of them) in the aid policies of individual governments.

They maintain a vigilant watch on the activities of multi-national corporations, such as those in Holland and the USA which have been buying up small seed-supply firms to enable them to develop a monopoly in the new high-tech breeds of seeds which, when sold in the Third World, will require farmers to buy large amounts of the chemical fertilisers made by the same multinationals. They run specific campaigns, in which they invite participation, to lobby politicians by letter or in person. Issues vary from constantly pressing for changes in aid policy to specific matters, like the abolition of the infamous Multi-Fibre Agreement, under which, for example, US textiles have to pay smaller tariffs to enter the European Community than do those from Bangladesh.

Such bodies also provide information on the activities of direct action groups such as the boycott campaigns run against products like Nescafé coffee to pressure the manufacturers, Nestlé, into ending marketing strategies in the Third World which attempt to push powdered baby milk in situations where breast-feeding would be healthier and cheaper for the poor. A similar campaign against another multinational, Coca-Cola, in 1984, helped bring a satisfactory resolution to a vicious dispute between the company and its workers in Guatemala which had led to the murder of a number of prominent local trade union leaders. Other single-issue bodies include those groups who purchase small shareholdings in multinational companies in order to go along to annual shareholders' meetings to raise moral questions among the dividend debate.

What is to be done? In truth the list of options is endless. Having some insight into the complexity of the burdens placed on the Third World by international finance, and our own role in profiting from them, should not make us despair at the intractability of the problem. The first step to a global conversion must be global acknowledgement that wrong is being done. Our new knowledge is a cause for optimism and a spur to action. Are those of us with two coats now prepared to give one away?

NOTES

Introduction

1. *The State of the World's Children* 1990 report, Unicef.
2. ibid.
3. *World Debt Tables 1989–90*, World Bank, 1990.
4. Richard Jolly, deputy executive director of Unicef, 'The Human Dimensions of International Debt', in Adrian Hewitt and Bowen Wells, eds, *Growing Out of Debt*, Overseas Development Institute, London, 1989.
5. Nigel Lawson, when British Chancellor of the Exchequer, in Hewitt and Wells, op. cit.
6. *The State of the World's Children* report 1990, Unicef.
7. *World Debt Tables 1989–90*.
8. Sadly the changes in Eastern Europe seem likely to be bad news for the Third World. By July 1990 some Western aid was already being switched from developing countries to those in Eastern Europe. If the Third World is to compete for cash it will come under increased pressure to follow IMF orthodoxy, the Organisation for Economic Co-operation and Development (OECD) said in its annual survey of Third World debt: The *Independent*, 12 July 1990.
9. Gunnar Myrdal, *Asian Drama*, Penguin, London, 1972.

Chapter One

1. *shamma*: a heavy garment, of coarse white wool, like a cross between a cloak and a blanket.

2. *birr*: Ethiopian currency. At the time the official rate was 2.5 per $US, though the black market rate was treble that.

3. *Médecins Sans Frontières*: this agency of medical volunteers was later expelled from Ethiopia after being the only group prepared to jeopardise its work in the country in order to make a strong public protest about the deaths occurring under the government's enforced resettlement policy.

4. The beginning of the day of twenty-four hours is reckoned, in Semitic fashion, from sunset and sunrise, rather than from midnight and midday. What we call 7 a.m. they call one o'clock. See Edward Ullendorff, *The Ethiopians*, Oxford University Press, 1960.

5. *goitre*: a massive swelling of the thyroid gland, caused by a deficiency of iodine, usually in drinking water. It is common to poor highland areas. Easily eradicable by adding iodine to the diet, usually in salt; without that it produces blindness and cretinism in offspring of the goitred woman. It was common until recent centuries in Switzerland. Today goitre affects 200 million people in the Third World: World Development Movement, *New Deal for the Poorest*, London, 1986.

6. see David Blundy and Paul Vallely, *With Geldof in Africa*, Times Books/Band Aid, London, 1985.

7. *triage* from the French expression meaning to sort or to grade. In this usage it dates from a battlefield practice by French surgeons during the First World War, who graded patients by their chances of survival: they then operated only on those likely to live; the rest were allowed to die.

Chapter Two

1. A general figure given by Unicef in *The State of the World's Children* 1990 report, Oxford University Press. There are no up-to-date detailed figures. One of the best studies, by the World Bank, estimated that as long ago as 1965, 840 million people, some 56 per cent of the populations studied, had diets deficient by more than 250 calories a day; extrapolations would indicate this figure is now well over one billion. The UN's Food and Agriculture Organisation (FAO), in a study during 1972–74, estimated that 455 million people suffer from insufficient protein; quoted in Keith Griffin, *World Hunger and the World Economy*, Macmillan, London 1987.

2. There is no general agreement on the exact number who die from hunger each year. Jon Bennett, *The Hunger Machine*, Polity Press, Cambridge, 1987, estimates between 14–18 million; *The Hunger Project*, 1984, says 13–18 million, of which 75 per cent are children. The Unicef estimate of 17 million is quoted here. In a moral sense a precise figure is meaningless in any case.

3. *The State of the World's Children* 1989 report, Unicef.

4. See Charles Elliott, *Comfortable Compassion?* Hodder & Stoughton, London, 1987.

5. Mahmound Mohamed Taha, the regime's only remaining critic of stature, was hanged at Kober prison in Khartoum, after declaring that Nimeiri was using *sharia* law for political ends. Nimeiri had removed other political opponents in other ways.

6. 700 Falashas were airlifted from a refugee camp near Gedaref. The plan had been worked out at a meeting between Nimeiri and vice-president George Bush who visited Khartoum on 6 March 1985. A similar route may have been used for 7,800 other Falashas taken to Israel between November 1984 and January 1985. Christopher Thomas, Washington, *The Times*, 25 March 1985.

7. International Monetary Fund, see chapter 5, p. 178.

8. Dante, *The Inferno*, Canto XIV, author's translation.

9. *Children First*, Unicef, London, Autumn 1987.

10. The name traditionally given to a child born after the death of its sibling. Edward Ullendorff, *The Ethiopians*, Oxford University Press, 1960.

11. See Dervla Murphy, *In Ethiopia with a Mule*, Century Publishing, London, 1968; also Ullendorff, op. cit.

12. ibid. Also see Donald Levine, *Wax and Gold*, University of Chicago Press, 1965.

13. Counterpart funds: under the US Public Law 480 the US gives food aid (known as Title II food) to the government of a country which can then give away the food or sell it internally and use the funds for some other approved purpose (see p. 78). In this case the funds were to be used to pay for the transport costs of food distribution.

14. *The Times*, 17 July 1985.

15. Ken Willis, manager, Arkel-Talab, at Kosti: *The Times*, London, 17 July 1985.

16. Oxfam internal report by Nigel Taylor, nutritionist, Darfour, 1985.

17. El Geneina, *The Times*, London, 26 July 1985.

18. Lloyd Timberlake, *Africa in Crisis*, Earthscan, London, 1985.

19. ibid.

20. This is undoubtedly an important area of concern. For Christians it raises in a different, temporal, context the question of our stewardship of the planet for future generations; in the parable of the Talents the reward for good stewardship was not the easier life of increased consumption but the gift of a greater responsibility. We will deal with this later, p. 215. But our concern here is that climate and drought are not in any case the prime causes of hunger, which are political and economic.

21. H. Daniel, *Man and Climatic Variability*, World Meteorological Organisation, 1980.

22. Independent Commission on International Humanitarian Issues, *Famine: A Man-Made Disaster?*, Pan, London & Sydney, 1985. As much as 742 million hectares in Africa, 26 per cent of the total land area, is undergoing moderate or severe desertification. This represents no less

than 85 per cent of the dryland area in Africa which is populated by 61 million people: Paul Harrison, *The Greening of Africa*, Grafton Books, London, 1987.

23. UNEP report, quoted in *Famine: A Man-Made Disaster?*

24. Amartya Sen, *Poverty and Famines: An Essay on Entitlement and Deprivation*, Oxford, Clarendon Press, 1981.

25. David Blundy and Paul Vallely, *With Geldof in Africa*, Times Books/ Band Aid, London, 1985.

26. Michael Beenstock, Professor of Finance and Investment, City University Business School, London, in *The Times*, 31 October 1985.

27. ibid.

28. Figure based on estimates of population experts in Kenya given to the author in Nairobi in May 1987. 1989 Unicef figures claim an average of 4.1 per cent between 1980–86.

29. *World Development Report*, World Bank, 1987.

30. *The Times*, 26 May 1987.

31. Paul Harrison, *Inside the Third World*, Penguin, London, 1979.

32. All information based on interviews by the author with population experts in Nairobi in May 1987. On Islamic opposition to contraception: the 1975 meeting of the World Moslem League declared birth control had been 'invented by the enemies of Islam' and urged the faithful to 'pro-create, avoid abortion and reject the pill'.

33. Irene Dankelman and Joan Davidson, *Women and the Environment in the Third World*, Earthscan, London, 1988.

34. The United States grew at 1.6 per cent a year for most of this century and industrialising Europe at only 0.6 per cent a year: Harrison, *Inside the Third World*, op. cit.

35. Some movement in this direction was made in the Third World before the election of Pope John Paul II. Despite the central tenet of the notorious papal encyclical *Humanae Vitae* that 'every conjugal act must remain open to the transmission of life' the Vatican did give quiet approval to a statement commissioned by the Catholic conference of bishops in Kenya which proposed that when Catholic hospitals were integrated into the Kenyan national system Catholic doctors and nurses could co-operate with the government's family planning programme.

36. Susan George, *How the Other Half Dies*, Penguin, London, 1976.

37. Nigel Twose, *Cultivating Hunger: An Oxfam Study of Food, Power and Poverty*, Oxfam, Oxford, 1984.

38. ibid.

39. George, *How the Other Half Dies*.

40. Frances Moore Lappe and Joseph Collins, *World Hunger: Twelve Myths*, Grove Press, USA, 1986.

41. Timothy King, *Population Policies and Economic Development*, a World Bank staff report, Johns Hopkins University Press, Baltimore, 1974.

42. *The State of the World's Children* reports, 1986, 1987, and 1988, Unicef.
43. Quoted in William W. Murdoch, *The Poverty of Nations*, Johns Hopkins University Press, Baltimore, 1980.
44. *The State of the World's Children* 1987 report, Unicef.
45. Harrison, *Inside the Third World*.
46. See interesting chapter 'Tackling Runaway Populations' in Paul Harrison, *The Greening of Africa*.
47. Deut. 26:5–8.
48. Exod. 22:21–4.
49. Jer. 22:13–19.
50. Matt. 11:5.
51. Luke 4:18.
52. Matt. 5:3.
53. Figures given to the author by the Mozambican finance minister, Abdul Magid Osman. See *The Times*, 23 December 1987.
54. The answer to that question was, as we shall come to see, all too predictable. By 1988 Mozambique owed in those debt repayments which were immediately due, fifteen times more than it had managed to earn in total for all its exports: *Banking on the Poor*, Christian Aid, London, 1989.
55. A highly-placed Zambian copper industry executive, in an interview with the author. All the statistics and quotations here are from this source. *The Times*, 20 March 1987.
56. ibid.
57. Source: Dunlop's managing director, Kit Blease, in an interview with the author, *The Times*, 23 March 1987.
58. John Clark, *Zambia – Oxfam Experience with Structural Adjustment*, internal report, Oxfam, November 1986.
59. From an interview with President Kaunda by the author, *The Times*, 25 March 1987.
60. Source: an international banker, who asked not to be named, in an interview with the author in Lusaka, see *The Times*, 17 March 1987.
61. From an interview with President Kaunda by the author, *The Times*, 25 March 1987.
62. *The Times*, 3 January 1989.
63. In an interview with the author, see *The Times*, 22 October 1985.

Chapter Three

1. Luke 10:29ff.
2. Matt. 15:32–8, Mark 8:1–10; Matt. 14:15–21, Mark 6:35–44.
3. 30 December 1987.
4. P. T. Bauer, *Equality, the Third World and Economic Delusion*, Methuen, London, 1982.

5. Jon Bennett, *The Hunger Machine*, Polity Press, Cambridge, 1987. For the UK the proportion was around 60 per cent throughout the late 1980s.
6. Quoted in Wayne G. Bragg, 'From Development to Transformation' in Vinay Samuel and Chris Sugden, eds., *The Church in Response to Human Need*, Regnum Books, Oxford, 1987.
7. Most US food aid is given bilaterally; most UK food is given through multilateral agencies.
8. Nigel Twose, *Cultivating Hunger*, Oxfam, Oxford, 1984.
9. Teresa Hayter, *The Creation of World Poverty*, Pluto Press, London, 1981.
10. Bennett, *The Hunger Machine*.
11. John Clark, *For Richer, For Poorer*, Oxfam, Oxford, 1986.
12. Bennett, *The Hunger Machine*.
13. Susan George, *How the Other Half Dies*, Penguin, London, 1976.
14. Suzanne C. Toton, *World Hunger*, Orbis, Maryknoll, NY, 1982.
15. Rehman Sobhan, *Politics of Food and Famine in Bangladesh*, quoted in Hayter, *The Creation of World Poverty*.
16. Frances Moore Lappe and Joseph Collins, *World Hunger: Twelve Myths*, Earthscan, London, 1988.
17. Japan, which is now the world's largest aid donor, persists with loans rather than grants.
18. Figures provided from budget estimates by US Embassy in London, February 1990. Official figures show that ten countries received more than half of all US aid in the years 1981–85. They were: Egypt ($5,444m), Israel ($5,215m), El Salvador ($1,286m), Pakistan ($1,153m), Turkey ($1,103m), India ($1,084m), Bangladesh ($857m), Sudan ($819m), Costa Rica ($655m) and the Philippines ($637m).
19. Overseas Development Administration, London, *British Overseas Aid in 1985* and *British Aid Statistics, 1985*, analysed in Clark, *For Richer, For Poorer*.
20. Bennett, *The Hunger Machine*.
21. *The Observer*, 12 May 1985.
22. Lappe and Collins, *World Hunger*.
23. Clark, *For Richer, For Poorer*.
24. Michael Lipton, Institute of Development Studies, University of Sussex, quoted in Clark, *For Richer, For Poorer*. Hayter, *The Creation of World Poverty*, estimates that the average price of goods financed by aid is 25 per cent above world market prices.
25. *Missed Opportunities*, Independent Group on British Aid, London, 1986.
26. 'In many developing countries, the poor have not been the main beneficiaries of economic growth,' Robert Cassen and associates in *Does Aid Work?*, a report for the Joint Ministerial Committee of the Board of Governors of the World Bank and the International Monetary Fund, Oxford University Press, 1986. Also see Clark, *For Richer, For Poorer*:

'It is Oxfam's experience, however, that the benefits of this sort of "development" rarely reach the poor . . . national prosperity by no means automatically leads to individual survival. Desperate levels of poverty co-exist with opulence in some of the world's wealthier countries, such as South Africa. The poor need justice as much as they need economic growth.'

27. Griffin, *World Hunger and the World Economy*.
28. See Cassen, *Does Aid Work?*
29. See Harry Magdoff, *Imperialism: From the Colonial Age to the Present*, Monthly Review Press, 1978.
30. Estimate by the Ministry for Economic Co-operation, Federal Republic of Germany, *Bundesministerium fur wirtschaftliche Zusammenarbeit, Journalisten-Handbuch*, Entwicklungspolitik, Bonn, 1982, p. 201; quoted in P. T. Bauer, *Reality and Rhetoric*, Weidenfeld & Nicolson, London 1984.
31. Bauer, *Reality and Rhetoric*.
32. US Agency for International Development, Congressional Presentation Fiscal Year 1987, quoted in Lappe and Collins, *World Hunger*.
33. ibid.
34. Based on data in Ruth Leger Sivard, *World Military and Social Expenditures 1983*, World Priorities, Washington DC, 1983, quoted in Lappe and Collins, *World Hunger*.
35. Lappe and Collins, *World Hunger*.
36. Bauer, *Equality, the Third World and Economic Delusion*.
37. Aristotle, Ethics IX.7, trans. Sir David Ross, Oxford University Press, 1954.
38. Matt. 23:27, 28, Revised Standard Version.
39. Matt. 21:13 RSV
40. Griffin, *World Hunger and the World Economy*.
41. Cassen, *Does Aid Work?*
42. Bennett, *The Hunger Machine*.
43. ibid.
44. R. H. Tawney, *Religion and the Rise of Capitalism*, Penguin, London, 1938.
45. Paul Harrison, *Inside the Third World*, Penguin, London, 1979.
46. Clark, *For Richer, For Poorer*.
47. Hayter, *The Creation of World Poverty*.
48. See Hayter, op. cit., for a succinct account.
49. Peter Donaldson, *Worlds Apart*, Penguin, London, 1985.
50. Harrison, *Inside the Third World*.
51. Adam Smith, *An Inquiry into the Nature and Causes of the Wealth of Nations*, 1776.
52. W. S. Woytinsky and E. S. Woytinsky, *World Commerce and Governments*, Twentieth Century Fund, 1955, quoted in Hayter, op. cit.
53. Hayter, *The Creation of World Poverty*.

54. Ernest Mandel, *Marxist Economic Theory*, Merlin Press, 1962, quoted in Hayter, op. cit.

55. Donaldson, *Worlds Apart*. It was a process which Stalin imposed on the Soviet Union in the 1930s, which was used to build the industrial strength of the Japanese, and which Third World dictators like Colonel Mengistu are pursuing today in Ethiopia.

56. 'The division of labour is limited by the extent of the market,' Adam Smith, *The Wealth of Nations*.

57. Hayter, *The Creation of World Poverty*.

58. Jer. 22:13 RSV.

59. Eph. 6:12.

60. Richard Jolly, of Unicef, in Adrian Hewitt and Bowen Wells, eds., *Growing out of Debt*, Overseas Development Institute, London, 1989.

61. Ironically, the example which Ricardo used to demonstrate the pure workings of free trade was already burdened with an extra-market inequality. It was the principle of comparative advantage, he said, which determined that wine would be made in Portugal and manufactured goods in England. In fact the import of Portuguese wine into England, and the traffic of textiles the other way, was governed in terms favourable to Britain by the Methuen Treaty of 1703 in which Portugal ceded advantages to England in return for military protection against Spain.

62. Amos 6:12 RSV.

63. Ezek. 16:49 RSV.

64. Amos 6:4 RSV.

65. Amos 2:6–7 RSV.

66. Vincent Donovan, *Christianity Rediscovered: an Epistle from the Masai*, Orbis, New York, 1982.

67. Harrison, *Inside the Third World*.

68. For a fuller account see Stephen Neill, *A History of Christian Missions*, Penguin, London, 2nd edition 1986.

69. This section draws extensively on Neill, op. cit.

70. J. K. Galbraith, *The Age of Uncertainty*, BBC/Andre Deutsch, London, 1977.

71. Quoted in Bennett, *The Hunger Machine*.

72. Neill, *A History of Christian Missions*.

73. Galbraith, *The Age of Uncertainty*.

74. Charles Elliott, *Comfortable Compassion?*, Hodder & Stoughton, London, 1987.

75. Donovan, *Christianity Rediscovered*.

76. Judith Listowel, *The Making of Tanganyika*, Chatto & Windus, London, 1965, quoted in Donovan, op. cit.

77. See Jack Nelson-Pallmeyer, *The Politics of Compassion*, Orbis, New York, 1986, p. 20.

78. Quoted in Harrison, *Inside the Third World*.

79. Frantz Fanon, *Black Skin, White Masks*, Paladin, London, 1973.

80. Donovan, *Christianity Rediscovered*.
81. See Donovan, op. cit., for an examination of this phenomenon.
82. Amos 5:21–4 rsv.
83. In Bauer, *Equality, the Third World and Economic Delusion*.
84. Bauer, *Reality and Rhetoric*.
85. ibid.
86. Martin Meredith, *The First Dance of Freedom*, Hamish Hamilton, London, 1984.
87. Matt. 7:16.
88. Ulrich Duchrow, *Global Economy: A Confessional Issue for the Churches*, World Council of Churches, Geneva, 1986.
89. Twose, *Cultivating Hunger*.
90. United Nations Environment Programme, *The State of the Environment 1984*, Nairobi.
91. *World Bank News*, January 1986.
92. Clark, *For Richer, For Poorer*.
93. Alberto Masferrer, quoted in Nelson-Pallmeyer, *The Politics of Compassion*.
94. Lloyd Timberlake, *Africa in Crisis*, Earthscan, London, 1985.
95. Economist Intelligence Unit, *Quarterly Report* No 4, 1985.
96. Clark, *For Richer, For Poorer*.
97. Edward Mayo, *Beyond 1992*, World Development Movement, London, June 1989.
98. *World Bank Annual Report*, 1985.
99. *World Development Report*, World Bank, 1986.
100. Ronald J. Sider, *Rich Christians in an Age of Hunger*, Hodder & Stoughton, London, 1978.
101. Toton, *World Hunger*.
102. *Presidential Commission on World Hunger*, US Government Printing Office, Washington, 1980.
103. Clark, *For Richer, For Poorer*.
104. Toton, *World Hunger*.
105. ibid.
106. Clark, *For Richer, For Poorer*.
107. Isa. 10:1 *New Jerusalem Bible*
108. *North–South: A Programme for Survival*, report of the Independent Commission on International Development Issues under the Chairmanship of Willy Brandt, Pan Books, London, 1980.
109. Gunnar Myrdal, *The Challenge of World Poverty*, Penguin, London, 1970.
110. Clark, *For Richer, For Poorer*.
111. Brian Bolton, *The Common Agricultural Policy, African Food and International Trade*, Catholic Institute for International Relations, London, 1987.
112. These are often given in Export Processing Zones which are usually

346   BAD SAMARITANS

cut off from the rest of the country and where foreign companies enjoy
perks like five- or ten-year tax holidays, no tariffs or customs duties,
freedom to repatriate profits, compulsory no-strike agreements with the
workforce, cheap electricity and water, and training and cheap loans
subsidised by the government: see *Work*, Development Education Project,
Manchester, 1986, for interesting details on the Bataan Free Trade Zone
in the Philippines, including interviews with workers.

113. *Work*.
114. FAO Production and Trade Year Books and Commodity Reviews.
115. Clark, *For Richer, For Poorer*.
116. ibid.
117. Lappe and Collins, *World Hunger*.
118. See account given to Jack Nelson-Pallmeyer, *The Politics of Compassion*.
119. See stories from Brazil in Bennett, *The Hunger Machine*.
120. Hayter, *The Creation of World Poverty*.
121. Samir Amin, *Accumulation on a World Scale*, Harvester Press, Sussex, 1978, quoted in Hayter, op. cit.
122. *Change the World*, World Development Movement, London, 1986.
123. Frances Moore Lappe and Joseph Collins, *Food First*, 1980 edition, Souvenir Press, London.
124. For a fuller account see Lappe and Collins, *Food First*.
125. *Work* (see n. 112).
126. Bolton, *The Common Agricultural Policy*.
127. *Economic and Political Weekly*, Bombay, xiii, no 37, 16 September 1986, quoted in Clark, *For Richer, For Poorer*.
128. Lappe and Collins, *Food First*.
129. Timberlake, *Africa in Crisis*.
130. See Bennett, *The Hunger Machine*.
131. Richard J. Barnet and Ronald E. Muller, *Global Reach: the Power of the Multinational Corporation*, Simon & Schuster, New York, 1974.
132. Harrison, *Inside the Third World*.
133. Hayter, *The Creation of World Poverty*.
134. Brandt report, *North–South*.
135. Hayter, *The Creation of World Poverty*.
136. *Nestlé Bulletin*, No. 20, International Union of Food and Allied Workers, Geneva, quoted in Lappe and Collins, *Food First*.
137. *UK Prices Commission Report* No. 24, *Coffee*, HMSO, 1977, quoted in Lappe and Collins, *Food First*.
138. *Nestlé Bulletin*, No. 20.
139. Isa. 5:8 RSV.
140. Mic. 2:2 *New Jer.*
141. Amos 8:4–6 *New Jer.*
142. Introduction to Bennett, *The Hunger Machine*.
143. *Spur*, World Development Movement, September 1987.

144. Donaldson, *Worlds Apart*.
145. Brandt report, *North–South*.
146. Jas. 5:4 *New Jer*.
147. Isa. 3:12–15 RSV.
148. Research by Dr Dan Lashof of the National Resource Defence Council, Washington, DC. Previously scientists thought that CO_2 was responsible only for 50 per cent of the problem. See *The Sunday Correspondent*, 4 February 1990.
149. John Mitchell, World Development Movement, London.
150. Gen. 2:9, 15 RSV.
151. *World Development Crisis*, Catholic Institute for International Relations, London, 1987.

Chapter Four

1. J. M. Keynes, *Collected Writings*, Vol XXV, London, Macmillan, 1980.
2. ibid.
3. Anthony Sampson, *The Money Lenders*, Coronet, London, 1988.
4. Sue Branford and Bernado Kucinski, *The Debt Squads: the US, the Banks and Latin America*, Zed Books, London, 1988.
5. *The Economic Report of the President*, February 1975.
6. Branford and Kucinski, *The Debt Squads*.
7. ibid.
8. *The Economic Report of the President*, February 1975.
9. *Wall Street Journal*, 7 January 1986.
10. In an interview with Jan Joost Teunissen of the Transnational Institute in Amsterdam, *Alternatives*, Vol XII, July 1987, pp. 359–95.
11. Teunissen, in *Alternatives*.
12. *The Future of the Dollar as a Reserve Currency*, Barclays Bank Review, February 1979.
13. Teunissen, in *Alternatives*.
14. ibid.
15. ibid.
16. C. S. Gwynne, *Selling Money*, Weidenfeld & Nicolson, New York, 1986; Branford and Kucinski, *The Debt Squads*; and Sampson, *The Money Lenders*.
17. See Sampson, *The Money Lenders*, for an intriguing account.
18. Branford and Kucinski, *The Debt Squads*.
19. Between 1973 and 1981 growth rates in non-oil Third World countries averaged 5.1 per cent, only slightly less than the 5.8 per cent of the period 1967–72. The industrial countries by contrast showed only 2.8 per cent, compared with 4.4 per cent: Harold Lever and Christopher Huhne, *Debt and Danger: the World Financial Crisis*, Penguin, London, 1987.
20. OECD, *The Internationalization of Banking: The Policy Issues*, Paris,

1983; the Bank of International Settlements: Fourth Quarter 1984, Basle, 1985: quoted in Lever and Huhne, *Debt and Danger.*

21. Speech to the International Monetary Conference, London, 11 June 1979.

22. Lever and Huhne, *Debt and Danger.*

23. Jackie Roddick, *The Dance of the Millions: Latin America and the Debt Crisis,* Latin America Bureau, London, 1988.

24. For a discussion of this see Ronald Preston, 'Is There a Christian Ethic of Finance?', in *Finance and Ethics,* Centre for Theology and Public Issues, University of Edinburgh, 1987.

25. Tim Congdon, *The Debt Threat,* Basil Blackwell, Oxford, 1988.

26. IMF, *International Capital Markets, Developments and Prospects,* 1982.

27. According to the Brazilian economist, Prof. Maria da Conceicao Tavares, in Teunissen, *Alternatives.*

28. Sampson, *The Money Lenders.*

29. *The Guardian,* 15 March 1975.

30. Teunissen in *Alternatives.*

31. Later, after interest rates rose steeply, private banks in Latin America were particularly keen to continue borrowing so that they could re-lend locally at rates of interest which had been forced even higher by the 'adjustment' policies of the International Monetary Fund. Eventually the governments of the region were forced to take over this debt. See Chapter Five.

32. Gwynne, *Selling Money,* see note 16.

33. Sampson, *The Money Lenders.*

34. David Lomax, *The Developing Country Debt Crisis,* Macmillan, London, 1986.

35. Lever and Huhne, *Debt and Danger.*

36. See Roddick, *The Dance of the Millions.*

37. *State of the World's Children* 1990 report, Unicef.

38. William Cline, *International Debt and the Stability of the World Economy,* Institute for International Economics, Washington DC, 1983.

39. *Financial Times,* 7 August 1987.

40. *Statistical Abstract of the United States 1987,* Washington DC, 1986.

41. *The Guardian,* 10 March 1986.

42. Gwynne, *Selling Money.*

43. BIS Annual Report, 1983.

44. *Profits out of Poverty?* War on Want, London, 1986.

45. Susan George, *A Fate Worse than Debt,* Penguin, London 1988.

46. ibid.

47. Karen Lissakers, 'Money in flight: bankers drive the getaway cars', *International Herald Tribune,* 7 March 1986.

48. One 1982 study by the Inter-American Development Bank suggested that the region's currencies were over-valued, for a decade, at 2.3 per cent per year: see Congdon, *The Debt Threat,* p 122.

49. *World Development Report*, World Bank, 1985, Oxford University Press.

50. Stockholm International Peace Research Institute: Rita Tullberg, 'Military-related debt in non-oil developing countries, 1972–82', SIPRI *Year Book 1985*, Taylor & Francis, London and Philadelphia.

51. *State of the World's Children* 1990 report, Unicef.

52. Catholic Fund for Overseas Development (Cafod) projects.

53. Jack Nelson-Pallmeyer, *The Politics of Compassion*, Orbis, New York, 1986.

54. John Clark, *For Richer, For Poorer*, Oxfam, Oxford, 1986.

55. Anthony Sampson, *The Arms Bazaar*, Hodder & Stoughton, London, 1988.

56. World Bank, *World Development Report 1985*; Ruth Leger Sivard, *World Military and Social Expenditures 1985*: quoted in George, *A Fate Worse Than Debt*.

57. SIPRI *Year Book 1985*, Table 12.5.

58. Deger and Smith, *IDS Bulletin*, October 1985.

59. SIPRI *Year Book 1985*.

60. The Brandt report, *North–South: A Programme for Survival*, Pan Books, London, 1970.

61. Clark, *For Richer, For Poorer*.

62. The Brandt Report, *North–South*, p. 121.

63. *We ask why they are hungry*, Catholic Fund for Overseas Development (Cafod) and Christian Aid, London, 1987.

64. *Link*, Cafod Development Education Newsletter, Autumn 1988, Catholic Fund for Overseas Development, London.

65. Sampson, *The Arms Bazaar*.

66. Brandt Report, *North–South*

67. Quoted in Sampson, *The Arms Bazaar*.

68. George, *A Fate Worse Than Debt*.

69. Comparing 1962–71 with 1972–81 the actual increase in arms to Latin America was some $6 billion, in 1975 prices: Lever and Huhne, *Debt and Danger*.

70. Sampson, *The Arms Bazaar*.

71. Lever and Huhne, *Debt and Danger*.

72. Helen Boaden, Brendan McCarthy and Gerry Northam, *File on Four*, BBC Radio 4, 17 January 1989; by the end of 1984 US military spending had been rising by 8.6 per cent a year in real terms, for four years, giving an aggregate rise of 39.9 per cent.

73. ibid.

74. ibid.

75. Paul Vallely, *The Tablet*, London, 19 March 1988.

76. *Profits out of Poverty?*, War on Want, 1986.

77. Lever and Huhne, *Debt and Danger*.

78. *Profits out of Poverty?*

79. See Chapter Eight, page 321, and notes 46, 47, 48.
80. Congdon, *The Debt Threat*.
81. Branford and Kucinski, *The Debt Squads*.
82. *Change the World*, World Development Movement, London, 1986.
83. Lever and Huhne, *The Debt Threat*.
84. *From Debt to Development*, The Debt Crisis Network, Institute for Policy Studies, Washington DC, 1985.
85. *The Debt Crisis and the World Economy*, Report by a Commonwealth Group of Experts, Commonwealth Secretariat, London.
86. F. Clairmonte and J. Cavanagh, *Third World Network* feature, Penang, Malaysia, 1987.
87. ibid.
88. *Spur*, World Development Movement, London, quoting World Bank annual report, September 1988 and World Bank annual report 1987.
89. Branford and Kucinski, *The Debt Squads*.
90. ibid.
91. Gwynne, *Selling Money*.
92. *Latin American Weekly Report*, 31 March 1983.

Chapter Five

1. *African Concord*, 16 July 1987.
2. John Clark, *Oxfam: An NGO reaction to the World Bank paper – 'Protecting the poor during periods of adjustment'*, private paper for the World Bank, 20 February 1987.
3. John Clark, *NGOs and Structural Adjustment*, United Nations Non-Governmental Liaison Service, Geneva, 1987.
4. John Clark, *Zambia – Oxfam's experience with structural adjustment*, Oxfam internal memorandum, November 1986.
5. *Banking on the Poor*, Christian Aid, London, 1989.
6. *Spur*, World Development Movement, London, October 1987.
7. *The Times*, 3 January 1989.
8. G. A. Cornia, ed., *Adjustment with a Human Face*, vol. 1, *Protecting the Vulnerable and Promoting Growth*, Oxford University Press, 1987.
9. *The State of the World's Children* 1989 report, Unicef.
10. This and the other examples in this paragraph are taken from *From Debt to Development*, The Debt Crisis Network, The Institute for Policy Studies, Washington DC, 1985.
11. The IMF has before required that governments cut subsidies on fertilisers, pesticides, and other essential agricultural resources. In 1978 such cuts in Zambia resulted in a dramatic drop in maize production and an increase in malnutrition.
12. 800,000 in the US alone by 1985, according to testimony before the Joint Economic Committee of Congress in June 1985.

13. NGO lobbying document, IMF annual meeting, Berlin, September 1988.
14. *Profits out of Poverty?*, War on Want, London, 1986.
15. ibid.
16. *World Development Crisis*, Catholic Institute for International Relations, London, August 1987.
17. *Profits out of Poverty?*
18. *The Debt Crisis and Brazil*, Commission on the Churches' Participation in Development (CCPD), World Council of Churches, 1987.
19. *The Financial Famine*, World Development Movement and Unicef UK, London, summer 1988.
20. *Banking on the Poor.*
21. *The Financial Famine.*
22. *Profits out of Poverty?*
23. *The State of the World's Children* 1988 report, Unicef.
24. *Banking on the Poor.*
25. ibid.
26. ibid.
27. NGO lobbying document, IMF annual meeting, Berlin, September 1988.
28. For details see Peter Korner, Gero Maass, Thomas Siebold and Rainer Tetzlaff, *The IMF and the Debt Crisis*, Zed Books, London, 1986.
29. Cornia, *Adjustment with a Human Face.*
30. ibid.
31. *The State of the World's Children*, 1990 Report, Unicef.
32. *Banking on the Poor.*
33. NGO lobbying document, IMF annual meeting, Berlin, September 1988.
34. Evidence given 9 March 1987, published by Interfaith Action for Economic Justice, Washington.
35. Ismail-Sabra Abdalla, *The inadequacy and loss of legitimacy of the IMF*, Development Dialogue, Uppsala, 1980; quoted in Anthony Sampson, *The Money Lenders*, Coronet, London, 1988.
36. Testimony before the Senate subcommittee on International Finance and Monetary Policy, Committee on Banking, Housing and Urban Affairs, 14 February 1983; quoted in Susan George, *A Fate Worse Than Debt*, Penguin, London, 1988.
37. From the French word *tranche*, meaning slice.
38. see page 170.
39. *Reinforcing International Support for African Recovery and Development*, Commonwealth Secretariat paper, London, August 1987.
40. Internal World Bank report.
41. Father J. Bryan Hehir, adviser on debt to US Catholic Bishops Conference, testimony to US House of Representatives Committee on Banking and Currency, 4 January 1989.

42. For the Third World's non-oil-exporting countries: George, *A Fate Worse than Debt*.

43. *Profits out of Poverty?*

44. Sue Branford and Bernado Kucinski, *The Debt Squads: the US, the Banks and Latin America*, Zed Books, London, 1988.

45. See Professor Bade Onimode, of Nigeria, Opening Address, Conference on the Impact of IMF and World Bank Policies on the People of Africa, City University, London, September 1987.

46. See page 65 above.

47. F. Clairmonte and J. Cavanagh, *Third World Network* feature, Penang, Malaysia, 1987. See also Chapter 4, n. 59.

48. ibid.

49. Bright E. Okogu, Hertford College, Oxford: *Structural Adjustment Policies in African Countries*, Conference on the Impact of IMF and World Bank Policies on the People of Africa, City University, London, September 1987.

50. *Executive Intelligence Review*, 5 October 1982.

51. Harold Lever and Christopher Huhne, *Debt and Danger: The World Financial Crisis*, Penguin, London, 1987.

52. *The State of the World's Children* 1988 report, Unicef.

53. Laurence Harris, *The Bretton Woods System and Africa*, Conference on the Impact of IMF and World Bank Policies on the People of Africa, City University, London, September 1987.

54. ibid.

55. *From Debt to Development*, The Debt Crisis Network, Institute for Policy Studies, Washington DC, 1985.

56. Professor Bade Onimode, see note 45.

57. ibid.

58. *Financial Times*, 23 September 1983.

59. Professor Bade Onimode, see note 45.

60. Although the existence of IMF mechanisms to try to stabilise the price of Third World raw materials seems to indicate that the IMF does recognise a basic unfairness in the system of global trade and finance.

61. Professor Bade Onimode, see note 45.

62. Arthur Schlesinger, *A Thousand Days*, Houghton Mifflin, New York, 1965.

63. Branford and Kucinski, *The Debt Squads*.

64. George, *A Fate Worse Than Debt*.

65. *Financial Times*, 4 May 1984.

66. See Chapter Eight, page 293.

67. Maria da Conceicao Tavares, quoted by Jan Joost Teunissen, see Chapter Four, note 10.

68. Richard Thomson, *The Times*, 26 August 1987; Branford and Kucinski, *The Debt Squads*.

69. Branford and Kucinski, *The Debt Squads*.

70. Susan George, *New Statesman*, London, 26 February 1988.
71. Jackie Roddick, *The Dance of the Millions: Latin America and the Debt Crisis*, Latin America Bureau, London, 1988.
72. Speech to the All Party Parliamentary Group on Overseas Aid, 22 July 1987.
73. *Spur*, World Development Movement, London, September 1987.
74. World Bank, *World Debt Tables 1988–89*.
75. *The Economist*, 18 March 1989.
76. *The Independent*, 3 March 1989.
77. *The Times*, 3 March 1989.
78. *The Times*, 22 February 1989.
79. *The Independent*, 25 February 1989.
80. *The Times*, 24 February 1989.
81. *The Independent*, 4 August 1989.
82. *Financial Times*, 24 February 1990.
83. NatWest had 75 per cent cover, Lloyds 72 per cent, Barclays 70 per cent (or 64 per cent when its debts to South Africa are included). Only the Midland was less secure; its cover was now 50.2 per cent of its debt: *Financial Times*, 24 February 1990 and 2 March 1990. Lloyds raised its cover by £66m to 73 per cent in July 1990. By this point the banks considered the debt crisis behind them. They had 70 per cent provision plus a further 20 per cent of the debt covered by other agreements, including the Brady Plan: *Financial Times*, 28 July 1990.
84. *The Times*, 21 February 1990.
85. *The Independent*, 28 January 1990. Barclays sold off almost £1 billion of its £2.5 billion debt in the eighteen months up to March 1990: *Financial Times*, 2 March 1990.
86. *World Bank News*, extract from World Debt Tables 1988–89, 22 December 1988.
87. ibid.

Chapter Six

1. Brian Griffiths, *The Creation of Wealth: a Christian's Case for Capitalism*, Downers Grove, Inter Varsity Press, 1984.
2. Eph. 6:5–8 and 1 Cor. 7:17–24 were frequently quoted to justify slavery. In the early nineteenth century in Bristol, the home port for many British slave ships, the church bells used to ring out in triumph whenever a Bill to abolish the slave trade was defeated in Parliament: Horace Dammers, *A Christian Lifestyle*, Hodder & Stoughton, London, 1986.
3. Mark 2:27.
4. Deut. 22:6–7 *Jerusalem Bible*. Later they were to lose this complete harmony with their environment. As settled farmers they developed a more combative attitude. Palestine in the twelfth century BC was little like

the dusty eerie rockscapes which the visitor to Israel sees today; much of it was covered in thick forests of pines and deciduous and evergreen oaks which the settlers had to clear to cultivate. In the intervening years these have disappeared through over-cultivation – the fate which now threatens many of the world's equatorial regions. The first chapters of Genesis, probably written later than some of the Deuteronomy prescriptions, parallel the settlers' own activity when they speak of creation in terms of God bringing order out of chaos and of Paradise as a garden made from wilderness. Their instruction is to take the earth and 'subdue it' (Gen. 1:28).

5. Num. 26:54; 33:54; 34:16–29; Josh.18–19.
6. For further details see John Rogerson and Philip Davies, *The Old Testament World*, Cambridge University Press, 1989.
7. Lev. 25:23; see also Deut. 10:14.
8. 'Christianity and Capitalism' in Digby Anderson, ed., *The Kindness that Kills*, SPCK, London, 1984.
9. Lev. 25:16–17.
10. Lev. 25:25–28.
11. Lev. 25:8–10. Some scholars believe that this chapter was written in the fifth century, at the time of Nehemiah, to consolidate what he believed were the views of the early settlers.
12. Donald Hay, 'International Socio-Economic Order and Lifestyle' in *Lifestyle in the Eighties*, ed. Ronald Sider, Paternoster Press, Exeter, 1982.
13. Exod. 23:10–11.
14. Deut. 24:19–22.
15. Lev. 25:14–17.
16. Exod. 21:2; Deut. 15:12–18.
17. Lev. 25:54–5.
18. Deut. 15:12–14.
19. Deut. 15:1–6.
20. Deut. 15:9.
21. Deut. 14:28–9.
22. Exod. 22:25; Deut. 23:19–20; Lev. 25:35–8.
23. Exod. 22:26–7; Deut. 24:6.
24. Donald Hay, *A Christian Critique of Socialism*, Grove Books, Nottingham, 1982.
25. Gen. 13:2. It is also said at the same point (12:10ff.) that, fearing his life is in danger, he allows his wife Sarai to sleep with the Pharaoh. Presumably those who claim that Abraham's wealth is here specifically sanctioned by God would not say the same about his conduct.
26. Gen. 26:12–15.
27. Gen. 30:43.
28. Deut. 28:1ff.
29. Paul Gifford, Department of Theology in the University of Leeds and

former lecturer at the University of Zimbabwe, 'The Gospel of Prosperity', *The Tablet*, 3 December 1988. See also chapter on Korea and the Full Gospel Church in Charles Elliott, *The Sword and The Spirit*, BBC Books, London, 1989.

30. For further details see Rogerson and Davies, *The Old Testament World*.

31. Roland De Vaux, *Ancient Israel: Its Life and Institutions*, Darton, Longman and Todd, London, 1968.

32. Rogerson and Davies, *The Old Testament World*.

33. 1 Sam. 8:11–18 RSV.

34. 1 Kgs. 5:13–16.

35. 1 Kgs. 9:10–11.

36. 2 Sam. 24:18–25; 1 Kgs. 16:24.

37. 1 Kgs. 21:1ff.

38. Vinay Samuel and Chris Sugden, 'A Just and Responsible Lifestyle – An Old Testament Perspective', in Sider, *Lifestyle in the Eighties*.

39. H. K. Henry, 'Land Tenure in the Old Testament', *Palestine Exploration Society Quarterly*, 86, 1954.

40. Introduction to the Wisdom Books, *The New Jerusalem Bible*, Darton, Longman & Todd, London, 1985.

41. Prov. 14:35 and 16:10; Eccles. 5:9.

42. Eccles. 10:19; Prov. 10:3–4; 10:15; 21:5; 22:7.

43. Prov. 18:23.

44. Robert W. Wall, Professor of Theology at Seattle Pacific University, 'Social Justice and Human Liberation', in Vinay Samuel and Chris Sugden, eds., *The Church in Response to Human Need*, Regnum Books, Oxford, 1987.

45. For further details see Rogerson and Davies, *The Old Testament World*.

46. Thomas Cullinan, reflecting on Isaiah 53 in *The Passion of Political Love*, Sheed & Ward, London, 1987.

47. Jer. 22:13.

48. Job 24:3–11.

49. Amos 5:11.

50. Mic. 6:11.

51. Job 24:3–11.

52. Mic. 2:2.

53. Isa. 10:1–4.

54. Amos 3:15.

55. Isa. 3:14.

56. Amos 5:11.

57. Jer. 22:13–15.

58. Amos 6:4.

59. Amos 6:4–6.

60. Amos 4:1.

61. Isa. 3:16–26.
62. Amos 8:4–5.
63. Jer. 5:26–9.
64. Amos 5:7–10; Micah 3:9–12.
65. Neh. 5:1–5.
66. Neh. 5:8.
67. Gen. 2:18.
68. Exod. 20:15–17; Deut. 5:19–21; Deut. 27:17; Prov. 22:28; and others.
69. Lev. 19:9–10; Deut. 24:19–22.
70. Harvey Perkins, 'The Poor and Oppressed', in Vinay Samuel and Chris Sugden, eds., *Evangelism and the Poor*, Regnum Books, Oxford, 1983.
71. Francis Bacon, 'Of Adversity', The *Essays*, London, 1625.
72. Ernst Troeltsch, *The Social Teachings of the Christian Churches*, 1911, quoted in Stephen Mott, *Jesus and Social Ethics*, Grove Books, Nottingham, 1984.
73. ibid.
74. Rudolf Bultmann, *Jesus and the Word*, quoted in Mott, op. cit.
75. Luke 4:16–21 *New Jer.*
76. John Howard Yoder in *The Politics of Jesus* (Eerdmans, 1972) sees allusions to the Jubilee Year in several of Jesus's sayings: on leaving the soil to fallow, on remission of debts and liberation of slaves and on the redistribution of land.
77. Luke 6:20–26.
78. Matt. 5:17.
79. Luke 16:29–31.
80. Matt. 6:25–32.
81. Matt. 14:16.
82. Luke 19:11–27 and Matt. 25:14ff., where the discussion of the use of the Talents is followed immediately by the judgement of the sheep and goats in which the crucial test is helping the poor and needy.
83. Matt. 25:37–8, and the story of the rich man and Lazarus in Luke 16:19ff.
84. Mark 7:21–2.
85. Matt. 20:1–16.
86. Karl Marx, *Critique of the Gotha Programme*, in Karl Marx and Frederick Engels, *Selected Works*, Lawrence & Wishart, London, 1968.
87. Matt. 25:44ff.
88. Luke 7:22.
89. Matt. 5:3.
90. C. René Padilla, 'New Testament Perspectives on Simple Lifestyle', in Sider, *Lifestyle in the Eighties*.
91. Christ's full words, of course, are 'For you always have the poor with you, and whenever you will, you can do good to them' Mark 14:7.
92. Matt. 11:5.

93. Luke 2:7.
94. See p. 220.
95. Luke 2:24.
96. Matt. 2:14.
97. John 1:46.
98. John 7:41.
99. Geza Vermes, *Jesus the Jew*, William Collins, London, 1973.
100. ibid.
101. ibid.
102. Matt. 8:20.
103. Luke 8:2–3.
104. Mark 2:8; 7:15.
105. Matt. 5:46–48; 6:7,32; 10:5.
106. Vinay Kumar Samuel, *The Meaning and Cost of Discipleship*, Bombay Urban Industrial League for Development, Bombay.
107. ibid.
108. See Ahn Byung Mu, 'Jesus and the Minjung', in Samuel and Sugden, *Evangelism and the Poor*. Minjung theology is being developed in Asia along much the same lines as liberation theology in Latin America. See page 248.
109. Mott, *Jesus and Social Ethics*.
110. Luke 11:37.
111. Luke 8:41.
112. There is an interesting insight into the relationship between poverty and status in the Indonesian language where 'poor' is translated not by the phrase 'those who have not' but 'those who are not': see Chavannes Jeunnes, 'Justice, Freedom and Social Transformation' in Samuel and Sugden, *The Church in Response to Human Need*.
113. Matt. 11:19; 21:32; Mark 2:16; Luke 7:33–50; 15:1; 19:2.
114. Luke 19:1–10.
115. Mark 1:40–45; Luke 17:11–19.
116. Matt. 8:5–13; John 4:46–54.
117. Matt. 8:5–13; 9:20–26.
118. See Elisabeth Schussler, *In Memory of Her*, Crossroad, New York, 1984.
119. Mark 9:37.
120. Mark 10:13–16.
121. Mark 2:11; 5:19; 5:34; 8:26.
122. Luke 8:43–48; Mark 5:24–34; for details on the extent of the uncleanliness of women see Lev. 15:19–30. See Vermes, *Jesus the Jew*, and Jane Williams, 'Jesus the Jew and Women', in Monica Furlong, ed., *Feminine in the Church*, SPCK, London, 1984.
123. Quoted in Mott, *Jesus and Social Ethics*.
124. Matt. 23:23–4 RSV.
125. Mark 2:27 RSV.

126. Luke 22:35–8.
127. Mark 12:38–40 RSV.
128. François Houtart, 'Palestine in Jesus' Time', *Social Scientist* No. 42.
129. Matt. 19:21.
130. We see this also in his silence before the Sanhedrin and Herod when he is brought to trial.
131. Mott, *Jesus and Social Ethics*.
132. Luke 4:29.
133. Mark 3:21.
134. Mark 6:44; 8:9.
135. John 11:53.
136. John 5:2–18.
137. Vishal Mangalwadi, 'Compassion and Social Reform: Jesus the Troublemaker', in Samuel and Sugden, *The Church in Response to Human Need*.
138. John 9:1–41.
139. Mangalwadi, 'Compassion and Social Reform'.
140. John 11:42 RSV.
141. John 12:9–11.
142. Mangalwadi, 'Compassion and Social Reform'.
143. Ronald H. Preston, 'The End of the Protestant Work Ethic?' in *The Future of Christian Ethics*, SCM, London, 1987.

Chapter Seven

1. E. Troeltsch, *The Social Teaching of the Christian Churches*, Harper & Row, Torchbook, New York, 1960.
2. Acts 4:36–7.
3. Acts 2:43–7; 4:32–7; 6:1–7.
4. Acts 5:1–11.
5. 1 Pet. 4:10 *New English Bible*.
6. 1 John 4:20 NEB.
7. 1 Cor. 6:10; Rom. 1:29.
8. Eph. 5:5.
9. 1 Tim. 6:10.
10. 1 Cor. 16:1–2.
11. 2 Cor. 8:1–6.
12. 2 Cor. 8:8.
13. 2 Cor. 8:13–14 RSV.
14. Jas. 5:1–5.
15. 1 Cor. 11:21–9.
16. 2 Cor. 8:1–5.
17. Quoted in Martin Hengel, *Property and Riches in the Early Church: Aspects of a Social History of Early Christianity*, SCM, London, 1974.

18. ibid.
19. See Redmond Mullin, *The Wealth of Christians*, Orbis, New York, 1984.
20. Ronald H. Preston, *The Future of Christian Ethics*, SCM, London, 1987.
21. Rule, Chapter 33.
22. R. H. Tawney, *Religion and the Rise of Capitalism*, Penguin, London, 1938.
23. E. M. Tillyard, *The Elizabethan World Picture*, Chatto & Windus, London, 1943.
24. Barbara Tuchman, *A Distant Mirror*, Macmillan, London, 1979.
25. Lev. 25:35–8; Deut. 15:1–11; 23:19–20; Ezek. 18:5–13.
26. Tawney, *Religion and the Rise of Capitalism*.
27. Tuchman, *A Distant Mirror*.
28. N. E. Lipson, *An Economic History of England*, quoted in G. M. Trevelyan, *Illustrated English Social History*, vol 1, Penguin, London, 1964.
29. Tawney, *Religion and the Rise of Capitalism*.
30. ibid.
31. *Selected Writings of Martin Luther*, Philadelphia, 1967.
32. Preston, *The Future of Christian Ethics*.
33. C. B. Macpherson, *The Political Theory of Possessive Individualism*, 1962, quoted in 'Capitalism, Socialism and Individualism' in Ronald H. Preston, *Religion and the Persistence of Capitalism*, SCM, London, 1979.
34. Max Weber, *Wirtschaft und Gesellschaft*, Tübingen, 1972, translated in Ulrich Duchrow, *Global Economy: A Confessional Issue for the Churches*, World Council of Churches, Geneva, 1986.
35. Quoted in Mullin, *The Wealth of Christians*.
36. Donald Hay, *A Christian Critique of Capitalism*, Grove Books, Nottingham, 1975.
37. *Encyclopaedia Britannica*, 1947.
38. J. Wesley Bready, *England: Before and After Wesley*, Hodder & Stoughton, London, 1938.
39. Preston, *The Future of Christian Ethics*.
40. Mullin, *The Wealth of Christians*.
41. See R. H. Bainlain, 'The Left Wing of the Reformation', *Journal of Religion* 21, 1941.
42. R. Goudzwaard, 'Centrally Planned Economies: Strengths, Weaknesses and the Future', *Transformations* vol. 4, Nos 3 and 4, Philadelphia, 1987.
43. W. Rauschenbusch, *A Theology for the Social Gospel*, New York, 1917.
44. Ulrich Duchrow, *Global Economy: A Confessional Issue for the Churches*.
45. David Jenkins, 'Doctrines Which Drive One to Politics', in Haddon

Wilmer, ed., *Christian Faith and Political Hopes*, Epworth, London, 1979.

46. Gustavo Gutierrez, essay 'Liberation Praxis and Christian Faith' in his *The Power of the Poor in History*, Orbis, New York, 1983.

47. Quoted by Philip Berryman in *Liberation Theology*, Taurus, London, 1987.

48. A Peruvian bishop quoted by Jon Sobrino in *Reflections on Puebla*, CIIR, London, 1980.

49. Paulo Freire, *Pedagogy of the Oppressed*, Penguin, London, 1972.

50. Charles Elliott, *Comfortable Compassion?*, Hodder & Stoughton, London, 1987.

51. Gustavo Gutierrez, *A Theology of Liberation*, Orbis, New York, 1973.

52. Gutierrez, 'Liberation Praxis and Christian Faith'.

53. Gutierrez, *A Theology of Liberation*.

54. In the following section I have drawn widely on the work of P. T. Bauer, 'Ecclesiastical Economics', in *Reality and Rhetoric*, Weidenfeld & Nicolson, London, 1984; Ulrich Duchrow, *Global Economy: A Confessional Issue for the Churches*; Brian Griffiths, *Morality and the Market Place*, Hodder & Stoughton, 1982, and *Christianity and Capitalism*, SPCK, London, 1984; Donald Hay, *A Christian Critique of Capitalism*, and *A Christian Critique of Socialism*, both Grove Books, Nottingham, 1975 and 1982, and 'International Socio-Economic Order and Lifestyle' in Ronald Sider, ed., *Lifestyle in the Eighties*, Paternoster Press, Exeter, 1982; Peter Hill, Stephen Mott, William Stent and others in 'Christian Faith and Economics', *Transformations* vol. 4, Nos. 3 and 4, Philadelphia, 1987; Ronald H. Preston, *Religion and the Persistence of Capitalism*, SCM, London, 1979, and *The Future of Christian Ethics*, SCM, London, 1987; and T. E. Utley, 'Capitalism the Moral Case' in *Politics Today* No. 16, CRDP, London, 1980.

55. Donald Hay, 'International Socio-Economic Order and Lifestyle'.

56. Utley, 'Capitalism the Moral Case'.

57. Literally: 'let do'; in this sense used to mean 'let things take their course'.

58. See page 240.

59. Adam Smith, *An Inquiry into the Nature and Causes of the Wealth of Nations*, 1776.

60. F. A. von Hayek, *The Road to Serfdom*, Routledge, London, 1944.

61. Lord Harris of High Cross, *Morality and Markets: Gospel of an Economist*, Centre for Policy Studies, London, 1986.

62. Milton Friedman, *Capitalism and Freedom*, University of Chicago Press, 1962.

63. Utley, 'Capitalism the Moral Case'.

64. Hay, *A Christian Critique of Capitalism*.

65. Duchrow, *Global Economy*.

66. Lord Harris of High Cross, *Morality and Markets*. Ralph Harris is a thin man, which perhaps explains his choice of metaphor.

67. Utley, 'Capitalism the Moral Case'.

68. Nigel Lawson, *The New Conservatives*, Centre for Policy Studies, London, 1980.

69. Griffiths, *Christianity and Capitalism*. There is, as Charles Elliott has pointed out, an ambiguity in this concession.

70. Hill, 'Christian Faith and Economics'. Hill takes no account here of the massive transfers of capital and technology from Europe to the United States early in this period which are currently denied to the Third World.

71. *Christianity and Capitalism*; this is the source of all Griffiths quotations in this section.

72. David Sheppard, *Bias to the Poor*, Hodder & Stoughton, London, 1983.

73. Geoffrey Dawson, 'God's Creation, Wealth Creation and the Idle Redistributors', in Digby Anderson, ed., *The Kindness that Kills*, SPCK, London, 1984. Ronald Preston dubs this attitude 'the paradoxical doctrine that the rich need their wealth increased to induce them to work effectively, whilst the poor need their wages reduced in order to make them do so': 'The New Right: a Theological Critique', in *The Future of Christian Ethics*.

74. Quoted in Utley, 'Capitalism the Moral Case'.

75. Utley, op. cit.

76. For a fuller discussion see Robert Goudzwaard, 'Centrally Planned Economies'.

77. Hay, *A Christian Critique of Socialism*.

78. This is not a question of degree: Hayek argues that freedom can only survive in a market economy and that socialism is *per se* inimical to it; Friedman maintains that freedom is indivisible and that all freedoms are interconnected, with personal and political freedoms being dependent upon economic freedom. Conversely the liberation theologians see a distinct hierarchy of freedoms: they ask how important is freedom of the press in a country where 80 per cent of the people cannot afford to buy a newspaper? They argue that certain of the political and human rights freedoms are secondary to the freedom to survive, to eat and to work.

79. Hay, *A Christian Critique of Socialism*.

80. Hay argues that queues are not necessarily a sign of systemic inefficiency so much as an indication that the socialist planners see a greater priority elsewhere and have diverted the limited resources to ends other than consumer goods. Queues are thus seen as a more just form of rationing by time rather than the rationing by price which happens in a market economy. But if planners are diverting resources away from the production of the most basic foodstuffs then this must indicate, at the very least, a dubious sense of priority.

81. Reinhold Niebuhr, *Moral Man and Immoral Society*, SCM, London, 1963.

82. Quoted in Goudzwaard, 'Centrally Planned Economies'.

83. See Hay, *A Christian Critique of Socialism*.

84. Herbert Marcuse, *Soviet Marxism*, Penguin, London, 1971.

85. Walter Wink, *Naming the Powers: the Language of Power in the New Testament*, Fortress, Philadelphia, 1984.

86. Elliott, *Comfortable Compassion*.

87. Matt. 7:15–16 RSV.

88. André Gunder Frank, *Capitalism and Underdevelopment in Latin America*, Penguin, London, 1971. The thesis is indebted to Lenin's Theory of Imperialism which claims that world-wide capitalism produces 'super-profits' for a handful of countries and that capitalists there then pass on part of this to important sections of their working class who remain 'quite philistine in their way of life' but who now form an international 'labour aristocracy'. The prosperity of the First World, he claimed, was achieved entirely from the 'super-profits' of colonial exploitation. V. I. Lenin, *Imperialism: The Highest Stage of Capitalism*, in *Selected Works*, Foreign Languages Publishing House, Moscow, 1952.

89. Vinay Samuel and Christopher Sugden, 'Theology of Development', in Ronald J. Sider, ed., *Evangelicals and Development*, Paternoster Press, Exeter, 1981.

90. 'Higher rates of growth cannot by themselves be relied upon to achieve a reduction in absolute poverty,' Griffiths, *Christianity and Capitalism*. See also Chapter Three p. 81 and Notes 26 and 27.

91. 'Economic growth may eventually lead to an increase in employment but there can be no guarantee that this will occur quickly, nor that it will occur in those areas where poverty is greatest. On the contrary, if the economic growth is associated with technological change, it might even lead to a decrease in employment,' William Stent (see note 54). An example of this is the Green Revolution in India where new hybrid crops and new fertilisers boosted production on the larger farms of the better-off farmers but forced peasants who could not afford to buy the new technology into bankruptcy. Many were forced to sell their land and join the growing number of landless labourers and the destitute. Many more who had previously rented poor land from rich farmers were thrown off it because the Green Revolution meant it was now profitable for the owner to farm it himself.

92. William Temple, *Christianity and Social Order*, Penguin, London, 1942.

93. Preston, 'Capitalism, Socialism and Individualism', in *Religion and the Persistence of Capitalism*.

94. Donald Hay, *A Christian Critique of Capitalism*.

95. Goudzwaard, 'Centrally Planned Economies'.

96. *The Times*, 27 February 1989.

97. Amartya Sen, 'Starvation and Exchange Entitlements', *Cambridge Journal of Economics*, vol 1, 1976, and *Ingredients of Famine Analysis*, Oxford University and Cornell University, Working Paper no. 210, 1979.

98. Tawney, *Religion and the Rise of Capitalism*.

99. H. E. Daly, *Toward a Steady-State Economy*, Freeman, San Francisco, 1973.
100. F. Hirsch, *The Social Limits to Growth*, Routledge & Kegan Paul, London, 1979.

Chapter Eight

1. Bishop Cyprian Bamwoze of Jinja in Uganda, quoted in Charles Elliott, *Comfortable Compassion?*, Hodder & Stoughton, London, 1987.
2. See page 120 above; for full details see *Beyond Dependency: The Developing World Speaks Out*, Overseas Development Council, Washington DC, 1975.
3. Wayne G. Bragg, 'From Development to Transformation' in Vinay Samuel and Chris Sugden, eds., *The Church in Response to Human Need*, Regnum Books, Oxford, 1987.
4. Cited by John G. Sommer, *US Voluntary Aid to the Third World*, Overseas Development Council, Washington DC, 1975.
5. This is one of the main arguments of his provocative book, *Comfortable Compassion?*
6. Tom Sine, 'Development: Its Secular Past and its Uncertain Future', in Samuel and Sugden, *The Church in Response to Human Need*; also in Ronald J. Sider, ed., *Evangelicals and Development*, Paternoster Press, Exeter, 1981.
7. Conversation with the author.
8. Herbert Butterfield, *Christianity and History*, Fontana, London, 1957.
9. Précis by the author of a speech to St Margaret's church, Twickenham, 10 May 1989.
10. Jackie Roddick, *The Dance of the Millions: Latin America and the Debt Crisis*, Latin America Bureau, London, 1988. From 1981 the amount declined annually thus: $30.5 billion, $12.1b (1982), $7.8b (1983), $5.7b (1984), $1.3b (1985) to minus $0.5 billion in 1986.
11. Charles Elliott, *The Ethics of International Debt*, Finance and Ethics, Paper 11, Centre for Theology and Public Issues, University of Edinburgh, 1987.
12. Charles Schumer and Alfred Watkins, 'Faustian Finance', *The New Republic*, 11 March 1985.
13. *The Times*, 28 September 1987.
14. *Spur*, World Development Movement, September 1987.
15. *The Times*, 29 September 1988.
16. John Williamson, Institute for International Economics, Washington DC, in 'Debt Reduction: Half a Solution', Adrian Hewitt and Bowen Wells, eds., *Growing Out of Debt*, All Party Group on Overseas Development, London, 1989.
17. *Financial Times*, 22 March 1989.

18. *The Guardian*, 16 March 1988.
19. *The Economist*, 18 March 1989.
20. *The Independent*, 23 January 1989.
21. *The Guardian*, 4 August 1989.
22. *Financial Times*, 31 July 1989.
23. In the Paul VI Memorial Lecture, in *Proclaim Jubilee*, Cafod, London, 1987.
24. Elliott, *The Ethics of International Debt*.
25. ibid.
26. *Populorum Progressio*, 1967, quoted in *Proclaim Jubilee*.
27. R. T. MacNamara, deputy secretary, reported in *Fortune* magazine, quoted in Susan George, *A Fate Worse Than Debt*, Penguin, London, 1988.
28. Anatole Kaletsky, *The Costs of Default*, a Twentieth Century Fund Paper, Priority Press Publication, New York, 1985.
29. ibid.
30. The US Catholic bishops list eight principles which any solution must observe, in *Relieving Third World Debt*, US Catholic Conference, October 1989. But in essence these can be reduced to the same two fundamentals.
31. George, *A Fate Worse Than Debt*.
32. It can mean changing structures too: the International Fellowship of Evangelical Students gains most of its income from its Northern members yet its executive committee, which makes the spending decisions, is made up of four members from the North and eight from the South.
33. *The State of the World's Children*, 1990 report, Unicef.
34. Tim Congdon, *The Debt Threat*, Basil Blackwell, Oxford, 1988.
35. Sue Branford and Bernado Kucinski, *The Debt Squads: The US, the Banks and Latin America*, Zed Books, London, 1988.
36. Except for the Midland, see Chapter Five, note 83.
37. *Financial Times*, 31 July 1989.
38. Hewitt and Wells, *Growing Out of Debt*.
39. Speech to All Party Parliamentary Group on Overseas Development, December 1988, quoted in Hewitt and Wells op. cit.
40. *Wall Street Journal*, 20 September 1984, quoted in Kaletsky, *The Costs of Default*.
41. Christopher Huhne, *The Guardian*, 16 March 1988.
42. John Denham of War on Want, in *The Guardian*, 2 August 1989.
43. See John Denham's paper *Debt Relief Not Tax Relief*, War on Want, mimeo, 1987.
44. Stephen Fidler, 'Forgive but not forget', *Financial Times*, 6 July, 1990.
45. See Harry L. Freeman, Amex Executive Vice-President, 'US National Security and the LDC Debt Crisis', in Hewitt and Wells, *Growing out of Debt*.
46. 'Marcos linked to $80 million; Westinghouse paid "commission" for nuclear plant in 76', *International Herald Tribune*, New York Times news

service, 8/9 March 1986, quoted in George, *A Fate Worse Than Debt*.

47. 'Westinghouse denies charge', *International Herald Tribune*, New York Times news service, 10 March 1986, quoted in George, *A Fate Worse than Debt*.

48. NGO lobby document for World Bank/IMF meeting in Berlin, 1988.

49. George, *A Fate Worse than Debt*.

50. NGO lobby document for World Bank/IMF meeting in Berlin, 1988.

51. Testimony to Congress in June 1985 estimated that 800,000 jobs had been lost in the United States because Latin America could not afford to buy as many US products as before. Other estimates are of 1.1 million jobs. See *From Debt to Development*, The Debt Crisis Network, Institute for Policy Studies, Washington DC, 1985.

52. See Harry L. Freeman, in Hewitt and Wells, *Growing out of Debt*.

53. See G. A. Cornia, ed., *Adjustment with a Human Face*, Oxford University Press, 1987.

54. See Hernando de Soto, *The Other Path*, I. B. Taurus, London, 1989, for an interesting account by this Peruvian economist who estimates that in Peru street vendors and black-market businesses work 61 per cent of the nation's man-hours and create 38 per cent of the GDP. They are often prevented from entering the mainstream economy by excessive bureaucracy and government restriction.

55. In Hewitt and Wells, *Growing out of Debt*.

56. See Kaletsky, *The Costs of Default*.

57. 'Brady Plan stalled by rudderless negotiations', *The Times*, 5 June 1989.

58. 'Banks on verge of debt accord with Mexico', *The Guardian*, 10 August 1989.

59. *The Independent*, 4 August 1989.

Epilogue

1. Jorgen Lissner, *Ten Reasons for Choosing a Simpler Life Style*, quoted in Horace Dammers, *A Christian Lifestyle*, Hodder & Stoughton, London, 1986.

2. Ulrich Duchrow, *Global Economy: A Confessional Issue for the Churches*, World Council of Churches, Geneva, 1986.

3. Teilhard de Chardin, *The Phenomenon of Man*, Collins, London, 1959.

4. Rob van Drimmelen, *Homo Oikumenicus and Homo Economicus*, in *Transformations* vol. 4, nos. 3 and 4, Philadelphia, 1987.

5. See Chapter Eight, pages 284–293.

6. *Sollicitudo Rei Socialis*, 1988.

Index

famine; and Ethiopia-Egypt
meat deal 21; British aid
during Ethiopian 31–2;
and exodus of Ethiopians
to Sudan 36; drought
triggers 40; named by
nomads 48; in
mid-western US 50; lack
of co-relation with
population density 55
Fanon, Frantz 101
Fanta, soft drink 114–15
Farias, Romario 301
farmers; and Korem 9; and
drought 26, 50; and food
prices 51, 171; and badly
managed food aid 52;
smuggling out of Zambian
maize 65; and peasant
committees in Burkina
Faso 68; and development
projects 82; dispossessed
94, 113, 241; protection of
European 109–10; *colonia*
system 116
Federal Reserve Board 191,
193
feeding programmes 12, 23,
24
female circumcision 54
fertility 53, 54, 56
Finney, Charles 245
First Chicago 141
First City Bank Corporation
193
Fischer, Stanley 197
food aid 77–9
Food and Agriculture
Organisation (FAO) 76
Food for Peace programme
see Public Law 480
Food for Work programme
12
food prices; fixing of 51, 60;
rises 64, 174, 177
food production, women
and 280–81
forestry, and aid 50
France 11; and colonialism
89, 96; and slave trade 89;
bank provision for
covering default 315
Francis of Assisi 72
Frank, André Gunder 267
free trade 88, 92–3, 120,
325–16
Freire, Paulo 250

Friedman, Milton 256
Funk, Dr Walter 126, 127

Gabon 158
Galbraith, J. K. 98–9, 155
Gandhi, Rajiv 81
Geldof, Bob 243, 244
General Agreement on
Tariffs and Trade
(GATT) 108–9, 129, 335
General Electric 321
General Foods 112
General System of
Preferences (GSP) 120
George, Susan 55, 116, 121,
155, 311
Germany, colonisation of
Africa 89
Ghana 82, 116, 175, 176,
292, 293
Gifford, Paul 204
Global Economy (Duchrow)
105
global warming 48, 123
gold 88, 89, 126, 129, 130,
132, 133, 134, 138, 143
Good Samaritan 215, 216;
rich world's role as Bad
Samaritan 4–5; and relief
workers 29; and
journalism 39–40; as
model for personal charity
71–2; and new parables
72–3; Calvin and
Gutierrez 249
'Gospel of Prosperity' 204
Goudzwaard, Professor
Robert 245, 270
grain; prices 41; pilferage
44; speculation 45, 67; EC
export of 110
Great Benghal Famine
(1943) 272
Great Crash 194
Great Depression 131, 132
Green Revolution 117
greenhouse effect 48, 123,
293
Griffin, Dr Keith 82, 84
Griffiths, Professor Brian
199, 201, 259–62, 268
Guatemala 79, 84, 336
Guinea-Bissau 176
Gurria, Angel 148
Gutierrez, Gustavo 249,
250
Gwynne, S. C. 144–7

Habgood, Dr John,
Archbishop of York 271,
272
Harris, Professor Laurence
185–6, 187
Harris, Lord Ralph, of High
Cross 256, 258
Harrison, Paul 97, 119
Hawaii 116
Hay, Donald 202, 254, 257,
263
Hayek, Professor Frederick
von 256, 264
health care 3, 29, 60, 64,
152, 153, 171–2, 174–5,
324
Herzog, Jesus Silva 163
Hill, Peter 259
Hirsch, Professor Fred 275
*History of Christian
Missions, A* (Neill) 98
Hobbes, Thomas 239
Holland; population density
55; and Indian spice trade
88–9
Honduras 79
Horlicks 114
Houston summit (July 1990)
319
Houtart, François 224
Howard, John 245
Huhne, Christopher 139,
148, 303
hunger; statistics 3, 173; and
natural causes 40; and
population density 55;
as domestic political
issue 71; and
characteristics of growth
82

IBRD loans 161
imports; debt 60; Chinese
concessions 89; rates of
import duty 107–8;
import-substitution
strategies 186
Incarnation 212, 216
Independent Group on
British Aid 81
India; lack of
famine/population
co-relation 55; British aid
to 80, 81; textile trade 86,
91; spice trade; 88;
advertising in 114; US
arms 155; and IDA 180